D1617089

Washington Wildflowers

Including A Color Guide Of Wildflowers Most Commonly
Found In The State Of Washington And Adjacent Areas
Of Oregon, Idaho, And British Columbia

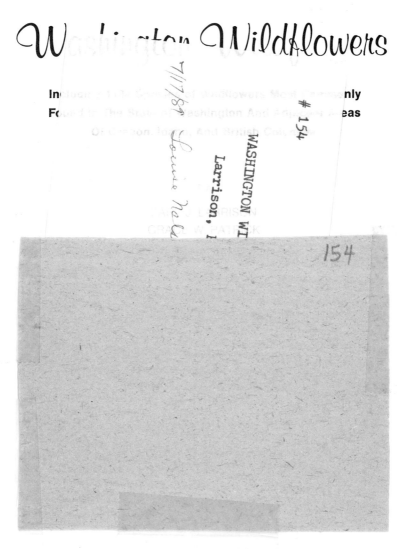

THE SEATTLE AUDUBON SOCIETY

1st Printing, May, 1974

2nd Printing, August, 1977

SPONSORS

Agnes E. Arnold
Constance E. Bain
John W. Beaufort
A. Kenneth Benedict
J. W. Bitterman
Bob and Elsie Boggs
Henry Broderick
Clifford C. Brown
Elroy D. Burnett
Beatrice Buzzetti
Ruth E. Campbell
Norma H. Christoferson
Hilah R. Conklin
Louisa Pike Crook
Florence Culp
Jack E. Davis
Mr. and Mrs. Lawrence A. Dewey
Mr. and Mrs. Jesse Epstein
Patricia Evans
Gunnar Fagerlund
Leslie Fishwick
Mabel Foise
Mrs. Henry T. Fowler
Mr. and Mrs. Ralph D. Hagenbuch
Pauline Hager
Anona Hales
Chester J. Higman

Patricia L. Hill
Margaret Hilty
Evelyn M. Kiehl
Patricia E. Knopp
T. R. Kurtz
Mabel Larrison
Katherine M. Laupp
Mrs. William T. Patten
Evelyn Peaslee
Bertine Pigott
Mr. and Mrs. Zachary Price
Bob and Georgia Ramsey
Marjorie M. Reynolds
William F. Rotecki
Olive P. Sahlstrom
Donna J. Scaman
Mrs. James G. Shakman
Nancy Solibakke
Mrs. Gordon Speck
Ethel Telban
Mr. and Mrs. Thornton Thomas
Adrian C. Thrupp
Elizabeth Tuttle
Dr. and Mrs. Thomas W. Weir
Winifred E. Weter
A. Geraldine Whiting
Robert E. Woodley

In Memory of Mary Compton

Nancy A. Hacker

Emily (Mrs. George W.) Scholl

In Memory of Al Forsman

Ruth Anderson
Ruth Boyle
Violet Cannon

Doris Jelliffe
Mary Nero
Hazel A. Wolf

In Memory of Mrs. Arthur R. Robinson

Mrs. Neil Haig

Organizations

Eastside Garden Club, Wenatchee
Blue Mountain Audubon Society
Kitsap Audubon Society
Lower Columbia Basin Audubon Society
North Cascades Audubon Society
North End Flower Club, Seattle

Palouse Audubon Society
Pilchuck Audubon Society
Spokane Audubon Society
Tahoma Audubon Society
Yakima Valley Audubon Society

ISBN 0-914516-02-7

Library of Congress Catalog Card Number: 73-94499

DEDICATION

It might have been the loosestrife in the Union Bay marsh, the late summer composites on Yellow Aster Butte, the oxyrias on Burroughs Mountain, the Indian paintbrushes on Kaleetan, the balsamroots in the Owyhees, or the marsh marigolds peeking from under the lips of melting snowbanks beside Lake 22 on Mount Pilchuck—it was always the same . . . the patient explanation of the floral characters, the careful taking of the photographs, the painstaking preparation of the pressed specimens.

Those days with the small, slightly-stooped and, in his latter years, the limping man who loved the wild things with an intensity imparted to few and who could write of them with such masterly prose . . . those days when the blue haze of autumn's Indian summer made the mountains such holy cathedrals of beauty that one almost hesitated to enter them . . . those were the days that some of us were privileged to spend with

Harry Wentworth Higman

(1883-1969)

to whom this book is dedicated

by

THE SEATTLE AUDUBON SOCIETY

In recognition of his services as former president, constant advisor, and benefactor.

Figure 1.
"Consider the lilies of the field, how they grow; they toil not, neither do they spin; yet I say unto you, that even Solomon in all his glory was not arrayed like one of these."
(Photo by Larrison)

PREFACE

The publishing of a guide to the wildflowers of the state of Washington has long been a goal of the Seattle Audubon Society. This was especially a fond project of Harry W. Higman, originator of the "Trailside Series" which he conceived of as a self-supporting line of field guides, usable by the non-specialist, which would deal with the various aspects of local natural history. Some six years ago, at one of the Wenas Audubon campouts, an informal steering committee of Hazel Wolf, Ruth Anderson, Zella Schultz, Grace Patrick, and the senior author laid preliminary plans for such a flower guide. Considerable study was made as to just exactly the type of guide that would be useful to the average student of natural history, follow the previous pattern of the *Trailside* books in being more or less complete, and lie within the financial feasibility of the Society. In this study, Larrison and Dr. William H. Baker, then curator of the herbarium of the University of Idaho, worked together. The plan of the present volume was accepted by the SAS editorial committee and work then proceeded at an active pace. Larrison prepared the original draft of the keys which was checked in detail by Baker and then field tested by a number of knowledgeable amateurs as to usability on the non-professional level. A second, expanded draft was prepared which was also exhaustively field tested. Copies of the two drafts were carried throughout Washington and adjacent areas in the packs of humans and horses in this endeavor. Grace Patrick, besides doing field work and photography, carefully checked the text against her many years of experience with the floras of the Cascades and with the literature. James A. Yaich spent the summer of 1972 in the field with Larrison, photographing the flowers and field checking the manuscript. He also prepared the enlargements for the black and white photographs.

The writing of this guide has been a long and difficult job, but it has been made pleasurable by the wonderful cooperation and encouragement of a number of persons. The enthusiasm and support of Pauline Hager of Naches, Washington, has been particularly helpful. Her knowledge of plant systematics and understanding of field identification, plus devoted field work, have been most useful. Careful attention to details along with her considerable field experience made Zella M. Schultz a particularly knowledgeable chairman of the editorial committee. She also prepared the line drawings of flower parts. Robert and Arta Clawson of Sequim, Washington, have encouraged the authors and aided in field work in the Olympics, as well as contributing a number of excellent color photographs.

Thanks are due also to Patricia Evans, Thais Bock, Evelyn Peaslee, Zella M. Schultz, Ruth Anderson, Eleanor Stopps, Anona Hales, and Emily Haig for field and editorial assistance.

Kenneth Batchelder of the Portland Audubon Society has offered many suggestions for the promotion and sales of the book, giving liberally of both his enthusiasm for nature and his wealth of business experience. Donald Durham of Durham and Downey, the printers, has afforded us every possible cooperation.

Finally, though certainly not least, the authors wish to express their heartfelt gratitude to Hazel Wolf, secretary of the Seattle Audubon Society, for her support and encouragement of the project during the years of its progress. The many hours she has spent in the planning, initiating, and promoting of the book are countless. Her never-ending enthusiasm helped solve a number of problems, human as well as physical, that appeared from time to time. It is no exaggeration to say that without Mrs. Wolf's support, this book would never have been published.

Earl J. Larrison	William H. Baker
Grace W. Patrick	James A. Yaich

CONTENTS

Page

INTRODUCTION

What This Book Includes

Wildflowers, as defined for this guide, include those species of flowering herbs which are native to the state of Washington. With very few exceptions, weeds and other exotics not native to the Evergreen State are not listed, nor are flowering shrubs and trees. To have done so would have greatly increased the size of this book. Basically, the guide covers the more commonly seen wildflowers in Washington. Some of the rare or very local species have not been included. In spite of these restrictions, the coverage (1134 species) is more than 90%. We feel that we have produced a book which is sufficiently complete to satisfy most of its users, in addition to one that is convenient and low-priced. Students of flowers in adjacent areas of Oregon, Idaho, and British Columbia will find the book of considerable value, though obviously the farther one goes from the boundaries of the state of Washington, the less inclusive it becomes.

The flowers of Washington, or parts thereof, have been treated in the past by a number of books and pamphlets. Generally, these fall into two categories, the detailed, technical manual and the colorfully illustrated—but brief—brochure of some local area. The latter have often been of the "101 Flowers of X National Park" type. The technical manuals are for the most part sparsely, if at all, illustrated and require some considerable botanical knowledge to use. The park brochures contain only a fraction of the species occurring in their areas and usually have no keys or adequate descriptions, being mainly purchased as "souvenirs" of a visit to that park. It is the hope of the Seattle Audubon Society that this book will meet the needs of most non-professional flower students, yet be as easy for the beginner to use as possible.

How To Enjoy The Wildflowers

There is hardly a more esthetic subject than a wildflower. It is usually simply appreciated for its appearance and often pleasing fragrance. Literally, beauty for its own sake. An increasing number of persons, however, wish also to be able to name the flower so they can remember it and add it to their cache of identified natural history objects. With the advent of high quality color films and single lens reflex cameras, flower photography has come into its own. This is a splendid way to "collect" flowers and and still leave them intact in their natural habitat for others to enjoy. More about techniques of flower photography in the Appendix. Finding the flowers, then, would seem to be the name of the game. This involves visiting a variety of habitats at all different times of the growing season, because flowers do not occur universally but exhibit an amazing diversity of environmental preferences and times of blooming during the spring, summer, and fall. It would follow that each species of flower shows a greater or lesser tendency to occur consistently in a particular place. Marsh marigolds are found in wet spots in subalpine meadows while cactuses are to be encountered in desert terrain. Arnicas frequently bloom in the shade of coniferous trees, while the saxifrages hug rocky slopes. To be a successful flower finder, one must develop an ecologic awareness of the distribution of flower species. One may come to measure his knowledge of wildflowers by his ability to find certain species or to amass a list of "finds." The environmental notes given for each species in this book should help considerably in this pursuit.

With the hobby of flower photography and the satisfaction of finding and identifying, there should be little if any need to pick wildflowers. Not only is it against the law in many places, but wild species wilt easily and are often difficult to transplant. Keeping qualities and the ability to withstand uprooting and re-planting in alien soils are qualities that have been built into tame plants via the domestication process. Leave them where they grow, so that others may enjoy them also! Let's make that the golden rule of flower finding. Or,

Pick, if you must, one flower face
If nine more blooms are left in place.
Two feet square must hold that many!
Otherwise, just look, but don't pick any.

How To Use This Guide

The most satisfactory system of plant identification is through the use of keys. Those that have been prepared for this book are as simple to use as possible, yet should serve the beginner who, with a minimum amount of technical knowledge, can separate the various species and arrive, with a little practice, at the determination of the flower in question. The authors gave considerable study to the best means of flower identification. In a book containing well over a thousand species, obviously all could not be illustrated. It would be an impossible task to sort through such a plethora of pictures to find the one matching the flower in hand. Grouping by flower color is not feasible, either, as there are relatively few flower colors. While the beginner, if he knows not what family his plant belongs to, will have to start with the family key and then turn to the particular family indicated and sort through genus and species keys, he eventually will be able to recognize more and more families and genera, so that the actual amount of keying will gradually be reduced.

The keys used here are two-branched ones with pairs of alternate leads. To begin an identification, the reader compares his plant with the two leads at the beginning of a key which will be opposite in meaning. One of the leads should match a condition in his specimen—the other should not. The matching statement will refer him by a number at the end of the line to a second pair (numbered at the beginning of the lines) of leads and so on. A few minutes practice will enable one to handle the key technique easily and to identify a plant with reasonable certainty. Brief descriptions have been included in many of the genus and species accounts for further verification. Technical terminology has been kept to a minimum and a glossary and set of illustrations of flower parts, leaf shapes, etc., immediately follows this introduction. To further familiarize the reader with family characters, a synopsis summarizing characteristic features of each family along with a list of genera is included. The family key immediately following the summary may be used for identifying the family if one does not know that fact to begin with.

The user of the guide is warned that flower identification is not always easy. Some plants have striking characters and may belong to small groups, making their determinations relatively simple. Others bear hidden, less obvious, characters and may belong to large genera with many species. Some flower groups are notoriously difficult. Do not feel discouraged if you have difficulty in identifying certain plants to species. It is sufficient, often, to be satisfied with identification to genus. Some groups even stump the experts! Plant identification cannot be learned in a single day, but the progress one gradually makes is an increasing case for satisfaction and a feeling of real achievement.

In the species account in this book, the common name is given first, followed by the scientific name. Some flowers have many names. It does not seem advisable to prolong such confusion, so a name commonly used or seemingly most appropriate has been selected. The scientific nomenclature follows, for the most part, the recent five volume monograph on Northwest flora by Hitchcock et al, as well as the more recently issued single volume Northwest flora by Hitchcock and Cronquist. The plant names are followed by a brief description which, while not complete, should be sufficient to "clinch" the key identification. Next is given the geographic distribution in the state. "East. Wash." refers to those areas east of the Cascades but often including the east slopes of that range. "West. Wash." includes the region west of the Cascade crest. A brief habitat statement then follows. Finally the average season of flowering is presented. "Spring" covers March, April, and May; "summer," June, July, and August; "fall," September, October and November; "winter," December, January, and February.

SUMMARY OF WILDFLOWER FAMILIES

1. CALLA LILY FAMILY (*Araceae*) Perennial, swamp-inhabiting plants with very large leaves and stout rootstocks. "Flower" consists of fleshy spike (spadix) containing many small flowers which is partly surrounded by a yellow hood-shaped bract (spathe). Leaves and stems with skunk-like odor.

    skunk cabbages (*Lysichitum*)

2. LILY FAMILY (*Liliaceae*) Perennial plants with parallel-veined leaves, and bulbs, corms, or rootstocks. Flowers bell-shaped or triangular with parts in 6's or 3's (rarely 4's). Sepals and petals often similar in shape and color. Flower groups (inflorescences) variable, but individual flowers usually lily-like. Ovary compound, superior.

onions (*Allium*)	false lilies of the valley (*Maianthemum*)
brodiaeas (*Brodiaea*)	false solomon's seals (*Smilacina*)
mariposa lilies (*Calochortus*)	bronze bells (*Stenanthium*)
camasses (*Camassia*)	twisted-stalks (*Streptopus*)
queen's cups (*Clintonia*)	lamb's lilies (*Tofieldia*)
fairy bells (*Disporum*)	trilliums (*Trillium*)
avalanche lilies (*Erythronium*)	veratrums (*Veratrum*)
fritillaries (*Fritillaria*)	bear grasses (*Xerophyllum*)
lilies (*Lilium*)	death camasses (*Zigadenus*)
alp lilies (*Lloydia*)	

3. IRIS FAMILY (*Iridaceae*) Perennial plants with flat, sword-like or grass-like leaves, creeping rootstocks, and large showy flowers which may be irregular (3 broad, downward pointing, petal-like sepals, 3 erect petals, and 3 petal-like style branches) in true irises; or regular (sepals and petals similar) in the blue-eyed grasses. Stamens 3; ovary compound, inferior.

    irises (*Iris*)   blue-eyed grasses (*Sisyrinchium*)

4. ORCHID FAMILY (*Orchidaceae*)   Perennial plants with corms, bulbs, tubers, or rootstocks. Flowers irregular with 3 similar sepals and 3 petals consisting of 2 lateral ones and 1 lower lip-like or sack-like petal (often spurred). Stamens united with style to form a "column." Flowers may be single, or in spikes or clusters. Flower pattern reminiscent of that of domestic orchids. Stamens 1 or 2.

calypsos (*Calypso*)
coralroots (*Corallorhiza*)
lady's-slippers (*Cypripedium*)
phantom orchids (*Eburophyton*)
giant helleborines (*Epipactis*)

evergreen orchids (*Goodyera*)
bog orchids (*Habenaria*)
twayblades (*Listera*)
ladies' tresses (*Spiranthes*)

5. NETTLE FAMILY (*Urticaceae*)   Perennial plants with creeping rootstocks, simple leaves, and small greenish flowers without petals, arranged in drooping panicles from leaf axils. Lax, green, toothed leaves distinctive. Foliage covered with numerous stinging hairs which produce an intense burning sensation on bare skin.

nettles (*Urtica*)

6. BIRTHWORT FAMILY (*Aristolochiaceae*)   Perennial plants with trailing aromatic rootstocks and large, heart-shaped, long-petioled, entire leaves occurring in pairs with a single perfect flower borne between them on or near the surface of the ground. Flower lacks petals but contains 3 brownish-purple sepals flaring outward from a swollen, cup-shaped, 6-celled ovary.

wild gingers (*Asarum*)

7. POLYGONUM FAMILY (*Polygonaceae*)   Annual or perennial plants with alternate, usually entire leaves, swollen stipular sheaths or joints ("knots") where leaves are attached, and small, more or less insignificant flowers which lack petals (sepals often colored and petal-like) and are arranged in clusters or heads; or axillary.

chorizanthes (*Chorizanthe*)
buckwheats (*Eriogonum*)
mountain sorrels (*Oxyria*)

oxythecas (*Oxytheca*)
knotweeds (*Polygonum*)
docks (*Rumex*)

8. GOOSEFOOT FAMILY (*Chenopodiaceae*)   Annual or perennial plants with usually alternate, simple leaves, and small, regular, inconspicuous, greenish flowers which lack petals. Foliage is often fleshy (succulent) and either greenish or mealy-white. Plants often with clustered weedy growth form. Leaves sometimes not well developed or fleshy scales (*Salicornia*).

saltbushes (*Atriplex*)
goosefoots (*Chenopodium*)
winterfats (*Eurotia*)

poverty weeds (*Monolepis*)
saltworts (*Salicornia*)
suaedas (*Suaeda*)

9. FOUR-O'CLOCK FAMILY (*Nyctaginaceae*)   Annual or perennial plants with fleshy leaves that are simple, opposite, and entire. One member of each pair of leaves smaller than the other. Flowers arranged in large showy heads. Individual flowers with long-tubed calyx and no petals. Our species occurring on sand dunes along saltwater beaches or in desert areas. Ovary superior; fruit winged.

sand verbenas (*Abronia*)

10. PURSLANE FAMILY (*Portulacaceae*) Small annual or perennial plants with more or less fleshy leaves that are opposite or basal and entire (some with alternate bracts). Flowers with usually 5 or more petals and 2 sepals, except *Lewisia*. Stamens opposite the petals, if the same number; ovary 1-celled.

red maids (*Calandrinia*)
spring beauties (*Claytonia*)
lewisias (*Lewisia*)
miner's lettuces (*Montia*)
pussy-paws (*Spraguea*)

11. PINK FAMILY (*Caryophyllaceae*) Annual or perennial plants with opposite, simple, entire leaves; regular, usually perfect flowers; and petals and sepals in 4's or 5's. Stamens usually twice as many as sepals. Joints (nodes) of stem often swollen. Tips of petals frequently notched (pinked), hence the name. Stamens alternate if the same number.

sandworts (*Arenaria*)
cardionemas (*Cardionema*)
field chickweeds (*Cerastium*)
honkenyas (*Honkenya*)
pearlworts (*Sagina*)
wild pinks (*Silene*)
sand spurries (*Spergularia*)
common chickweeds (*Stellaria*)

12. WATER LILY FAMILY (*Nymphaeaceae*) Perennial, aquatic plants with stout rootstocks from which project long stalks rising to floating or emergent, platter-like leaves and large or small, though often showy, flowers. Flowers perfect, regular, and solitary, and either large and yellow or small and purplish. Found in ponds, lakes, sloughs, and other standing waters.

water-shields (*Brasenia*)
yellow pond lilies (*Nuphar*)

13. PEONY FAMILY (*Paeoniaceae*) Perennial plants with fleshy leaves, stems, and roots. Bluish-green leaves dissected into numerous finger-like lobes. Flowers solitary with 5 leathery greenish-purple sepals and 5 fleshy brownish-purple petals surrounding a dense cluster of many yellowish stamens. Pistils 5. Bracts, sepals, and petals tend to intergrade.

peonies (*Paeonia*)

14. BUTTERCUP FAMILY (*Ranunculaceae*) Perennial or annual plants with alternate (rarely opposite) or basal leaves which may be simple, deeply lobed, or compound. Flowers are regular or irregular with 2-5 sometimes petal-like sepals and 4 or more (occasionally none) petals and numerous stamens and pistils forming a button or cluster in the center of the flower. Flowers of the various genera are quite diverse and are perhaps best learned genus by genus.

monkshoods (*Aconitum*)
baneberries (*Actaea*)
anemones (*Anemone*)
columbines (*Aquilegia*)
marsh marigolds (*Caltha*)
bugbanes (*Cimifuga*)
clematises (*Clematis*)
gold-threads (*Coptis*)
larkspurs (*Delphinium*)
mouse-tails (*Myosurus*)
buttercups (*Ranunculus*)
meadow rues (*Thalictrum*)
false bugbanes (*Trautvetteria*)
globeflowers (*Trollius*)

15. BARBERRY FAMILY (*Berberidaceae*) Perennial herbs (as included in this book) with rootstocks and basal or alternate 3-parted, compound leaves. Petals and sepals, 6 each—or none—borne opposite petals, if petals are

present. Stamens 6. Plants of shady, moist woods.

vanilla-leaves (*Achlys*)   inside-out flower (*Vancouveria*)

16. POPPY FAMILY (*Papaveraceae*) Annual or perennial plants with leaves divided several times into 3's and large showy flowers with 4 petals and numerous stamens. Sap is watery and bitter. Sepals united into a cap which is pinched off as the petals unfold. Color of flower, yellow to deep orange.

California poppies (*Eschscholzia*)

17. FUMITORY FAMILY (*Fumariaceae*) Annual or perennial, delicate, woodland plants with alternate, finely-dissected, compound leaves. Flowers perfect, but irregular, with one or both outer petals spurred and the 2 inner petals with crested and united tips. Deep woods or old glacial moraines, as well as gravelly streamsides. Stamens in 2 sets of 3.

corydalises (*Corydalis*)   dicentras (*Dicentra*)

18. MUSTARD FAMILY (*Cruciferae*) Annual or perennial plants with 4 petals forming a cross-shaped flower (cruci+fer="cross-bearing") and perfect, regular flowers often arranged in racemes. Stamens usually of 2 kinds: 4 long and 2 short, or 4 or 2. Ovary developing into a short or long, slender seed pod which often points upward. Flowers frequently yellow-colored.

rock cresses (*Arabis*)	peppergrasses (*Lepidium*)
sand weeds (*Athysanus*)	bladder-pods (*Lesquerella*)
wintercresses (*Barbarea*)	dagger-pods (*Phoenicaulis*)
bittercresses (*Cardamine*)	physarias (*Physaria*)
cochlearias (*Cochlearia*)	marsh-cresses (*Rorippa*)
tansy mustards (*Descurainea*)	smelowskias (*Smelowskia*)
whitlow grasses (*Draba*)	false twisted flowers (*Streptanthella*)
wallflowers (*Erysimum*)	thelypodies (*Thelypodium*)
hutchinsias (*Hutchinsia*)	penny-grasses (*Thlaspi*)
idahoas (*Idahoa*)	fringe-pods (*Thysanocarpus*)

19. CAPER FAMILY (*Capparidaceae*) Annual plants with alternate, 3-parted, compound leaves and the 4-parted, cross-shaped flowers grouped in terminal clusters. Very much favored by bees which are usually in abundant attendance upon the flowers. Stamens alike, differentiating capers from the mustards.

bee plants (*Cleome*)

20. SUNDEW FAMILY (*Droseraceae*) Low-lying, reddish-brown plants, usually found in bogs, with spoon- or spatula-shaped leaves containing sticky, glandular hairs used for capturing insects. Flowers small, on separate stalks; white, pink, or purple.

sundews (*Drosera*)

21. STONECROP FAMILY (*Crassulaceae*) Low-growing, fleshy-leaved plants with spreading, mat-like growth form and usually found in rocky or otherwise exposed places. Flowers are grouped in cymes and are usually yellowish (less commonly reddish). Small, succulent leaves are characteristic. Stamens definite in number.

stonecrops (*Sedum*)

22. SAXIFRAGE FAMILY (*Saxifragaceae*) Perennial plants usually character-ized by a rosette of basal leaves and smallish flowers grouped on the upper parts of tall, slender flowering stalks. Commonly grow in rocky, cliff-like habitats, particularly in the mountains. Stamens definite in number; less than 12, borne on a disk.

boykinias (*Boykinia*)
elmeras (*Elmera*)
heucheras (*Heuchera*)
golden carpets (*Chrysosplenium*)
false saxifrages (*Leptarrhena*)
prairie-stars (*Lithophragma*)
mitreworts (*Mitella*)

grasses-of-parnassus (*Parnassia*)
saxifrages (*Saxifraga*)
suksdorfias (*Suksdorfia*)
fringe-cups (*Tellima*)
foamflowers (*Tiarella*)
youth-on-ages (*Tolmiea*)

23. ROSE FAMILY (*Rosaceae*) Mostly perennial herbs (as included here) with alternate leaves and regular, usually perfect flowers characterized by generally 5 roundish petals (absent in burnets), 5 sepals, and many (com-monly 20) stamens. A variable group and many not always "rose-like" on gross inspection. When stamens = 10, fruit is an achene; if ovary is inferior, fruit is a pome.

goatsbeards (*Aruncus*)
mountain avens (*Dryas*)
strawberries (*Fragaria*)
geums (*Geum*)
horkelias (*Horkelia*)
ivesias (*Ivesia*)

partridge-foots (*Luetkea*)
rock-spiraeas (*Petrophytum*)
cinquefoils (*Potentilla*)
burnets (*Sanguisorba*)
sibbaldias (*Sibbaldia*)

24. PEA FAMILY (*Leguminosae*) Perennial or annual plants with a typically irregular, pea-shaped flower consisting of a broad, upper petal (the *banner* or *standard*), 2 lateral petals (the *wings*), and 2 lower petals joining to-gether to form the *keel* at bottom. Leaves alternate and usually compound and stipulate; seeds in a long or short pod technically called a *legume*.

locoweeds (*Astragalus*)
wild licorices (*Glycyrrhiza*)
sweet-brooms (*Hedysarum*)
peas (*Lathyrus*)
lotuses (*Lotus*)
lupines (*Lupinus*)

stemless locos *Oxytropis*)
prairie-clovers (*Petalostemon*)
psoraleas (*Psoralea*)
yellow peas (*Thermopsis*)
clovers (*Trifolium*)
vetches (*Vicia*)

25. GERANIUM FAMILY (*Geraniaceae*) Annual or perennial plants with deeply cleft, palmately lobed leaves and regular, symmetrical flowers with 5 petals, 5 sepals, 10 fertile stamens, and usually red, pink, or white in color. Fruits long-beaked at maturity.

geraniums (*Geranium*)

26. WOOD SORREL FAMILY (*Oxalidaceae*) Annual or perennial plants with large, clover-like leaves (3 leaflets) on slender stalks and large regular, flower parts in 5's. Juice of plant acidic to taste. Stamen filaments joined at base.

wood sorrels (*Oxalis*)

27. FLAX FAMILY (*Linaceae*) Annual plants with slender stems, narrow leaves, and delicate roundish-petaled, showy flowers, which may be blue or yellow in color.

flax (*Linum*)

28. SPURGE FAMILY (*Euphorbiaceae*) Small, often low-lying, annual or perennial plants with milky juice and greenish or whitish flowers which lack petals and sepals. The "flower" consists of petal-like bracts.

spurges (*Euphorbia*)

29. TOUCH-ME-NOT FAMILY (*Balsaminaceae*) Thin-leaved, fleshy-stemmed annual plants with showy, irregular flowers, each consisting of a large, colored, bell-shaped sepal, 2 small greenish sepals, and 4 petals united into 2 pairs. Juice watery.

touch-me-not (*Impatiens*)

30. MALLOW FAMILY (*Malvaceae*) Annual or perennial plants with large, showy (often hollyhock-like) flowers containing numerous stamens united into a tube or cluster surrounding the several to many pistils. The 5-lobed calyx may have a circle of small bracts around its base.

mountain hollyhocks (*Iliamna*)   sidalceas (*Sidalcea*)
alkali mallows (*Sida*)   globe mallows (*Sphaeralcea*)

31. ST. JOHN'S WORT FAMILY (*Hypericaceae*) Annual or perennial plants with opposite, black-dotted (glands), sessile (no petioles), leaves and deep yellowish, 5-petaled flowers. Stamens numerous, often grouped in 3's or 5's. Juice is resinous and sticky. Ovary superior; fruit a capsule.

St. John's worts (*Hypericum*)

32. VIOLET FAMILY (*Violaceae*) Small, perennial plants with showy, pansy-like flowers and heart-shaped or strongly-cleft, often basal leaves. The irregular flowers have a wide, often heavily-veined lower petal (with a basal spur), 2 lateral petals which are sometimes bearded, and 2 smaller upper petals. Pistil has a thickened head with a short beak. Stamens irregular; the filaments dilated above the anthers.

violets (*Viola*)

33. BLAZING-STAR FAMILY (*Loasaceae*) Annual or perennial plants with alternate or opposite, dandelion-like leaves and large yellowish flowers on the tips of tall stems. Foliage rough, with rigid, barbed hairs. Stems often whitish and shining. Petals spreading in "sunburst" pattern.

blazing-stars (*Mentzelia*)

34. CACTUS FAMILY (*Cactaceae*) Perennial plants with thickened, fleshy stems (no obvious leaves) and numerous sharp spines. Flowers large, colorful, and cup-shaped with numerous petals and stamens. Ovary inferior.

prickly pears (*Opuntia*)   hedgehog cactuses (*Pediocactus*)

35. LOOSESTRIFE FAMILY (*Lythraceae*) Annual or perennial plants with opposite leaves on tall stems and showy flowers placed either in axils of leaves or in terminal spikes. Petals 5 to 7 in number and purple, pink, or

14

whitish. Plants of moist, marshy habitats.

loosestrifes (*Lythrum*)

36. EVENING PRIMROSE FAMILY (*Onagraceae*) Annual or perennial plants with flower parts in 2's or 4's. Flowers large and showy, often with a 4-branched stigma forming a characteristic cross. A somewhat variable family and best recognized by genus. Carpels 4 or 2.

boisduvalias (*Boisduvalia*)
enchanter's nightshades (*Circaea*)
clarkias (*Clarkia*)
willow-herbs (*Epilobium*)

gauras (*Gaura*)
gayophytums (*Gayophytum*)
water purslane (*Ludwigia*)
evening primroses (*Oenothera*)

37. WATER MILFOIL FAMILY (*Haloragaceae*) Aquatic, emergent plants with whorled leaves, those below the water's surface with fine filaments while those above the surface much less divided or entire. Flower parts usually in 4's.

water milfoils (*Myriophyllum*)

38. MARE'S-TAIL FAMILY (*Hippuridaceae*) Perennial plants with narrow, whorled leaves located along simple stems projecting above shallow, in-shore waters or from wet, subalpine meadows. Flowers with 1 stamen and 1 pistil, but lacking sepals or petals and located in leaf axils.

mare's-tails (*Hippuris*)

39. GINSENG FAMILY (*Araliaceae*) Woody herbs or sub-shrubs with large, compound leaves and many small, greenish-white flowers arranged in simple whorls. Juice from roots and underground stems is aromatic.

wild sarsaparilla (*Aralia*)

40. PARSLEY FAMILY (*Umbelliferae*) Annual or perennial plants with hollow stems and small flowers arranged in umbrella-like clusters (umbels). Leaves usually finely divided (like those of the carrot). Flower parts usually in 5's. Ovary inferior. Plants best learned by genus.

angelicas (*Angelica*)
hedge-parsleys (*Caucalis*)
water-hemlocks (*Cicuta*)
hemlock-parsleys (*Conioselinum*)
Indian parsnips (*Cymopterus*)
silver-tops (*Glehnia*)
cow-parsnips (*Heracleum*)
lovages (*Ligusticum*)
lilaeopsises (*Lilaeopsis*)

desert parsleys (*Lomatium*)
water parsleys (*Oenanthe*)
turkey peas (*Orogenia*)
sweet cicelies (*Osmorhiza*)
yampahs (*Perideridia*)
sanicles (*Sanicula*)
hemlock water-parsnips (*Sium*)
tauschias (*Tauschia*)

41. DOGWOOD FAMILY (*Cornaceae*) As included here, small, low herbs with a "whorl" of small, heavily-veined, oval-shaped, often evergreen leaves at tip of stem (a second whorl near middle of stem). Flowers greenish-purple, arranged in dense head, and surrounded by 4-6 white petal-like bracts. Red fruits conspicuous in season. Ovary inferior.

dogwoods (*Cornus*)

42. HEATH FAMILY (*Ericaceae*) Variable family ranging from green-leaved to non-green, fungus-like, saprophytic herbs, shrubs, and trees. The herbs (included here) usually found in dense, dark, relatively underbrush-free coniferous forests. Best learned by genus. Flower parts in 4's or 5's, free or united.

candy sticks (*Allotropa*)   Indian pipes (*Monotropa*)
prince's pines (*Chimaphila*)   fringed pinesaps (*Pleuricospora*)
cone plants (*Hemitomes*)   pine-drops (*Pterospora*)
many-flowered Indian pipe (*Hypopitys*) wintergreens (*Pyrola*)

43. PRIMROSE FAMILY (*Primulaceae*) Perennial plants with perfect, regular flowers and stamens attached to the centers of the petals, instead of between petals. Leaves simple and entire. Petals united at the base.

shooting-stars (*Dodecatheon*)   yellow loosestrifes (*Lysimachia*)
douglasias (*Douglasia*)   star-flowers (*Trientalis*)
saltworts (*Glaux*)

44. PLUMBAGO FAMILY (*Plumbaginaceae*) Perennial seashore plants with basal, tuft-like leaves and naked stems bearing roundish clusters of flowers, each cluster surrounded by a papery bract. Calyx papery; petals partly united.

beach thrifts (*Armeria*)

45. GENTIAN FAMILY (*Gentianaceae*) Smooth perennial plants with simple, opposite, entire leaves and 4- or 5-lobed fused petals to form a tube-shaped, often bell-like, corolla. Ovary superior. Stamens on the petals, alternate with corolla lobes. Stigmas 2.

centauries (*Centaurium*)   gentians (*Gentiana*)
fraseras (*Frasera*)   swertias (*Swertia*)

46. BUCKBEAN FAMILY (*Menyanthaceae*) Perennial plants usually found standing in shallow, quiet water or wet meadows with leaves containing 3 prominent leaflets or else simple and not compound. Flowers perfect, regular and arranged in racemes or cymes.

buckbeans (*Menyanthes*)   deer-cabbage (*Nephrophyllidium*)

47. DOGBANE FAMILY (*Apocynaceae*) Perennial plants with milk juice and simple, opposite leaves and clusters of small, nodding, bell-shaped flowers. Flower parts in 5's. Ovary superior; 2 pistils in each flower (ours). Anthers converging.

dogbanes (*Apocynum*)

48. MILKWEED FAMILY (*Asclepiadaceae*) Perennial plants with thick milky juice, opposite or whorled leaves, and perfect, regular flowers arranged in umbel-like clusters. Pattern of the flower with 5 swept-back petals and 5-parted cup with 5 tiny horns projecting in central structures of united stamens and stigmas in form of a fly trap.

milkweeds (*Asclepias*)

49. MORNING-GLORY FAMILY (*Convolvulaceae*) Annual or perennial, twining, often prostrate plants with showy, funnel-shaped flowers and

alternate leaves. Flowers open during sunshine, but close at night or in shadow.

morning-glories (*Convolvulus*)

50. PHLOX FAMILY (*Polemoniaceae*) Annual or perennial plants with alternate or opposite, simple or divided leaves and regular flowers with partly fused petals. Stamens alternate with the corolla lobes. Plants often shrubby at base.

collomias (*Collomia*)   microsterises (*Microsteris*)
gilias (*Gilia*)   navarretias (*Navarretia*)
leptodactylons (*Leptodactylon*)   phlox (*Phlox*)
linanthastrums (*Linanthastrum*)   polemoniums (*Polemonium*)
linanthuses (*Linanthus*)

51. WATERLEAF FAMILY (*Hydrophyllaceae*) Herbs (as included here) with usually opposite or alternate leaves—all basal in a few species (often appearing water-stained). Flowers perfect and regular in 5 parts. Petals and sepals both partly united into a fused corolla and calyx. Foliage often hairy and stamens often projecting conspicuously beyond the petal tips. Ovary superior, with 2 locules, 2 carpels. Inflorescence often coiled or head-like.

hesperochirons (*Hesperochiron*)   phacelias (*Phacelia*)
waterleaves (*Hydrophyllum*)   romanzoffias (*Romanzoffia*)
namas (*Nama*)   nemophilas (*Nemophila*)

52. BORAGE FAMILY (*Boraginaceae*) Annual or perennial herbs (as included here) with rough-hairy foliage and mostly alternate, entire leaves. Flowers of most species arranged in 1-sided cymes originally rolled inward, but unrolling during flowering. Flower parts in 5's; regular; fruit of 4 nutlets.

tarweeds (*Amsinckia*)   gromwells (*Lithospermum*)
coldenias (*Coldenia*)   mertensias (*Mertensia*)
cryptanthas (*Cryptantha*)   mouse-ears (*Myosotis*)
hound's-tongues (*Cynoglossum*)   pectocaryas (*Pectocarya*)
stickseeds (*Hackelia*)   popcorn-flowers (*Plagiobothrys*)

53. VERBENA FAMILY (*Verbenaceae*) Annual or perennial herbs with opposite or whorled, toothed or lobed leaves with perfect, but irregular flowers in flat clusters or slender spikes. Petals often flat, as lobes of a tubular corolla. Sepals 5 and unequal; stamens 4 with 1 pair often sterile (not fully developed).

verbenas (*Verbena*)

54. MINT FAMILY (*Labiatae*) Annual or perennial herbs with usually square stems, opposite leaves, and "minty," aromatic odor to the foliage. Flowers are irregular, small, and generally arranged in spikes or clusters in the axils of the leaves. Many have 2-lipped flowers with the upper lip 2-lobed and the lower 3-lobed.

giant hyssops (*Agastache*)   sages (*Salvia*)
dragon's-heads (*Dracocephalum*)   yerba buenas (*Satureja*)
water horehounds (*Lycopus*)   skull-caps (*Scutellaria*)
mints (*Mentha*)   hedge nettles (*Stachys*)
moldavicas (*Moldavica*)   wood sages (*Teucrium*)
balms (*Monardella*)   blue curls (*Trichostema*)

55. FIGWORT FAMILY (*Scrophulariaceae*) Annual or perennial herbs (as treated here) with the flowers often with partly united petals forming a swollen corolla tube with 2 lips (upper lip with 2 lobes; lower lip with 3), resembling somewhat the garden snapdragon. Flowers mostly irregular. Stamens vary in number (4, 5, or 2) with one or more sterile. Leaves opposite or whorled.

bessyas (*Bessya*)
Indian paintbrushes *(Castilleja)*
collinsias (*Collinsia*)
bird's-beaks (*Cordylanthus*)
toadflaxes (*Linaria*)
mimetanthes (*Mimetanthe*)
monkey-flowers (*Mimulus*)

owl's-clovers (*Orthocarpus*)
louseworts (*Pedicularis*)
penstemons (*Penstemon*)
figworts (*Scrophularia*)
synthyrises (*Synthyris*)
tonellas (*Tonella*)
speedwells (*Veronica*)

56. BROOMRAPE FAMILY (*Orobanchaceae*) Low, fleshy, leafless (scales instead of leaves) plants which are root parasites. Corollas are usually 2-lipped as result of fusion near the tips of the 5 petals. The more common broomrapes present a gentian-like or penstemon-like flower (1 or more) at the tip of a short, leafless stem mostly below ground, the flowers often borne on peduncles.

ground-cones (*Boschniakia*)   broomrapes (*Orobanche*)

57. BLADDERWORT FAMILY (*Lentibulariaceae*) Small aquatic or semi-aquatic plants with 2-lipped flowers having hollow spurs at the base of the corolla. Bladderworts characterized by feathery underwater leaves and short, leaf-less flower stalks projecting above the surface. Butterworts show rosettes of fleshy, curl-edged, basal leaves with usually some entrapped insects on upper surfaces. Leaves in either case are characteristic.

butterworts (*Pinguicula*)   bladderworts (*Utricularia*)

58. MADDER FAMILY (*Rubiaceae*) Slender, annual or perennial plants with opposite or whorled leaves. Flower parts in 4's. The more widely-distrib-uted bedstraws have slender, square stems, small whitish or greenish flowers, 4-lobed corollas, and whorls of leaves. Stems often somewhat bristly to the touch.

bedstraws (*Galium*)   kelloggias (*Kelloggia*)

59. HONEYSUCKLE FAMILY (*Caprifoliaceae*) Perennial, somewhat woody, trailing vines with opposite leaves and bell-shaped or tubular flowers. Corolla expanding into 5 regular (twinflower) or irregular (honeysuckles) lobes. Ovary inferior.

twinflowers (*Linnaea*)   honeysuckles (*Lonicera*)

60. VALERIAN FAMILY (*Valerianaceae*) Perennial plants with opposite leaves and tall upright stems crowned with crowded clusters of very small flowers. Corollas tube-like with stamens and styles noticeably protruding beyond lobes of corolla. Stamens 3; ovary inferior—at first with 3 cells; only 1 cell at maturity.

corn-salads (*Plectritis*)   valerians (*Valeriana*)

61. CUCUMBER FAMILY (*Cucurbitaceae*) Trailing or climbing plants with conspicuous tendrils and palmately-shaped, maple-like leaves paired with flowering stalks. Fruits are prickly, green balls about 2 inches in diameter. Flowers small and whitish, and of 2 kinds, male and female.

wild cucumbers (*Marah*)

62. HAREBELL FAMILY (*Campanulaceae*) Annual or perennial plants with alternate leaves and usually bluish bell-shaped flowers (the corolla lobes often flaring). Sap usually milky. Corolla sometimes 2-lipped (lobelias). Ovary inferior. Fruit a capsule.

bluebells (*Campanula*)
downingias (*Downingia*)
bluecups (*Githopsis*)
heterocodons (*Heterocodon*)
howellias (*Howellia*)
lobelias (*Lobelia*)
venus's lookingglasses (*Triodanis*)

63. SUNFLOWER FAMILY (*Compositae*) An immense family of annual or perennial plants mostly characterized by composite flower heads made up of numerous tiny flowers appearing to represent a single flower with a center or eye of tube flowers, "petal" of ray flowers, and a "calyx" of scales. The flowers are usually yellow, less commonly white, blue, or red; ovary inferior; fruit an achene.

rattlesnake-roots (*Prenanthes*)
skeleton-weeds (*Lygodesmia*)
apargidiums (*Apargidium*)
saussureas (*Saussurea*)
blanketflowers (*Gaillardia*)
false sunflowers (*Helianthella*)
woolly sunflowers (*Eriophyllum*)
hulseas (*Hulsea*)
tansies (*Tanacetum*)
jaumeas (*Jaumea*)
rabbit-leaves (*Lagophylla*)
bristle-heads (*Rigiopappus*)
gold-stars (*Crocidium*)
blepharipappuses
    (*Blepharipappus*)
yarrows (*Achillea*)
townsendias (*Townsendia*)
sunflowers (*Helianthus*)
balsamroots (*Balsamorhiza*)
gum plants (*Grindelia*)
lasthenias (*Lasthenia*)
tar-weeds (*Madia*)
golden-weeds (*Haplopappus*)
arnicas (*Arnica*)
groundsels (*Senecio*)
goldenrods (*Solidago*)
daisies (*Erigeron*)
golden-asters (*Chrysopsis*)
coltsfeet (*Petasites*)
asters (*Aster*)
layias (*Layia*)
pearly everlastings (*Anaphalis*)
trail plants (*Adenocaulon*)
hymenopappuses (*Hymenopappus*)
sliver-leaves (*Chaenactis*)
lettuce (*Lactuca*)
dandelions (*Taraxacum*)
hawkweeds (*Hieracium*)
hawksbeards (*Crepis*)
agoserises (*Agoseris*)
microserises (*Microseris*)
rush pinks (*Stephanomeria*)
thistles (*Cirsium*)
beggar-ticks (*Bidens*)
wyethias (*Wyethia*)
rudbeckias (*Rudbeckia*)
thoroughworts (*Brickellia*)
luinas (*Luina*)
cudweeds (*Gnaphalium*)
pussy-toes (*Antennaria*)
ragweeds (*Ambrosia*)
woolly-heads (*Psilocarphus*)
poverty-weeds (*Iva*)
wormwoods (*Artemisia*)

KEY TO THE FAMILIES OF WASHINGTON WILDFLOWERS

1. Flower parts nearly always in 3's, rarely in 4's, and never in 5's; stems in cross-section showing the vascular bundles irregularly distributed throughout the pith or around a central cavity; leaves usually parallel-veined....2
1. Flower parts usually in 5's or 4's, very rarely in 3's or 6's; stems in cross-section showing a central pith or cavity surrounded by a circle of vascular bundles; leaves usually net-veined...............................4

2. Ovary superior; flowers regular (symmetrical)....LILY FAMILY (*Liliaceae*)
2. Ovary inferior; flowers regular or irregular (asymmetrical)..............3

3. Flowers regular; leaves alternately folded over each other in 2 ranks.
                                              IRIS FAMILY (*Iridaceae*)
3. Flowers irregular; leaves not alternately folded over each other in 2 ranks.
                                         ORCHID FAMILY (*Orchidaceae*)

4. Petals present 5
4. Petals absent; the sepals sometimes arranged like petals...........64

5. Petals wholly or partly united...................................6
5. Petals separate to the base....................................28

6. Stamens more than 5..7
6. Stamens 5 or less...8

7. Flowers butterfly-like (upper petal large and spreading, lateral petals smaller, and the 2 lower petals joining to form a keel).
                                        PEA FAMILY (*Leguminosae*)
7. Flowers not as above..............FUMITORY FAMILY (*Fumariaceae*)

8. Ovary inferior..9
8. Ovary superior..14

9. Stamens not distinct, but united in a tube around the style; flowers in dense head surrounded by an involucre....SUNFLOWER FAMILY (*Compositae*)
9. Stamens distinct; usually separated to base......................10

10. Leaves opposite or whorled....................................11
10. Leaves alternate 13

11. Stamens fewer in number than lobes of corolla.
                                   VALERIAN FAMILY (*Valerianaceae*)
11. Stamens same number as corolla lobes and alternate with them (stamens 1 less in genus *Linnaea*)..12

12. Herbs with whorled leaves; not vine-like...MADDER FAMILY (*Rubiaceae*)
12. Leaves opposite; climbing or trailing sub-shrubs or vines.
                           HONEYSUCKLE FAMILY (*Caprifoliaceae*)

13. Plants climbing with tendrils; flowers perfect or imperfect.
                              CUCUMBER FAMILY (*Cucurbitaceae*)
13. Plants not climbing; tendrils absent; flower perfect.
                              HAREBELL FAMILY (*Campanulaceae*)

14. Corolla regular (all petals equal)..............................15
14. Corolla slightly irregular to strongly 2-lipped..................24

21

33. Plants spiny.........................CACTUS FAMILY (*Cactaceae*)
33. Plants not spiny.................BLAZING-STAR FAMILY (*Loasaceae*)

34. Stamens hypogynous (stamens attached to the receptacle below and free from the ovary—"below the ovary")..............................35
34. Stamens perigynous (stamens attached to the calyx or hypanthium cup—"around the ovary"; condition where the ovary is neither entirely superior nor entirely inferior)..62

35. Stamens more than 10 in number..................................36
35. Stamens 10 or less in number...................................42

36. Pistils 2 to many and distinct (though 1 in genus *Actaea*)............37
36. Pistil 1 in number...39

37. Leaves shield-shaped, with petiole attached to middle (or nearly so) of leaf........................WATER-LILY FAMILY (*Nymphaeaceae*)
37. Leaves not as above................................. 38

38. Sepals leathery; stamens burne on margins of lobed disk not attached to calyx.............................PEONY FAMILY (*Paeoneaceae*)
38. Sepals and stamens not as above..BUTTERCUP FAMILY (*Ranunculaceae*)

39. plants aquatic; petals 10-20 in number.
    WATER-LILY FAMILY (*Nymphaeaceae*)
39. Plants not aquatic; petals 10-20 in number.

40. Leaves alternate; petals 4.............POPPY FAMILY (*Papaveraceae*)
40. Leaves alternate or opposite; petals 5...........................41

41. Leaves opposite and dotted..ST. JOHN'S WORT FAMILY (*Hypericaceae*)
41. Leaves alternate and not dotted........MALLOW FAMILY (*Malvaceae*)

42. Flowers regular (symmetrical) in shape and structure..............43
42. Flowers irregular (asymmetrical) in shape and structure.............58

43. Pistils more than 1 per flower.................................44
43. Pistils 1 per flower..48

44. Pistils distinct; not even partly united..........................45
44. Pistils not distinct; more or less united.........................47

45. Pistils more in number than petals or sepals.
    BUTTERCUP FAMILY (*Ranunculaceae*)
45. Pistils same number as, or fewer than, the petals or sepals.........46

46. Pistils equal in number to petals or sepals.
    STONECROP FAMILY (*Crassulaceae*)
46. Pistils fewer in number than either petals or sepals.
    SAXIFRAGE FAMILY (*Saxifragaceae*)

47. Leaves entire and distinctly dotted.
    ST. JOHN'S WORT FAMILY (*Hypericaceae*)
47. Leaves not as above..............GERANIUM FAMILY (*Geraniaceae*)

48. Ovary with 1 chamber (cell or locule)...........................49
48. Ovary with 2 to several chambers...............................55

49. Sepals 2 per flower................PURSLANE FAMILY (*Portulaceae*)
49. Sepals 4-6 per flower...50

69. Plants with saprophytic life form; leaves reduced and often scale-like.
HEATH FAMILY (*Ericaceae*)
69. Plants photosynthetic, not saprophytic, and with normal leaves........70
70. Stamens numerous and irregular in number.
BUTTERCUP FAMILY (*Ranunculaceae*)
70. Stamens few in number (usually 4, 5, or 6)........................71
71. Style or stigma 1 (single); fruit a pod.....MUSTARD FAMILY (*Cruciferae*)
71. Styles or stigmas several (2-3)................................72
72. Fruit a dry, 1-celled, 3-cornered achene.
POLYGONUM FAMILY (*Polygonaceae*)
72. Fruit a thin-walled, bladder-like 1-seeded structure.
GOOSEFOOT FAMILY (*Chenopodiaceae*)
73. Leaves whorled; ovary inferior..WATER MILFOIL FAMILY (*Haloragaceae*)
73. Leaves not whorled; ovary superior.............................74
74. Plants with stamens and pistils in separate flowers on the same plant
(monoecious) 75
74. Plants not as above...76
75. With disagreeable, stinging hairs; stamens 4.
NETTLE FAMILY (*Urticaceae*)
75. Without disagreeable, stinging hairs; stamen 1.
SPURGE FAMILY (*Euphorbiaceae*)
76. Style 1 in number; the calyx petal-like..........................77
76. Styles 2-4; calyx not petal-like................................78
77. Stamens hypogynous; fruit an achene.
FOUR-O'CLOCK FAMILY (*Nyctaginaceae*)
77. Stamens attached to calyx; fruit a capsule.
PRIMROSE FAMILY (*Primulaceae*)
78. Leaves with small, rounded teeth; stamens on a conspicuous disk.
SAXIFRAGE FAMILY (*Saxifragaceae*)
78. Leaves entire, not as above; stamens hypogynous.
PINK FAMILY (*Caryophyllaceae*)

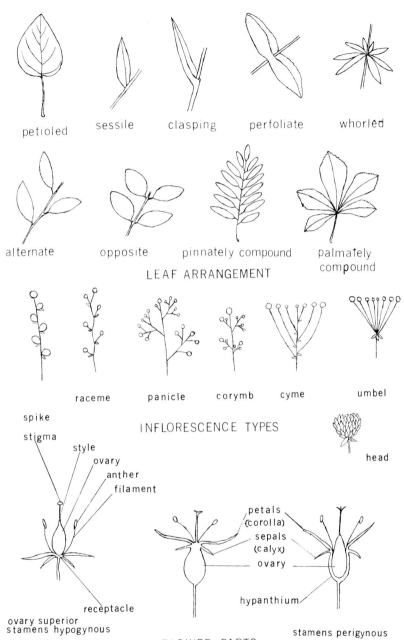

petioled   sessile   clasping   perfoliate   whorled

alternate   opposite   pinnately compound   palmately compound

LEAF ARRANGEMENT

raceme   panicle   corymb   cyme   umbel

spike

INFLORESCENCE TYPES

head

stigma
style
ovary
anther
filament

receptacle

ovary superior
stamens hypogynous

petals (corolla)
sepals (calyx)
ovary
hypanthium

stamens perigynous

FLOWER PARTS

25

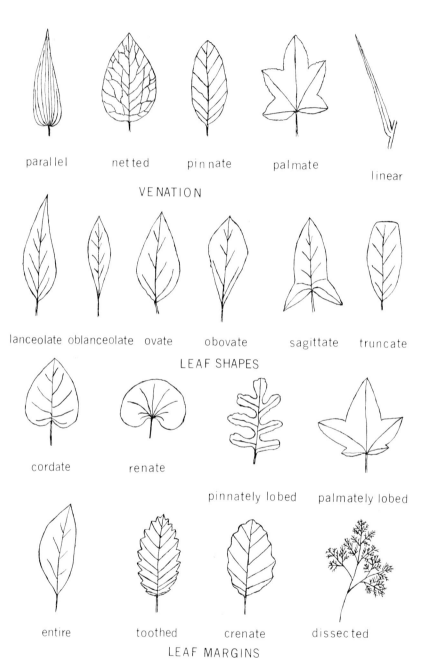

parallel   netted   pinnate   palmate

linear

VENATION

lanceolate oblanceolate ovate   obovate   sagittate   truncate

LEAF SHAPES

cordate   renate

pinnately lobed   palmately lobed

entire   toothed   crenate   dissected

LEAF MARGINS

GLOSSARY

Achene A small, dry, 1-seeded fruit which does not split when mature.

Alternate As in leaves in which there is only one at a node; not opposite.

Annual A plant which lives for only 1 year.

Anterior Toward the head, or front, end.

Anther The part of the stamen (toward the tip) bearing the pollen.

Aquatic Occurring in the water.

Asymmetrical One side not similar to the other side.

Axil The angle between a leaf and the stem.

Banner (=standard) The upper petal of a pea flower.

Basal (leaves) Located at the base (usually of a stem).

Beak A pointed projection.

Beard A tuft of hairs.

Bearded Possessing a beard.

Biennial A plant which lives for 2 years.

Bladder An expanded, balloon-like structure.

Bloom The waxy coating on a fruit or leaf.

Bract A small, modified leaf near the base of a flower or flower cluster.

Bulb An underground leaf bud with fleshy coats or scales for food storage and reproduction.

Bulblet A small bulb, sometimes occurring in leaf axils.

Burr A seed case with sharp points or prickles.

Calyx The cluster of sepals, united or separate, about the petals in a flower.

Capsule (fruit) A dry, multi-carpeled fruit which splits at maturity.

Chaff Thin, dry scales, as in the flowers of composites.

Chamber A compartment or section, as of an ovary.

Column A structure formed of the fused stamens and styles in the center of a flower, as in orchids.

Compound A structure composed of 2 or more similar parts, usually joined together.

Cordate Heart-shaped.

Corm The solid, fleshy base of a stem.

Corolla The group fused or separate, of petals.

Crenate Condition in leaves where the teeth are rounded.

Crenulate Condition in leaves where the teeth are small and rounded.

Crown The base of a perennial plant where the stem arises from the root.

Cyme A flat flower cluster (inflorescence) in which the central flowers bloom first.

Dioecious Stamens and pistils in different individual plants.

Disk-shaped (=discoid) Referring to composite heads composed of only tubular flowers.

Distal Toward the end of a structure.

Dorsal Toward the back, or upper side, of a structure.

Emergent Plants arising above the surface of the water.

Entire (leaf) Leaf margins without teeth, lobes, or other divisions.

Evergreen Bearing leaves throughout the year.

Exotic Non-native.

Fertile (stamen) Capable of reproduction; a stamen bearing pollen.

Fibrous Consisting of fibers.

Filament The stalk of a stamen.

Fleshy Thick, juicy.

Foliage Collectively, the leaves of a plant.

Fruit A ripened ovary; the seed-bearing structure of a plant.

Fused (petals, sepals) Joined together.

Gibbous The swollen part of a structure.

Gland A secreting body or structure.

Glandular With glands (usually sticky).

Glandular hairs Hairs bearing glands.

Hair Small, usually short, thread-like structures.

Head (flower) A dense, compact cluster of flowers in which the outer buds open first.

Heart-shaped Cordate, with petiole joining leaf in a notch and the tip pointed.

Herb Plants in which the parts above the ground surface die at end of growing season.

Hypanthium cup An enlarged, cup-shaped receptacle surrounding the ovary which bears the sepals, petals, and stamens.

Hypogynous Condition in which the sepals, petals, and stamens are attached directly to the receptacle.

Inferior ovary Condition where the ovary is below the pistil and stamens.

Infertile stamen Not bearing pollen.

Imperfect flower Condition where stamens and pistils are not borne in the same flower.

Inflorescence The flower cluster.

Involucre The circle of bracts at the base of a flower cluster or head of a composite.

Irregular flower A flower in which not all the petals are the same in shape, size, and pattern of location.

Joint See node.

Keel The lower 2 petals of a pea flower.

Keeled Having a keel.

Kidney-shaped As in a leaf shaped in the form of a kidney.

Lance-shaped (=lanceolate) As in a long, narrow leaf that is broadest at its base and narrows gradually to its tip.

Lateral Pertaining to the sides of a structure.

Leaflet A leaf-like division or section of a compound leaf.

Legume A member of the pea family; a fruit consisting of a single carpel and splitting along both upper and lower seams.

Ligule Flattened, elongated part of some composite flowers; a condition producing "ray flowers".

Linear (leaf) As in a long, narrow leaf with parallel margins.

Lip One of the parts of a 2-lobed corolla.

Lobe A shallow (less than one-half way to mid-vein) subdivision of a leaf.

Mat-like Plant growth form in which the plants are closely clustered together to form a solid mass.

Monoecious Condition where stamens and pistils are contained in separate flowers borne on the same plant.

Net-veined Leaves in which the veins cross or are joined more or less at right angles to each other, rather than occurring in a parallel pattern.

Node (=joint) The place on a stem which bears a leaf (or leaves).

Nodding Condition where the flower (or fruit) bends over to face downward.

Nutlet A small nut; a small, dry, thick-walled, non-splitting, usually single-celled, fruit.

Obcordate Heart-shaped, but with the notch at the tip of the leaf.

Oblanceolate A condition where the leaf is widest near the tip and tapers gradually to the base.

Opposite Condition where 2 leaves are located across from each other at the same node.

Ovary The part of the pistil containing the seeds.

Ovate Egg-shaped and broadest below the middle (as in a leaf).

Panicle A branched flower cluster consisting of several, elongated racemes.

Pappus The hairs, bristles, scales, etc., occurring on the seeds of composites.

Parallel-veined Condition where the veins of a leaf do not intersect, but are parallel to each other.

Pedicel The stalk of a single flower in a flower cluster.

Peduncle The stalk of a single flower or flower cluster.

Perennial A plant living and reproducing for years.

Perfect (flower) Having both stamens and pistils in the same flower.

Perfoliate Condition where the leaf surrounds the stem; i.e., the stem goes through the body of the leaf.

Perianth The calyx and corolla considered together.

Perigynous Condition where the calyx, corolla, and stamens are united into a basal disk or cup separate from the ovary, but surrounding it.

Petal A unit (actually a modified leaf) of the corolla which is usually colored; a part of the flower.

Petiole The stalk of a leaf.

Photosynthetic Green, food-producing, as in leaves.

Pinnate A compound leaf, with leaflets arranged on each side of a common petiole.

Pistil Central organ of a perfect flower containing the ovary, style, and stigma.

Pistillate flowers Flowers having pistils, but no stamens.

Pod (seed) A dry fruit which splits or otherwise opens.

Posterior Toward the back or rear of a structure.

Prostrate Lying flat on the ground.

Proximal Toward the base or beginning of a structure.

Raceme An elongate flower cluster along a single stalk with each flower on a separate pedicel and the youngest blooms toward the top of the common stalk.

Rachis The axis of an inflorescence or compound leaf.

Radiate A composite head in which the marginal flowers are ligulate (ray-like) and the central flowers tubular.

Rays The marginal flowers of a composite head; the branches of an umbel.

Receptacle The distal end of the flower stalk which bears the flowers.

Reflexed Turned back, as in a banner.

Regular Flowers in which all members of a group of structures are alike.

Rootstock A root-like, underground stem which may produce regular, upright stems.

Rosette A circular cluster of leaves, usually at the base of a stem or plant.

Saprophyte A non-chlorophyll-bearing plant which receives its nutrients from dead plant or animal material.

Scale A thin, flat, often leaf-like structure.

Scalloped Crenulate.

Sepal One of the units of the calyx.

Sessile Stalkless.

Sheath A tubular envelope, as a part of a leaf surrounding a stem.

Silicle A fruit resembling a silique, but scarcely longer than wide.

Silique A long capsule in which the 2 valves separate from a central, seed-bearing partition.

Simple Condition in a leaf where the body of the structure is one piece and not divided.

Spadix A spike with a fleshy axis containing small flowers.

Spathe A large bract inclosing a flower cluster.

Spatula-shaped Spoon-shaped.

Spike An elongate flower cluster where the flowers are attached very close to the stem.

Spine A sharp, usually woody, projection from a stem or leaf.

Spur A hollow projection of a calyx or corolla.

Stamen The pollen-bearing organ of a flower, containing an anther and a filament.

Staminate flower A flower bearing stamens, but no pistil.

Standard See banner.

Stigma The (usually) terminal, pollen-receiving part of the pistil.

Stipe A stalk.

Stipule One of a pair of appendages on each side of the base of the petiole of certain leaves.

Stolon (=runner) A long-creeping stem on the surface of the ground.

Style The narrowed portion of the pistil between the stigma and the ovary.

Sub-shrub A partly wooded, partly herbaceous plant.

Succulent Fleshy.

Superior (ovary) Where the ovary is located above the attachment of the corolla and calyx.

Taproot The stout, principal root descending vertically from the stem.

Teeth Usually more or less sharp-pointed projections on the margins of certain leaves.

Tendril A slender, coiling structure used by certain plants as holdfasts in climbing.

Terminal At the top.

Truncate Square-cut.

Tuber A short-thickened, underground branch or stem used for food storage.

Tufted Located in compact clusters.

Twining Ascending by coiling around a support, as in certain vines.

Umbel A more or less flat-topped flower cluster in which all the pedicels arise from the same point.

Vascular bundles Strands of cells in stems and veins for conducting fluids and solutes.

Veins The ribs (vascular bundles) in a leaf.

Ventral On the under side of a structure.

Whorl Usually, a group of 3 or more leaves radiating from the same node.

Wing A thin, membranous extension from a structure.

IDENTIFICATION KEYS

TO

WASHINGTON WILDFLOWERS

Figure 2.
Broad, green leaves of the skunk cabbage, *Lysichitum.* (Larrison)

Chapter 1—The Calla Lily Family (*Araceae*)

Members of this family are perennial herbs with large, broad leaves; stout rhizomes; and many, small flowers located on a fleshy stalk which is often partly surrounded by a large, colored bract or spathe. Sepals 4-6, or none. Fruit is a many-seeded berry. One native species in Washington. (Color Plate 1) (Fig. 2)

SKUNK CABBAGE (*Lysichitum americanum*) Yellow, corolla-like spathe partly inclosing a club-like spike of small, greenish flowers. Leaves, when crushed, give off strong, skunk-like odor. East. and West. Wash.; common in swampy, boggy places, often in woodland openings or in sedgy, half-drowned areas along pond and stream margins, in lowlands and up to intermediate elevations in mountains. Early spring to early summer; one of the earliest blooming wildflowers in the state.

Though far smaller in area than such monster neighbors as Idaho and Montana, the state of Washington possesses more ecologic diversity than does any other of the contiguous United States. This is due to several environmental factors. Altitudinally, the land varies from sea level to 14,410 feet at the summit of Mount Rainier. Latitudinally speaking, the state lies in the critical transitional belt between the sub-Arctic northern forest zone and the warmer, drier regions to the south, such that the northernmost parts of the state contain elements of the Canadian spruce forest biome, while the southernmost reaches dip into desert floral and faunal types, at least in the eastern portion.

While moist, temperate air masses sweep onto the state's west coast, these are modified by the Olympic and Cascade ranges, such that prominent rain shadows cover large portions of the land while various thermodynamic and air flow phenomena further complicate the climatic picture.

The very rocks and soil themselves are tremendously varied, presenting great mountainous uplifts of andesite, argillite, or granite in certain ranges, while shallow forest soils contrast with windblown sand and loess, the latter often interrupted by basaltic outcroppings.

Such variant factors as these, and many others, have produced a richly diversified flora of which this book reflects a part. A series of short essays are included through the body of the following keys to briefly expand on these interesting and important phenomena.

Figure 3.
Parallel veining in monocot leaves, as illustrated by the false solomon's seals,
Smilacina. (Larrison)

Chapter 2—The Lily Family (*Liliaceae*)

Members of this family are perennial herbs, often with bulbs, corms, or rhizomes, that are commonly found growing in open or semi-open places. The flowers may be large and showy or very small and perfect or imperfect, but usually the floral parts are in 3's. The stamens may be 3 to 6. A variable family, some plants lily-like, others not. (Color Plates 1-5)

1. Petals and sepals totalling 4, similar; 1/8 inch long.
WILD LILY-OF-THE-VALLEY
1. Petals and sepals totalling 6, similar or dissimilar; more than 1/8 inch long 2

2. Leaves in a single whorl of 3 at top of stem; sepals green; petals white or purplish . . . . .TRILLIUMS (*Trillium*)
2. Leaves not in a single whorl of 3 at top of stem; sepals and petals not color differentiated 3

3. Sepals and petals dissimilar in size . . . . .MARIPOSA LILIES (*Calochortus*)
3. Sepals and petals similar in size. 4

4. Flowers numerous, in umbels or heads; bulbs present; leaves linear and basal 5
4. Flowers solitary or in racemes or panicles, but never in single umbel or head on leafless stem. 6

5. Bulbs and leaves with onion odor. .ONIONS (*Allium*)
5. Bulbs and leaves without onion odor. . . . . BRODIAEAS (*Brodiaea*)

6. Leaves linear, stiff, and lasting for several years. . . . . .BEAR GRASS
6. Leaves various and not as above. 7

7. Leaves basal 8
7. Leaves not basal but on flowering stems. 14

8. Styles 3 in number, distinct to ovary. 9
8. Styles 1; or if 3, then fused for at least half their length. 11

9. Plants with rootstocks, rather than bulbs. . . . . .WESTERN TOFIELDIA
9. Plants with bulbs. 10

10. Stems slender and weak; flowers in racemes and nodding on slender pedicels . . . . .BRONZE BELLS
10. Stems stout; flowers in racemes or panicles, stiffly erect and not nodding.
DEATH CAMASSES (*Zigadenus*)

11. Leaves linear and very narrow (less than 1/8 inch wide). . . . . . .ALP LILY
11. Leaves oblong and broad, or if linear, more than 1/8 inch wide. 12

12. Flowers 1 to 5; leaves in 2's or 3's. 13
12. Flowers 10 or more in a raceme; leaves several. .CAMASSES (*Camassia*)

13. Flowers white; petals and sepals not turned backward. . . .QUEEN'S CUP
13. Flowers white, yellow, or pink; petals and sepals strongly turned backward.
AVALANCHE LILIES (*Erythronium*)

14. Plants with bulbs; flowers mostly large; leaves linear or lanceolate. 15
14. Plants with rootstocks; flowers mostly small; leaves oval. 16

15. Petals more than 1 inch in length. . . . . .COLUMBIA LILY
15. Petals less than 1 inch in length. . . . . .FRITILLARIES (*Fritillaria*)

16. Flowers numerous in terminal raceme or panicle on single stem 17
16. Flowers 1 to few, occurring along stem or in small groups at tips of branches of stem 18
17. Plants large; styles 3; leaves prominently veined . . VERATRUMS (*Veratrum*)
17. Plants medium size; style 1; leaves not prominently veined.
FALSE SOLOMON'S SEALS (*Smilacina*)
18. Flowers at tips of branches of stem . . . . FAIRY BELLS (*Disporum*)
18. Flowers scattered along stem and usually hidden under the leaves.
TWISTED-STALKS (*Streptopus*)

             *   *   *

WILD LILY-OF-THE-VALLEY (*Maianthemum dilatatum*) Spike of small, white flowers rising above 1 to 3 shiny, green, prominently eared, pointed-tipped leaves. East. and West. Wash.; stream banks and moist woods from lowlands to intermediate elevations. Late spring to early summer. (Color Plate 3)

BEAR GRASS (*Xerophyllum tenax*) Basal leaves tough, linear, grass-like; in thick clump. Stout flower stalk to 5 feet, topped by globe-shaped head of tiny creamy-white flowers. East. and West. Wash.; open woods and meadows, often occurring in large conspicuous patches; increasing in elevation from sea level along ocean coast to subalpine areas on eastern border mountains. Late spring and summer. (Color Plate 5)

WESTERN TOFIELDIA (*Tofieldia glutinosa*) Leaves linear, grass-like. Stem sticky, 4 to 20 inches tall, topped by bistort-like cluster of creamy-white flowers, 1/4 inch in diameter; followed by heads of glistening, wine-red seeds. East. and West. Wash.; moist meadows, bogs, streamsides, and road-side ditches, from sea level to (mostly) subalpine areas in mountains. Summer. (Color Plate 4)

WESTERN BRONZE BELLS (*Stenanthium occidentale*) Leaves grass-like, mostly basal, to 12 inches long; stem to 18 inches tall. Flowers in loose raceme of nodding, narrow, bell-shaped blooms, 1/3 to 1/2 inch long, and brownish purple in color. East. and West. Wash.; moist wooded slopes and mossy streamsides; sea level (Olympic Peninsula) to (mostly) subalpine areas. Mid to late summer. (Color Plate 4)

ALP LILY (*Lloydia serotina*) Flower single on 6-inch stems, white with pink vein and yellow spot at base of each petal. Leaves long, grass-like, and very narrow. West. Wash. in Cascades and Olympics; usually in the highest places in the mountains, where scattered among the rocks; rare. Early to mid summer. (Color Plate 3)

QUEEN'S CUP (*Clintonia uniflora*) 2 or 3 inch wide, oblong basal leaves; single, large, white, 6-petalled flower. Dark, blue berry in fruit. East. and West. Wash.; common in the moist, montane forests. Early to mid summer. (Color Plate 2)

COLUMBIA LILY (*Lilium columbianum*) Large (2 inch long), 6-parted, re-curved-petalled flowers, which are orange, spotted with purplish brown. East. and West. Wash.; lowlands to subalpine areas; open places to forests. Early to late summer. (Color Plate 3)

TRILLIUMS (*Trillium*) (Color Plate 5)

Plants marked by 3 leaves in a whorl at tip of stem. Flowers large with 3 green sepals and 3 white or purple petals.

1. Flowers sessile, without stems (pedicels); leaves long-petioled or mottled. 2
1. Flowers on pedicels, not sessile; leaves without petioles.
WESTERN TRILLIUM

2. Leaves long-petioled and not mottled; flowers usually purple.
ROUND-LEAVED TRILLIUM
2. Leaves sessile, without petioles, and mottled; flowers usually white, rarely pink . . . . .MOTTLED TRILLIUM

*   *   *

ROUND-LEAVED TRILLIUM (*Trillium petiolatum*) Leaves round-tipped with long petioles; flowers purple, but occasionally greenish or yellowish. East. Wash.; moist places in woods, such as streambanks and wet swales. Late spring to early summer.

MOTTLED TRILLIUM (*Trillium chloropetalum*) Flower stemless in center of three, brownish, mottled, green leaves; narrow petals are upright and are white, less commonly pink or reddish. West. Wash.; moist lowland woods. Early spring to early summer.

WESTERN TRILLIUM (*Trillium ovatum*) Flower on noticeable stalk projecting from cluster of three leaves; petals white, turning to pink or reddish in age. East. and West. Wash.; mostly woods and semi-open places. Early spring to early summer.

MARIPOSA LILIES (*Calochortus*) (Color Plate 1)

Plants with few, but showy, flowers at tips of short stems arising from 1 or 2 basal leaves. Petals broad, often hairy, and with prominent gland.

1. Basal leaf relatively broad and flat; ovary and fruit oblong to roundish. . . . 2
1. Basal leaf very narrow and not flat; ovary and fruit long and narrow.
LARGE-FLOWERED MARIPOSA LILY

2. Fruits nodding 3
2. Fruits erect 5

3. Gland on base of petal straight, not curved, and black.
KOOTENAI MARIPOSA LILY
3. Gland on base of petal curved and not black. 4

4. Sepals lacking basal, glandular spot; flowers greenish white with purple crescent on each petal; extreme East. and Southeast. Wash.
ELEGANT MARIPOSA LILY
4. Sepals with basal, glandular spot; flowers yellowish white with narrow purple crescent on each petal; southern Cascades. . SUBALPINE MARIPOSA LILY

5. Petals pointed at tip and triangular; flowers white or purplish with dark purple crescent on each petal. . . . . LYALL'S MARIPOSA LILY
5. Petals broad near tip and not pointed; flowers creamy white with reddish blotch on each petal. . . . . BIG-POD MARIPOSA LILY

LARGE-FLOWERED MARIPOSA LILY (*Calochortus macrocarpus*) Large, tulip-like, purple to pink flowers with green stripe on each petal; sepals long and narrow; plants large, 8 to 20 inches tall. East. Wash.; dry, open places. Late spring to mid summer.

KOOTENAI MARIPOSA LILY (*Calochortus apiculatus*) Flowers only slightly pointed and yellowish white, occasionally streaked with purple. Northeast. Wash.; rocky slopes in yellow pine woods. Early summer.

ELEGANT MARIPOSA LILY (*Calochortus elegans*) Flowers greenish white with purple crescent on each petal. Extreme East. and Southeast. Wash.; grassy hillsides and open woods. Late spring to early summer.

SUBALPINE MARIPOSA LILY (*Calochortus subalpinus*) Flowers yellowish white with narrow purple crescent on each petal; purple gland at base of petal. Southern Cascades; pumice areas in subalpine zone, especially on Mounts Adams and St. Helens. Summer.

LYALL'S MARIPOSA LILY (*Calochortus lyallii*) Petals triangular and pointed; anthers blunt. Flowers white to purplish with dark, purple crescent on each petal. East. Wash.; open yellow pine forests. Late spring to mid summer.

BIG-POD MARIPOSA LILY (*Calochortus eurycarpus*) Petals very broad and rounded at tip. Flowers creamy white. Southeast. Wash.; grassy meadows and open forests. Summer.

ONIONS (*Allium*) (Color Plate 1)

Onion-like plants with characteristic onion odor, linear leaves, and smallish flowers in terminal umbel. Plants growing from bulb.

1. Bulb coat with network of coarse, branching fibers......GEYER'S ONION
1. Bulb coat without fibers or with parallel fibers, but never a branching network 2

2. Bulbs elongate with heavy rootstocks................................3
2. Bulbs more or less roundish or oval-shaped; rootstock, if present, small and slender 4

3. Flower head (umbel) nodding......................NODDING ONION
3. Flower head (umbel) erect, not nodding...........TALL SWAMP ONION

4. Leaves narrow, often concave, and more than 2.......HOOKER'S ONION
4. Leaves broad and flat; 2 or 1 in number............................5

5. Stem roundish; leaves concave-convex..............................6
5. Stem more or less flattened; leaves thick and flat.....................8

6. Stamens shorter than petals...........................JONES' ONION
6. Stamens as long as, or longer than, the petals.......................7

7. Leaves slender; longer than stem......................ROCK ONION
7. Leaves thick; shorter than stem.....................DOUGLAS' ONION

8. Margins of petals strongly in-turned..................TOLMIE'S ONION
8. Margins of petals not, or hardly, in-turned..........................9

9. Bulbs twisted sideways and not symmetrical........CRENULATED ONION
9. Bulbs not twisted sidewise, but symmetrical...........FOOTHILL ONION

GEYER'S ONION (*Allium geyeri*) Some plants have flowers replaced by tiny bulbs. Flowers rose-colored. East. Wash.; grassy, rocky meadows, scabrock areas, on moist slopes and streamsides; often common. Late spring to early summer.

NODDING ONION (*Allium cernuum*) Flowering head turned downward ("nodding"). Flowers pink. East. and West. Wash.; dry, rocky hillsides where snow banks leave spots of spring moisture. Early to mid summer.

TALL SWAMP ONION (*Allium validum*) Bulb on a long, stout rhizome. Flowers rose or white. Wet meadows in upper parts of Cascades and mountains eastward; prefers higher elevations. Summer.

HOOKER'S ONION (*Allium acuminatum*) Tips of petals and sepals curved backward. Flowers pink to deep rose. East. and Northwest. Wash.; dry, gravelly, open places, such as exposed hillsides and bluffs. Late spring to mid summer.

JONES' ONION (*Allium fibrillum*) Flowers white. East. Wash.; in moist, open places. Late spring to mid summer.

ROCK ONION (*Allium macrum)* Flowers white to pale reddish. East. Wash.; dry, open, rocky places. Spring.

DOUGLAS' ONION (*Allium douglasii*) Flowers reddish purple. East. Wash.; dry, gravelly areas that are moist in spring; irregular in distribution. Spring.

TOLMIE'S ONION (*Allium tolmiei*) Flowers white to pink. East. Wash.; thin soil in rocky, open places. Mid spring to mid summer.

CRENULATED ONION (*Allium crenulatum*) Two flat, downward-curved leaves that are longer than flowering stem. West. and western part of East. Wash.; dry, rocky places, such as bald summits, on intermediate and higher elevations. Flowers deep red. Mid spring to mid summer.

FOOTHILL ONION (*Allium scilloides*) Flowers white, pink, or red. East. Wash.; dry, open, rocky slopes and foothills in western part of Columbia Basin. Early spring.

BRODIAEAS (*Brodiaea*) (Color Plate 1)

Plants with few, slender, basal leaves. Flowers in loose to compact umbels. Common in dry, open ground.

1. Fertile stamens 3 in number. 2
1. Fertile stamens 6 in number. 3
2. Flower head open, with individual flowers on pedicels at least 3/8 inch long. . . . . .HARVEST BRODIAEA
2. Flower head with individual flowers tightly bunched; pedicels less than 3/8 inch long . . . . .BUNCH-FLOWERED BRODIAEA
3. Flowers bell-shaped with ovary visible; flowers white with a green median strip on each petal. . . . . .HYACINTH BRODIAEA
3. Flowers tube-shaped, bluish, with ovary concealed. 4
4. Inner "petals" with ruffled margins. . . . . .DOUGLAS' BRODIAEA
4. Inner "petals" without ruffled margins. . . . . .HOWELL'S BRODIAEA

HARVEST BRODIAEA (*Brodiaea coronaria*) Leaves narrow and disappearing by time of flowering; not all flowers in head opening at same time; flowers 1 inch long and trumpet-shaped, being 6-cleft to 2/3 of length and erect on long pedicels; petals re-curved and violet purple; fertile stamens 3 in number. West. Wash. and southern part of East. Wash.; open, rocky or grassy places on dry hillsides; common in early summer. Early to mid summer.

BUNCH-FLOWERED BRODIAEA (*Brodiaea congesta*) Flower pedicels very short and united at base. Flowers light to dark purple. Mostly West. Wash. in dry, open places on fields and hillsides. Late spring to early summer.

HYACINTH BRODIAEA (*Brodiaea hyacinthina*) Flowers white and in dense umbels, with spreading, 6-lobed perianths. East. and West. Wash.; open, grassy or rocky places. Late spring to late summer.

DOUGLAS' BRODIAEA (*Brodiaea douglasii*) Flowers bluish, tubular and with short lobes. Plants often large (to 2 feet); leaves green and present at flowering. East. Wash.; grasslands, sagebrush, and open yellow pine woods. Mid spring to mid summer.

HOWELL'S BRODIAEA (*Brodiaea howellii*) Large, drooping flowers with dark blue tubes and white or pale blue lobes. East. and West. Wash.; grasslands and sagebrush in lowlands and foothills. Mid spring to early summer.

POISON CAMASSES (*Zigadenus*) (Color Plate 5)

1. Petals without petiole-like stems . . . . MOUNTAIN DEATH CAMAS
1. Petals with petiole-like stems 2

2. Flowers in panicles; petals about 1/8 inch long . PANICLED DEATH CAMAS
2. Flowers in racemes; petals about 1/4 inch long . . . . POISON CAMAS

*   *   *

MOUNTAIN DEATH CAMAS (*Zigadenus elegans*) Stout, grass-like leaves on lower stem. Flowers few in raceme and greenish white, about 3/8 inch long. Petals and sepals similar, each with greenish yellow gland spot at base. Each flower on separate petiole. West. Wash.; open, as well as forested areas in the middle and higher zones of the mountains. Summer.

PANICLED DEATH CAMAS (*Zigadenus paniculatus*) Plants small and slender with weak stems. Flower head small and loose; flowers white to buffy white. East. Wash.; sagebrush to open, coniferous forests. Early spring to early summer.

POISON CAMAS (*Zigadenus venenosus*) Plants with stout stalks and substantial leaves. Flowers white to buffy white and in tight heads which taper to the top. East. and West. Wash.; dry, open, often rocky, places. Early spring to mid summer.

AVALANCHE LILIES (*Erythronium*) (Color Plate 2) (Fig. 1)

Single-stemmed herbs with broad, nearly basal leaves and large, nodding, single or several, lily-like flowers. Usually growing in large patches.

1. Leaves uniformly green; flowers yellow or white 2
1. Leaves mottled, light green or dark green; flowers pink or white 3

2. Leaves broad at base with distinct petiole; flowers white.
ALPINE AVALANCHE LILY
2. Leaves narrow at base without distinct petiole; flowers pale to light yellow.
YELLOW AVALANCHE LILY
3. Flowers white and slightly down-turned........GREAT AVALANCHE LILY
3. Flowers pink and strongly down-turned........COAST AVALANCHE LILY

*　　*　　*

ALPINE AVALANCHE LILY (*Erythronium montanum*)   Broad leaf abruptly narrowing to long petiole. Flowers white. Cascades and Olympics; subalpine, coniferous groves and meadows; often covering areas of many acres in extent. Summer to early autumn. Probably the most beloved of all wildflowers.

YELLOW AVALANCHE LILY (*Erythronium grandiflorum*) Flowers pale to strong yellow. East. and West. Wash.; variable, being found on grassy or sagebrush slopes, as well as in montane coniferous forests, and even to subalpine meadows. Early spring to late summer.

GREAT AVALANCHE LILY (*Erythronium oregonum*) Leaves mottled. Flowers white. West. Wash.; open to semi-open, moist, habitats (fields, meadows, woods), mostly at lower elevations. Early to late spring.

COAST AVALANCHE LILY (*Erythronium revolutum*) Leaves mottled; flowers pink and strongly down-turned. West. Wash.; irregular; in moist, semi-open places, such as edges of woods, at lower elevations. Spring.

CAMASSES (*Camassia*) (Color Plate 2)

1. Occurs in West. Wash.; petals, after withering, twisting about ovary; flower-bearing stems not, or little, longer than leaves............GREAT CAMAS
1. Occurs in both West. and East. Wash.; petals, after withering, separating and not covering ovary; flower-bearing stem longer than leaves.
COMMON CAMAS

*　　*　　*

GREAT CAMAS (*Camassia leichtlinii*) Stalks of individual flowers spreading outward. Flowers light to deep bluish violet; rarely cream-colored. West. Wash. and Col. Gorge; moist, open places, such as wet meadows; common. Spring.

COMMON CAMAS (*Camassia quamash*)   Stalks of individual flowers not spreading outward. Flowers white, pale blue, or dark blue. East. and West. Wash.; open, grassy places that are moist in early spring; common. Spring to early summer.

FRITILLARIES (*Fritillaria*) (Color Plate 3)

Plants with scaly bulbs and numerous, narrow leaves. Flowers 1 to several, bell-shaped, and nodding.

1. Flowers yellowish..............................YELLOW FRITILLARY
1. Flowers purplish 2
2. Petals not strongly mottled; flowers definitely bell-shaped and petals strongly fused............................KAMCHATKA FRITILLARY
2. Petals strongly mottled; flowers not so definitely bell-shaped and petals not strongly fused together.........................BROWN FRITILLARY

YELLOW FRITILLARY (*Fritillaria pudica*) Stem about 3-4 inches high; leaves narrow, pointed, concave, and growing on stem. Usually single, narrowly bell-shaped, down-turned, bright yellow flower. East. Wash.; grasslands, sagebrush, and open woods. Early to late spring; often one of the earliest of bloomers in arid country.

KAMCHATKA FRITILLARY (*Fritillaria camschatcensis*) 12-24 inches tall. Flowers usually in 2's and purplish in color. West. Wash.; moist, open places from sea level to subalpine areas. Late spring to mid summer.

BROWN FRITILLARY (*Fritillaria lanceolata*) 8-20 inch stem. Flowers 1 to several on stem and bowl-shaped, down-turned, and purplish brown, heavily speckled with greenish yellow on inside. Leaves lance-shaped and in whorls. East. and West. Wash.; open places, meadows as well as woods. Mid spring to early summer.

VERATRUMS (*Veratrum*) (Color Plate 5)

1. Flowers green, in drooping panicles. . . . . .GREEN VERATRUM
1. Flowers white, in erect panicles. . . . . .WHITE VERATRUM

*   *   *

GREEN VERATRUM (*Veratrum viride*) Panicle branches drooping. Flowers greenish. East. and West. Wash.; wet, boggy places in forests and mountain meadows. Summer to early autumn.

WHITE VERATRUM (*Veratrum californicum*) Panicle branches horizontal or ascending. Flowers white. East. and West. Wash.; lowlands as well as mountains, mostly in wet, boggy places. Summer.

FALSE SOLOMON'S SEALS (*Smilacina*) (Color Plate 4) (Fig. 3)

1. Leaves narrow; flowers about 1/4 inch long; stamens shorter than petals.
SMALL FALSE SOLOMON'S SEAL
1. Leaves broad; flowers about 1/8 inch long; stamens longer than petals.
GIANT FALSE SOLOMON'S SEAL

*   *   *

SMALL FALSE SOLOMON'S SEAL (*Smilacina stellata*) Leaves narrow. Large, creamy-white flowers, each on a single stalk in a few-flowered raceme. East. and West. Wash.; open hillsides. Late spring to early summer.

GIANT FALSE SOLOMON'S SEAL (*Smilacina racemosa*) Leaves broad (1½-3 inches) and long (3-8 inches). Flowers tiny, creamy white, and arranged in white plume at top of stem. East. and West. Wash.; moist woods, sea level to intermediate elevations. Mid spring to mid summer.

FAIRY BELLS (*Disporum*) (Color Plate 2)

Plants with oval, alternate leaves and drooping, whitish or greenish-yellow leaves that are terminal, occurring in 2's, 3's, or singles.

1. Flowers distinctly bell-shaped (petals more united) and petals longer than
stamens. . . . . .LARGE-FLOWERED FAIRY BELLS

1. Flowers not so bell-shaped (petals more separated); petals shorter than stamens. 2
2. Leaves smooth on upper surface. . . . . . ROUGH-FLOWERED FAIRY BELLS
2. Leaves hairy on upper surface. . . . . .HOOKER'S FAIRY BELLS

*   *   *

LARGE-FLOWERED FAIRY BELLS (*Disporum smithii*) Stamens not protruding beyond tips of petals. Flowers whitish. West. Wash.; common in moist, shaded woods. Spring to early summer.

ROUGH-FLOWERED FAIRY BELLS (*Disporum trachycarpum*) Stamens longer than petals; hairs on leaf margins spreading laterally. Flowers buffy white. East. Wash.; moist, shaded woods. Late spring to mid summer.

HOOKER'S FAIRY BELLS (*Disporum hookeri*) Stamens projecting beyond tips of petals; hairs on leaf margins pointing sharply forward. Flowers cream white. East. and West. Wash.; moist, dense woods. Mid spring to mid summer.

TWISTED-STALKS (*Streptopus*) (Color Plate 4)

Plants with leafy stems and small, solitary or paired, axillary, nodding flowers characterized by peduncles which are bent or twisted near the middle.

1. Petals less than 1/4 inch long; entire petal spreading.
SMALL-FLOWERED TWISTED-STALK
1. Petals more than 1/4 inch long; only tips of petals spreading. 2

2. Plants large (to 40 inches tall); stems branching. .LARGE TWISTED-STALK
2. Plants small (to 12 inches tall); stems seldom branching.
SMALL TWISTED-STALK

*   *   *

SMALL-FLOWERED TWISTED-STALK (*Streptopus streptopoides*) Small, flattened, saucer-shaped, greenish (occasionally tinged with purple) flowers. East. and West. Wash.; dense, coniferous woods in mountains. Late summer.

LARGE TWISTED-STALK (*Streptopus amplexifolius*) Underside of leaves grayish; bases of leaves clasping the stem. Thread-like flower pedicel with sharp kink or twist in the middle. Flowers greenish white. East. and West. Wash.; moist areas, mostly in forests of lowlands and mountains. Late spring.

SMALL TWISTED-STALK (*Streptopus roseus*) Underside of leaves not grayish; leaves not clasping the stem. Flower stalk only slightly curved. Flowers white or greenish yellow, marked with reddish, or, reddish or purplish with white tips. Cascades and West. Wash.; also the Blue Mountains; mostly in damp places, such as moist woods and streambanks, in the mountains. Early summer.

Figure 4.
Blue-eyed grass, *Sisyrinchium.* (Yaich)

44

Chapter 3—The Iris Family (*Iridaceae*)

Members of this family, as treated here, are perennial plants with flat, sword-like leaves, creeping rootstocks, and large showy flowers which may be irregular (3 broad, downward pointing, petal-like sepals, 3 erect petals, and 3 petal-like style branches) in true irises; or regular (sepals and petals similar) in the blue-eyed grasses. They favor open places that are moist in spring and early summer, but become dry or arid later in the season. Certain species may occur in beds or patches of considerable size to form striking, though temporary, floristic aspects in the environment. (Color Plate 6)

1. Petals, as well as sepals, similar in shape and size.
BLUE-EYED GRASSES (Sisyrinchium)
2. Petals, like sepals, dissimilar in shape and size; styles petal-like.
IRISES (Iris)

BLUE-EYED GRASSES (*Sisyrinchium*) (Color Plate 6) (Fig. 4)

1. Flowers yellow . . . . GOLDEN-EYED GRASS
1. Flowers various in color, but not yellow 2

2. Flowers bluish . . . . BLUE-EYED GRASS
2. Flowers reddish purple or white 3

3. Flowers deep reddish purple; filament tube not strongly inflated above base; flowers somewhat conical at base . . . . PURPLE-EYED GRASS
3. Flowers light magenta to pinkish purple or albino (white); filament tube strongly inflated (bulb-like) above base; flowers flat and more spreading at base . . . . GRASS WIDOW

*   *   *

GOLDEN-EYED GRASS (*Sisyrinchium californicum*) Flowers golden yellow, about 3/4 inch in diameter. Seed pods rather oblong, cylindrical, and 3-chambered. West. Wash.; moist areas, as at the edge of water, in the lowlands. Early to mid summer.

BLUE-EYED GRASS (*Sisyrinchium angustifolium*) Flowers deep bluish and smaller, about 1/2 inch in diameter. Seed pods round. East. and West. Wash.; sea level to intermediate elevations in mountains, preferring open areas with abundant spring moisture in the soil. Spring to mid summer.

PURPLE-EYED GRASS (*Sisyrinchium douglasii*) Flowers deep rose purple and large, 1½ inches in diameter. West. Wash.; the Columbia Gorge, and northward along the east base of the Cascades; open, often rocky or dry areas, which are wet in spring; from sea level to subalpine. Early spring to early summer.

GRASS WIDOW (*Sisyrinchium inflatum*) Flowers light magenta to pale pinkish purple or white (the albino form) and about 1¼ inches in diameter. East. Wash.; grassy places in sagebrush or yellow pine woods where temporarily moist in spring; low to intermediate elevations in lowlands and foothills. Early spring to early summer.

IRISES (*Iris*) (Color Plate 6)

1. Flowering stems shorter, usually under 16 inches tall and with several leaves . . . . PURPLE IRIS
1. Flowering stems longer, usually over 16 inches tall and leafless or with one leaf per stem . . . . WESTERN IRIS

*   *   *

PURPLE IRIS (*Iris tenax*) Flowers lavender, purple, or blue; rarely white, pinkish, or yellowish. West. Wash.; open sunny areas, such as pastures, roadsides, meadows, logged land, and forest clearings; entirely in lowlands. Spring to early summer.

WESTERN IRIS (*Iris missouriensis*) Flowers pale to deep blue. East. Wash. and some islands in the northern part of Puget Sound; sagebrush, grasslands, and open yellow pine woods where spring moisture is abundant. Spring to mid summer.

Chapter 4—The Orchid Family (*Orchidaceae*)

Members of this family are woodland or deep coniferous forest flowers that are mostly perennial herbs with perfect, irregular flowers and corms, rhizomes, tubers, or bulbs. The flowers of many species resemble those of horticultural orchids, but are smaller and much less showy. Sepals 3 and similar; petals 3, with median one (the "lip") usually larger and often spurred. The stamens are often more or less united with the style. (Color Plates 6-8)

1. Plants with green foliage leaves....................................2
1. Plants without green foliage leaves..............................8

2. Flowers single to few and showy.................................3
2. Flowers numerous, in spikes or racemes.........................4

3. Flowers pinkish ....CALYPSO
3. Flowers brownish, purplish, or yellowish. . LADY'S-SLIPPERS (*Cypripedium*)

4. Leaves 2, located near middle of stem...........TWAYBLADES (*Listera*)
4. Leaves more than 2, alternate or basal...........................5

5. Flowers with prominent spurs..............BOG ORCHIDS (*Habenaria*)
5. Flowers without prominent spurs.................................6

6. Flowers white or greenish and arranged in spikes.....................7
6. Flowers greenish and brownish purple and arranged in a raceme.
GIANT HELLEBORINE

7. Spikes twisted; leaves not mottled...........HOODED LADIES-TRESSES
7. Spikes not twisted; leaves mottled................EVERGREEN ORCHID

8. Stem and flowers whitish (with yellow patch on lip)....PHANTOM ORCHID
8. Stem and flowers yellowish green, reddish, or brownish...............9

9. Flowers with prominent spurs; "roots" not reddish.
BOG ORCHIDS (*Habenaria*)
9. Flowers lacking prominent spurs; "roots" commonly reddish.
CORALROOTS (*Corallorhiza*)

*   *   *

CALYPSO (*Calypso bulbosa*) Typically one shiny leaf at base of flowering stem (sometimes 2). Flower pink with purple, slipper-like lip about 1 inch long. Distinctive, pleasing fragrance. East. and West. Wash.; prefers rich leaf mold in deep, cool, coniferous forests from sea level to middle elevations; often found on well-shaded banks near streams. Early spring to early summer. An endangered flower species. (Color Plate 6)

GIANT HELLEBORINE (*Epipactis gigantea*) Stem leafy with numerous, oval to lanceolate, sheathing, deeply concave leaves. Flowers few (2-10), greenish to reddish purple, lacking spurs, and in loose raceme. Lip veined and purplish. Sepals and petals similar; pouch-like lip is pinched in the center with tip hanging down loosely as if on hinge. East. and West. Wash.; streambanks and lake shores; uncommon and irregular. Spring to late summer. (Color Plate 7)

HOODED LADIES'-TRESSES (*Spiranthes romanzoffiana*) Leaves basal and on lower part of stem, narrowly lance-shaped. Pearly greenish-white to pale cream flowers in tightly-packed, spirally-twisted raceme. Sepals and petals form a "hood" over the lip. East. and West. Wash.; moist places in lowlands to intermediate mountain elevations. Mid summer to late summer. (Color Plate 8)

47

Figure 5.
Lady's-slippers, *Cypripedium.* (Larrison)

EVERGREEN ORCHID (*Goodyera oblongifolia*) Leaves long-oval, greenish with creamy stripe down the middle and mottled, evergreen, and in flat rosette on ground surface around base of stem. Flowers small, white; in one-sided raceme on stalk. Petals and 1 sepal form "hood" over sac-like lip. East. and West. Wash.; deep, mossy woods, though occasionally in dry, open forests. Mid summer to early autumn. (Color Plate 7)

PHANTOM ORCHID (*Eburophyton austiniae*) Saprophytic species with entire plant (stalk, flowers, and bract-like leaves) a pure, waxy white, except for a yellow spot on the lip of each flower. Flowers are miniature, white orchids. Pleasing vanilla-like fragrance. East. and West. Wash.; dry, dense, shady woods in lowlands and mountains. Summer. (Color Plate 7) (Fig. 6)

LADY'S-SLIPPERS (*Cypripedium*) (Color Plate 7) (Fig. 5)

Stems erect and leafy, supporting at tip 1 to several showy, orchid-like flowers with large, sac-like, lower petals.

1. Leaves 2, opposite on stem; flowers several, in cluster.
   CLUSTERED LADY'S-SLIPPER
1. Leaves more than 2, alternate on stem; flowers 1-3, not clustered, but widely spaced 2
2. Lip white, occasionally purplish tinged . . . . . .MOUNTAIN LADY'S-SLIPPER
2. Lip yellow, streaked or dotted with reddish purple.
   YELLOW LADY'S-SLIPPER

*   *   *

CLUSTERED LADY'S-SLIPPER (*Cypripedium fasciculatum*) One pair of broad, ovate, opposite leaves, spread horizontally. Flowers in drooping cluster of 1 to 4 blooms; lip a roundish pouch, greenish, streaked with purple. Sepals and petals narrow, pointed, and reddish purple. East. Wash.; yellow pine woods, mostly along lower east slopes of Cascades. Mid spring to mid summer.

MOUNTAIN LADY'S-SLIPPER (*Cypripedium montanum*) Three sepals and 2 petals are brownish purple, narrow strap-like, and twisted. Lip white, slipper-like, and 1 inch or more long. Leaves several, oblong, and clasping. Flowers fragrant. East. Wash. and Columbia Gorge; habitat variable, being found in dry to moist, open to dense woods in lowlands and mountains. Irregular in distribution. Spring to mid summer.

YELLOW LADY'S-SLIPPER (*Cypripedium calceolus*) Leaves oval, pointed, and 3-5 on stem. Sepals and 2 petals greenish yellow to purple, long, narrow, and spirally twisted. Lip slipper-shaped, yellow, and streaked with reddish purple. Flowers fragrant. East. Wash.; damp situations in woods, swamps, or along streambanks. Late spring and early summer.

TWAYBLADES (*Listera*) (Color Plate 8)

Small herbs with 2 opposite leaves located near middle of stem and small flowers in terminal racemes.

Figure 6.
Eburophyton, the phantom orchid, "ghost of the forest." (Patrick)

1. Leaves somewhat heart-shaped; lip cleft for half its length.
HEART-LEAVED TWAYBLADE
1. Leaves not heart-shaped; lip not cleft or only slightly so 2

2. Lip not at all cleft and tapering gradually to base. . WESTERN TWAYBLADE
2. Lip slightly, but noticeably, cleft and narrowing abruptly to base.
BROAD-LEAVED TWAYBLADE

*   *   *

HEART-LEAVED TWAYBLADE (*Listera cordata*) Leaves heart-shaped, shiny above, paler below. Flowers tiny, orchid-like, yellowish green or purplish; lip deeply divided into 2 lobes. East. and West. Wash.; damp, mossy, but also fairly dry, coniferous woods; occasionally in damp, boggy places. Summer.

WESTERN TWAYBLADE (*Listera caurina*) Plants tall and slender. Leaves not heart-shaped. Flowers green or greenish yellow; lip wedge-shaped and not cleft. East. and West. Wash.; moist, shadowy, forest floors in mountains. Summer.

BROAD-LEAVED TWAYBLADE (*Listera convallarioides*) Plants taller than other twayblades. Flowers yellowish green with petals and sepals strongly back-turned. Lip slightly notched. East. and West. Wash.; damp, dense forests, as well as stream and lake margins. Early to mid summer.

BOG ORCHIDS (*Habenaria*) (Color Plate 8)

Stems tall and leafy at base; flowers greenish or white in terminal raceme or spike. Lip of flower spreading or drooping with spur-like base.

1. Leaves basal 2
1. Leaves scattered along stem, not basal 4

2. Basal leaves roundish . . . . ROUND-LEAVED BOG ORCHID
2. Basal leaves not roundish 3

3. Spike slender and sparsely flowered; spur shorter than ovary.
SHORT-SPURRED BOG ORCHID
3. Spike densely flowered; spur much longer than ovary.
ELEGANT BOG ORCHID

4. Flowers white, rarely greenish . . . . WHITE BOG ORCHID
4. Flowers greenish 5

5. Spur long and tube-shaped; leaves relatively long and narrow.
GREEN-FLOWERED BOG ORCHID
5. Spur short and bag-like; leaves short and oval shaped.
SLENDER BOG ORCHID

*   *   *

ROUND-LEAVED BOG ORCHID (*Habenaria orbiculata*) Two opposite, round, basal leaves. Flowers whitish green in loose raceme. Lip long and narrow; spur long and cylindrical. East. and West. Wash.; moist, mossy forest floors, mostly in mountains. Summer.

SHORT-SPURRED BOG ORCHID (*Habenaria unalascensis*) Two to 4 oblong to lance-shaped basal leaves, often withering by time of flowering. Flowers tiny, yellowish green, in tall, slender spike. Lip and spur only slightly longer

51

than sepals and petals. Flowers twisted sideways on stalk. East. and West. Wash.; dry to semi-moist woods and slopes, mostly in mountains. Summer.

ELEGANT BOG ORCHID (*Habenaria elegans*) Spur about twice as long as lip. Spike densely flowered and flowers larger than in Short-spurred Bog Orchid. Flowers white to greenish white. East. and West. Wash.; dry woods to edges of meadows and clearings. Summer to early autumn.

WHITE BOG ORCHID (*Habenaria dilatata*) Tall, stout, leafy stem often more than 12 inches high. Flowers numerous in raceme, pure white, showy, and fragrant. Upper sepal and 2 petals curving to form hood; lip projecting outward. Spur equal to or longer than lip. East. and West. Wash.; boggy areas and spring seeps, shaded or in the open; mostly in the lower mountains. Summer to early autumn.

GREEN-FLOWERED BOG ORCHID (*Habenaria hyperborea*) Leaves lanceolate, and scattered along stem—not basal. Flowers greenish, on tall, narrow, few- to many-flowered, bracted spike. Spur shorter than lip. East. Wash.; moist, boggy places; occasionally in shady woods. Summer.

SLENDER BOG ORCHID (*Habenaria saccata*) Flowers greenish. Spur short and bag-shaped. East. Wash.; moist, boggy places, mostly in mountains. Summer.

CORALROOTS (*Corallorhiza*) (Color Plate 6)

Saprophytic or parasitic on roots with large, coral-like rhizomes. Flowers small, numerous, and in terminal racemes.

1. Flowers pink, prominently striped with reddish brown or purple.
STRIPED CORALROOT
1. Flowers reddish or purplish, but not prominently striped 2

2. Sepals yellowish to whitish, with 1 nerve . . . . NORTHERN CORALROOT
2. Sepals reddish, with 3 nerves 3

3. Lip white, usually spotted with purple . . . . SPOTTED CORALROOT
3. Lip purple . . . . WESTERN CORALROOT

*　　*　　*

STRIPED CORALROOT (*Corallorhiza striata*) Flowers pale pink to buffy with purple stripes on petals and sepals and lacking spurs. Lip not lobed. East. and West. Wash.; deep, moist to dry, coniferous woods. Spring to late summer.

NORTHERN CORALROOT (*Corallorhiza trifida*) Lip 3-lobed; plant small and slender. Flowers greenish yellow; stem yellowish. East. and West. Wash.; deep, moist, shady woods. Summer.

SPOTTED CORALROOT (*Corallorhiza maculata*) Flowers pinkish or reddish; lip usually purple spotted. Spur sometimes missing. Stem yellowish and short. East. and West. Wash.; moist to semi-moist to often dry (yellow pine), coniferous woods. Late spring to late summer.

WESTERN CORALROOT (*Corallorhiza mertensiana*) Flower (including lip) as well as stem reddish. Chin-like projection from underside of calyx tube. East. and West. Wash.; moist coniferous woods. Mid to late summer.

Chapter 5—The Nettle Family (*Urticaceae*)

The single member of this family in our area is a perennial herb with simple, opposite leaves; small, greenish, single-sexed flowers placed in axillary clusters; and lacking petals but possessing 4 sepals per flower. Sap is a watery juice. The Washington species is characterized by stinging hairs which produce an intense burning sensation on the bare skin; the plant is to be avoided. (Color Plate 8)

STINGING NETTLE (*Urtica dioica*) Plant is a single, unbranched stalk, to 4 feet tall. Leaves bright greenish and coarsely toothed. Usually growing in dense patches. Flowers greenish. East. and West. Wash.; often common in moist or boggy places along streams and springy areas from sea level to subalpine and in humid as well as arid regions. Spring to early autumn.

The weather forces that affect the state of Washington are controlled largely by the various air masses that visit it. If we can think of great chunks of air lying over particular parts of the earth, taking on the characteristics of those areas, then passing to and over the land mass of the state, we may gain some idea of the tremendous phenomena operating on it. Depending on the nature of the air mass, the land may be visited by humid gales, drying breezes, or chilling winds. These factors, having great effect on the distributional patterns of vegetation, will be discussed in this and the following two essays.

In summer, the prevailing westerlies sweep on shore bringing mild, cool, relatively dry breezes which pass over the state. In Western Washington, the effect is that of cool, clear weather, with some heating due to diurnal solar input. In Eastern Washington, these air masses have been modified, by heating upon descending the east slope of the Cascades and stagnating in the Columbia Basin. Injections of moisture aloft from the south in the form of thermal troughs may cause orographic thunderstorms to form, giving moisture to the mountains and nearby areas during late May and June. For most of the summer, however, many days of cloudless skies prevail in Eastern Washington to produce the typical summer drought. Much of the same dry spell occurs in the western part of the state, but about the first of August low stratus or "high fogs" form during the early morning hours, burning off in the late morning. These are produced by cool air from the ocean passing inland and rising due to the action of the warm land with some of the water vapor changing to fog. The effect of this late summer stratus is to slow the day's temperature progression, making for cooler days.

As the great Pacific high pressure field moves to the south, storm tracks reach the state from the north, subjecting it to colder, moister weather conditions with the occasional invasion of a cold air mass from the north or east. Winter conditions, which are much more complex than those of the summer, will be treated in the next essay in the series.

Figure 7.
The buried flower of the wild ginger, *Asarum*. (Yaich)

54

Chapter 6—The Birthwort Family (*Aristolochiaceae*)

The single member of this family in our area is a perennial herb with creeping rootstocks with alternate leaves; perfect, regular flowers without petals; and a 3-lobed calyx. Stamens 12. Flowers are solitary and the leaves are more or less heart-shaped. Plant smells of ginger. (Color Plate 9)

WILD GINGER (*Asarum caudatum*)   Dark, green kidney-shaped or heart-shaped leaves. Flowers large, solitary, bell-like, and brownish purple to greenish yellow. Sepals taper to a long point. Stems covered with fine hairs. East. and West. Wash.; moist shaded woods where there is thick leaf mold which often hides the flowers. Spring to mid summer. (Fig. 7)

With the coming of September and October, the great Pacific storm track shifts southward and a series of low pressure areas with associated weather fronts bring mild, marine air masses interspersed with colder, wetter masses from the northern part of the Pacific Ocean. Punctuating this progression of weather disturbances and associated air masses will be a series of cold, continental Arctic outbreaks from the northeast. This sequence continues through the winter, reaching an intensity in late December and January and gradually tapering off to late spring.

Weather fronts (usually of the occluded type by the time they reach Washington) bring a definite precipitation pattern, starting with a high, overriding, prefrontal cloud shield which gradually lowers to a rain-dropping stratus. The warm sector may bring warm, mild, moist air from the central Pacific. The passage of the front is marked by heavier rain and a wind shift, usually to the northwest. Showers and cooler temperatures follow the front with eventual clearing of the skies. Rain during the frontal episode will be heavy on the windward sides of the coast ranges and Cascades, particularly at the mouths of mountain river valleys. Here, the funneling of air masses may produce very heavy precipitation. An often-occurring convergence zone east of Everett accounts in part for the heavy rainfall in the Pilchuck-Stillaguamish area. Adding the Olympic Mountains rain shadow to other local variations, the precipitation patterns may be seen reflected in the variant vegetation.

Part of the moisture borne in the westerly airflow has been wrung out by passage over the Cascades. With a drying and warming movement down the east slopes, the masses deposit little moisture over the Columbia Basin. Precipitation does not begin to increase till rising land in the eastern border region is encountered, just before these masses leave the state.

Figure 8.
Flower heads of the buckwheat, *Eriogonum*. (Yaich)

Chapter 7—The Polygonum Family (*Polygonaceae*)

Members of this family are herbs or shrubs with simple, alternate (less commonly basal or opposite), entire leaves. The flowers are small and regular, but without petals. Sepals 4-9, often petal-like; stamens 3-9; ovary superior. (Color Plates 9-10)

1. Leaves with collar-like sheathing stipules surrounding bases of petioles of leaves...2
1. Leaves without collar-like sheathing stipules surrounding bases of petioles of leaves 4

2. Leaves kidney-shaped; calyx 4-lobed..............MOUNTAIN SORREL
2. Leaves not kidney-shaped; calyx not 4-lobed.......................3

3. Calyx with 5 (rarely 4) lobes (sepals).........KNOTWEEDS (*Polygonum*)
3. Calyx with 6 lobes (sepals).........................DOCKS (*Rumex*)

4. Involucre (the bracts, here usually fused, surrounding the floral parts) with spine-tipped lobes or teeth..5
4. Involucre without spiny lobes or teeth........BUCKWHEATS (*Eriogonum*)

5. Sepals divided to base; flowers more than 1 in an involucre.
NORTHERN OXYTHECA
5. Sepals divided less than halfway from edge to base of perianth; flowers single in an involucre.....................WATSON'S CHORIZANTHE

*   *   *

MOUNTAIN SORREL (*Oxyria digyna*) Fleshy, basal, kidney-shaped leaves. Small flowers are greenish, tinged with reddish and in upright clusters. Leaves with acid taste. East. and West. Wash.; moist to somewhat dry, rocky places in alpine zone of high mountains. Summer. (Color Plate 9)

NORTHERN OXYTHECA (*Oxytheca dendroides*) Leaves basal, bristly, and sharp-pointed. Stem leaves much smaller. Involucres 2-flowered; white to dark pink in color. East. Wash.; dry, sandy habitats in the sagebrush plains. Summer.

WATSON'S CHORIZANTHE (*Chorizanthe watsonii*) Foliage grayish, hairy. leaves basal with slender petioles. Involucres with single, tiny, yellowish flowers. East. Wash.; sagebrush plains. Late spring to mid summer.

KNOTWEEDS (*Polygonum*) (Color Plate 9)

Herbs with alternate leaves bearing conspicuous, sheathing stipules. Sepals often colored and petal-like. Stem with numerous joints.

1. Plants as annuals (with small roots) and usually occurring in dry to semi-moist areas 2
1. Plants perennials, with strong rootstocks; often occurring in or near water 15

2. Stipules as large collar-like sheathes with leaves branching off from near base of stipule..3
2. Stipules not as large collar-like sheathes..........................4

3. Leaves with purplish spot in middle of blade............LADY'S-THUMB
3. Leaves not so spotted.....................PUNCTATE SMARTWEED

57

4. Pedicel (stalk of flower) strongly down-turned; flowers not bunched, but scattered along the stem.......................................5
4. Pedicels not strongly down-turned; flowers often bunched in terminal racemes...6

5. Sepals ("flower") more than 1/8 inch long............WIRY KNOTWEED
5. Sepals less than 1/8 inch long................DOUGLAS' KNOTWEED

6. Flowers closely crowded in terminal spike-like racemes; leaves very narrow—less than 1/8 inch wide.................................7
6. Flowers located mostly in axils of leaves; leaves more than 1/8 inch wide...11

7. Achenes (seeds) black and glossy...............................8
7. Achenes brownish or yellowish and not glossy.....................9

8. Flowers more than 1/8 inch long...................FALL KNOTWEED
8. Flowers less than 1/8 inch long...............NUTTALL'S KNOTWEED

9. Anther-bearing stamens 8 in number.............................10
9. Anther-bearing stamens 3 in number..........KELLOGG'S KNOTWEED

10. Flower clusters longer than broad.............WATSON'S KNOTWEED
10. Flower clusters broader than long.......WHITE-MARGINED KNOTWEED

11. Plants very small, less than 4 inches tall............LEAFY KNOTWEED
11. Plants larger, more than 4 inches tall...........................12

12. Sepals joined for less than 1/2 their length; achenes black and glossy..13
12. Sepals joined for at least half their length; achenes yellowish or brownish...14

13. Leaves mostly narrow and linear..............NUTTALL'S KNOTWEED
13. Leaves not linear, but broader.................SAWATCH KNOTWEED

14. Plants partly prostrate; flower lobes not yellowish; leaves broader.
COMMON KNOTWEED
14. Plants strongly upright; flower lobes yellowish; leaves narrow.
BUSHY KNOTWEED

15. Leaves mostly basal; flowers borne in single tight head at tip of stalk...16
15. Leaves not basal; flowers not as above...........................17

16. Flower head 3 times as long as broad................ALPINE BISTORT
16. Flower head less than 3 times as long as broad......COMMON BISTORT

17. Plants with woody stems........................BLACK KNOTWEED
17. Plants with herbaceous stems...................................18

18. Plants erect; usually found in alpine habitats.....................19
18. Plants prostrate or floating in water; usually not found in alpine habitats.20

19. Flowers in showy panicles.......................ALPINE KNOTWEED
19. Flowers in inconspicuous clusters in axils of leaves.
NEWBERRY'S KNOTWEED

20. Flowers reddish and in 1 or 2 spikes.............................21
20. Flowers whitish, pinkish, or greenish, and in several panicles........22

21. Flower head several times longer than broad.......SWAMP PERSICARIA
21. Flower head not much longer than broad..........WATER SMARTWEED

58

22. Flowers strongly "warty"....................PUNCTATE SMARTWEED
22. Flowers not "warty" 23

23. Stamens usually 6; flowers reddish...................LADY'S-THUMB
23. Stamens not 6 in number; flowers greenish............WATER-PEPPER

*   *   *

LADY'S-THUMB (*Polygonum persicaria*) Dark, V-shaped blotch in middle of each leaf. Short, thick spike of reddish to (rarely) white flowers is the "thumb." East. and West. Wash.; weedy, in moist, cultivated or wastelands, as well as wet, marshy places. Spring and summer.

PUNCTATE SMARTWEED (*Polygonum punctatum*) Leaves dotted, lanceolate, and sharp-pointed. Flowers greenish with white margins. East. and West. Wash.; moist places, mostly in the lowlands. Summer to early autumn.

WIRY KNOTWEED (*Polygonum majus*) Stems slender and sharply angled. Leaves long and narrow with curled margins. Flowers greenish with white or pink margins. East. Wash.; dry places in sagebrush and yellow pine areas, in lowlands and lower montane elevations. Late spring and summer.

DOUGLAS' KNOTWEED (*Polygonum douglasii*) Flowers greenish with white margins on calyx lobes and in slender spikes in leaf axils. East. and West. Wash.; variable, though mostly on dry, rocky wasteland. Summer and early autumn.

FALL KNOTWEED (*Polygonum spergulariaeforme*) Flower lobes pinkish or whitish with greenish midvein. West. and Southeast. Wash.; gravelly or sandy soil in lowlands and foothills. Summer and early autumn.

NUTTALL'S KNOTWEED (*Polygonum nuttallii*) Flowers very small and pinkish. Styles separate. West. Wash.; dry, open, lowland prairies and bald hills. Late spring to early fall.

KELLOGG'S KNOTWEED (*Polygonum kelloggii*) Flowers in compact, terminal spikes and greenish in color with white or pink margins. East. (mostly) and West. Wash.; meadows, moist flats, and subalpine ridges. Summer.

WATSON'S KNOTWEED (*Polygonum watsonii*) Plants erect. Fertile stamens 6. Flowers greenish with white or pink margins. East. Wash.; lowland, moist meadows, especially where there are vernal pools. Late spring and summer.

WHITE-MARGINED KNOTWEED (*Polygonum polygaloides*) Involucre bracts greenish with white or pink curled margins. Perianth lobes bright pink. East. Wash.; moist meadows and flats in lowlands and mountains; also occasionally on rocky ridges. Summer.

LEAFY KNOTWEED (*Polygonum minimum*) Stems reddish and much branched. Flowers greenish with white or pinkish margins. East. and West. Wash.; barren subalpine areas in the high mountains. Late summer to early autumn.

SAWATCH KNOTWEED (*Polygonum sawatchense*) Stems branched, dull green. Flowers greenish with white margins and present along entire stem. East. Wash.; open slopes of foothills and lower mountains. Summer.

COMMON KNOTWEED (*Polygonum aviculare*) Stems prostrate; leaves bluish. Flowers greenish with white or pink margins to calyx lobes and located 1 to 3 in leaf axils. East. and West. Wash.; common weed on hard, waste ground. Mid summer to early autumn.

BUSHY KNOTWEED (*Polygonum ramosissimum*) Flowers greenish with yellow margins. East. Wash.; waste areas, both dry and moist. Mid summer to early autumn.

ALPINE BISTORT (*Polygonum viviparum*) Basal leaves more or less heart-shaped. Flowers white. East. and West. Wash.; moist mountain areas, such as streambanks, meadows, and deep woods. Mid summer to early autumn.

COMMON BISTORT (*Polygonum bistortoides*) Flowers white, in dense, club-like clusters at tips of long stems. Leaves wedge-shaped at base. East. and West. Wash.; moist alpine meadows, slopes, and streambanks in mountains. Late spring to late summer.

BLACK KNOTWEED (*Polygonum paronychia*) Stems prostrate and woody with upturned ends. Leaves numerous and narrow, with down-turned edges. Flowers whitish or pinkish. West. Wash.; sand dunes along sea coast. Spring to early autumn.

ALPINE KNOTWEED (*Polygonum phytolaccaefolium*) Stout, bushy plant. Leaves with funnel-shaped stipules. Flowers whitish. East. and West. Wash.; subalpine meadows and rocky ridges. Summer.

NEWBERRY'S KNOTWEED (*Polygonum newberryi*) Plants to 12 inches, often prostrate. Dull, yellowish-green, oval, tapering leaves. Flowers greenish white to pinkish, usually in short racemes. East. and West. Wash.; open, rocky areas in high mountains. Summer. Often common.

SWAMP PERSICARIA (*Polygonum coccineum*) Leaves long and pointed. Flowers reddish in slender spikes. East. and West. Wash.; moist, often flooded, ground in lowlands and foothills. Mid summer to early fall.

WATER SMARTWEED (*Polygonum amphibium*) Leaves oval to elliptic. Flowers reddish. Flowering spikes 1 or 2 and densely flowered. Leaves not pointed. East. and West. Wash.; widespread and common, floating in ponds. Summer to early autumn.

WATER-PEPPER (*Polygonum hydropiperoides*) Leaves lanceolate. Flowers greenish, pinkish, or whitish, in several raceme-like spikes. East. and West. Wash.; wet, swampy places, often growing in mud. Mid summer to early autumn.

DOCKS (*Rumex*) (Color Plate 10)

Plants with entire, undulate, or crisped leaves with thin, sheathing stipules. Flowers greenish or reddish in whorls on jointed pedicels.

(Many species are introduced weeds and are not included here)

1. Leaves mostly basal; male and female plants; flowers imperfect; occurring in montane or alpine areas....................ALPINE SHEEP-SORREL
1. Leaves more or less not basal; plants usually not sexually separated; flowers usually perfect; lowland species...................................2

2. Leaves very leathery in texture; stems from large rootstocks. WINGED DOCK
2. Leaves various, but usually not leathery; stems from taproots rather than rootstocks (rhizomes) 3
3. Perianth lobes toothed or bristled 4
3. Perianth lobes not toothed or bristled 5
4. Plants prostrate; flowers less than 1/8 inch long . . . . GOLDEN DOCK
4. Plants erect; flowers more than 1/4 inch long . . . . BITTER DOCK
5. Leaf base narrowing gradually to petiole . . . . NARROW-LEAVED DOCK
5. Leaf base cordate; not narrowing gradually to petiole . . . . WESTERN DOCK

*　　*　　*

ALPINE SHEEP-SORREL (*Rumex paucifolius*)　Leaves lanceolate, on long petioles, and mostly basal. Flowers reddish, several, and in axils of bracts. East. Wash.; moist places in the subalpine and alpine areas of the eastern Cascades and eastward. Summer.

(Note: RED SORREL, *Rumex acetosella,* is a similar species, but has the lower leaves lobed near their bases; a very widely spread exotic weed from sea level to timberline. Another common weedy exotic in this genus is the CURLY-LEAVED DOCK, *Rumex crispus,* identifiable by the curled edges of its leaves.)

WINGED DOCK (*Rumex venosus*)　Sturdy plants to 12 inches. Large, leathery leaves. Inner parts of perianth 1 inch wide and bright red. Flowers developing to brilliant clusters of rose-red, 3-sided, winged seeds. East. Wash.; sagebrush and grassy plains, preferring sand dunes and rocky places. Spring to early summer.

GOLDEN DOCK (*Rumex maritimus*)　Leaves narrow, with short petioles. Sepals with bristly edges. Flowers greenish brown. East. and West. Wash.; sea beaches and wet areas. Summer to early autumn.

BITTER DOCK (*Rumex obtusifolius*)　Tall plants (to 4 feet). Leaves large (to 12 inches), on long petioles, and notched at base. Flowers greenish brown. West. Wash.; waste places such as old fields and roadsides. Early spring to early autumn.

NARROW-LEAVED DOCK (*Rumex salicifolius*)　Stems tufted. Leaves lance-shaped and pointed at both ends. Flowers greenish brown or pinkish. East. and West. Wash.; moist places from sea level to subalpine. Summer and early autumn.

WESTERN DOCK (*Rumex occidentalis*)　Plants large, with stalks reaching several feet. Leaves fleshy, smooth, glossy, bluish-green, and heart-shaped at base. Flowers pinkish. Conspicuous seed heads. West. Wash.; wet, swampy meadows and bogs from sea level to intermediate elevations. Summer.

BUCKWHEATS (*Eriogonum*) (Color Plate 9) (Fig. 8)

Herbs or sub-shrubs with entire, alternate or whorled leaves. Flowers small, often yellowish, and in dense clusters. Plants low in stature; often with many branches.

1. Plants annual with small, slender roots 2
1. Plants perennial with large, well-developed roots 3

2. Leaves basal and roundish . . . . WIRE-STEMMED BUCKWHEAT
2. Leaves linear and not basal . . . . HAIR-STEMMED BUCKWHEAT

3. Flower stems arising from 2 linear bracts; sepals with rosy-red hairs on outer surfaces . . . . ALPINE BUCKWHEAT
3. Flower stems not arising from 2 linear bracts; sepals without reddish hairs on outer surface 4

4. Calyx (perianth) narrowing to a slender, tube-like stalk at its base and jointed to pedicel by a conspicuous collar 5
4. Calyx not narrowing to a slender, tube-like stalk at its base and not con-spicuously jointed to pedicel 10

5. Perianth conspicuously hairy externally, being covered with long, down-ward-pointing, white hairs . . . . THYME-LEAVED BUCKWHEAT
5. Perianth not conspicuously covered externally with long, downward-pointing, white hairs 6

6. Perianth covered externally with short hairs 7
6. Perianth usually not hairy externally 9

7. Leaves oval-shaped, not much longer than broad.
SULFUR-FLOWERED BUCKWHEAT
7. Leaves narrow and linear (much longer than broad) 8

8. Flowering stem with circle of leaves at mid-length.
DOUGLAS' BUCKWHEAT
8. Flowering stem without circle of leaves at mid-length.
ROUND-HEADED BUCKWHEAT

9. Leaves triangular or heart-shaped . . . . HEART-LEAVED BUCKWHEAT
9. Leaves long and narrow, not triangular or heart-shaped.
CREAMY BUCKWHEAT

10. Flowering stem covered with leaves for much of its length.
BUSHY BUCKWHEAT
10. Flowering stem not covered with leaves 11

11. Single tight head of flowers at tip of flowering stem.
OVAL-LEAVED BUCKWHEAT
11. Flowering stem branching and not single with tight head of flowers at tip.
WHITE BUCKWHEAT

*   *   *

WIRE-STEMMED BUCKWHEAT (*Eriogonum vimineum*) Leaves 1/2 inch long, basal, and covered with white, woolly hairs. Flowers white, pink, or yellow. East. Wash.; sandy or gravelly places in sagebrush plains. Summer to early autumn.

HAIR-STEMMED BUCKWHEAT (*Eriogonum spergulinum*) Plants to 12 inches with very narrow leaves. Flowers very small, white, veined with reddish. East. Wash.; sandy or rocky places in arid areas. Summer.

ALPINE BUCKWHEAT (*Eriogonum pyrolifolium*) Small, loosely-tufted plant less than 4 inches tall. Oval leaves in basal cluster. White, pink, or rose-colored flowers in small, dense umbels on 3 inch to 4 inch stems. Inflor-escences with strong, unpleasant odor. Cascades and possibly high mountains near eastern border; rocky habitats in subalpine and alpine areas. Often common. Mid to late summer.

THYME-LEAVED BUCKWHEAT (*Eriogonum thymoides*) Miniature shrubs with gnarled, woody branches. Tiny grayish green leaves in tufts at ends of branches. Flower color variable, white, yellow, creamy, pinkish, or reddish. East. Wash.; sagebrush and open grassy places in lowlands and lower montane areas. Spring to early summer.

SULFUR-FLOWERED BUCKWHEAT (*Eriogonum umbellatum*) Stems woody near base and much branched. Leaves white-hairy below—smooth and green above. Flowers pale to deep yellow. East. Wash.; sagebrush and grassy, rocky plains to alpine ridges. Summer.

DOUGLAS' BUCKWHEAT (*Eriogonum douglasii*) Dense, matted branches. Leaves small and spatulate. Flowers bright yellow or pinkish with filaments and ovary hairy. East. Wash.; sagebrush plains, grassy slopes, and open yellow pine forests. Late spring to mid summer.

ROUND-HEADED BUCKWHEAT (*Eriogonum sphaerocephalum*) Large, shrubby plant (to 24 inches). Short, lance-shaped leaves at bases and tips of branches and in rosette halfway along flowering stem. Flowers yellowish to whitish. East. Wash.; sagebrush, grassy slopes, and open yellow pine woods. Late spring to mid summer.

HEART-LEAVED BUCKWHEAT (*Eriogonum compositum*) Tall, erect plant to 14 inches. Leaves broad, arrow-shaped, with heart-shaped base and long stems. Leaves green above and felted with white hairs on undersides. Creamy-white to yellow flowers in large umbels 3 to 6 inches in diameter. East. Wash.; rocky places in open arid regions. Late spring to mid summer.

CREAMY BUCKWHEAT (*Eriogonum heracleoides*) Slender, tufted stems (8-20 inches tall). Leaves mostly basal and lance-shaped. Flowers yellowish white. East. Wash.; sagebrush and grassy areas, mountain ridges, and yellow pine woods, often preferring rocky places. Late spring to mid summer.

BUSHY BUCKWHEAT (*Eriogonum microthecum*) Shrubby plant to 24 inches. Young branches hairy. Leaves numerous with often curled margins, white hairy below and only sparsely hairy above. Involucres few-flowered and white to pinkish. East. Wash.; sagebrush plains and slopes. Summer to early fall; often lasting till the first frost.

OVAL-LEAVED BUCKWHEAT (*Eriogonum ovalifolium*) Short, tufted plant, to 8 inches tall. Densely covered with white, woolly hairs. Flowers few in a head, creamy white to yellowish, sometimes colored with pinkish. East. and West. Wash.; sagebrush, yellow pine forests, montane meadows, and alpine ridges. Late spring and summer.

WHITE BUCKWHEAT (*Eriogonum niveum*) Woody stems with lance-shaped to oval leaves that are densely white woolly on both surfaces, as are flowering stems. The involucres are scattered, with white or light yellow flowers. East. Wash.; sagebrush, grasslands, and open yellow pine woods. Late summer to early autumn.

Figure 9.
Larrison field checking the *Washington Wildflowers* manuscript on Umptanum Ridge.
(Yaich)

64

Chapter 8—The Goosefoot Family (*Chenopodiaceae*)

Members of this family are annual or perennial herbs or shrubs with alternate leaves and perfect flowers. Sepals 2-5; petals absent; ovary superior; stamens 1-5. Foliage of these plants is often grayish or whitish and granular in texture. A number of exotic weeds belonging to this family occur in Washington, but only the commoner, herbaceous, native flowers are treated. (Color Plate 10)

1. Leaves reduced to small scales; stems jointed and fleshy.
SALTWORTS (*Salicornia*)
1. Leaves not scale-like; stems not jointed and not so fleshy..............2
2. Leaves long and very narrow, not toothed, and densely covered with grayish hairs..WINTERFAT
2. Leaves not long and very narrow; often toothed, and not covered with grayish hairs 3
3. Flowers borne in axils of leaves and not on spikes or panicles.
SUEDAS (*Sueda*)
3. Flowers borne on spikes or panicles...............................4
4. Perianth a single, bract-like lobe, partly including stamen and pistil.
NUTTALL'S POVERTY WEED
4. Perianth 3-5 lobed in staminate flowers...........................5
5. Flowers perfect, with 5-lobed perianth.....GOOSEFOOTS (*Chenopodium*)
5. Flowers not perfect; perianth 3-5 lobed in staminate flowers; no perianth in pistillate flowers...............................SALTBUSHES (*Atriplex*)

*   *   *

WINTERFAT (*Eurotia lanata*) White, woolly appearing plant, often in dense patches. East. Wash.; dry, open, alkaline areas. Flowers whitish. Late spring to mid summer. (Color Plate 10)

NUTTALL'S POVERTY WEED (*Monolepsis nuttalliana*) Low-growing annual with spear-shaped leaves and small, greenish flowers. East. Wash.; alkaline areas in open deserts and in lower and intermediate parts of mountains. Late spring to mid summer.

SALTWORTS (*Salicornia*) (Color Plate 10)

1. Occurs mostly in Eastern Washington.................RED SALTWORT
1. Occurs in Western Washington..................COMMON SALTWORT

*   *   *

RED SALTWORT (*Salicornia rubra*) Spreading, matted plants with thick, jointed stems. Leaves are tiny scales at the joints. Plants turn bright red at maturity. East. Wash.; very rarely in West. Wash.; alkaline or salty soils and shores of stagnant, alkaline lakes and ponds. Greenish flowers. Mid summer to early autumn.

COMMON SALTWORT (*Salicornia europaea*) Joints longer than wide (unlike *S. rubra* where they are about as wide as long). Otherwise similar to that species. West. Wash.; very common in salt marshes and wet meadows along salt water. Flowers greenish. Summer and early autumn.

(Note: The GLASSWORT, *Salicornia virginica,* also occurs in marsh and beach areas along the ocean coast and differs from the above two in its more matted habit and perennial life form.)

SUADEAS *(Suaeda)*

1. Occurs in Western Washington . . . . BEACH SEA BLITE
1. Occurs in Eastern Washington 2
2. Foliage and stems covered with waxy, powdery bloom imparting grayish or bluish appearance . . . . PAHUTE WEED
2. Foliage and stems not as above, but yellowish green in appearance.
SLENDER WESTERN BLITE

*   *   *

BEACH SEA BLITE *(Suaeda maritima)* Flowers greenish. West. Wash.; marshes and wet meadows along salt water. Mid summer to early autumn.

PAHUTE WEED *(Suaeda depressa)* Fleshy plants with cylindrical leaves of which those of the inflorescences are broader than those of the stems. Becoming reddish when mature. Flowers greenish. East. Wash.; alkali flats. Mid summer to early autumn.

SLENDER WESTERN BLITE *(Suaeda occidentalis)* Bracts of inflorescences not broader than leaves. Flowers greenish. East. Wash.; alkali flats and salt marshes. Summer.

GOOSEFOOTS *(Chenopodium)* (Color Plate 10)

1. Leaves large (to 4 inches). Reddish, raspberry-like fruits.
STRAWBERRY BLITE
1. Leaves smaller (to 2 inches). Fruits not as above 2
2. Leaves narrow; much longer than wide; never lobed.
NARROW-LEAVED GOOSEFOOT
2. Leaves not narrow, but lobed and about as wide as long.
FREMONT'S GOOSEFOOT

*   *   *

STRAWBERRY BLITE *(Chenopodium capitatum)* Leaves roughly arrow-shaped, irregularly lobed and toothed. Greenish flowers followed by unusual red fruits resembling raspberries which grow closely against the stems. East. and West. Wash.; widely occurring in lowlands. Summer.

NARROW-LEAVED GOOSEFOOT *(Chenopodium leptophyllum)* Flowers grayish green. East. Wash.; dry, desert areas. Late spring and summer.

FREMONT'S GOOSEFOOT *(Chenopodium fremontii)* Flowers grayish green. East. Wash.; sagebrush and open yellow pine. Summer and early autumn.

SALTBUSHES *(Atriplex)*

1. Leaves greenish and usually not powdered with grayish . . . . . SPEARSCALE
1. Leaves mealy in appearance, being powdered with grayish.
WEDGESCALE ORACHE

SPEARSCALE (*Atriplex patula*) Leaves long and narrow. Flowers greenish and confined mostly to upper part of stem. East. and West. Wash.; alkali flats and salty ground near salt water. Summer.

WEDGESCALE ORACHE (*Atriplex truncata*) Leaves short and broad. Flowers greenish and scattered along entire length of stems. East. Wash.; alkali flats. Summer.

———————

As with the alpine tundra, the sea beach and associated sand dune areas are often overlooked by the plant lover and in so doing, he misses one of the most interesting and unique floral habitats. The sand dunes area actually represents a series of habitats, each with its own method of origin, conditions for plant growth, and vegetational communities.

The area immediately above high tide line is moist and often buffeted by storm-driven waves and stranded logs. Nevertheless a few plants gain foothold in protected places on hummocks and foredunes. Two of the commonest of these are the yellow sand abronia and the silver ragweed. The first of these is often very abundant, its masses producing almost a literal ground cover. Several kinds of grasses and sedges are also present. Farther back from the tidal zone, in more stabilized locations, are to be found such plants, often in profusion, as the two peas, the gray beach pea and the Japanese beach pea; the beach morning-glory; the beach silver top; and the black knotweed.

Farther shoreward on more stable and longer established sites will be found such plants as the seashore lupine, western tansy, and the seacoast angelica. In the more established dune areas, shrubs and trees will be represented. Often they will grow in dense thickets and in such places there will be little herbaceous undercover.

Inside the dunes, may be a complex of very moist to relatively dry meadows, again with their characteristic flowers. The salt marsh contains certain sedges and rushes, but also such herbs as the Pacific cinquefoil, paintbrush owl's-clover, small creeping buttercup, and stiff gentian.

The rush meadow community is a somewhat drier zone with lower water table and less frequent standing surface water. Common wildflowers occurring here are the seashore lupine mentioned above, sea beach strawberry, pearly everlasting, and yarrow.

(continued on page 81)

Figure 10.
The sea beach, home of the sand verbenas, *Abronia*. (Larrison)

Chapter 9—The Four-O'Clock Family (*Nyctaginaceae*)

Members of this family possess opposite, fleshy leaves and perfect, regular flowers. The calyx is tubular, 4-5 lobed; petals absent. Plants typically sprawl over the ground. (Color Plate 11)

1. Plants not of saltwater beaches; not prostrate, but usually upright.
WHITE SAND VERBENA
1. Plants of saltwater beaches; strictly prostrate and creeping in life form...2
2. Flowers yellow; leaves almost as broad as long..YELLOW SAND VERBENA
2. Flowers pink; leaves much longer than broad......PINK SAND VERBENA

*　　*　　*

WHITE SAND VERBENA (*Abronia mellifera*) Flowers white, but not fragrant. Plants not prostrate or creeping, but decumbent and otherwise upright. Stems stout; leaves fleshy. East. Wash.; Columbia Gorge and central and southeastern parts of state. Dunes and other sandy places in lowlands. Late spring to mid summer.

YELLOW SAND VERBENA (*Abronia latifolia*) Fragrant, yellow flowers in umbels. Prostrate, thick, fleshy stems with sticky surfaces. Leaves wide and thick. West. Wash.; saltwater beaches. Summer. One of the most colorful of beach plants.

PINK SAND VERBENA (*Abronia umbellata*) Fragrant, pink flowers in umbels. Stems slender and prostrate; leaves oblong. West. Wash.; saltwater beaches. Summer.

Figure 11.
A trail in the Olympic rainforest. (Larrison)

Chapter 10—The Purslane Family (*Portulacaceae*)

Members of this family are annual or perennial herbs with fleshy, entire leaves and regular, perfect flowers. Sepals usually 2; petals 5, though as few as 2 and as many as 18. Stamens few to many and opposite the petals, if the same number. Ovary is superior. (Color Plates 11-12)

1. Flowers borne in dense, ball-like umbels................PUSSY-PAWS
1. Flowers not borne in dense, ball-like umbels........................2

2. Well-developed leaves scattered through flower clusters which are in the form of racemes.......................................RED MAIDS
2. Flower clusters either without leaves or with very small bracts; flowers either single or in racemes or cymes.....................................3

3. Plants annual or perennial but without thick, fleshy corms or taproots.
　　　　　　　　　　　　　　　　　　　　　MINER'S LETTUCE (*Montia*)
3. Plants perennial with very thick, fleshy corms or taproots..............4

4. Leaves, if present, usually in dense basal clusters or rosettes close to the ground surface, or lacking at time of flowering; petals 6 or more.
　　　　　　　　　　　　　　　　　　　　　　　LEWISIAS (*Lewisia*)
4. Leaves, if present, not in dense basal clusters or rosettes close to the ground, but opposite and on stems above the surface; not absent at time of flowering. Petals 5...............................SPRING BEAUTY

　　　　　　　*　　　*　　　*

PUSSY-PAWS (*Spraguea umbellata*) Thick, leathery, green, spatulate leaves in thick, basal tuft and prostrate. Fuzzy, rounded heads of white to pinkish-white flowers on smooth, reddish stalks, which recline like clock hands. Taproot large. Cascades and East. Wash.; dry, gravelly places on alpine slopes and ridges in high mountains, as well as in dry, sandy soil in yellow pine woods. Summer. (Color Plate 12)

RED MAIDS (*Calandrinia ciliata*) Leaves long (up to 3 inches), narrow, and grass-like; fringed with hairs along the margins. Flowers large and red, purple, or rarely white, with yellow centers. West. Wash.; moist ground in lowlands; weed-like. Spring. (Color Plate 11)

SPRING BEAUTY (*Claytonia lanceolata*) Few or no basal leaves (often a single pair of stem leaves present which are usually opposite, narrow, and lance-shaped). Loose, terminal cluster of dainty flowers, white or pinkish with darker veins, in pattern of 5 petals notched at the tips. East. and West. Wash.; moist woods, but often in dry places, such as sagebrush slopes and subalpine or alpine ridges and meadows. Mid spring and summer. One of the montane species that bloom along the edges of melting snowbanks. (Color Plate 11)

LEWISIAS (*Lewisia*) (Color Plate 11)

Low-growing, fleshy herbs with often inconspicuous leaves but with large, showy flowers, the latter in some species virtually on the ground surface.

1. Basal leaves lacking (except when plant is not in flower); rather, in flowering plants, a whorl of long, narrow leaves just below the flowers; root with ball-like corm...............................THREE-LEAVED LEWISIA
1. Basal leaves present; roots not as ball-like corms.....................2

71

2. Sepals 5 to 9; flowers borne singly on stems . . . . BITTERROOT
2. Sepals 2; flowers often 2 or more on a stem 3

3. Flowers single on unbranching stems; stems less than 4 inches tall.
DWARF LEWISIA
3. Flowers several on branching stems; stems more than 4 inches tall 4

4. Petals more than 1 inch long; leaves more than 1/2 inch wide; flowers pink
or peach-colored . . . . TWEEDY'S LEWISIA
4. Petals less than 3/4 inch long; leaves less than 1/2 inch wide; flowers
white or pink . . . . COLUMBIA LEWISIA

*   *   *

THREE-LEAVED LEWISIA (*Lewisia triphylla*) Basal leaves absent when flowering, except 2 or 3 leaves present on stem. Flowers in raceme-like cluster
with small bracts. Flowers white or pink, 1/4 inch long, with 5 to 9 petals.
Cascades and East. Wash.; damp, sandy or gravelly soils in sagebrush and
open yellow pine forests up to the subalpine section of mountains, often
bordering melting snowbanks. Late spring and summer.

BITTERROOT (*Lewisia rediviva*) Leaves fleshy, cylindrical, flat on ground and
radiating from rootstock; appear in early spring, but drying up and disappearing entirely by time of flowering. Flowers showy and up to 2 inches in diameter;
pink to rose, occasionally white. 10 to 18 wide-spreading petals. Narrow, cone-
shaped buds. East. Wash.; exposed gravelly or rocky places from sagebrush
up into foothills. Mid spring to mid summer. The famous "bitterroot," both a
beautiful wildflower and an important food plant of the Indians.

DWARF LEWISIA (*Lewisia pygmaea*) Basal tuft of linear leaves. Small pink,
whitish, or lavender flowers with 6-8 petals. Flowers single on unbranched
stems. East. and West. Wash.; rocky, open places in high mountains. Late
spring and summer.

TWEEDY'S LEWISIA (*Lewisia tweedyi*) Large, basal cluster of thick, green
leaves, wide oval in shape with long petioles. Numerous single flowers on
single stems, about 1½ inches in diameter, usually with 7-9 petals, and pale
pink or shades of pale peach or apricot in color. Central east slope of Cascades; rocky slopes and crevices, mostly in yellow pine woods. Late spring
to mid summer.

COLUMBIA LEWISIA (*Lewisia columbiana*) Basal tuft of fleshy, narrow, slightly
spatulate leaves. Flowers small, 1/2 in diameter, with 6-9 petals, on slender,
branching stems about 6 inches tall. Flowers white, pink, or magenta, with
pink veins. East. and West. Wash.; exposed, rocky places, mostly in the
mountains. Late spring and summer.

MINER'S LETTUCE (*Montia*) (Color Plate 12)

Smallish plants with smooth, slightly fleshy leaves. Flowers small, white or
pink, in racemes or umbels.

1. Stem leaves opposite 2
1. Stem leaves alternate 7

*　　*　　*

CHAMISSO'S MONTIA (*Montia chamissoi*) Stems weak, but very leafy. Bulblets often present at tips of stolons. Flowers white to pink. Cascades and East. Wash.; wet, boggy places in foothills and lower parts of mountains. Late spring and summer.

BROAD-LEAVED MONTIA (*Montia cordifolia*) Flowering stems 6-12 inches tall with 1 pair of opposite leaves below flowers; lower leaves blunt at tip. Flowers white. East. and West. Wash.; moist places, usually near water in foothills and mountains. Late spring to early autumn.

WESTERN SPRING BEAUTY (*Montia sibirica*) Lower leaves pointed at tips, long-stalked, and basal. Stem leaves pointed. Flowers white with pink veins and 1/3 to 1/2 inch long. East. and West. Wash.; damp, shady habitats in lowlands and lower parts of mountains; common. Early spring to early autumn.

SAND MONTIA (*Montia arenicola*) Pink flowers in racemes of 2-14 blooms, each arising from the axil of a small bract. Petals about 1/4 inch long. East. Wash.; hillsides and yellow pine woods; common along the Snake River. Spring and early summer.

MINER'S LETTUCE (*Montia perfoliata*) Fused, perfoliate condition of stem leaves distinctive. East. and West. Wash.; moist, sandy soils in open or wooded habitats in lowland and foothills. Flowers white to pink. Spring and early summer.

PALE MONTIA (*Montia spathulata*) Narrow, basal leaves in dense tufts. Stem leaves occasionally joined on one side to produce fork-like structure. Flowers tiny (1/8 inch long) and white to whitish pink. West. Wash.; fairly open habitats. Spring and early summer.

DWARF MONTIA (*Montia dichotoma*) Plants small with 1/4-3/4 inch long leaves. Flowers white and 1/10 inch long, hardly longer than sepals. East. and West. Wash.; moist, lowland soils. Spring and early summer.

NARROW-LEAVED MONTIA (*Montia linearis*) Numerous, alternate leaves on stem. Flowers white, 1/5 inch long, and in 1-sided raceme. East. and West. Wash.; sandy areas in lowlands and foothills. Mid spring to mid summer.

STREAMBANK SPRING BEAUTY (*Montia parvifolia*) Plant pinkish in color. Stems branched with numerous, alternate leaves. Flowers pink or white with pink veins, 1/4-1/2 inch long. Plants spreading by runners. East. and West. Wash.; moist habitats along streams in mountains. Late spring and summer.

BRANCHING MONTIA (*Montia diffusa*) Low, spreading plant with many branches. Leaves short and as broad as long. Flowers 1/4 inch long and white to pale pink. West. Wash.; moist, shady woods. Mid spring to mid summer.

HOWELL'S MONTIA (*Montia howellii*) Flowers in clusters of 3's, each cluster opposite a leaf. Petals white, tiny or absent. Stems spreading, runner-like. West. Wash.; moist habitats in lowlands. Spring.

Chapter 11—The Pink Family (*Caryophyllaceae*)

Members of this family are perennial, biennial, or annual herbs with opposite, simple, entire leaves, and regular, perfect or imperfect flowers. Sepals and petals 4 or 5; stamens 5-10; and styles 1-5. Ovary superior. Petals may be lacking in some members of the family. (Color Plates 12-13)

1. Perennial plants with large, broad, fleshy leaves occurring along the seashore; flower parts attached to a 10-lobed disk..............HONKENYA
1. Plants not as above; leaves, if fleshy, not large and broad, but narrow....2

2. Sepals united...................................WILD PINKS (*Silene*)
2. Sepals not united..3

3. Styles the same number as the sepals.............................4
3. Styles fewer in number than the sepals...........................5

4. Very low plants forming tufts or mats............PEARLWORTS (*Sagina*)
4. Plants not tufted or matted.......................FIELD CHICKWEED

5. Style single and 2-branched at the tip..............SAND CARDIONEMA
5. Styles 3 or 4 in number..6

6. Petals 2-lobed ....CHICKWEEDS (*Stellaria*)
6. Petals entire, not lobed...7

7. Papery stipules at bases of leaf petioles..........BEACH SAND SPURRY
7. No papery stipules at bases of leaf petioles.......SANDWORTS (*Arenaria*)

*   *   *

HONKENYA (*Honkenya peploides*)   Plant large, to 24 inches. Leaves and stems thick and fleshy. Flowers small, greenish, with 5-6 petals and growing in axils of leaves or in clusters at tips of stems. West. Wash.; coastal beaches along saltwater. Late spring to early fall. (Color Plate 13)

FIELD CHICKWEED (*Cerastium arvense*)   Leaves downy, narrow, pointed. Flowers 1/2 inch in diameter, white, and borne on slender stems; petals 5, deeply notched. Petals at least twice as long as sepals. Stamens 10. East. and West. Wash.; open, grassy, rocky, or waste places. Mid spring and summer. (Color Plate 12)

SAND CARDIONEMA (*Cardionema ramosissima*)   Stems prostrate, 2-8 inches long, covered with wooly hairs and sharp, needle-like leaves. Lobes of calyx tipped with spines. Petals scale-like and not colored. West. Wash.; sandy beaches along saltwater. Summer.

BEACH SAND SPURRY (*Spergularia macrotheca*)   Leaves very fleshy and linear, sharp-pointed. Stems long (to 16 inches) and spreading or prostrate. Petals shorter than sepals, and pink or white. West. Wash.; shores and marshes along saltwater. Summer. (Color Plate 13)

Figure 12.
Wild pinks, *Silene*. Note the sac-like calyxes. (Yaich)

WILD PINKS (*Silene*) (Color Plate 13) (Fig. 12)

Plants characterized by the often bladder-like calyx in the flowers which may be strongly marked with conspicuous nerves. Foliage often sticky.

1. Calyx large, inflated, bladder-like, and conspicuously marked with 15-20 veins . . . . BLADDER SILENE
1. Calyx not as above. 2
2. Plants annual, weed-like, and growing mostly on disturbed soil.
SLEEPY CATCHFLY
2. Plants perennial, not weed-like, and growing mostly on undisturbed soil. .3
3. Calyx smooth; plants low (less than 4 inches tall). . . . . . . MOSS CAMPION
3. Calyx hairy; plants higher (mostly over 4 inches). 4
4. Flowers less than 1/2 inch long and borne in open, leafy cymes.
MENZIES' CAMPION
4. Flowers more than 1/2 inch long and not borne in open, leafy cymes. . . .5
5. Petal blades less than 1/8 inch long, notched, but not lobed.
SPALDING'S CAMPION
5. Petal blades more than 1/8 inch long and noticeably lobed. 6
6. Petals equally 4-lobed, sometimes with deeper cleft between the 2 middle lobes . . . . OREGON CAMPION
6. Petals either 2-lobed or if 4-lobed, then lobes unequal. 7
7. Petals with 2 lobes. 8
7. Petals with 4 lobes. 9
8. Sides of petals with prominent humps or "shoulders."
DOUGLAS' CAMPION
8. Sides of petals without prominent humps or "shoulders."
TRAILING CAMPION
9. Sides of petals without prominent humps or "shoulders."
SCOULER'S CATCHFLY
9. Sides of petals with prominent humps or "shoulders". 10
10. Lateral shoulders of petal weakly toothed. . . . . PARRY'S CAMPION
10. Lateral shoulders of petal sharply toothed. . . . . . SUKSDORF'S CAMPION

*   *   *

BLADDER SILENE (*Silene cucubalus*) Inflated, bladder-like calyx distinctive. East. and West. Wash.; introduced into waste and disturbed places in lowlands and occasionally in mountains. Flowers white. Summer.

SLEEPY CATCHFLY (*Silene antirrhina*) Narrow, lanceolate leaves, to 2½ inches long. Flowers white to pink and only slightly longer than the calyx. Sticky bands around stem between leaves often catch insects or fallen seeds. East. and West. Wash.; lowlands to high mountains.

MOSS CAMPION (*Silene acaulis*) Low, cushion-like plants with crowded, needle-like leaves. Petals notched, less than 1/2 inch long, and pink, lavender, or white. East. and West. Wash.; moist slopes and swales in alpine zone of high mountains. Summer.

MENZIES' CAMPION (*Silene menziesii*) Spreading, matted plant with broadly lance-shaped leaves. Inflorescence leafy, with flowers white and petals mostly

2-lobed. East. and West. Wash.; in moist woods of mountains. Late spring and summer.

SPALDING'S CAMPION (*Silene spaldingii*) Plants very sticky-hairy. Leaves numerous, to 2¾ inches long. Flowers greenish white. Extreme East. Wash.; rocky habitats in sagebrush and yellow pine woods. Summer.

OREGON CAMPION (*Silene oregana*) About 6 basal leaves with those of stem smaller. Flowers pinkish white. Columbia Gorge and East. Wash.; open areas in sagebrush plains and slopes and yellow pine woods up into the subalpine zone. Summer.

DOUGLAS' CAMPION *(Silene douglasii)* A large plant (to 16 inches) with leaves tufted and matted near ground. Leaves large, reaching 3 inches in length. Calyx large (to 1/2 inch long) and petals long (3/4 inch) and white, pink, or purple in color. East. and West. Wash.; open places in lowlands and mountains. Late spring to mid summer.

TRAILING CAMPION (*Silene repens*) Plant matted with trailing, prostrate branches giving rise to erect stems. Leaves narrow, reaching 1½ inches in length. Exposed petals white, reddish, or purplish and 1/4 inch long. East. Wash.; rocky places in the high mountains. Summer.

SCOULER'S CATCHFLY (*Silene scouleri*) Large plant (over two feet) with 6 inch leaves, becoming smaller farther up stem. Calyx 1/2-3/4 inch long and covered with soft hairs. Petals greenish white to reddish. East. and West. Wash.; open to semi-open habitats, mostly in lowlands. Summer.

PARRY'S CAMPION (*Silene parryi*) Leaves narrow and basal. Petal blades short (1/4 inch) and white, greenish, or purplish. East. and West. Wash.; mostly in the mountains.

SUKSDORF'S CAMPION (*Silene suksdorfii*) Low alpine plant with very short (1/2 inch) leaves. The very short petals are white, greenish, or lavender. Cascades; open alpine areas in high mountains. Summer.

PEARLWORTS (*Sagina*)

1. Leaves and stems fleshy; occurring along seashore.
                                    THICK-STEMMED PEARLWORT
1. Leaves and stems not fleshy; not occurring along the seashore.
                                    WESTERN PEARLWORT

                    *   *   *

THICK-STEMMED PEARLWORT (*Sagina crassicaulis*) Fleshy leaves and erect stems. Flowers white. West. Wash.; sand and rocks along seashore. Summer and early autumn.

WESTERN PEARLWORT (*Sagina occidentalis*) Small plant (less than 4 inches high) with thread-like leaves. Flowers white and very small. East. and West. Wash.; moist places in the lowlands. Summer.

78

CHICKWEEDS (*Stellaria*) (Color Plate 13)

Mostly small plants with prostrate or partially-prostrate branches. Flowers are small and white, the petals 2-cleft. Flowers sometimes absent.

1. Petals much longer than sepals; stem very glandular. .STICKY CHICKWEED
1. Petals not much longer than sepals, shorter than sepals, or sometimes petals absent; stem not strongly glandular. 2

2. Petals usually much shorter than sepals; leaves broad. 3
2. Petals similar in length to sepals, or slightly larger or slightly shorter; leaves long and narrow 6

3. Plant as a thin-stemmed annual; upper part of stem lacking leaves.
SHINING CHICKWEED
3. Plants perennial; stems leafy throughout. 4

4. Flowers borne singly in axils of leaves. 5
4. Flowers borne in cymes in axils of leaves or at tip of stem.
MOUNTAIN BOG STARWORT

5. Margins of leaves wrinkled or scalloped. . . . . .CRISPED STARWORT
5. Margins of leaves not wrinkled or scalloped.
CLUSTERED MOUNTAIN STARWORT

6. Flowers single, in axils of leaves; petals as long as sepals.
LONG-STALKED STARWORT
6. Flowers several to many and arranged in cymes; petals often shorter than sepals 7

7. Cymes with leaves; petals shorter than sepals.
MOUNTAIN BOG STARWORT
7. Cymes not leafy; petals longer than sepals. 8

8. Leaves narrowing slightly at base; leaves not stiff.
LONG-LEAVED STARWORT
8. Leaves not narrowing at base; leaves stiff. . . .LONG-STALKED STARWORT

*   *   *

STICKY CHICKWEED (*Stellaria jamesiana*)   Flowers white. Cascades and East. Wash.; variable, shady or open woods, subalpine meadows, and dry, rocky ridges. Late spring to mid summer.

(Note: In members of this genus, the petals, when present, are 5 in number and deeply cleft. Stamens 10 or less.)

SHINING CHICKWEED (*Stellaria nitens*)   Petals present or absent. East. and West. Wash.; grassy slopes and prairies, as well as stream margins. Spring and early summer.

MOUNTAIN BOG STARWORT (*Stellaria calycantha*)   Leaves ovate to ovate-lanceolate. Petals tiny or absent. East. and West. Wash.; wet places in lowlands and lower montane areas. Summer.

CRISPED STARWORT (*Stellaria crispa*)   Stems weak. Leaves thin and egg-shaped and with crisped margins. Petals usually missing. East. and West. Wash.; moist meadows and shady woods in lowlands. Summer.

CLUSTERED MOUNTAIN STARWORT (*Stellaria obtusa*)   Short, clustered stems (to 4 inches). Leaves oval, 1/2 inch long. Petals usually lacking. East. and West. Wash.; wet meadows and streamsides, mostly in the mountains. Summer.

LONG-STALKED STARWORT (*Stellaria longipes*)   Stems matted. Leaves narrow and stiff, 1 inch or less. Petals short and white. East. and West. Wash.; wet meadows and stream margins, as well as rocky slopes, mostly in the mountains. Late spring and summer.

LONG-LEAVED STARWORT (*Stellaria longifolia*)   Leaves linear-lanceolate. Sepals shorter than petals. Flowers white. East. and West. Wash.; wet meadows and stream margins. Late spring and summer.

SANDWORTS (*Arenaria*) (Color Plate 12)

Small, fine-stemmed, often tufted or matted plants, commonly with many, narrow leaves. Flowers small and white. Frequently grows on open, exposed, often sandy soil surfaces.

(Note: A difficult group in which to identify species, as there is much variation and interbreeding.)

1. Leaves more than 1/8 inch wide; not so long and narrow.
                                                LARGE-FLOWERED SANDWORT
1. Leaves less than 1/16 inch wide; long and narrow....................2
2. Plants annual, without well-developed roots.........................3
2. Plants perennial with well-developed roots; often occurring in mat-like life form 4
3. Smaller leaves in axils of larger leaves...........SLENDER SANDWORT
3. No smaller leaves in axils of larger leaves..........DWARF SANDWORT
4. Plants occurring in low, mat-like life form..........................5
4. Plants not occurring in low, mat-like life form......................6
5. Flowering stems densely leafy and not strongly upright. Sepals and leaves not prominently veined......................NUTTALL'S SANDWORT
5. Flowering stems not densely leafy but strongly upright above leaf mat. Sepals and leaves prominently veined.............VERNAL SANDWORT
6. Flowers many, in a tightly-congested head.
                                                DENSE-FLOWERED SANDWORT
6. Flowers few, not in a tightly-congested head.
                                                NEEDLE-LEAVED SANDWORT

                        *   *   *

LARGE-FLOWERED SANDWORT (*Arenaria macrophylla*)   Lanceolate leaves 1/2-1½ inches long and narrow; pointed at each end. Flowers white and few and borne in a cyme. East. and West. Wash.; open to semi-open, or even dense, moist woods, as well as meadows, and dry, sandy places in lowlands and moderate elevations in mountains. Late spring and summer.

SLENDER SANDWORT (*Arenaria stricta*)   Leaves narrow and pointed, with smaller leaves in axils of the larger ones. Flowers white with petals longer than sepals. East. and West. Wash.; occurs in variety of open habitats, such as meadows, in the lowlands. Late spring to mid summer.

DWARF SANDWORT (*Arenaria pusilla*) Plants short, to 2 inches tall, with tiny leaves (to 1/6 inch). Petals white and shorter than sepals. East. and West. Wash.; dry areas, such as sagebrush and yellow pine woods. Mid spring to early summer.

NUTTALL'S SANDWORT (*Arenaria nuttallii*) Stems leafy and semi-prostrate. Flowers numerous and white. East. and West. Wash.; rock slides and open, exposed plateaus, mostly in the higher mountains. Late spring and summer.

VERNAL SANDWORT (*Arenaria rubella*) Stems 2-6 inches tall. Leaves needle-shaped, strongly veined, and 1/4 to 1/2 inch long. Flowers white. East. and West. Wash.; open, exposed, rocky places and meadows in the higher mountains. Common. Summer.

DENSE-FLOWERED SANDWORT (*Arenaria congesta*) Stems long (to 10 inches) with sharp-pointed basal leaves occasionally reaching 2 inches in length. Flowers white and borne in congested head-like inflorescences. East. Wash.; open, exposed habitats from sagebrush plains to alpine areas. Summer.

NEEDLE-LEAVED SANDWORT (*Arenaria capillaris*) Leaves basal and very narrow and grass-like. Petals white and much longer than sepals. East. and West. Wash.; rocky slopes in higher mountains. Summer.

*   *   *

The sea beach continued:

On still higher and drier ground is located the dry meadow habitat with its seashore lupine, beach silver-top, black knotweed, and gray beach pea, species found also in the sand dune community. In all these habitats, other species will be present to a lesser degree. An example of the latter would be the dwarf montia (*Montia dichotoma*).

Probably the best place to study seashore flowers in Washington is the Leadbetter Point area at the tip of the Long Beach peninsula on Willapa Bay. Here a large tract of land, including the various sand dune and sea beach habitats, has been set aside as a park (after a valiant effort by conservationists!) and natural history preserve. Birding is also excellent in this area and there are a number of motels a few miles south for housing.

A good introduction to seashore plants is contained in the book, PLANTS OF THE OREGON COASTAL DUNES, by Alfred M. Wiedemann, LaRea J. Dennis, and Frank H. Smith, published by OSU Bookstores, Inc., in 1969. While mainly treating Oregon beaches, it applies almost as well to those of Washington. Seashore plants, like seashore animals, have a certain cosmopolitan nature, being bound together around the world by the interconnecting saltwater beaches. For a detailed discussion of the origin of sand dunes, we recommend COASTAL SAND DUNES OF WASHINGTON AND OREGON, Geological Society of America Memoir No. 72, 1958, by W. S. Cooper.

For the finding and identification of organisms on the seashore in general, consult the new SEASHORE LIFE OF PUGET SOUND, THE STRAIT OF GEORGIA, AND THE SAN JUAN ARCHIPELAGO by Eugene N. Kozloff, published by the University of Washington Press.

Figure 13.
Water lily family growth habit, as shown by the water shield, *Brasenia.* (Larrison)

Chapter 12—The Water Lily Family (*Nymphaeaceae*)

Members of this family are perennial, aquatic herbs with stout rhizomes or tubers anchored into the mud of ponds or lakes and with long stalks reaching to the surface and headed with platter-like, emergent or floating leaves. The flowers are perfect, regular, and solitary. Sepals 3-12; petals and stamens few to many. (Color Plate 14)

1. Flowers purplish and very small; leaves with stalk attached to underside near the middle, like an umbrella, floating, and 3-4 inches long; pistils several and simple..................................WATER-SHIELD
1. Flowers yellow and large; leaves heart-shaped, not umbrella-like; emergent or floating, and 4-12 inches long; pistil 1, compound.
WESTERN YELLOW WATER LILY

*　　*　　*

WATER-SHIELD (*Brasenia schreberi*) East. and West. Wash.; lowland ponds, small lakes, and slow-moving water. Flowers purplish. Mid summer to early autumn. (Color Plate 14) (Fig. 13)

WESTERN YELLOW WATER LILY (*Nuphar polysepalum*) Flowers yellow. East. and West. Wash.; lowland lakes and slow streams. (Color Plate 14)

Occurring some 6 to 8 times during the winter is a series of outbreaks of cold, dry air from the Yukon and northern Canada which visit Washington, particularly its eastern and northeastern parts. Even though these outbreaks may be occasionally stalled along the Canadian border by a stationary front, some leakage of cold air will move down the north-south river valleys in northeastern Washington to give that region added chill.

Arctic air invasions are characterized by the coldest temperatures of the winter and seem to be necessary for the production of snow in any quantity in the lowlands. They may come in one-two blows with snow along the advancing Arctic front, especially if it collides with a Pacific weather system, and then again when the Arctic front retrogrades as a warm front. Exposed plains and ridges are often swept by these northern winds and if the snow cover is quite light, their vegetation will be sparse.

It is obvious from these brief accounts that a very interesting and important pattern of climatic conditions occurs in Washington. For those readers interested in further information on weather and its effects on the environment, we recommend UNDERSTANDING OUR ATMOSPHERIC ENVIRONMENT by Morris Neiburger, James G. Edinger, and William D. Bonner, and published by W. H. Freeman and Company in 1973.

Figure 14.
Flower study camp of Larrison and Yaich along Wenas Creek. (Yaich)

Chapter 13—The Peony Family (*Paeoniaceae*)

Members of this family, as treated here, are stout, perennial herbs with large, regular, perfect flowers and fleshy ternately or palmately compound leaves. Sepals, 5-6; petals, 5-10. Not commonly, though widely distributed, but easily recognizeable by their deeply dissected, fleshy leaves, and fleshy, brownish or purplish flowers. One species in our area. (Color Plate 14)

WILD PEONY (*Paeonia brownii*) Petals reddish purple with greenish-yellow borders; sepals green; numerous stamens with golden anthers. In center of flower are 5 egg-shaped ovaries with apparently no styles but with a little, cream-colored stigma. Leaves are light gray-green or bluish green with a bit of a bloom. East. Wash.; sagebrush and yellow pine woods in lowlands and foothills; most numerous in the Blue Mountains of southeastern Washington and in the yellow pine woods along the lower east slope of the Cascades. Late spring and early summer.

———————

Among the multitude of duties assigned to the Lewis and Clark expedition which visited the Pacific Northwest in 1805-06 was the collection of plant specimens and the recording of information on the various floras encountered. Although some of the materials collected were destroyed by moisture when buried in caches in the ground earlier in the trip, about 200 pressed plants were brought back by the group. These were subsequently examined by Frederick Pursh, a European botanist who had been living in Philadelphia while working on the flora of North America. From the Lewis and Clark material, he described 4 new genera and 123 new species in 1814. Some 188 of the pressed plants are still in existence in the collection of the Philadelphia Academy of Sciences.

In addition to the specimens, commentaries were made on a number of plant species, especially those used by the Indians for food or medicines. Lewis prepared detailed notes on the common camas (*Camassia quamash*), its beautiful flowers as well as its food qualities and how the Indians prepared it. The cous (*Lomatium cous*) was also described, though it was suspected of causing dysentery among members of the expedition!

Some of the plants discovered by Lewis were the elegant mariposa lily (*Calochortus elegans*), yellow avalanche lily (*Erythronium grandiflorum*), mountain death camas (*Zigadenus elegans*), red globe mallow (*Sphaeralcea coccinea*), and balsamroot (*Balsamorhiza sagittata*). Two plants, the bitterroot (*Lewisia rediviva*) and the large-flowered clarkia (*Clarkia pulchella*) were named after the leaders of the expedition.

Figure 15.
A moist meadow, typical habitat of the buttercups. (Larrison)

Chapter 14—The Buttercup Family (*Ranunculaceae*)

Members of this family are herbs (as included here) and shrubs with mostly alternate, simple or compound leaves and regular or irregular flowers. Sepals 2-5, sometimes petal-like; petals 4, more than 4, or none. Stamens are numerous. Ovary superior. (Color Plates 14-17)

1. Flowers irregular, large, and very conspicuous......................2
1. Flowers regular, often small and rather inconspicuous...............3

2. Petals 4, extending beyond sepals; upper sepal spurred.
LARKSPURS (*Delphinium*)
2. Petals mostly 2, more or less covered by hood; upper sepal prominently hooded—but not spurred..................COLUMBIA MONKSHOOD

3. Petals prominently spurred and large; perennial. COLUMBINES (*Aquilegia*)
3. Petals not prominently spurred and/or smaller; annual or perennial.....4

4. Plants very small with tiny flowers; sepals 5, and spurred; annual.
MOUSE-TAILS (*Myosurus*)
4. Plants and flowers larger; perennials..............................5

5. Pistil 1....................................WESTERN BANEBERRY
5. Pistils 2 or more..6

6. Fruit small, dry, 1-seeded, and not splitting at maturity (achene).......7
6. Fruit larger, dry, 2- to several-seeded, and splitting when mature (follicle) 11

7. Flower (perianth) consisting of both corolla and calyx, with corolla the more dominant of the two.................BUTTERCUPS (*Ranunculus*)
7. Flower (perianth) of calyx, or calyx and small, subordinate corolla......8

8. Plants climbing, with somewhat woody vines....CLEMATISES (*Clematis*)
8. Plants not as above...9

9. Flowers often imperfect.................MEADOW RUES ((*Thalictrum*)
9. Flowers perfect 10

10. Stem leaves in whorls of 3's..................ANEMONES (*Anemones*)
10. Stem leaves not in whorls of 3's....................FALSE BUGBANE

11. Leaves divided (1 to several times) into 3's........................12
11. Leaves simple or compound, but not divided into 3's................13

12. Leaves leathery and evergreen; "roots" (rhizomes) yellowish.
GOLD-THREADS (*Coptis*)
12. Leaves neither leathery or evergreen; roots not yellowish.
TALL BUGBANE

13. Leaves simple.........................MARSH MARIGOLDS (*Caltha*)
13. Leaves 5-lobed to almost compound..................GLOBEFLOWER

*   *   *

COLUMBIA MONKSHOOD (*Aconitum columbianum*) Plants 1½ to 5 feet tall. Leaves circular, palmately divided into several sections with many lobes. Sepals colored, 5; the upper sepal forming a peaked hood. Only 2 small petals, almost hidden by hood. Flowers deep purple, bluish, greenish, or white. East. and West. Wash.; moist places in forests and subalpine meadows; usually on streambanks. Summer. (Color Plate 14)

WESTERN BANEBERRY (*Actaea rubra*) Plants to 3 feet. Leaves divided in several separate sections and irregularly toothed; long petioles. Tiny white flowers (petals) in short, dense racemes rounded on top. Sepals white or purplish. Numerous stamens give fuzzy appearance to flower heads. Fruit a cluster of shiny, red berries. East. and West. Wash.; moist places in woods and along streams. Late spring to mid summer. (Color Plate 16)

FALSE BUGBANE (*Trautvetteria carolinensis*) Plants robust, to 36 inches. Leaves palmately lobed, wide, 5-9 lobes; toothed. Large, flat flower heads of feathery, creamy white flowers containing no petals, but numerous spreading stamens. Flowers resemble "spoon" chrysanthemums, when viewed very closely. East. and West. Wash.; moist, open woods and streambanks. Late spring and summer. (Color Plate 17)

TALL BUGBANE (*Cimicifuga elata*) Plants tall, to 7 feet. Leaves large and compound; lobed and toothed. Numerous, cream-colored flowers in tall, branched racemes. Petals absent; "flower" of stamens and sepals. West. Wash.; moist, deep woods in lowlands. Summer.

GLOBEFLOWER (*Trollius laxus*) Plants usually less than 12 inches. Leaves basal, with long petioles and several smaller, sessile leaves on stalk, just below the single flower which is about 1½ inches in diameter with 5-6 white to creamy or rose-greenish sepals. Tiny, yellow petals resembling stamens, in a ring around the many true stamens. East. and West. Wash.; wet, swampy or boggy areas in mountains, including moist, subalpine meadows. Late spring and summer. (Fig. 16)

LARKSPURS (*Delphinium*) (Color Plate 16)

Plants with flowers containing 5 large, colored sepals, the upper one prominently spurred. The 4 petals are much smaller and less conspicuous than the sepals and form a tuft in the center of the latter. Stamens numerous. Leaves palmately cleft.

1. Plants occurring east of the Cascade crest..........................2
1. Plants occurring west of the Cascade crest..........................6
1. Plants occurring in moist woods and along streams in the Columbia Gorge.
POISON LARKSPUR

2. Plants taller—usually more than 16 inches high......................3
2. Plants shorter—usually less than 16 inches tall.....................4

3. Lower stem and leaves with long, soft hairs; all the leaves more or less alike..TALL LARKSPUR
3. Lower stem and leaves with very fine, tiny hairs; lower and upper leaves different in shape...........................BURKE'S LARKSPUR

4. Plants occurring in Northeastern Washington.....BICOLORED LARKSPUR
4. Plants occurring elsewhere than in Northeastern Washington..........5

5. Plants occurring in sagebrush, grassland, and (mostly) yellow pine woods of lower, east slope of Cascades.............YELLOW PINE LARKSPUR
5. Plants occurring in subalpine and alpine areas of the Cascades.
LARGE-FLOWERED LARKSPUR

6. Stems larger, plants more than 36 inches tall . . . . PALE LARKSPUR
6. Stems smaller, plants less than 36 inches tall 7
7. Lower petals with notch at least 1/8 inch deep; roots fibrous.
LARGE-FLOWERED LARKSPUR
7. Lower petals with shallow notch, less than 1/8 inch deep; roots tuber-like . 8
8. Spurs and sepals large, more than 1/2 inch in length.
MENZIES'S LARKSPUR
8. Spurs and sepals small, less than 1/2 inch in length.
NUTTALL'S LARKSPUR

                                   *   *   *

POISON LARKSPUR (*Delphinium trolliifolium*) Leaflets broad and toothed. Flowers violet purple to deep blue in long, open, loosely-flowered racemes. Moist, shaded woods in Columbia Gorge. Mid spring to early summer.

TALL LARKSPUR (*Delphinium multiplex*) Plants tall (to 40 inches) and clammy to the touch. Basal and lower stem leaves thick and fleshy. Sepals bluish purple; petals bluish. East-central Cascades; sagebrush and yellow pine woods, usually along streams, in foothills and lower montane areas. Summer.

BURKE'S LARKSPUR (*Delphinium burkei*) Sepals bluish purple and cupped forward, rather than flaring; upper petals white; lower petals blue. East. Wash.; wet meadows and spring flats in foothills and montane areas, as well as sagebrush and yellow pine woods. Summer.

BICOLORED LARKSPUR (*Delphinium bicolor*) Sepals bluish purple; petals bluish. Northeast. Wash.; grasslands and yellow pine zones to subalpine meadows and rockslides. Late spring to mid summer.

YELLOW PINE LARKSPUR (*Delphinium nuttallianum*) Leaves small and mostly basal. Flowers strikingly colored (sepals white to bluish; petals white, yellow, or purple) in open racemes, on outward-spreading stalks. East. Wash.; dry, rocky soil in yellow pine woods and adjacent grasslands and sagebrush in foothills and lower mountain areas. Early spring to mid summer.

LARGE-FLOWERED LARKSPUR (*Delphinium glareosum*) Plants low (under 16 inches); bushy. Leaves small and 3-lobed. Sepals bluish purple; petals blue. Cascades and Olympics; rock slides and alpine ridges in the high mountains; common. Summer.

PALE LARKSPUR (*Delphinium glaucum*) Plants tall, to 7 feet. Leaves divided into 5-7 lobes; lobes toothed. Sepals dark purple; petals pale blue; in tall, loosely-arranged raceme. Olympics and southern and central Cascades; meadows and stream sides in the subalpine zone. Summer.

MENZIES'S LARKSPUR (*Delphinium menziesii*) Plants low, to 20 inches. Lower pair of petals notched. Sepals and petals blue. West. Wash.; bluffs along saltwater, glacial outwash prairies, and grassy foothill slopes. Mid spring to mid summer.

NUTTALL'S LARKSPUR (*Delphinium nuttallii*) Plants to 24 inches. Sepals bluish purple; upper petals light blue; lower petals dark bluish purple. Flowers in spike-like raceme. West. Wash. and Columbia Gorge; glacial prairies around southern end of Puget Sound and basaltic cliffs in the Columbia Gorge. Late spring and early summer.

Figure 16.
The globeflower, *Trollius.* (Yaich)

COLUMBINES (*Aquilegia*) (Color Plate 15)

1. Sepals yellow; spurs curved inward . . . . YELLOW COLUMBINE
1. Sepals reddish; spurs nearly straight . . . . RED COLUMBINE

*   *   *

YELLOW COLUMBINE (*Aquilegia flavescens*) Flowers yellow, rarely pale pink East. and West. Wash.; moist, subalpine meadows and slopes. Summer.

RED COLUMBINE (*Aquilegia formosa*) Flowers bicolored; petals yellow; sepals red. East. and West. Wash.; moist places in open woods and edges of clearings, in lowlands and lower mountains. Late spring and summer.

MOUSE-TAILS (*Myosurus*)

Small, inconspicuous plants characterized by a tall (1/2 to 1 inch) column in the middle of the flower which bears the numerous pistils.

1. Sepals narrow, with one nerve per sepal; spikes shorter, less than 1/2 inch long . . . . BRISTLY MOUSE-TAIL
1. Sepals wider, with 3 nerves; spikes longer, more than 3/4 inch long.
WESTERN MOUSE-TAIL

*   *   *

BRISTLY MOUSE-TAIL (*Myosurus aristatus*) Leaves linear to linear-spatulate. Achenes with long beak. Flowers greenish to yellowish. East. Wash.; moist swales in sagebrush and grasslands; mostly in the lowlands, though sometimes to subalpine areas. Spring and early summer.

WESTERN MOUSE-TAIL (*Myosurus minimus*) Leaves thread-like. Achenes with short beak. Flowers greenish or yellowish. East. and West. Wash.; moist areas. Spring and early summer.

BUTTERCUPS (*Ranunculus*) (Color Plate 17)

Flowers with usually yellow, waxy petals and a single series of green sepals; growing singly on a long stalk from leafy base. Stamens and pistils numerous. Usually found in wet to moist habitats.

1. Leaves entire to weakly toothed 2
1. Leaves (at least some on a plant) deeply lobed to compound 4

2. Leaves broad; almost as wide as long . . . . SEASIDE BUTTERCUP
2. Leaves narrow, several times longer than wide 3

3. Plants creeping; stems weak; rooting at the nodes.
SMALLER CREEPING BUTTERCUP
3. Plants erect; not rooting at nodes . . . . . . PLANTAIN-LEAVED BUTTERCUP

4. Achenes covered with spines . . . . DOWNY BUTTERCUP
4. Achenes not covered with spines 5

5. Petals mostly white 6
5. Petals mostly yellow 7

6. Leaves sessile on stipules (which are attached to stem); leaves stiff.
STIFF-LEAVED WATER BUTTERCUP
6. Leaves attached to stem by slender petioles; leaves weak.
COMMON WATER BUTTERCUP

7. Plants mainly aquatic in habitat and often with deeply-lobed, submerged leaves. 8
7. Plants not aquatic and leaves not deeply lobed or dissected. 10

8. Plants annual with erect life form, usually more than 6 inches tall.
CELERY-LEAVED BUTTERCUP
8. Plants perennial with floating life form, usually less than 6 inches tall. . . .9

9. Leaves usually more than 3/4 inch long; petals more than 3/8 inch long.
YELLOW WATER BUTTERCUP
9. Leaves usually less than 3/4 inch long; petals less than 3/8 inch long.
GMELIN'S BUTTERCUP

10. Achenes only slightly flattened, with width not less than 1/3 the length of the achene. 11
10. Achenes very flattened and disk-shaped. 17

11. Petals more than 1/4 inch long. . . . . SAGEBRUSH BUTTERCUP
11. Petals less than 1/4 inch long. 12

12. Achenes usually covered with fine hairs. 13
12. Achenes smooth, without covering of fine hairs. 14

13. Most basal leaves finely scalloped, but not deeply lobed.
MOUNTAIN MEADOW BUTTERCUP
13. Most basal leaves deeply lobed. . . . . .SNOW BUTTERCUP

14. Basal leaves all deeply lobed. . . . . .SNOW BUTTERCUP
14. Basal leaves not all deeply lobed or cleft, but some or all merely scalloped 15

15. Stems not strongly erect, but spreading and seldom more than 6 inches tall. . . . . .TALUS SLOPE BUTTERCUP
15. Stems strongly erect and usually more than 6 inches tall. 16

16. Bases of lower leaves not tapering gradually to petiole but blunt.
MOUNTAIN MEADOW BUTTERCUP
16. Bases of lower leaves not tapering gradually to petiole but blunt.
KIDNEY-LEAVED BUTTERCUP

17. Basal leaves pinnately compound or divided.
WESTERN SWAMP BUTTERCUP
17. Basal leaves palmately compound or divided. 18

18. Petals much longer than sepals. . . . . .WESTERN BUTTERCUP
18. Petals not much longer than, or shorter than, sepals. 19

19. Basal leaves simple and deeply, but not completely, cleft.
WOODS BUTTERCUP
19. Basal leaves compound (lobes completely cleft to base to form leaflets). 20

20. Stem leaves usually more than 4. . . . . .BRISTLY BUTTERCUP
20. Stem leaves usually 4 or less. . . . . .MACOUN'S BUTTERCUP

*   *   *

SEASIDE BUTTERCUP (*Ranunculus cymbalaria*) Plants to 12 inches. Leaves to 1½ inches long, oval or heart-shaped, pale green, with scalloped margins, on 2 inch petioles. Flowers pale yellow; sepals and petals 1/3 inch long. East.

and West. Wash.; wet meadows, bogs, marshes, ditches, etc. Late spring and summer.

SMALLER CREEPING BUTTERCUP (*Ranunculus flammula*) Plants to 6 inches (flowering branches from creeping stems). Leaves thread-like to lance-shaped or grass-like. Petals twice as long as sepals. Flowers yellow. East. and West. Wash.; wet, muddy places from lowlands to foothills. Late spring to mid summer.

PLANTAIN-LEAVED BUTTERCUP (*Ranunculus alismaefolius*) Plants to 24 inches. Stems hollow and branching, erect or prostrate, Leaves long (to 6 inches), narrow, and lanceolate, with long petioles ("plantain-like"); entire or toothed. Flowers light yellow; petals 3/8 inch long. East. and West. Wash.; wet habitats, such as moist meadows and the shores of streams and ponds. Late spring to mid summer.

DOWNY BUTTERCUP (*Ranunculus hebecarpus*) Plants to 12 inches. Leaves 3-parted with 3-5 cleft lanceolate to ovate segments. Foliage downy. Petals 1/16 inch long, yellow, and 5, less than 5, or absent. East. Wash.; hillside slopes and yellow pine woods. Early to late spring.

STIFF-LEAVED WATER BUTTERCUP (*Ranunculus subrigidus*) Leaves sub-merged, dissected into thread-like divisions, without petioles, and firm—not collapsing when lifted from the water. Flowers white; 3/16 to 1/4 inch long. East. and West. Wash.; aquatic; occurs in ponds and slow-moving streams. Late spring and summer.

COMMON WATER BUTTERCUP (*Ranunculus aquatilis*) Leaves below the water surface finely divided into thread-like segments; those above surface merely lobed. Sub-surface leaves collapse and mat together when raised above water. Numerous tiny, white, floating flowers. East. and West. Wash.; aquatic; occurring in ponds and sluggish streams. Late spring and summer.

CELERY-LEAVED BUTTERCUP (*Ranunculus sceleratus*) Plants, when erect, to 12 inches. Stems fleshy. Lower leaves "celery-like," 3-lobed. Flowers yellow. East. and West. Wash.; wet meadows and shores of streams and ponds; also in shallow water. Late spring to early autumn. Poisonous to touch; sap may raise blisters on the skin.

YELLOW WATER BUTTERCUP (*Ranunculus flabellaris*) Aquatic or terrestrial. Submerged leaves ternately dissected into thread-like segments. Above-surface leaves roundish, 5-7-parted into wedge-shaped lobes. Petals bright yellow; 5-8 in number. East. Wash. and Columbia Gorge; ponds, mudflats, and bogs in lowlands. Late spring and summer.

GMELIN'S BUTTERCUP (*Ranunculus gmelinii*) Plants wholly or partly sub-merged. Above-surface plants hairy. Submerged leaves cleft into long, mem-branous segments. Petals oval, bright yellow, and less than 1/3 inch long. East. and West. Wash.; shallow water in ponds and marshes. Late spring and early autumn.

SAGEBRUSH BUTTERCUP (*Ranunculus glaberrimus*) Foliage smooth. Plants to 4-6 inches high; some stems prostrate or upward-curving. Basal leaves round or elliptical, 1¼ to 2 inches long. Occasionally some leaves lobed and some entire and linear on the same plant. Petals deep yellow, broadly oval-shaped, 1/3 to 3/5 inch long. East. Wash.; sagebrush and yellow pine woods.

Early spring to early summer. One of the earliest of the east-side wildflowers to bloom. Frequently appearing in spring seeps on south-facing slopes that have been melted free of snow.

MOUNTAIN MEADOW BUTTERCUP (*Ranunculus inamoenus*) Plants smooth to hairy; to 12 inches tall. Basal leaves fleshy and broadly oval, 3/4 to 1½ inches long. Petals yellow; 5, or missing. East. Wash.; montane and subalpine meadows and streambanks. Early and mid summer.

SNOW BUTTERCUP (*Ranunculus eschscholtzii*) Plants to 10 inches with yellowish or brownish down on stems. Leaves fleshy, shiny, somewhat kidney-shaped, and irregularly lobed. Whorl of narrowly-lobed leaves on upper part of stem. Flowers large and yellow. East. and West. Wash.; subalpine meadows and rockslides. Often found blooming at edges of melting snowbanks. Summer.

TALUS SLOPE BUTTERCUP (*Ranunculus verecundus*) Plants to 8 inches. Leaves small (1/3 to 3/4 inch), scalloped to even palmately lobed; flowers yellow, with sepals purple tinged, and very small (petals only 1/5 inch long). Cascades and East. Wash.; rockslides and meadows of the high alpine country. Mid to late summer.

KIDNEY-LEAVED BUTTERCUP (*Ranunculus abortivus*) Plants to 20 inches. Basal leaves oval, kidney-shaped, or cordate (1½ inches long), with long petioles. Sepals greenish yellow, tinged with purple. Petals yellow, 3/16 inch long. Northeastern Wash.; moist woods, streambanks, and subalpine meadows in lowlands and mountains. Mid summer.

WESTERN SWAMP BUTTERCUP (*Ranunculus orthorhynchus*) Plants downy, with long (to 40 inches) erect or prostrate stems; stems often tufted. Basal leaves pinnately compound with 3-7 leaflets which may reach 4-5 inches. Petals yellow, 1/3 to 3/4 inch long, and sometimes tinged with reddish. Sepals bent downward. East. and West. Wash.; moist meadows, bogs, and streambanks from lowlands up into the mountains. Mid spring to mid summer.

WESTERN BUTTERCUP (*Ranunculus occidentalis*) Plants large (to 24 inches) and downy. Leaves to 2 inches, deeply cleft into 3 toothed lobes. Flowers yellow with 1/3 to 1/2 inch petals. Sepals down-turned. West. Wash.; open, lowland fields and meadows; common. Mid spring to early summer.

WOODS BUTTERCUP (*Ranunculus uncinatus*) Plants tall, to 36 inches. Leaves 3-cleft; coarsely toothed. Flowers yellow, small (1/10 to 1/4 inch long). East. and West. Wash.; moist, lowland woods, especially along streams. Mid spring to mid summer.

BRISTLY BUTTERCUP (*Ranunculus pensylvanicus*) Plants hairy, to 30-40 inches tall. Leaves 3-cleft, toothed, and up to 5 inches. Flowers yellow and small (petals 1/10 to 1/6 inch long). East. and West. Wash.; moist habitats, such as river bottoms, in the lowlands. Summer.

MACOUN'S BUTTERCUP (*Ranunculus macounii*) Plants erect or prostrate, with stems up to 24 inches. Leaves 3-cleft, and again lobed. Foliage strongly hairy. Leaves up to 3 inches long. Petals roundish; yellow. Stems stout, sometimes drooping and rooting at nodes; lower leaves often heart-shaped. East. and West. Wash.; moist woods, wet meadows, and streambanks in lowlands and foothills. Late spring and summer.

CLEMATISES (*Clematis*) (Color Plate 16)

Large, often twining, plants with numerous, conspicuous flowers. Leaves are paired and the numerous, large stamens are distinctive.

1. Sepals bluish to reddish or brownish purple..........................2
1. Sepals whitish yellow or creamy......................WILD CLEMATIS
2. Plants as woody vines; flowers borne on short axillary stems; leaves divided into 3 leaflets (ternate).....................PURPLE VIRGIN'S BOWER
2. Plants not woody vines; flowers borne singly at tips of stems; leaves pinnate ....SUGER BOWLS

*   *   *

PURPLE VIRGIN'S BOWER (*Clematis columbiana*) Sepals petal-like, 4 in number and blue to purplish or reddish, and long and pointed. Flowers 2-4 inches in diameter. Rounded, compact tuft of stamens in center. East. Wash., including Blue Mountains; moist woods and rockslides in mountains. Late spring to mid summer.

SUGAR BOWLS (*Clematis hirsutissima*) Plants with single, upright stem to 1-2 feet. Flower is bell-shaped, down-turned with 4 thick, petal-like sepals that are brownish purple, with bloom of fine, whitish hairs on outside. Leaves finely dissected, fern-like. East. Wash.; sagebrush, grasslands, and yellow pine woods in lowlands and foothills. Mid spring to mid summer.

WILD CLEMATIS (*Clematis ligusticifolia*) Plants trailing or climbing, often on cliffs or trees to 30-40 feet. Leaves pinnately compound, with 5-7 lanceolate segments. Flowers often abundant, with the many stamens often giving a decided fringe-like appearance to the inflorescence. Flowers yellowish white or cream colored. East. Wash. and Columbia Gorge; streamside growth in sagebrush, grasslands, and yellow pine woods in lowlands and foothills. Early and mid summer.

MEADOW RUES (*Thalictrum*) (Color Plate 17)

Tall, graceful plants with fringe-like flowers (due to numerous stamens; the sepals fall at opening and petals are lacking) and large, compound leaves, resembling those of columbines. The plants are often dioecious.

1. Flowers perfect (both stamens and pistils present in the same flower).
FEW-FLOWERED MEADOW RUE
1. Flowers imperfect (known as *dioecious* with staminate and pistillate flowers on different plants)...2
2. Pistillate flowers open and leafy; veins in leaflets indistinct.
WESTERN MEADOW RUE
2. Pistillate flowers bunched in tight heads; veins in leaflets prominent.
VEINY MEADOW RUE

*   *   *

FEW-FLOWERED MEADOW RUE (*Thalictrum sparsiflorum*) Plants to 40 inches. Leaves smooth, 3-4 ternate, with leaflets and subdivisions 3-cleft. Flowers perfect; inflorescences leafy. Sepals whitish to greenish. East. Wash.; moist woods. Summer.

WESTERN MEADOW RUE (*Thalictrum occidentale*) Plants to 40 inches with tall, very slender stalks. Leaves with long petioles, ternately divided and compounded into small, round-lobed leaflets. Tiny flowers with green sepals, no petals, and numerous thread-like stamens and pistils. Male (staminate) flowers purplish; female (pistillate) flowers greenish. Young sprouts and stems are dark purplish and very distinctive in this stage. East. and West. Wash.; moist woods. Late spring to mid summer.

VEINY MEADOW RUE (*Thalictrum venulosum*) Plants smooth but grayish, to 24 inches. Leaflets strongly veined on underside. East. Wash.; moist meadows and woods. Summer.

ANEMONES (*Anemone*) (Color Plate 15)

Plants with large, pastel-colored flowers consisting only of sepals. Leaves may be finely divided. Often a circle of 3+ leaves on the stem forming an "involucre."

1. Style long (more than 5/8 inch) and hairy...........................2
1. Style short (less than 5/8 inch) and not hairy........................3
2. Sepals bluish or purplish, but usually not white; leaves cleft in 3's but not pinnate...WILD CROCUS
2. Sepals white or purplish tinged; leaves cleft in 3's and leaflets pinnately arranged..............................MOUNTAIN PASQUE FLOWER
3. Stem leaves sessile, simple to deeply toothed........................4
3. Stem leaves compound in 3's or cleft into narrow segments; when compound, the leaflets with short petioles...............................5
4. Stem leaves occasionally cleft to mid length; single basal leaf.
WESTERN WHITE ANEMONE
4. Stem leaves cleft to mid length or deeper; several basal leaves.
NORTHERN ANEMONE
5. Plants with a number of tuft-like basal leaves arising from single roots; seeds very woolly..6
5. Plants with leafy flowering stalks arising singly from elongate underground stems; leaves single or few, but neither tufted nor basal; seeds not woolly.7
6. Styles slender and yellowish; leaves several times distinctly divided into 3's; 1 flower per stem........................DRUMMOND'S ANEMONE
6. Styles thick at base and pink or red; leaves not distinctly divided into 3's; 2 or more flowers on a stem........................CLIFF ANEMONE
7. Rhizomes ascending (upright) and dark brown in color; mostly plants of Eastern Washington.............................PIPER'S ANEMONE
7. Rhizomes horizontal, not ascending, and pale brown in color; mostly occurring in Cascades and Western Washington.........................8
8. Flowers usually white; sepals less than 3/8 inch long.
LITTLE MOUNTAIN ANEMONE
8. Flowers usually bluish; sepals more than 3/8 inch long.
OREGON ANEMONE

WILD CROCUS (*Anemone nuttalliana*) Foliage hairy; leaves divided palmately. Flowers blue, purple, or rarely white. Petals 3/4 to 1½ inches long. Plants to 12-14 inches high. Northern and Central Cascades; fairly dry slopes, mostly in the mountains. Late spring and summer.

MOUNTAIN PASQUE FLOWER (*Anemone occidentalis*) Plants to 24 inches. Leaves finely dissected and fern-like; stems covered with soft hairs. Flowers about 1½ inches in diameter, creamy white (occasionally very pale purple). Sepals 5-7, 3/4 to 1¼ inches long. Stamens many; the gold anthers in a ring. Fruiting heads are distinctive, upright, frowzy mops of silky hairs. East. and West. Wash.; mountain meadows. Summer and early autumn.

WESTERN WHITE ANEMONE (*Anemone deltoidea*) Plants to 12 inches. Single white flower 1½ inches wide borne at tip of stem. 3 oval, toothed, sharp-pointed, triangular leaves in whorl halfway up the stem. West. Wash.; and Columbia Gorge (absent from the Olympic Peninsula); open to often thick woods, as well as dry, brushy slopes. Spring.

NORTHERN ANEMONE (*Anemone parviflora*) Plants to 14 inches. Basal and involucral leaves 3-cleft into lobes. Flowers small and white or pale bluish; petals 1/2 inch long; hairy on outer surface. East. and West. Wash.; streambanks and moist meadows in the mountains. Summer.

DRUMMOND'S ANEMONE (*Anemone drummondii*) Plants to 12 inches. Foliage hairy. Leaves compound, finely divided, and long stemmed. Flowers white, tinged with blue or lavender. West. (mostly) and East. Wash.; meadows and rocky cliffs in the high mountainous areas. Summer.

CLIFF ANEMONE (*Anemone multifida*) Plants to 24 inches; silky-hairy throughout. The 3 involucral leaves divided into linear segments. Flower yellowish, often tinged with red, blue, or purple; borne on long stems. East. and West. Wash.; mountains, especially high, open, rocky places. Late spring and summer.

PIPER'S ANEMONE (*Anemone piperi*) Plants to 14 inches; smooth to sparsely silky. Leaves 3- to 5-cleft and toothed; up to 2 inches long. Flowers white, pinkish, or purplish. Sepals 4-7; 1/2 to 3/4 inch long. East. Wash.; moist, deep woods. Mid spring to late summer.

LITTLE MOUNTAIN ANEMONE (*Anemone lyallii*) Plants small and delicate, to 4 inches. Involucral leaves 3, with oval or lance-shaped, bluntly-toothed leaflets. Flowers white, bluish, or pale reddish. West. Wash.; prairies, woods, and subalpine slopes, from lowlands to high mountains. Early spring to mid summer.

OREGON ANEMONE (*Anemone oregana*) Plants to 10 inches; smooth. Involucral leaves 3, more or less lobed or toothed, and stalked. Sepals bluish, purplish, pale pink, or white; 1/2 to 3/4 inches long. Eastern Cascades, Blue Mountains, Columbia Gorge, and Southwestern Wash.; moist, open woods and brushy slopes in the mountains and also sphagnum bogs in Southwestern Wash. Spring and early summer.

GOLD-THREADS *(Coptis)* (Color Plate 16)

Small, ground-cover plants with bright, golden-yellow roots; the distinctive color to be revealed by scraping off some of the root skin.

1. Leaves divided into 3 groups of 5 pinnately-arranged leaflets; flowering stems (scapes) longer than leaves plus petioles.
                                            FERN-LEAVED GOLD-THREAD
1. Leaves with 3 deeply-lobed leaflets; flowering stems (scapes) shorter than leaves and petioles. 2
2. Leaflets deeply cleft, being lobed almost to their bases.
                                            COASTAL GOLD-THREAD
2. Leaflets not so deeply cleft, being lobed not more than half their length.
                                            INTERIOR GOLD-THREAD

*   *   *

FERN-LEAVED GOLD-THREAD *(Coptis asplenifolia)* Plants just a few inches tall. Flowers tiny, white. Northern Cascades as far south as Mount Pilchuck; also in Olympics; moist woods in mountains. Spring and early summer.

COASTAL GOLD-THREAD *(Coptis laciniata)* Plants to 6 inches. Flowers white, borne singly or in pairs at tips of leafless stems; sepals 1/5 to 2/5 inches long; petals 5-7 in number. Southwestern Wash.; moist woods and rocky places in foothills and mountains. Mid spring to late summer.

INTERIOR GOLD-THREAD *(Coptis occidentalis)* Plants to 10 inches. Leaves evergreen. Sepals linear, 3-nerved, white. Petals 1/4 inch long. Extreme East. Wash.; moist woods in the foothills and mountains; common. Spring and early summer.

MARSH MARIGOLDS *(Caltha)* (Color Plate 16)

Moderately low, clustered plants growing in very wet or even temporarily standing-water habitats. Leaves mostly large, basal, fleshy, and coarsely toothed. Flowers without petals, but large and showy; whitish or yellowish. Leaves shiny green.

1. Flowers yellow; stems with several leaves and often creeping.
                                            WESTERN MARSH MARIGOLD
1. Flowers whitish; stems erect and leafless or with only 1 or 2 leaves. 2
2. Flowers usually 2 on a stem; leaves nearly as broad as long.
                                            BROAD-LEAVED MARSH MARIGOLD
2. Flowers usually 1 on a stem; leaves noticeably longer than broad.
                                            HEART-LEAVED MARSH MARIGOLD

*   *   *

WESTERN MARSH MARIGOLD *(Caltha asarifolia)* Leaves kidney-shaped, smooth. Flowers with 6-8 yellow, petal-like sepals; numerous yellow stamens. Plants to 24 inches. West. Wash.; bogs along the ocean coast. Summer.

BROAD-LEAVED MARSH MARIGOLD *(Caltha biflora)* Plants to 12 inches. Flowers whitish, very similar to those of following species, but usually 2 on a stem. Leaves more rounded and kidney-shaped. East. and West. Wash.; mostly subalpine meadows; often found leafing out or flowering under edges of melting snowbanks. Late spring and summer.

HEART-LEAVED MARSH MARIGOLD (*Caltha leptosepala*) Flowers about 1 inch wide; sepals shining white and petal-like; varying in number from 6 to 12. Smooth, heart-shaped leaves, often folded or rolled. West. Wash.; moist, subalpine meadows in Cascades and Olympics; often flowering at edge of melting snowbanks. Late spring and summer.

Chapter 15—The Barberry Family (*Berberidaceae*)

Members of this family, as included here, are herbs with compound leaves and regular, perfect flowers. Sepals and petals present or absent, but 6 in number when present. Fruit a berry or pod. Stamens generally 6. (Color Plates 17-18)

1. Leaflets in 3's; flowers in a spike; no sepals or petals......VANILLA-LEAF
1. Leaflets not in 3's, but numerous; flowers in a panicle, with sepals and petals ....INSIDE-OUT FLOWER

*   *   *

VANILLA-LEAF (*Achlys triphylla*) Large, umbrella-like leaves divided into 3 roughly triangular, fan-shaped parts, on long, slender, upright petioles. Flowers lacking petals and sepals but with numerous, delicate white stamens in dense, narrow terminal raceme on straight stem which is much taller than the leaves. Cascades and West. Wash.; deep to semi-open woods, particularly on streambanks and in moist hollows. Mid spring to mid summer. (Color Plate 17)

INSIDE-OUT FLOWER (*Vancouveria hexandra*) Plants 12-18 inches tall. Leaves divided into a number of thin, delicate leaflets on tall, wiry stems. Flowers borne in a panicle, drooping, with sepals and petals strongly reflexed. Flowers white and small. Southwest. Wash.; dense, moist woods, in lowlands and lower mountain areas. Late spring to early summer. (Color Plate 18)

Flowers, like other organisms, have two names, a common name and a scientific, or technical, name. The common name is usually in the English language, except for a few, like *cous,* that bear a native Indian designation. The common name may be descriptive (yellow aster), a translation of the scientific name (mouse-tail), or possibly some name derived from mythology or tradition (St. John's wort). In species belonging to a large genus, the common name (or colloquial name, as it is sometimes called) may consist of a noun (usually the genus name) plus an adjective specially describing or at least denoting that particular species. An example would be the *woodland violet.* Occasionally, flowers have been named after persons, often the one who collected the first specimens or someone prominent in the field of botany whom the describer wished to honor (*Flett's violet*). The common names used in this book are those that have been widely published in the Pacific Northwest. An attempt in the past to standardize plant names did not meet with much acceptance, for a variety of reasons. It is only good sense that if the purpose of the scientific name is to provide a universal name, then the common epithet may be more local or regional in nature and use.

Figure 17.
In the rainforest. (Larrison)

Chapter 16—The Poppy Family (*Papaveraceae*)

Members of this family are annual or perennial herbs (ours) with very finely cleft, singly born leaves and large, brightly-colored flowers. In the single species in Washington, the sepals are united into a cup which is discarded as the petals develop. Petals 4, with numerous stamens; pistils 2; ovary superior. (Color Plate 18)

CALIFORNIA POPPY (*Eschscholzia californica*) Native in Southern Wash.; as in the Columbia Gorge, but widely introduced or escaped elsewhere in state; open, grassy or weedy areas in lowlands; frequently along roadsides and railroads. Flowers deep yellow to orange. Late spring to early autumn.

Important as large-scale, state-wide weather phenomena are, they should be considered in relation to the variations and modifications they receive as the result of interaction with local topography. Nowhere is this better demonstrated than in a mountain range.

Mountains may be thought of as immense barriers of solid rock (which indeed they are!) that may lie athwart prevailing wind tracks or that thrust themselves and their thin veneers of soil, plants, and animals up into progressively higher climatic layers in the sky.

Let's examine the results of these factors. Most field naturalists, amateur or professional, are aware of the altitudinal life zones (such as those proposed by Merriam, which will be the subject of a future essay) that begin at the base of a mountain and cover variously the different elevations to its summit. An example of such a series would be a mixed coniferous belt at the base, followed above by a broad montane forest of hemlock, succeeded still higher by an open subalpine woods interspersed by meadows, to give way finally (if the mountain is high enough) to barren rocky fields and scattered snow and ice areas. The most noticeable local modification, as the result of differences of temperature and precipitation, will be the occurrence of each zone at a significantly lower elevation on the north side of the mountain, as compared with its location on the south slope.

Rainfall is often heavier on windward sides of mountain ranges, so that we commonly find the west side of a range, say the Cascades, to be much wetter than the east side. Air masses rising up the windward slope of a barrier are cooled, condensing and precipitating out a certain amount of moisture which the air can no longer hold as water vapor. The same air mass descending the lee side of the range is warmed by compression, enabling it to hold in gaseous form a greater amount of moisture and to produce less rainfall. Thus, vegetation is usually heavier and more lush on windward sides and more open and scattered on lee sides.

Figure 18.
Plant explorers' camp in the Juniper Forest, northeast of Pasco. (Larrison)

Chapter 17—The Fumitory Family (*Fumariaceae*)

Members of this family are mostly woodland flowers with delicate, finely-cut leaves. They may be perennial, biennial, or annual. The flowers are perfect, but irregular; the outer petals larger and one or both spurred at the base. Sepals 2; petals 4; stamens 6. Flowers usually arranged in racemes. (Color Plate 18)

1. Corolla 1-spurred at the base of the flower . . . . . CORYDALISES (*Corydalis*)
1. Corolla 2-spurred at the base of the flower . . . . DICENTRAS (*Dicentra*)

CORYDALISES (*Corydalis*) (Fig. 19)

1. Flowers yellow; stem prostrate along the ground, particularly at the base.
GOLDEN CORYDALIS
1. Flowers pink; stem erect, not prostrate . . . . WESTERN CORYDALIS

*   *   *

GOLDEN CORYDALIS (*Corydalis aurea*)   Flowers yellow, in short, terminal racemes. Leaves delicate and finely divided. East. and West. Wash.; woods of lowlands and foothills. Late spring and summer.

WESTERN CORYDALIS (*Corydalis scouleri*) Plants often 3-4 feet tall in dense patches. Flowers pink (rarely white) in terminal racemes. West. Wash. and the Cascades; moist, shaded woods; occasionally along streambanks. Mid spring to mid summer.

DICENTRAS (*Dicentra*) (Color Plate 18)

1. Single flower borne at tip of stem . . . . STEER'S-HEAD
1. Several flowers borne on stem 2
2. Flowers white, or pinkish at first, tipped with yellow; spurs elongate and divergent or slightly in-curved . . . . DUTCHMAN'S BREECHES
2. Flowers pink to lavender; the corolla heart-shaped at base with very short in-curved spurs . . . . BLEEDING-HEART

*   *   *

STEER'S-HEAD (*Dicentra uniflora*)   Plants very small and ground-hugging. Single flower (pale pink, lilac, or white) at tip of each leafless stem. Flower small (1/2 inch long). Cascades and East. Wash.; open woods and subalpine woods, favoring rocky slopes, from foothills to subalpine country. Early spring to early summer. Plant so-called from resemblance of flower to head of long-horned cow.

DUTCHMAN'S BREECHES (*Dicentra cucullaria*)   Flowers white or pale pink with long spurs and borne in racemes. Mostly in East. Wash.; moist woods in arid lowlands. Spring.

BLEEDING-HEART (*Dicentra formosa*) Plants to 18 inches high. Leaves basal, long-stalked. Flowers (pink to lavender) drooping from a branched inflorescence. Base of flower heart-shaped. West. Wash.; moist, shaded woods in lowlands, as well as mountains; often occurring on the rocky surface of old glacial moraines. Early spring to mid summer.

Figure 19.
The finely-divided leaves of corydalis. (Yaich)

Chapter 18—The Mustard Family (*Cruciferae*)

Members of this family are herbs with mostly alternate leaves and perfect, regular flowers usually arranged in racemes. Juice is watery and the flowers are often yellow in color. Petals 4, in the form of a cross (hence the name of the family) or rarely reduced; sepals 4; stamens 6, 4 long and 2 short (or 4 and 2); pistil 1; fruit a pod, usually longer than broad. (Color Plates 18-21)

1. Fruit borne on a stalk (stipe) at least 1/16 inch long.
THELYPODIES (*Thelypodium*)
1. Fruit either not borne on a stalk or stalk less than 1/16 inch long.......2

2. Pod consisting of 2 sections, the lower seed-bearing and the upper (distal) sterile...................................FALSE TWISTED-FLOWER
2. Pod consisting of 1 seed-bearing section.........................3

3. Pod a silicle, being scarcely longer than wide (not long and narrow)....4
3. Pod a silique, being considerably longer (at least 3 times) than wide....18

4. Pods flattened, not roundish or circular in cross section...............5
4. Pods not strongly flattened, but swollen and roundish in cross section; or flattened at right angles to the partition...........................11

5. Seeds 1 in a seed chamber (locule)..............................6
5. Seeds 2 or more in a locule....................................8

6. Pods with 2 locules....................WHITLOW-GRASSES (*Draba*)
6. Pods with 1 locule...7

7. Pods less than 3/16 inch long and covered with hooked hairs. SANDWEED
7. Pods more than 3/16 inch long, smooth or with unhooked hairs.
FRINGE-POD

8. Plants are white-flowered perennials with flower-bearing scapes (ped-uncles), less than 1⅛ inch tall, and with leathery pods.
WHITLOW-GRASSES (*Draba*)
8. Plants not entirely as above....................................9

9. Plants with scapes bearing single, terminal flowers; seeds with wings.
IDAHOA
9. Plants without scapes; or, if scapes present, then the scapes bearing 2 or more flowers; seeds without wings.............................10

10. Seed pods long, at least twice as long as broad.
WHITLOW-GRASSES (*Draba*)
10. Seed pods round or oval-shaped; less than twice as long as broad.
COLUMBIA BLADDER-POD

11. Plants with fleshy leaves and seashore habitat............COCHLEARIA
11. Plants not as above...12

12. Seed pods inflated or swollen...................................13
12. Seed pods flattened at right angles to the partition...................14

13. Pods 2-parted............................PHYSARIAS (*Physaria*)
13. Pods not 2-parted......................COLUMBIA BLADDER-POD

14. Plants covered with star-shaped hairs............................15
14. Plants smooth or covered with simple, non-star-shaped hairs.........16

Figure 20.
Lesquerella, the bladder-pod. (Larrison)

106

15. Pods 2-parted with prominent groove at apex..... PHYSARIAS (*Physaria*)
15. Pods not 2-parted or at least without prominent apical groove.
COLUMBIA BLADDER-POD

16. Pods with 1 seed in each seed chamber (locule).
PEPPERGRASSES (*Lepidium*)
16. Pods with 2 or more seeds in each seed chamber................... 17

17. Pods more than 1/8 inch long; stem leaves not tapering to stem at base.
FENDLER'S PENNY-GRASS
17. Pods 1/8 inch or less in length; stem leaves tapering to stem at base.
HUTCHINSIA

18. Flowers yellow to orange... 19
18. Flowers white, pinkish, or purple................................. 26

19. Plants hairy with 2-, 3-, or 4-branched hairs pressed to surface of leaves.
WALLFLOWERS (*Erysimum*)
19. Plants smooth, but if hairy, then the hairs not branched............... 20

20. Style with beak; basal leaves numerous and pinnately lobed.
WINTERCRESS
20 Style without beak.. 21

21. Seeds in 2 linear series in pods................................. 22
21. Seeds in 1 linear series in pods................................. 25

22. Plants smooth or with unbranched hairs........................... 23
22. Plants with branched or star-shaped hairs......................... 24

23. Leaves simple....................... WHITLOW-GRASSES (*Draba*)
23. Leaves pinnate or pinnately lobed.......... MARSH-CRESSES (*Rorippa*)

24. Leaves simple and entire................ WHITLOW-GRASSES (*Draba*)
24. Leaves pinnately lobed.............. TANSY MUSTARDS (*Descurainia*)

25. Basal lobes of upper leaves clasping the stem........... WINTERCRESS
25. Basal lobes of upper leaves not clasping the stem.
MARSH-CRESSES (*Rorippa*)

26. Seeds in 2 linear series in the pod............................. 27
26. Seeds in 1 linear series in the pod............................. 30

27. Flowering stems without leaves.......... WHITLOW-GRASSES (*Draba*)
27. Flowering stems with leaves................................... 28

28. Plants more or less aquatic or growing in wet places.
MARSH-CRESSES (*Rorippa*)
28. Plants not aquatic and not growing in wet places.................. 29

29. Pods short, less than 8 times as long as broad.
WHITLOW-GRASSES (*Draba*)
29. Pods long, more than 8 times as long as broad..ROCK CRESSES (*Arabis*)

30. Leaves long and narrow; pods not splitting their entire length at maturity.
FALSE TWISTED-FLOWER
30. Leaves not long and narrow; pods splitting their entire length at maturity. 31

31. Flowers borne on leafless stalks (scapes) arising from the ground; leaves
entire... DAGGER-POD
31. Flowers not as above... 32

Figure 21.
Penny-grasses, *Thlaspi.* (Larrison)

*　　　*　　　*

FALSE TWISTED FLOWER (*Streptanthella longirostris*)　Plants to 24 inches. Foliage smooth with whitish bloom. Leaves linear and some toothed. Flowers white; petals with purple veins. Southeast. Wash.; sagebrush plains and slopes. Spring.

SANDWEED (*Athysanus pusillus*)　Plants small, to 3-4 inches. Leaves basal, oval, to 1/2 inch, and somewhat toothed. Flower very small and white; petals sometimes absent. East. and West. Wash.; dry, sandy, or grassy places. Early spring to early summer.

FRINGE-POD (*Thysanocarpus curvipes*)　Plants to 24 inches; hairy. Basal leaves in rosette, 2-3 inches long; stem leaves with conspicuous, pointed, recurved lobes. Flower small, white, occasionally tinged with purple. East. and West. Wash.; dry, open places, especially warm hillsides. Mid spring to early summer. (Color Plate 21)

IDAHOA (*Idahoa scapigera*)　Plants to 6 inches. Leaves basal, oval, with 2 lobes near leaf base. Petals small and white; sepals red to purple. East. Wash.; sagebrush and grasslands in lowlands and foothills; often where the ground is moist and rocky. Spring.

COLUMBIA BLADDER-POD (*Lesquerella douglasii*) Foliage silvery-hairy. Leaves basal, oval, and more or less entire. Stem leaves smaller on spreading branches. Flowers yellow to yellowish orange. Large oblong pods are distinctive when plant is in fruit. East. Wash.; sagebrush and yellow pine woods; often on rocky cliffs. Early spring to mid summer. (Fig. 20)

COCHLEARIA (*Cochlearia officinalis*) Plants to 12 inches with upward-curving stems. Foliage smooth. Basal leaves scalloped, on long petioles; stem leaves larger and toothed. Flowers very small and white. West. Wash.; seashore along the coast. Summer.

FENDLER'S PENNY-GRASS (*Thlaspi fendleri*) Plants tufted with slender, 4-12 inch stems bearing racemes of small, white flowers. Most leaves basal. East. and West. Wash.; moist, rocky places, lowlands to high, alpine ridges. Late spring and summer. (Fig. 21)

HUTCHINSIA (*Hutchinsia procumbens*) Stems 8-10 inches, spreading or erect. Leaves small, occasionally lobed. Flowers very small and white. East. and West. Wash.; sagebrush, sand dunes, and moist, alkaline flats in arid lowlands and coastal seashore areas. Early spring to early summer.

WINTERCRESS (*Barbarea orthoceras*) Plants medium, to 16 inches. Basal leaves roundish, lobed or entire; stem leaves pinnately cleft. Stems fleshy and angled. Flowers terminal, yellow. East. and West. Wash.; moist habitats, such as streamsides, woods, and meadows, as well as road shoulders and ditches and pastures; lowlands and up into the mountains. Early spring to mid summer. (Color Plate 19)

DAGGER-POD (*Phoenicaulis cheiranthoides*) Leaves entire, tufted in dense rosettes; grayish-hairy. Flowering stems to 8 inches, with few leaves, and bearing showy, reddish-purple, pink, or rarely white flowers. East. Wash.; sagebrush areas in lowlands and foothills. Mid spring to early summer. (Color Plate 20)

THELYPODIES (*Thelypodium*) (Fig. 22)

Small, often fleshy plants with leaves with ear-like lobes at base. Flowers commonly in dense racemes.

1. Leaves on stems either sessile or with ear-like lobes partly enclosing the stem . . . . SAGITTATE THELYPODY
1. Leaves on stems with petioles or without ear-like lobes as above 2
2. Plants annual; pods pointing sharply downward, not ascending.
    CUT-LEAVED THELYPODY
2. Plants biennial; pods erect or spreading outward 3
3. Leaves on stems entire . . . . ENTIRE-LEAVED THELYPODY
3. Leaves on stems toothed or lobed . . . . DESERT THELYPODY

*   *   *

SAGITTATE THELYPODY (*Thelypodium sagittatum*) Flowers violet purple in color. East. Wash.; generally moist, often alkaline meadows in arid lowlands. Early and mid summer.

CUT-LEAVED THELYPODY (*Thelypodium lasiophyllum*) Plants tall, to 40 inches. leaves toothed to pinnately cleft. Flowers creamy white. West. Wash.;

burns, logged areas, and brushy places in coastal lowlands. Mid spring to early summer.

ENTIRE-LEAVED THELYPODY (*Thelypodium integrifolium*) Leaves lanceolate, entire, smooth, and grayish. Some plants to 6 feet. Flowers white, purplish, or reddish. East. Wash.; sagebrush plains, brushy places in foothills, and mountain streamsides. Summer.

DESERT THELYPODY (*Thelypodium laciniatum*) Plants tall, to 8 feet. Foliage smooth, succulent, with bloom. Leaves deeply cleft or lobed. Flowers white to violet in short, dense racemes. East. Wash.; cliffs and rockslides, often in river canyons. Mid spring to mid summer.

WHITLOW-GRASSES (*Draba*) (Color Plate 19)

Small, often tiny, plants with sparse foliage and very small, white or yellow flowers. Plants often tufted and some species very inconspicuous.

1. Plants annual with relatively weak taproots...........................2
1. Plants biennial or perennial with relatively stocky taproots.............8

2. Flowers white; petals deeply cleft into 2 lobes. VERNAL WHITLOW-GRASS
2. Flowers yellow or petals not deeply cleft into lobes..................3

3. Upper stems smooth, not hairy.....................................4
3. Upper stems hairy..7

4. Leaves almost all basal.............THICK-LEAVED WHITLOW-GRASS
4. Leaves both basal and located along the stem.......................5

5. Flowers white........................CAROLINA WHITLOW-GRASS
5. Flowers yellow...6

6. Pedicels of fruits usually several times as long as the fruits (pods).
   WOOD WHITLOW-GRASS
6. Pedicels usually not more than 1½ times as long as the fruits.
   SLENDER WHITLOW-GRASS

7. Plants occurring along the Snake and Columbia Rivers; pod broadest in distal half of length...................BROAD-POD WHITLOW-GRASS
7. Plants occurring in mountains; pod broadest in basal half of length.
   TALL WHITLOW-GRASS

8. Stems leaf-bearing; plants not matted or tufted......................9
8. Stems bearing leaves; plants usually matted and tufted..............13

9. Style either lacking or very short and inconspicuous.................10
9. Style visible and conspicuous.....................................12

10. Flowers white or creamy; leaves densely hairy above and below.
    TALL WHITLOW-GRASS
10. Flowers yellow; leaves usually hairy below, smooth above............11

11. Pedicels shorter than pods..........THICK-LEAVED WHITLOW-GRASS
11. Pedicels same length or longer than pods...SLENDER WHITLOW-GRASS

12. Flowers white ....TWISTED WHITLOW-GRASS
12. Flowers yellow ....GREAT ALPINE WHITLOW-GRASS

13. Style lacking or inconspicuous; plants not matted, though stems bearing leaves ....THICK-LEAVED WHITLOW-GRASS
13. Style present and conspicuous; plants matted.....................14

111

Figure 22.
The tall flowering spikes of the thelypodies, *Thelypodium.* (Larrison)

14. Pods swollen and oval-shaped; seeds at least 1/16 inch long.
DOUGLAS'S WHITLOW-GRASS
14. Pods not swollen nor oval-shaped; seeds less than 1/16 inch long.....15

15. Hairs on leaves simple and unbranched or in star-shaped clusters; sometimes sparse 16
15. Hairs on leaves comb-like with lateral branches at right angles to main axis of hair..18

16. Leaves with sparse and simple hairs; upper surface of leaves more or less smooth..........................NELSON'S WHITLOW-GRASS
16. Leaves hairy above and below...................................17

17. Flowers white ....TWISTED WHITLOW-GRASS
17. Flowers yellowish.....................PAYSON'S WHITLOW-GRASS

18. Leaves densely tufted; stems below inflorescence relatively short; usually 1½ times the length of the flower cluster; hairs on leaves closely pressed to leaf surface......................FEW-SEEDED WHITLOW-GRASS
18. Leaves loosely tufted; stems below inflorescence relatively long (twice or more the length of the flower clusters); leaf hairs not closely pressed to the leaf surface ....UNCERTAIN WHITLOW-GRASS

*   *   *

VERNAL WHITLOW-GRASS (*Draba verna*) Plants 2-7 inches. Leaves basal. Flowers white; petals deeply cleft. East. and West. Wash.; grassy hillsides and lower mountainous areas, as well as sagebrush and grasslands, east of the Cascades. One of the earliest of the spring flowers. Early to late spring.

THICK-LEAVED WHITLOW-GRASS (*Draba crassifolia*) Plants 1-6 inches. Leaves numerous in basal rosette. Flowers yellow, fading to white. Cascades and West. Wash.; rock slides and high, barren ridges in the subalpine and alpine areas of the higher mountains. Summer.

CAROLINA WHITLOW-GRASS (*Draba reptans*) Plants to 5 inches high. Leaves basal, spatulate to roundish. Flowers white. East. Wash.; dry, open flats and slopes in lowlands and foothills. Spring.

WOOD WHITLOW-GRASS (*Draba nemorosa*) Plants to 10 inches. Leaves toothed and numerous on lower part of stem. Flowers pale yellow to whitish, 10-20 in raceme. East. and West. Wash.; dry, open flats and slopes in lowlands and foothills. Spring and early summer.

SLENDER WHITLOW-GRASS (*Draba stenoloba*) Plants to 12 inches. Leaves 10-25, mostly in basal rosette. Flowers yellow or cream colored, fading to white. East. and West. Wash.; moist or dry meadows and streambanks from foothills to subalpine. Late spring and summer.

BROAD-POD WHITLOW-GRASS (*Draba curvifolia*) Plants to 10 inches. Leaves mostly basal and sparsely toothed. Flowers white in loose racemes of few to many flowers. Southern Wash.; along the Snake and Columbia Rivers; sagebrush and grasslands in lowlands and foothills, particularly favoring rocky river canyons. Early spring to early summer.

LOW ALPINE WHITLOW-GRASS (*Draba praealta*) Plants very small (to 1½ inches high). Leaves mostly in downy, basal rosettes. Flowers tiny, white, or cream colored. Cascades and East. Wash.; varying from moist dense woods to more open subalpine ridges in middle and higher parts of mountains. Summer.

TWISTED WHITLOW-GRASS (*Draba lonchocarpa*) Slender tufted alpines with white flowers. Leaves grayish. Plants to 5 inches. East. and West. Wash.; slides and outcroppings on the high alpine ridges. Summer.

GREAT ALPINE WHITLOW-GRASS (*Draba aureola*) Small plants (2-6 inches) covered with white hairs. Leaves willow-like and 1/2 inch long. Cascades from Mount Rainier southward; barren, open slopes and ridges in high alpine country. Summer.

DOUGLAS'S WHITLOW-GRASS (*Draba douglasii*) Plants small, 1/2 to 2 inches tall, growing in tufts. Leaves thick, leathery, and nearly smooth, but with marginal hairs. Flowers small and white. East. Wash.; rocky places in sagebrush, lowlands and foothills. Mid spring to early summer.

NELSON'S WHITLOW-GRASS (*Draba densifolia*) Plants small and tufted (to 4-5 inches high). Leaves smooth, but fringed with stiff hairs. Flowers yellow. Eastern Cascades and East. Wash.; open, rocky ridges and outcroppings in higher parts of mountains. Summer.

PAYSON'S WHITLOW-GRASS (*Draba paysonii*) Plants low and tufted (to 2½ inches) with leaves hairy above and below and fringed on margins. Flowers yellow, 10 or less in short racemes. East. and West. Wash.; subalpine and alpine ridges. Summer.

FEW-SEEDED WHITLOW-GRASS (*Draba oligosperma*) Densely-tufted alpine plants with short, linear leaves and slender 2-inch flowering stems bearing yellow to cream-colored flowers. Leaves hairy. Cascades and East. Wash.; open ridges and slopes in higher and intermediate parts of mountains. Late spring to mid summer.

UNCERTAIN WHITLOW-GRASS (*Draba incerta*) Plants low with clustered, 2-inch stems. Leaves basal, broad-linear, and hairy above and below. Flowers yellow, fading to white. East. and West. Wash.; subalpine and alpine ridges and slopes. Summer.

PHYSARIAS (*Physaria*) (Color Plate 20)

1. Plants occurring in Snake River Canyon of Southeastern Washington; pods (silicles) more than 3/8 inch long...................OREGON PHYSARIA
1. Plants occurring in Eastern Washington, but not in the Snake River Canyon; pods (silicles) less than 3/8 inch long..............GEYER'S PHYSARIA

*   *   *

OREGON PHYSARIA (*Physaria oregana*) Flowers light yellow. Southeast. Wash.; dry, rocky slopes in Snake River Canyon and in Blue Mountains. Mid spring to early summer.

GEYER'S PHYSARIA (*Physaria geyeri*) Flowers yellow, aging to reddish. East. Wash.; sandy or gravelly places, as streambanks, scattered outcroppings on hillsides, and ballast along railroad embankments. Late spring to mid summer.

114

PEPPERGRASSES (*Lepidium*) (Color Plate 20) (Fig. 23)

Mostly small plants with small, white or yellow flowers, arranged in racemes. Seed pods usually winged at apex.

1. Stem leaves perfoliate, that is, lower parts of leaves surrounding the stem.
                                                    PERFOLIATE PEPPERGRASS
1. Stem leaves not perfoliate...2
2. Pedicels (stalks) of seed pods strongly flattened; stems not stiffly upright (vertical).. 3
2. Pedicels of seed pods somewhat, but not strongly, flattened; stems stiffly upright (vertical) 4
3. Seed pods with smooth, shining surfaces and inconspicuous veins.
                                                    SHINING PEPPERGRASS
3. Seed pods smooth or hairy, but not shining, and with conspicuous veins.
                                                    VEINY PEPPERGRASS

4. Petals missing or very tiny and poorly formed.......DULL PEPPERGRASS
4. Petals conspicuous........................VIRGINIA PEPPERGRASS

*   *   *

PERFOLIATE PEPPERGRASS (*Lepidium perfoliatum*) Leaves perfoliate. Flowers yellowish. East. (mostly) and West. Wash.; over-grazed and wasteland; a very common, exotic weed. Early spring to early summer.

SHINING PEPPERGRASS (*Lepidium nitidum*) Plants to 16 inches; foliage often reddish purple. Leaves mostly smooth. Lower leaves oblanceolate, toothed to cleft. Flowers tiny and white. Southern Wash.; open, often bare or wasteland. Spring.

VEINY PEPPERGRASS (*Lepidium dictyotum*) Plants low with short, spreading branches. Basal leaves cleft into narrow segments and hairy. Petals of flowers minute, white, and even occasionally missing. East. Wash.; alkaline flats and spring sloughs in lowlands. Spring.

DULL PEPPERGRASS (*Lepidium densiflorum*) Plants medium (to 20 inches). Basal leaves toothed to pinnately cleft and in dense rosettes. Foliage dull green. Flowers tiny; petals usually absent. East. (mostly) and West. Wash.; open, lowland areas. Mid spring to early summer.

VIRGINIA PEPPERGRASS (*Lepidium virginicum*) Plants tall for peppergrasses (to 24 inches). Lower leaves oblanceolate to obovate; slightly toothed or entire. Flowers whitish, numerous, and in long racemes. East. and West. Wash.; open lowland areas, including upper sea beaches along saltwater. Early spring to early summer.

WALLFLOWERS (*Erysimum*) (Color Plate 19)

Medium-sized plants with showy, yellow or orange flowers, arranged in dense flowering heads. Seed pods long and narrow. Very similar to the domestic wallflowers.

1. Flowers larger, petals usually more than 3/8 inch long.................2
1. Flowers smaller, petals usually less than 3/8 inch long.................4

Figure 23.
Peppergrass, *Lepdidium*. Note the perfoliate leaves. (Larrison)

116

2. Plants occurring on high, open, subalpine and alpine ridges in Cascades and Olympics.............................MOUNTAIN WALLFLOWER
2. Plants not occurring on high, open, subalpine ridges in Cascades and Olympics 3
3. Seed pods 4-angled in cross-section; seeds without wings or only slightly winged at tip; petals hairy on underside near base; leaves usually toothed.
ROUGH WALLFLOWER
3. Seed pods flattened, not 4-angled; seeds prominently winged; petals smooth on underside; leaves usually entire..........PALE WALLFLOWER
4. Pedicel more or less as thick as the pod it supports; petals more than 1/4 inch long ....BUSHY WALLFLOWER
4. Pedicel only half as thick as the pod it supports; petals often less than 1/4 inch long..5
5. Flowers in relatively tight head; leaves broadening conspicuously near mid-length; petals less than 1/4 inch long.......WORM-SEED WALLFLOWER
5. Flowers in relatively loose head; leaves not conspicuously broadening at all along their length; petals usually more than 1/4 inch long.
INCONSPICUOUS WALLFLOWER

*   *   *

MOUNTAIN WALLFLOWER (*Erysimum arenicola*)   Plants 10-20 inches tall. Flowers bright lemon yellow in dense racemes on erect, gray-haired stems. Leaves narrow and toothed. Olympic and Cascade Mountains; barren ridges and rocky slopes in the subalpine and alpine areas of the high mountains. Summer and early fall.

ROUGH WALLFLOWER (*Erysimum asperum*)   Plants tall, to 30 inches. Basal leaves lanceolate, toothed, with hairs on upper surface. Flowers yellow, orange, or reddish; in terminal cluster. East. Wash. and Columbia Gorge; open, arid habitats; common. Late spring and summer.

PALE WALLFLOWER (*Erysimum occidentale*)   Plants to 20 inches; foliage with harsh hairs. Basal leaves numerous, linear to linear-lanceolate; entire or weakly toothed. Flowers pale yellow. East. Wash.; sagebrush in lowlands and foothills. Early to late spring.

BUSHY WALLFLOWER (*Erysimum repandum*)   Plants to 16 inches, bushy, and with spreading branches. Leaves linear-oblanceolate. Flowers pale yellow. East. Wash.; waste places, pastures, and grain fields, in lowlands and foothills; a common weed. Mid spring to early summer.

WORM-SEED WALLFLOWER (*Erysimum cheiranthoides*)   Plants tall, to 40 inches. Leaves narrow-lanceolate; mostly on the stems; toothed or entire. Flowers pale yellow, in terminal clusters (as is characteristic with wallflowers). East. and West. Wash.; roadsides, moist pastures, and other waste places; weedy in nature. Summer.

INCONSPICUOUS WALLFLOWER (*Erysimum inconspicuum*)   Flowers pale yellow, in loose terminal heads. East. Wash.; alkali areas in lowlands. Early and mid summer.

MARSH-CRESSES (*Rorippa*)

Plants with pinnately lobed or finely dissected leaves on numerous branches and yellowish flowers. Prefers moist habitats.

1. Flowers white, sometimes tinged with purplish . . . . WATER-CRESS
1. Flowers yellow 2
2. Plants perennial with spreading rhizomes; petals more than 1/8 inch long.
SPREADING YELLOW CRESS
2. Plants annual or biennial; rhizomes not present; petals less than 1/8 inch long 3
3. Pedicels as long as the fruits they bear; plants and stems mostly erect.
BOREAL YELLOW CRESS
3. Pedicels noticeably shorter than the fruits they bear; plants mostly with spreading or prostrate life form 4
4. Fruits (seed pods) oval to oblong, but not curved.
BLUNT-HEADED YELLOW CRESS
4. Fruits (seed pods) long, narrow, and curved . . . WESTERN YELLOW CRESS

*   *   *

WATER-CRESS (*Rorippa nasturtium-aquaticum*) Plants with smooth, fleshy foliage; creeping stems; round leaflets. Flowers white to purplish tinged. East. and West. Wash.; aquatic, growing in cold, slow-moving streams; common. Early spring to mid fall. The familiar water-cress, often used for greens in salads.

SPREADING YELLOW CRESS (*Rorippa sinuata*) Branches spreading. Leaves oblong, lobed. Flowers light yellow. East. and West. Wash.; banks of streams and rivers, wooded swales, road ditches, and other moist places in the lowlands. Late spring to early autumn.

BOREAL YELLOW CRESS (*Rorippa islandica*) Stems erect, branching above, but not from base. Leaves pinnately cleft. Petals light yellow, very small. East. and West. Wash.; wet places in lowlands. Summer and early fall.

BLUNT-HEADED YELLOW CRESS (*Rorippa obtusa*) Stems densely branched near base. Foliage smooth. Branches spreading or prostrate. Leaves oblong and cleft. Flowers pale yellow. East. and West. Wash.; moist, muddy, or sandy habitats in lowlands. Summer and early autumn.

WESTERN YELLOW CRESS (*Rorippa curvisiliqua*) Tall, many-branched stems with pinnately-lobed leaves. Stems branching from base. Flowers yellow. East. and West. Wash.; wet ground, including shallow water, in lowlands; often common. Late spring to early autumn.

TANSY MUSTARDS (*Descurainia*) (Color Plate 19)

1. Seed pods with blunt tip and not constricted at intervals along the pod.
TANSY MUSTARD
1. Seed pods pointed at tip and sharply constricted at intervals along the pod.
WESTERN TANSY MUSTARD

TANSY MUSTARD (*Descurainia pinnata*) Flowers yellow to pale yellow. East. Wash.; common and weedy in open places in the lowlands. Mid spring to mid summer.

WESTERN TANSY MUSTARD (*Descurainia richardsonii*) Flowers yellow to pale yellow. East. Wash.; dry, rocky places in foothills and lower mountainous areas. Summer.

ROCK CRESSES (*Arabis*) (Color Plate 18)

Plants with stem leaves usually entire and commonly sessile or clasping. Flowers white, yellow, or purple. Growth form erect with flowers terminal on leafy stems.

1. Seeds either without wings or with a very small, narrow wing; seed pods (siliques) erect and often tightly pressed to the stem..................2
1. Seeds conspicuously winged; seed pods erect or turned downward.....4

2. Upper leaves with basal lobes partly surrounding the stem; plants taller, usually more than 12 inches high...............................3
2. Upper leaves without basal lobes surrounding the stem; plants shorter, usually less than 12 inches tall..............NUTTALL'S ROCK CRESS

3. Seeds in 1 linear series in pod; plant hairy throughout; sepals pouched at base......................................HAIRY ROCK CRESS
3. Seeds in 2 linear series in pod; plants more or less smooth, except at base; sepals not pouched at base......................TOWER MUSTARD

4. Seed pods more than 1/8 inch wide; plants woody at base.
                          WOODY-STEMMED ROCK CRESS
4. Seed pods 1/8 inch wide or less, or if wider, then plant not woody at base 5

5. Lower leaves long, narrow, and very hairy; leaves on stems numerous; seed pods erect, but spreading...............CUSICK'S ROCK CRESS
5. Lower leaves not so long and narrow, nor hairy, but if so, then the seed pods spreading broadly or down-turned...........................6

6. Plants smaller, usually less than 12 inches tall; perennial, with several-headed root crown..7
6. Plants larger, usually more than 12 inches tall; or, if shorter, then with simple, not multiple, root crowns................................8

7. Basal leaves usually toothed; flowering stems very slender and narrow; basal leaves often very hairy............SMALL-LEAVED ROCK CRESS
7. Basal leaves entire and usually smooth; stems not so slender and narrow.
                          LYALL'S ROCK CRESS

8. Lower leaves densely covered with small hairs branching in root-like fashion; seed pods spreading or somewhat downward-turned; stem leaves with basal lobes partly surrounding the stem......HOARY ROCK CRESS
8. Lower leaves with 2- or 3-forked hairs (not branching in root-like fashion); or, hairs in star-shaped clusters; if the hairs root-like, then the pods sharply down-turned or stem leaves without enclosing basal lobes.............9

9. Seed pods with seeds in 2 complete, linear series; seed pods held sharply erect (vertical)........................DRUMMOND'S ROCK CRESS
9. Seed pods with seeds in 1 linear series; seed pods held erect or down-turned...10

10. Hairs on leaves 3-branched; seed pods held more or less erect or spreading.........................SPREADING-POD ROCK CRESS
10. Hairs on leaves variously branched; seed pods mostly down-turned, rarely ascending 11

11. Seed pods sharply curved and sickle-shaped.SICKLE-POD ROCK CRESS
11. Seed pods straight, or very nearly so........HOLBOELL'S ROCK CRESS

*   *   *

NUTTALL'S ROCK CRESS (*Arabis nuttallii*) Plants tufted, to 10 inches. Leaves sparsely hairy and mostly entire. Flowers white, often tinged with lavender. East. Wash.; moist meadows in lowlands and mountainous terrain. Spring and summer.

HAIRY ROCK CRESS (*Arabis hirsuta*) Foliage rough-hairy. Basal leaves clustered; stem leaves heart-shaped. Flowers white, creamy, to pale pinkish. East. and West. Wash.; sea level to montane areas, in a variety of open and shaded habitats. Mid spring to mid summer.

TOWER MUSTARD (*Arabis glabra*) Plants tall, to 5 feet. Stem leaves with conspicuous basal lobes. Basal leaves often toothed. Flowers cream colored. East. and West. Wash.; edge of denser vegetation, meadows, and rocky slopes in lowlands and foothills. Late spring to mid summer.

WOODY-STEMMED ROCK CRESS (*Arabis suffrutescens*) Plants small to medium (8-20 inches). Leaves narrow (without lobes) and mostly basal. Leaves mostly smooth. Flowers few, pink to purplish. East. Wash.; rocky places in sagebrush and yellow pine woods. Late spring to mid summer.

CUSICK'S ROCK CRESS (*Arabis cusickii*) Stems tufted, to 6 inches. Leaves linear-oblanceolate to spatulate, entire or slightly toothed, and sparsely haired. Flowers white, deep pink, or bright purple. East. Wash.; sagebrush and yellow pine woods. Spring.

SMALL-LEAVED ROCK CRESS (*Arabis microphylla*) Stems slender, numerous, and to 7 inches. Leaves mostly basal, narrow, slightly toothed, and mostly somewhat less than 1 inch long. Flowers pink or purple. East. Wash.; dry, open, rocky places from lowlands to subalpine areas. Mid spring to mid summer.

LYALL'S ROCK CRESS (*Arabis lyallii*) Plants small, 2-6 inches high, and arising from branching base. Plants tufted with numerous, green, fleshy leaves. Flowers medium to deep purple. East. and West. Wash.; dry, often rocky, habitats in the higher mountains. Summer.

HOARY ROCK CRESS (*Arabis puberula*) Plants to 20 inches; stems and foliage densely downy or hoary. Flowers white to reddish pink. East. Wash.; dry areas in foothills and higher mountains. Spring.

DRUMMOND'S ROCK CRESS (*Arabis drummondii*) Plants 12-30 inches tall. Basal leaves spatulate, smooth to sparsely hairy, and entire. Stem leaves clasping and lance-shaped. Flowers white, pale pinkish, or purplish. East. and West. Wash.; open, rocky places in the higher parts of the mountains. Late spring to mid summer.

SPREADING-POD ROCK CRESS (*Arabis divaricarpa*) Plants tall, to 32 inches. Leaves narrow; cauline (stem) leaves with basal lobes. Leaves sparsely toothed and more or less hairy. Flowers pink or purplish. East. Wash.; open areas in the mountains. Summer.

SICKLE-POD ROCK CRESS (*Arabis sparsiflora*) Plants tall, to 48 inches. Basal leaves oblanceolate, hairy, with long petioles. Pods often strongly curved. Flowers white to purple. East. Wash.; rocky places in sagebrush and yellow pine woods; common. Mid spring to early summer.

HOLBOELL'S ROCK CRESS (*Arabis holboellii*) Plants variable in height (4-40 inches). Basal leaves narrow-oblanceolate, grayish-haired, and sparsely toothed. Stem leaves with clasping lobes. Flowers white, pink, or purple. East. Wash. and the Cascades; sagebrush, yellow pine woods, and open montane and subalpine areas, mostly in rocky habitats. Late spring and summer.

BITTERCRESSES (*Cardamine*) (Fig. 24)

Similar to the genus *Arabis* but with seeds in 1 row in the seed pod and stems of uniform thickness throughout their length.

1. Plants with simple leaves. 2
1. Plants with some of the leaves, at least, compound .3
2. Leaves oval-shaped and entire, and in form of a loose rosette.
ALPINE BITTERCRESS
2. Leaves roundish and scalloped and heart-shaped at base.
HEART-LEAVED BITTERCRESS
3. Flowers larger, petals more than 1/4 inch long 4
3. Flowers smaller; petals 1/4 inch or less in length. .5
4. Upper stem leaves long and narrow (at least 3 times as long as wide) and mostly entire. . . . . .LARGE-FLOWERED BITTERCRESS
4. Upper stem leaves broader and shorter (not more than twice as long as wide) and usually lobed. . . . . .ANGLE-LEAVED BITTERCRESS
5. Plants perennial with well-developed rhizomes; flowers showy with petals 1/8 to 1/4 inch in length. 6
5. Plants annual or biennial, growing from taproots, not rhizomes; flowers small, usually less than 1/8 inch long. 7
6. Basal leaves (at least some) roundish, heart-shaped at base, and simple.
BREWER'S BITTERCRESS
6. Basal leaves all compound and pinnate. . . . . . . .WESTERN BITTERCRESS
7. Leaflets oval or roundish and borne on noticeable stalks.
LITTLE WESTERN BITTERCRESS
7. Leaflets not roundish, but long and narrow and indistinctly stalked.
PENNSYLVANIA BITTERCRESS

*　　*　　*

ALPINE BITTERCRESS (*Cardamine bellidifolia*) Leaves simple, entire, fleshy, and mostly basal. Flowers white. Cascades and Northeast. Wash.; subalpine and alpine areas of the high mountains. Mid to late summer.

HEART-LEAVED BITTERCRESS (*Cardamine cordifolia*) Leaves simple and smooth and somewhat lobed or scalloped; heart-shaped. Flowers white. East.

Figure 24.
Bittercress, *Cardamine.* (Larrison)

and West. Wash.; moist habitats in higher mountains, such as subalpine meadows and streamsides. Summer and early autumn.

LARGE-FLOWERED BITTERCRESS (*Cardamine pulcherrima*)   Plants 6-14 inches tall. Flowers in racemes and pink, reddish, or purple. West. Wash.; including western Cascades and the Olympics; moist, deep woods. Spring.

ANGLE-LEAVED BITTERCRESS (*Cardamine angulata*)   Leaves all compound (3-5 leaflets) and coarsely toothed. Flowers white to pink. West. Wash.; deep, moist woods; commonly along streams, mostly in lowlands and foothills. Spring and early summer.

BREWER'S BITTERCRESS (*Cardamine breweri*)   Basal leaves simple; stem leaves compound (3-5 leaflets). Flowers white. East. and (mostly) West. Wash.; wet habitats in the lowlands and lower foothills. Mid spring to late summer.

WESTERN BITTERCRESS (*Cardamine occidentalis*)   All basal leaves pinnately compound. Rhizomes bearing tubers at tips. Flowers white. West. Wash.; wet habitats, particularly streambanks, in lowland and foothills. Mid spring to mid summer.

LITTLE WESTERN BITTERCRESS (*Cardamine oligosperma*)   Plants small (to 16 inches). Leaves pinnately divided into 5-11 segments and numerous on the branching stems. Leaflets rounded and smooth or sparsely hairy. Flowers white. East. and West. Wash.; moist spots in open to shady woods in lowlands and mountains; often common. Early spring to mid summer.

PENNSYLVANIA BITTERCRESS (*Cardamine pensylvanica*)   Plants to 24 inches with freely-branching stems. Basal leaves compound; leaflets of upper leaves very narrow. Seed pods extremely narrow. Flowers white. East. and West. Wash.; moist, shady places in lowland woods; often common. Mid spring to mid summer.

SMELOWSKIAS (*Smelowskia*) (Color Plate 20)

High alpine plants with pinnately-compound leaves on long, slender stalks and showy whitish, sometimes purple-tinged, flowers.

1. Seed pods oval-shaped (not more than twice as long as broad); sepals persistent; sepals and pedicels very hairy; petioles of leaves without stiff hairs . . . . SMALL-FRUITED SMELOWSKIA
1. Seed pods long and narrow (at least 3 times as long as wide); sepals dropping off after flowering; sepals and pedicels weakly and sparsely hairy; petioles of leaves with numerous stiff hairs . . . . DWARF SMELOWSKIA

*   *   *

SMALL-FRUITED SMELOWSKIA (*Smelowskia ovalis*)   Plants with tufted, matted habit. Leaves hairy, finely-dissected, and grayish green. Flowers small, white (sometimes tinged with purplish), and borne in racemes. Cascades and Olympics; rocky slides and slopes and ridges in the subalpine and alpine areas of the higher mountains. Summer. One of the highest occurring of all wildflowers.

DWARF SMELOWSKIA (*Smelowskia calycina*)   Basal leaves with long, stiff hairs fringing the petioles. Lower leaves finely divided and grayish-hairy.

Figure 25.
A barbed wire fence makes a handy holder in plant photography. (Larrison)

124

Flowers white, sometimes tinged with purple. East. and West. Wash.; rocky habitats in the subalpine and alpine areas of the higher mountains; mostly occurring above 6,000 feet. Late spring and summer.

Chapter 19—The Caper Family (*Capparidaceae*)

Members of this family have palmately divided leaves (usually into 3 leaflets). Petals and sepals in 4's; stamens 6. Flower clusters are large and showy for the size of the plants. Species in our area are annuals. These are plants of the open, often arid, wastelands. (Color Plate 21)

1. Flowers pink to purplish................ROCKY MOUNTAIN BEE PLANT
1. Flowers yellow...............................TALL YELLOW CLEOME

*   *   *

ROCKY MOUNTAIN BEE PLANT (*Cleome serrulata*) Plants tall (1-4 feet), branched. Showy clusters of pinkish or purplish (rarely white) flowers; petals 4 with 6 protruding, thread-like stamens. Leaves with 3 lance-shaped, entire leaflets; petioles long and slender. Seed pods long and narrow, hanging downward below flowers still blooming. East. Wash.; open, arid places. Summer.

TALL YELLOW CLEOME (*Cleome lutea*) Flowers similar to the above species, but bright yellow. Leaves with 5 leaflets. East. Wash.; open, arid areas, often on rocky soil. Late spring to mid summer.

Some of you, upon using this book for an introduction to the wildflowers of Washington, may wish to read further about such matters as geology and ecology. An understanding of these subjects as they affect the distribution of the various flower species and control the composition of the assorted flower communities that occur from the sea beach to the alpine tundra adds much more to flower "watching" than mere identification of individual plants. Two books are to be recommended highly for home study and field verification.

The first of these is an excellently written and beautifully illustrated book, *Cascadia: The Geologic Evolution of the Pacific Northwest* by Bates McKee of the Department of Geological Sciences of the University of Washington. Published in 1972 by McGraw-Hill, it sells for $12.95. This reference will probably tell you all you ever wanted to know about the geological make-up of the state and how it got that way.

The second volume, *Natural Regions of the United States and Canada,* by Charles B. Hunt (W. H. Freeman and Company, 1973, $15.00), treats in detail the various environments of the continent, their topography, geology, climates, soils, and geography. Among other things, this book will enable you to understand how Washington flowers fit into the entire North American complex and make it possible for you to broaden your wildflower perspective.

Chapter 20—The Sundew Family (*Droseraceae*)

Members of this family are insectivorous, perennial herbs with leaves in basal rosettes and covered with sensitive, glandular hairs and possessing long petioles. An insect touching the leaf is engulfed in a sticky liquid secreted by the hairs. Flowers are borne in a 1-sided raceme and are perfect and regular. Sepals and petals, 5; stamens 4-20; styles 2-5. (Color Plate 21)

1. Leaves spreading sideways from main part of plant and roundish in shape.
ROUND-LEAVED SUNDEW
1. Leaves more or less erect and noticeably longer than broad.
LONG-LEAVED SUNDEW

*   *   *

ROUND-LEAVED SUNDEW (*Drosera rotundifolia*) Flowers white. East. and West. Wash.; in lowland and montane swamps and bogs, the latter especially of the sphagnum type where the plants usually locate on the sphagnum mats. Summer and early autumn.

LONG-LEAVED SUNDEW (*Drosera anglica*) Flowers white. East. and West. Wash.; montane bogs.

———————

The following are some additional books on wildflowers of all or parts of the state of Washington that the advanced student may find interesting and useful. A few of the titles are out of print but are probably available in most libraries.

Brockman, C. Frank 1947 *Flora of Mount Rainier National Park.* Govt. Printing Office.
Clark, Lewis J. 1973 *Wildflowers of British Columbia.* Gray's Publishing Ltd.
Craighead, John J.; Craighead, Frank C.; and Ray J. Davis 1963 *A Field Guide to Rocky Mountain Wildflowers.* Houghton Mifflin Company.
Davis, Ray J. 1952 *Flora of Idaho.* Wm. C. Brown Company.
Fries, Mary A. 1970 *Wildflowers of Mount Rainier and the Cascades.* Mount Rainier Natural History Association and the Mountaineers.
Gilkey, Helen M. and LaRea J. Dennis 1967 *Handbook of Northwestern Plants.* Oregon State University Bookstores, Inc.
Hitchcock, C. Leo; Cronquist, Arthur; Ownbey, Marion; and J. W. Thompson 1955-1969 *Vascular Plants of the Pacific Northwest.* 5 vols. University of Washington Press. (The most detailed and up-to-date monograph on the flora of the Northwest.)
Hitchcock, C. Leo and Arthur Conquist 1973 *Flora of the Pacific Northwest.* University of Washington Press. (The best, single volume, technical manual on Northwest flowers; a must for the advanced student.)

(Continued in Chapter 27)

Chapter 21—The Stonecrop Family (*Crassulaceae*)

Members of this family are annual or perennial, fleshy herbs, with usually perfect flowers, that are low in stature and commonly to be found in rocky places. Floral parts are usually in 5's and the flowering heads as terminal cymes. Stamens are twice as many as the sepals and petals. One genus (*Sedum*) in our area. (Color Plate 21)

1. Flowers purplish .... ROSE-ROOT
1. Flowers yellow 2

2. Stem leaves mostly opposite .... SPREADING STONECROP
2. Stem leaves mostly alternate 3

3. Sepals less than 1/8 inch long .... LEIBERG'S STONECROP
3. Sepals more than 1/8 inch long 4

4. Distal half of leaf broader than proximal half and leaves strongly flattened . 5
4. Proximal half of leaf broader than distal half and leaves not strongly flattened 6

5. Petals more than 3/8 inch long .... OREGON STONECROP
5. Petals less than 3/8 inch long .... BROAD-LEAVED STONECROP

6. Leaves strongly keeled .... DOUGLAS'S STONECROP
6. Leaves not strongly keeled and more or less roundish.
                                    NARROW-LEAVED STONECROP

*   *   *

ROSE-ROOT (*Sedum roseum*) Plants to 6 inches. Leaves flattish, numerous, and scattered along stems. Flowers purple, in flat-topped cymes. East. and West. Wash.; rock outcroppings, cliffs, and slides, where there is some moisture. In the mountains. Summer.

SPREADING STONECROP (*Sedum divergens*) Leaves round and opposite; 1/4 to 1/2 inch in circumference and almost globular; growing tightly packed around the stems. Leaves and stalks waxy light green to rose red. Seed pods spreading (hence name). Flowers bright yellow, star-like, in flat-topped clusters. Cascades and Olympics: rocky slopes and cliffs in subalpine and alpine areas. Mid summer to early autumn.

LEIBERG'S STONECROP (*Sedum leibergii*) Plants erect, to 4 inches. Lower leaves narrow-spatulate; upper leaves oblong. Flowers greenish yellow, in crowded, terminal clusters. East. Wash.: rocky slopes in river canyons. Late spring to mid summer.

OREGON STONECROP (*Sedum oreganum*) Plants to 8 inches with smooth, green leaves that are somewhat spatulate, flattened, and mostly basal; a few smaller alternating on stem. Flowers pale yellow. East. and (mostly) West. Wash.; rocky slopes and outcroppings in mountainous areas. Summer.

BROAD-LEAVED STONECROP (*Sedum spathulifolium*) Plants to 12 inches with spatulate leaves covered with white bloom, giving gray-green appearance. Leaves flattened, in rosettes at ends of stems; a few reduced, alternate leaves on flower stems. Flowers yellow. West. Wash.; rocky places in lowlands and lower mountains. Late spring and summer.

Figure 26.
Typical habitat of the stonecrops, *Sedum.* (Larrison)

128

DOUGLAS'S STONECROP (*Sedum stenopetalum*) Plants low, 4-6 inches tall. Leaves narrow, lance-shaped, 1/4 to 1/2 inch long, mostly in tufts, basal or terminal. Foliage often reddish. Flowers yellow, in compact clusters. East. and West. Wash.; widely scattered, but uncommon, in rocky places in desert plains, foothill benches (open and semi-open), and subalpine ridges. Summer.

NARROW-LEAVED STONECROP (*Sedum lanceolatum*) Plants to 10 inches with leaves varying from narrow and round in cross section to oval and flat, depending on variety. Flowers yellowish. East. and West. Wash.; open, rocky places from sea level to subalpine. Summer.

Chapter 22—The Saxifrage Family (*Saxifragaceae*)

Members of this family are perennial, smooth-foliaged or hairy herbs with mostly basal or occasionally alternate leaves. Flowers are perfect and regular and usually white or whitish in color. Petals, sepals in 5's (rarely 4's); stamens, 5 to 10. Petals fringe-like in some species. (Color Plates 22-24)

1. Fertile stamens 5 or less (10 in *Mitella nuda*) 2
1. Fertile stamens 8 or 10 8

2. Stamens 2 or 3; petals thread-like, attached to calyx . . . . YOUTH-ON-AGE
2. Stamens 5; petals not thread-like or attached to calyx 3

3. Flowers single, at tip of flowering stem . . . . GRASS-OF-PARNASSUS
3. Flowers more than 1, in a group (inflorescence) 4

4. Plant bearing a cluster of bulbs at the base of the stem.
CLIFF SUKSDORFIA
4. Plants not bearing a cluster of bulbs at the base of the stem 5

5. Petals pinnately divided and feather-like or lobed 6
5. Petals entire, not divided as above 7

6. Petals with 5 or more short, blunt lobes; calyx more than 1/3 inch long.
ELMERA
6. Petals with feather-like lobes or with 3, short, blunt lobes; calyx lobes 1/4 inch or less in length . . . . MITREWORTS (*Mitella*)

7. Ovary divided into 2 chambers . . . . BOYKINIAS (*Boykinia*)
7. Ovary of 1 chamber . . . . HEUCHERAS (*Heuchera*)

8. Stamens 8, petals absent . . . . GOLDEN-CARPET
8. Stamens 10; petals usually present 9

9. Ovary of 2 chambers 10
9. Ovary of 1 chamber 11

10. Leaves leathery, broad, and more or less oval-shaped to oblong; inflorescence tightly bunched at tip of stem . . . . FALSE SAXIFRAGE
10. Leaves not leathery, but either palmately lobed or veined, or very finely dissected; inflorescence open and loose, not tightly bunched at tip of stem . . . . SAXIFRAGES (*Saxifraga*)

11. Petals entire . . . . FOAMFLOWERS (*Tiarella*)
11. Petals divided, lobed, or fringed 12

12. Petals pinnately divided or fringed . . . . FRINGE-CUP
12. Petals palmately divided . . . . PRAIRIE-STARS (*Lithophragma*)

Figure 27.
Rocky habitat of the saxifrages, *Saxifraga.* (Larrison)

YOUTH-ON-AGE (*Tolmiea menziesii*) Plants to 36 inches. Flowers inconspicuous and "bristly." Calyx cylindrical, greenish streaked purple; petals 4, curl-
ing, thread-like. Foliage hairy, leaves maple-shaped, lightly lobed and toothed.
West. Wash. (rare east of Cascade Crest); moist, shady woods. Late spring
and summer. So-called from habit of bearing a bud or young plant at base of
leaf blade. (Color Plate 24)

GRASS-OF-PARNASSUS (*Parnassia fimbriata*) Leaves kidney-shaped, glossy
green, and in basal cluster; 1 small clasping leaf half way or more up each
stem. Single white flowers facing the sky at tip of tall, slender stems with
unusual, geometric pattern: 5 petals with dainty fringe on lower edges; 5
fertile stamens with yellow anthers spreading alternately between petals;
clumps of sterile filaments forming green spot at base of each petal. East. and
West. Wash.; wet meadows and slopes and bogs; commonly along streams;
from lower parts of mountains to the subalpine areas. Mid summer to early
fall. (Color Plate 23)

CLIFF SUKSDORFIA (*Suksdorfia violacea*) Plants to 10 inches. Leaves small
and roundish and mostly basal with few on stem. Flowers violet (rarely white).
East. Wash. and Columbia Gorge; wet, rocky, or mossy cliffs. Spring and early
summer. (*S. ranunculifolia* has rounded, deeply-cleft, and lobed leaves; white
flowers; with characteristic basal bulbs. Mostly East. Wash.; subalpine slopes
and cliffs. We have found it just east of Chinook Pass.) (Color Plate 23)

ELMERA (*Elmera racemosa*) Dark green, hairy, basal leaves that are cordate
and slightly lobed with roundish teeth. Flowers white, bell-shaped and borne
in racemes. Cascades and Olympics; cliffs and gravel and rock slopes in high
mountains; frequently on shale becoming bare of snow in late summer.
Summer and early autumn. (Fig. 28)

GOLDEN-CARPET (*Chrysosplenium glechomaefolium*) To 8 inches tall;
though partly prostrate. Leaves small, fleshy, and paired (on non-flowering
stems). Petals absent; sepals greenish; stamens 8 in number; flowers axillary.
West. Wash.; moist, boggy habitats in lowlands and mountains. Spring.

FALSE SAXIFRAGE (*Leptarrhena pyrolifolia*) Plants to 12 inches with shining, leathery, rather thick leaves which are oval-shaped with toothed margins.
Short panicles of small, creamy flowers at tips of stems, followed by wine-red
seed clusters. East. and West. Wash.; moist habitats, such as wet meadows
(lowland to subalpine) and stream margins. Summer.

FRINGE-CUP (*Tellima grandiflora*) Plants to 40 inches. Bell-like greenish
calyx with small white, protruding, fringe-like petals in typical 1-sided racemes.
Flowers greenish white to red. Leaves roundish with toothed lobes. Foliage
coarsely hairy. East. and West. Wash.; moist, shady woods and streambanks,
from lowlands to near subalpine. Mid spring to mid summer (Color Plate 23)

MITREWORTS (*Mitella*) (Color Plate 22)

Plants with elongate, strongly-cleft, filamentous petals which are often feathery
in appearance. Leaves usually basal and flowers in slender racemes.

1. Stamens 10 . . . . NAKED MITREWORT
1. Stamens 5 2

2. Petals 3-lobed at tip. 3
2. Petals fringe-like, being pinnately divided into hair-like structures. 4
3. Lobes of petals long and narrow. . . . . .SIDE-FLOWERED MITREWORT
3. Lobes of petals short and broad. . . . . .THREE-TOOTHED MITREWORT
4. Leaves all basal 5
4. Leaves not only basal, but scattered along the stem.
                                        LEAFY-STEMMED MITREWORT
5. Stamens opposite the petals and alternating with the calyx lobes.
                                        FIVE-POINT MITREWORT
5. Stamens opposite the sepals and alternating with the petals. 6
6. Leaves round, but heart-shaped at base. . . . . .FEATHERY MITREWORT
6. Leaves oblong, though heart-shaped at base. .OVAL-LEAVED MITREWORT

                    *   *   *

NAKED MITREWORT (*Mitella nuda*) Plants to 8 inches with hairy foliage. Leaves small and scalloped. Petals greenish yellow, pinnately divided into usually 9 segments. West. Wash.; damp, shady woods, streambanks, and wet meadows. Summer.

SIDE-FLOWERED MITREWORT (*Mitella stauropetala*) Plants to 20 inches with round or kidney-shaped leaves with scalloped and toothed margins. Petals 2-3 times as long as calyx lobes; purplish. Racemes strongly 1-sided. Blue Mountains and extreme East. Wash.; moist spots in yellow pine and fir woods. Late spring and early summer.

THREE-TOOTHED MITREWORT (*Mitella trifida*) Plants to 14 inches. Leaves round with numerous small teeth. Leaves basal with hairy petioles. Petals white, often tinged with purple, and cleft at tip into 3 pointed lobes. East. and West. Wash.; moist, shady woods. Late spring to mid summer.

LEAFY-STEMMED MITREWORT (*Mitella caulescens*) Plants to 25 inches with leafy stems. Leaves 5-lobed and finely toothed. Flowers greenish. East. and West. Wash.; moist woods and meadows from sea level to moderate elevations in mountains. Spring and early summer.

FIVE-POINT MITREWORT (*Mitella pentandra*) Plants to 12 inches. Leaves basal, heart-shaped to roundish with round teeth. Stamens opposite petals (unique feature). Petals greenish yellow and finely divided. East. and West. Wash.; moist woods and meadows, and streamsides. Summer.

FEATHERY MITREWORT (*Mitella breweri*) Plants to 12 inches with basal, shiny green, kidney-shaped leaves with roundish teeth. Stamens alternating with petals. Flowers greenish yellow. East. and West. Wash.; moist woods and meadows, mostly in the mountains. Late spring and summer.

OVAL-LEAVED MITREWORT (*Mitella ovalis*) Plants to 16 inches with oval, weakly lobed or crenate margins; heart-shaped at base. Flowers greenish yellow. West. Wash.; moist, shady woods and streambanks; lowlands up into the mountains. Spring.

BOYKINIAS (*Boykinia*) (Color Plate 22)

Plants very leafy, with roundish, strongly lobed and toothed leaves on long petioles. Flower parts in 5's. Ovary with 2 chambers.

1. Stipules of upper leaves large and leaf-like.
                                                    LARGE-FLOWERED BOYKINIA
1. Stipules of leaves small and bristle-like . . . . SLENDER BOYKINIA

*   *   *

LARGE-FLOWERED BOYKINIA (*Boykinia major*) Leaves small, to 2½ inches wide. Flowers white with yellow centers (the ovary showing in throat of floral tube). East. and West. Wash.; moist meadows and streambanks. Summer and early autumn.

SLENDER BOYKINIA (*Boykinia elata*) Leaves large (to 8 inches wide) on long petioles. Flowers white. West. Wash.; moist woods and streambanks, lowlands and foothills. Summer.

ALUMROOTS (*Heuchera*) (Color Plate 22)

Rather loosely arranged plants with roundish, toothed, lobed, long-petioled leaves. The calyx is tube-like and incloses the ovary. The smallish flowers are borne in open or spike-like panicles. Plants commonly of rocky places. Leaves palmately veined, in basal clusters.

1. Flowers in spike-like group (borne close to stem) 2
1. Flower group not spike-like, but loose 3
2. Stems and petioles covered with large, brownish hairs.
                                                    NARROW-FLOWERED ALUMROOT
2. Stems and petioles smooth or covered by short, whitish hairs.
                                                    LAVA ALUMROOT
3. Leaves and petioles hairy; teeth of lobes of leaves mostly rounded.
                                                    SMALL-FLOWERED ALUMROOT
3. Leaves and petioles smooth, not hairy; lobes of leaves sharp-pointed.
                                                    SMOOTH ALUMROOT

*   *   *

NARROW-FLOWERED ALUMROOT (*Heuchera chlorantha*) Plants to 3 feet. Foliage densely hairy. Flowers greenish to cream colored, with some or all petals lacking. West. Wash. and Columbia Gorge; rocky prairies and open, wooded slopes of foothills. Late spring and summer.

LAVA ALUMROOT (*Heuchera cylindrica*) Plants to 30 inches. Plants quite variable according to variety. Sepals greenish yellow to cream colored; petals often lacking. East. Wash.; rocky slopes, slides, and cliffs. Mid spring to late summer. Also in Cascades.

SMALL-FLOWERED ALUMROOT (*Heuchera micrantha*) Plants to 36 inches. Stems covered with reddish hairs. Dainty panicle spray of tiny, white flowers on wiry stems a foot or more tall. East. and West. Wash.; rocky habitats from sea level to subalpine areas. Late spring and summer. Some alternate leaves (short-petioled) on stem.

SMOOTH ALUMROOT (*Heuchera glabra*) Stems and petioles not hairy. Leaf lobes triangular. Flowers white. East. and West. Wash.; moist, rocky places and streambanks. Summer.

SAXIFRAGES (*Saxifraga*) (Color Plate 23)

Flowers with mostly basal leaves, cup-shaped calyxes, 5 petals, and 10 stamens. Pistils 2 and joined at their base. The flowers are small and often borne in panicles. Commonly found growing on rocky ledges in hilly or mountainous country.

1. Leaves entire, not lobed or toothed, and not entirely basal.............2
1. Leaves lobed or toothed, or if entire, then basal....................3

2. Leaves leathery, with fringed margins.............MATTED SAXIFRAGE
2. Leaves thick and fleshy, without fringed margins...TOLMIE'S SAXIFRAGE

3. Some leaves with 3 sharp teeth at the leaf tip.......MATTED SAXIFRAGE
3. Leaves lobed or toothed, but not as above.........................4

4. Flowers on plant usually more than 10 in number; leaves seldom present on flowering stems; leaves usually wider than 3/4 inch.............. 5
4. Flowers on plant usually less than 10 in number; a few leaves on flowering stems; leaves less than 3/4 inch wide...........................12

5. Leaves round in shape and usually broader than long; may be cordate at base..6
5. Leaves not round in shape and usually much longer than broad........8

6. Leaves double-toothed (small teeth on many of the larger teeth); petioles very hairy..................................MERTEN'S SAXIFRAGE
6. Leaves singly toothed (no smaller teeth on the larger ones); petioles not, if at all, very hairy..7

7. Petals round; irregular in shape and size (some broader than others); upper part of flowering stem not strongly hairy (the hairs short and straight).......................MOUNTAIN MEADOW SAXIFRAGE
7. Petals oblong; more or less regular in shape and size (all of about the same width); upper part of flowering stem strongly hairy, with matted, curled, or twisted hairs.....................PUNCTATE SAXIFRAGE

8. Flowers in small compact group (head) at tip of long stem.
HOOKER'S SAXIFRAGE
8. Flowers in larger, looser group.................................9

9. Petals (at least some) narrowing to a short, slender claw.............10
9. Petals mostly rounded to a base with or without a claw..............11

10. Leaves with slender petioles; plant sparsely hairy...LYALL'S SAXIFRAGE
10. Leaves without slender petioles; plant very hairy.....RUSTY SAXIFRAGE

11. Leaves with narrow petioles.........WESTERN MOUNTAIN SAXIFRAGE
11. Leaves without narrow petioles................OREGON SAXIFRAGE

12. Leaves with long, narrow petioles................................13
12. Leaves lacking petioles, or their petioles very broad................14

13. Plants small, less than 4 inches tall; flowers often single at ends of flowering stems................................WEAK SAXIFRAGE
13. Plants larger, usually more than 4 inches tall; flowers or bulblets several on a flowering stem.........................NODDING SAXIFRAGE

14. Foliage in a tight tuft with several flowering stems arising therefrom.
TUFTED SAXIFRAGE

14. Foliage not tightly tufted, but merely basal, with usually a single flowering
    stem arising therefrom.....................ASCENDING SAXIFRAGE

*   *   *

MATTED SAXIFRAGE (*Saxifraga bronchialis*) Densely tufted or matted with 2-6 inch flowering stems bearing cymes of small, star-like flowers that are white, spotted with purple or yellowish. Leaves tiny, densely clustered, and fleshy. East. and West. Wash.; cliffs, rockslides, and open, rocky slopes from lowlands to high mountains. Summer.

TOLMIE'S SAXIFRAGE (*Saxifraga tolmiei*) Plants low, mat-like. Leaves small, round, thick, and fleshy (like those of a stonecrop). Flowers white; small and star-like; stamens with black anthers. East. and West. Wash.; moist subalpine meadows, cliffs, and rocky slopes. Mid to late summer.

MERTEN'S SAXIFRAGE (*Saxifraga mertensiana*) Plants to 20 inches. Leaf stipules inclosing the stem. Leaves doubly toothed. Foliage hairy. Flowers white. Cascades and West. Wash.; moist, rocky streambanks in lowlands and mountains. Mid spring to late summer.

MOUNTAIN MEADOW SAXIFRAGE (*Saxifraga arguta*) Plants to 24 inches. Leaves fleshy, basal, long-stemmed, and broader than long; coarsely toothed. Petals white and roundish. East. and West. Wash.; moist habitats along water in mountain forests and subalpine meadows; common. Mid summer to early autumn. Characterized by flowering stems 6-10 inches long with panicles of numerous flowers.

PUNCTATE SAXIFRAGE (*Saxifraga punctata*) Plants to 12 inches. Similar to above, but petals oblong in shape. Leaves with blunt teeth. Stems smooth. Flowers white. Cascades and Olympics; moist margins of streams and pools in the mountains. Summer.

HOOKER'S SAXIFRAGE (*Saxifraga integrifolia*) Plants to 14 inches. Leaves entire, basal, and fringed with hairs. Undersurface of leaves densely haired with reddish hairs. Flowers white, greenish, yellowish, or purple. East. and West. Wash.; grassy prairies and slopes, streambanks, and subalpine meadows from lowlands up into the mountains. Early spring to mid summer.

LYALL'S SAXIFRAGE (*Saxifraga lyallii*) Plants to 12 inches; mat-like. Leaves large and fan-shaped. Flower stalks and sepals reddish; petals white, turning pink. Northern Cascades and northeastern Wash.; moist meadows and stream margins in montane and subalpine areas. Mid and late summer.

RUSTY SAXIFRAGE (*Saxifraga ferruginea*) Plants 2-12 inches tall. Spatulate leaves in rosette at base of stems; leaves toothed on outer half. Flowers white, or rarely purplish. West. and northeastern Wash.; including the Cascades; streambanks in the mountains; common. Summer.

WESTERN MOUNTAIN SAXIFRAGE (*Saxifraga occidentalis*) Plants to 10 inches with oval, basal leaves possessing coarse, blunt teeth. Petals white, sometimes with pink or purple tinge, and with 2 yellowish spots at base. East. and West. Wash.; moist meadows, streambanks, and rocky slopes in montane and subalpine areas. Late spring and summer.

135

Figure 28.
Oxyria, growing in saxifrage habitat, may be confused with that family. (Larrison)

OREGON SAXIFRAGE (*Saxifraga oregana*) Plants sometimes to several feet. Petals white to greenish white and very small. Flowering stalks very glandular. Leaves variable, without much of a petiole. Cascades and West. Wash.; moist meadows, bogs, and streambanks in the mountains. Late spring to mid summer.

WEAK SAXIFRAGE (*Saxifraga debilis*) Plants small, to 4 inches, and some-what mat-like, in loose scattered patches. Leaves small, and 5-lobed. Petals white, with pink veins. East. and West. Wash.; moist rocky slopes, slides, and cliffs in the mountains. Summer.

NODDING SAXIFRAGE (*Saxifraga cernua*) Plants tufted, to 8 inches. Leaves with up to 7 lobes. Often a single flower in bloom at tip of stem. Flowers white, often with 3 purple veins per petal. Northern Wash.; streambanks and moist, rocky cliffs in the mountains. Mid to late summer.

TUFTED SAXIFRAGE (*Saxifraga caespitosa*) Plants matted or tufted, to 6 inches. Leaves cleft into usually 3, narrow lobes. Numerous white flowers on short stems projecting above the dense mat. East. and West. Wash.; rocky slopes and cliffs from lowlands to alpine areas in mountains. Mid spring to early autumn.

ASCENDING SAXIFRAGE (*Saxifraga adscendens*) Similar to above but leaves very bluntly or shallowly lobed or toothed into 3 parts; sometimes entire. Flowers white. Northern Wash.; rocky slopes, cliffs, and moraines in higher mountain areas. Mid and late summer.

FOAMFLOWERS (*Tiarella*) (Color Plate 24)

Plants with tiny flowers in loose, narrow racemes or "airy" panicles with simple or 3-cleft leaves. Foliage coarsely-hairy. One of the most abundant ground cover plants in the coniferous forests, often forming a continuous cover throughout the summer. An early to late summer bloomer. Leaves simple or compound, palmately lobed; lobes sharp-pointed, mostly basal on erect petioles. The following often considered as a single species.

1. Leaves mostly simple; lobed, but not compound. WESTERN FOAMFLOWER
1. Leaves compound, with 3 leaflets.....................................2
2. Leaflets cleft into lobes not more than half the length of the leaflet.
THREE-LEAVED FOAMFLOWER
2. Leaflets, especially the lower ones, cleft into lobes almost the entire length
of the leaflet............................LACINIATE FOAMFLOWER

*   *   *

WESTERN FOAMFLOWER (*Tiarella unifoliata*) Plants to 16 inches with palm-ately-lobed, but not cleft, leaves. Flowers white. East. and West. Wash.; moist, shady woods and streambanks in mountains. Summer. Common and widely distributed.

THREE-LEAVED FOAMFLOWER (*Tiarella trifoliata*) Plants to 16 inches. Leaves with 3 leaflets that are poorly, if at all, cleft. Delicate raceme of small, white flowers. West. Wash.; moist, shady woods and streambanks in lowlands and lower montane areas. Late spring and summer.

LACINIATE FOAMFLOWER (*Tiarella laciniata*) Plants to 12-16 inches. Leaves with deeply-cleft leaflets. Flowers white. West. Wash.; moist, shady woods. Late spring and summer.

PRAIRIE-STARS (*Lithophragma*) (Color Plate 22)

Small plants with mostly basal leaves and with flowers in terminal racemes on long stems. The flowers are usually white and characterized by the deeply-cleft petals. Flowers star-like, hence the name. One of the early spring bloomers.

1. Basal leaves smooth or sparsely hairy; petals usually 5-lobed; stem leaves often bearing bulblets. 2
1. Basal leaves strongly hairy; petals 3-5 lobed; stem leaves not bearing bulblets 3
2. Stem leaves bearing bulblets. . . . . .SLENDER PRAIRIE-STAR
2. Stem leaves not bearing bulblets. . . . . .GLABROUS PRAIRIE-STAR
3. Petals usually 3-lobed. . . . . .SMALL-FLOWERED PRAIRIE-STAR
3. Petals usually 5-lobed . . . . .STAR-FLOWER

* * *

SLENDER PRAIRIE-STAR (*Lithophragma bulbifera*) Stem leaves with tiny, axillary bulbs. Plants to 10 inches with reddish-purple foliage. Petals white to pinkish and lobed. East. Wash.; sagebrush, grassy slopes, and yellow pine woods in lowlands and foothills. Spring and early summer.

GLABROUS PRAIRIE-STAR (*Lithophragma glabra*) Plants to 12 inches. Stem leaves without bulblets. Foliage with fine, short hairs. Stems with 2 leaves only; basal leaves with deeply cleft leaflets. Flowers white to pinkish. East. Wash. and Columbia Gorge; sagebrush, grasslands, and yellow pine woods. Spring.

SMALL-FLOWERED PRAIRIE-STAR (*Lithophragma parviflora*) Plants to 14 inches. Basal leaves with 5 deeply-lobed leaflets. Flowers white, pinkish, or purplish and 2-5 on a stem. East. and West. Wash.; sagebrush, grassy prairies, and yellow pine and fir forests of lowlands and lower montane areas. Spring and early summer.

STAR-FLOWER (*Lithophragma tenella*) Plants to 10 inches. Flowers white or pinkish, scattered along stem, and with 5-lobed petals. East. Wash.; sagebrush, grasslands, and yellow pine woods in lowlands and foothills. Spring and early summer.

Chapter 23—The Rose Family (*Rosaceae*)

Members of this family are herbs, trees, or shrubs with regular, usually perfect flowers and generally alternate leaves. The calyx is usually of 5 sepals (though varying from 5 to 10) and the petals match the sepals in number. Stamens are numerous, though commonly 20; pistils are 1 to many. The sepals are often partly united to form a 5- or 4-lobed calyx. Sometimes the petals are absent. Ovary may be superior or inferior. This family contains many domestic fruits and plants of horticultural value, but only native Washington wildflowers are included here. (Color Plates 24-26)

1. Petals absent; pistils 1 or 2..................BURNETS (*Sanguisorba*)
1. Petals present; pistils more than 3..............................2

2. Leaves twice or 3-times divided into groups or 3 linear segments (lobes); most leaves in tight clusters at base of flowering stems, but with scattered leaves along stems right to the flowering heads......PARTRIDGE-FOOT
2. Leaves not as above..3

3. Leaves entire or scalloped (crenulate)...........................4
3. Leaves lobed or compound, not entire or merely scalloped...........5

4. Flowers single, at tips of branches or flowering stems..MOUNTAIN AVENS
4. Flowers numerous, in racemes.........ROCK-SPIRAEAS (*Petrophytum*)

5. Plants dioecious—with stamens and pistils on different individuals; leaves compound and divided into 3's; flowers tiny with petals less than 1/16 inch long...GOATSBEARD
5. Plants usually not dioecious; leaves not compound in 3's; flowers larger, petals more than 1/16 inch long.................................6

6. Stamens 5...7
6. Stamens 10 or more..8

7. Leaves palmately divided into 3 leaflets...................SIBBALDIA
7. Leaves pinnately divided...........................ALPINE IVESIA

8. Plants perennial with pinnate leaves; stamens 10; leaflets sharply cleft.
PINE WOODS HORKELIA
8. Plants annual or biennial (with thus weaker taproots); stamens usually more than 10; leaflets not cleft.................................9

9. Leaves divided into 3 leaflets; fruits strawberry-like; flowers white to pale pinkish; stems as runners (stolons), rooting at the joints.
STRAWBERRIES (*Fragaria*)
9. Leaves usually not divided into 3 leaflets; fruits not strawberry-like; flowers usually not white or pinkish, but yellow; stems rarely runner-like.......10

10. Leaves with terminal leaflet larger than the lower ones which are often arranged in 2 rows on opposite sides of the flowering stem and are pinnatifid...GEUMS (*Geum*)
10. Leaves usually not as above; the lower leaflets about the same size as the terminal one; thus often giving the appearance of being palmately compound ....CINQUEFOILS (*Potentilla*)

Figure 29.
A cascade of goat's-beard, *Aruncus*. (Larrison)

PARTRIDGE-FOOT (*Luetkea pectinata*) Low (2-4 inches), spreading plants forming extensive mats of moss-like foliage with finely-divided leaves. Attractive heads of creamy-white flowers. East. and West. Wash.; moist, shaded places in subalpine and alpine areas in the mountains. Summer. (Color Plate 25) (Fig. 30)

MOUNTAIN AVENS (*Dryas octopetala*) Low, mat-forming plants with thick, oval, round-toothed leaves that are deeply veined and white-hairy beneath. Flowers creamy white, like small, single roses with 8 petals. Seed heads are feathery plumes. East. and West. Wash.; rocky, gravelly places in upper montane forests, and subalpine and alpine areas in the higher mountains; also open meadows and exposed, rocky ridges. Summer. (Color Plate 24)

GOATSBEARD (*Aruncus sylvester*) Conspicuous, frothy plumes of tiny, white flowers topping tall, upright, leafy stalks reaching 3-6 feet. Leaves compound; leaflets ovate, doubly toothed. Cascades and West. Wash.; shady, moist woods, streambanks, and commonly along roadsides in the forested lowlands. Late spring to mid summer. (Color Plate 24) (Fig. 29)

SIBBALDIA (*Sibbaldia procumbens*) Mat-like plants with erect, 3-cleft leaves that are toothed at the ends. Flowering stems to 3 inches with terminal, pale yellow flowers. East. and West. Wash.; subalpine and alpine meadows and slopes. Early and mid summer. (Color Plate 26)

ALPINE IVESIA (*Ivesia gordonii*) Clustered plants to 6 inches with numerous basal leaves with numerous, crowded, deeply-cleft segments. Flowers as head-like blooms, yellow, and borne on mostly leafless (usually 1 leaf) stems. Central and Southern Cascades and Blue Mountains; high, rocky, subalpine and alpine ridges and slides down to river banks in adjacent lowlands. Summer.

PINE WOODS HORKELIA (*Horkelia fusca*) Plants to 24 inches. Leaves with numerous, roundish segments. Flowers white to dark pink with 1/4 inch long petals. Pistils 15-25. Lower slopes and foothills of the eastern Cascades; variable, meadows, rocky slopes, and yellow pine woods. Early and mid summer. (Color Plate 25)

BURNETS (*Sanguisorba*) (Color Plate 26)

1. Plants annual or biennial; stamens 2; leaflets sharply cleft; spikes greenish.
   WESTERN BURNET
1. Plants perennial; stamens 4; leaflets toothed, but not sharply cleft; spikes white or purplish 2
2. Calyx greenish white to pale pinkish; spikes greenish white to whitish.
   BROAD-LEAVED BURNET
2. Calyx reddish or purplish; spikes reddish purple . . . . . MENZIES'S BURNET

* * *

WESTERN BURNET (*Sanguisorba occidentalis*) Plants to 20 inches. Stems leafy with the leaves deeply-cleft into many lobes. Flowers greenish; borne in tight heads. East. Wash.; grassy flats, sagebrush areas, moist weedy places, and open woods. Early and mid summer.

141

BROAD-LEAVED BURNET (*Sanguisorba sitchensis*) Plants to 3 feet with leaves mostly basal. Leaflets roundish and toothed. Flowers greenish white or pale pinkish in very tight heads. Cascades and East. Wash.; wet places, such as swamps, bogs, and streambanks, in the mountains. Mid to late summer.

MENZIE'S BURNET (*Sanguisorba menziesii*) Plants to 20 inches with basal leaves with roundish, toothed leaflets and reddish or purplish terminal flower heads. Olympic peninsula; marshes and bogs. Summer.

ROCK-SPIRAEAS (*Petrophytum*) (Plate ??)

Plants tufted or mat-like with clusters of entire leaves widest in outer half. Flowers clustered in crowded spikes on projecting flowering stems. Petals 5, with numerous stamens.

1. Upper bracts on stems bearing rudimentary buds; stamens 20-25; sepals triangular and erect (surrounding petals)..........GRAY ROCK-SPIRAEA
1. Upper bracts on stem not bearing rudimentary buds; stamens 35-40; sepals oblong (not triangular) and bent downward, away from the petals.
HENDERSON'S ROCK-SPIRAEA

*   *   *

GRAY ROCK-SPIRAEA (*Petrophytum cinerascens*) Flowers white. East. Wash.; along the Columbia River in Chelan County; basaltic cliffs. Summer.

HENDERSON'S ROCK-SPIRAEA (*Petrophytum hendersonii*) Flowers white. Olympics; cliffs and rock slides at middle to higher elevations in mountains. Midsummer to early autumn.

STRAWBERRIES (*Fragaria*) (Color Plate 25)

Low-growing plants with the familiar strawberry-like, 3-leaflet leaves; 5-petalled, white flowers with numerous yellow stamens; and the typical reddish strawberry fruits.

1. Plants with deep green, leathery leaves; occurs along salt water.
SEA BEACH STRAWBERRY
1. Plants with light green or bluish green, non-leathery leaves; not occurring along salt water...2
2. Leaves grayish or bluish green; leaf surface not raised between veins.
VIRGINIA STRAWBERRY
2. Leaves yellow or bright green; leaf surface bulged or raised between the veins ....INTERIOR STRAWBERRY

*   *   *

SEA BEACH STRAWBERRY (*Fragaria chiloensis*) Flowers white. West. Wash.; beaches along salt water. Mid spring to early summer.

VIRGINIA STRAWBERRY (*Fragaria virginiana*) Flowers white, less commonly pink. East. and West. Wash.; streambanks, sandy soil in meadows and road-sides, and open woods in lowlands and foothills. Late spring and summer.

INTERIOR STRAWBERRY (*Fragaria vesca*) Flowers white to pinkish. East. and West. Wash.; sandy meadows, ditches, and roadsides, as well as stream-banks and moist, open woods. Mid spring to early summer.

GEUMS (*Geum*) (Color Plate 25)

Plants with mostly basal, pinnately-divided leaves. Leaflets often increasing in size toward tip of leaf. Foliage often thick and bushy. Flowers similar to those of the cinquefoils.

1. Sepals turned downward, not surrounding the petals.
LARGE-LEAVED GEUM
1. Sepals not turned downward, but upright and surrounding the petals.....2
2. Petals erect, producing a cup-shaped flower; stem leaves opposite.
THREE-FLOWERED GUEM
2. Petals spreading, producing a flat flower; stem leaves alternate.........3
3. Plants smaller, seldom more than 12 inches; leaflets about the same size (other than a few very small ones) on a stalk.............ROSS'S GEUM
3. Plants larger, more than 16 inches; outer leaflets on stalk much larger than lower ones...MARSH GEUM

*　　*　　*

LARGE-LEAVED GEUM (*Geum macrophyllum*) Plants tall and leafy, to 36 inches. Leaves large, irregularly lobed; foliage rough-hairy. Flowers yellow, 5-petalled, with single blooms or small clusters at ends of branches. East. and West. Wash.; moist woods, meadows, and stream sides from lowland to subalpine. Late spring and summer.

THREE-FLOWERED GEUM (*Geum triflorum*) Plants to 12 inches with finely-dissected leaves and reddish stems. Calyx of 5 sepals, bell shaped, dull wine-red or pinkish, and nodding; cream-colored petals inconspicuous. Flowers in 3's at tip of each stem. Seed heads in attractive, feather-like plumes. East. and West. Wash.; moist areas in lowlands (including sagebrush) up to the sub-alpine ridges of the mountains. Late spring and summer.

ROSS'S GEUM (*Geum rossii*) Plants to 12 inches. Leaves finely divided. Flowers yellow, large, and flat with spreading petals. East. and West. Wash.; rocky meadows and slopes in the high mountains. Summer.

MARSH GEUM (*Geum rivale*) Plants large, to 20 inches. Leaflets relatively few per leaf, with terminal 3 leaflets much larger than others. Flowers yellow to pink. Northwest. Wash.; moist places, such as streamsides, wet meadows, bogs, and the shores of ponds and lakes. Mid summer.

CINQUEFOILS (*Potentilla*) (Color Plate 26)

Flowers flat or slightly dished, yellow in most species; 5 petals, rounded, often notched. Green calyx appears to be 10-lobed—actually 5 lobes alternating with 5 smaller, narrow bractlets. Handsome leaves, always compound—pinnate in some species, palmate in others. These flowers are often mistaken for buttercups (*Ranunculus*), but the cinquefoils have non-waxy petals which are often notched and the "extra" calyx of bracts. Also, the cinquefoils tend to have a somewhat higher growth form. A large and somewhat difficult group —rely on the key.

1. Flowers purple or dark reddish.................MARSH CINQUEFOIL
1. Flowers not purple or reddish.....................................2

Figure 30.
The partridge foot-like foliage of *Luetkea*. (Yaich)

144

2. Plants more or less shrubby.................SHRUBBY CINQUEFOIL
2. Plants not shrubby 3
3. Plants annual or biennial, without stout rootstock; stamens 10-20.......4
3. Plants perennial with stout rootstocks; stamens 20-30................6
4. Leaflets less than 3/8 inch long............NEWBERRY'S CINQUEFOIL
4. Leaflets more than 3/8 inch long.................................5
5. Plants sticky-hairy; leaflets only slightly longer than broad.
BIENNIAL CINQUEFOIL
5. Plants woolly and not sticky; leaflets much longer than broad.
STREAMBANK CINQUEFOIL
6. Flowers borne singly on non-leaf-bearing stems; often with runners.....7
6. Flowers borne severally on often leaf-bearing flowering stems; plants without runners 8
7. Occurring mainly east of the Cascades......SILVER-WEED CINQUEFOIL
7. Occurring mostly near salt water...............PACIFIC CINQUEFOIL
8. Leaves pinnate; usually not more than 11 leaflets; stamens 25 or more...9
8. Leaves, particularly the upper ones, palmate; if pinnate, then usually with more than 11 leaflets; stamens usually 20........................10
9. Flower clusters consisting of tightly bunched flowers and their stems.
CONVALLARIA CINQUEFOIL
9. Flower clusters not tightly bunched, but the flowering stems spreading, and not vertical...............................STICKY CINQUEFOIL
10. Basal leaves mostly pinnate with odd number of leaflets; leaflets usually not arising at or very near the tips of the petioles....................11
10. Basal leaves usually arising at or very near the tip of the petioles and not pinnate...13
11. Leaves and stems very hairy; leaves white-woolly beneath.
SLENDER CINQUEFOIL
11. Leaves and stems not very hairy; leaves not white-woolly beneath.....12
12. Plants smaller, less than 12 inches tall.
MOUNTAIN MEADOW CINQUEFOIL
12. Plants larger, more than 12 inches tall......DRUMMOND'S CINQUEFOIL
13. Basal leaves with 3 leaflets....................RAINIER CINQUEFOIL
13. Basal leaves with 5 or more leaflets............................14
14. Plants larger, usually more than 16 inches tall and leaflets more than 1¼ inches long............................SLENDER CINQUEFOIL
14. Plants smaller, usually less than 16 inches tall and leaflets less than 1¼ inches long...................MOUNTAIN MEADOW CINQUEFOIL

*   *   *

MARSH CINQUEFOIL (*Potentilla palustris*) Stems prostrate with only the tips erect. Plants with stolons. Upper leaves divided into 3-7 leaflets. Flowers reddish to purple. West. Wash.; wet meadows, bogs, and stream and lake margins. Summer.

SHRUBBY CINQUEFOIL (*Potentilla fruticosa*) Stems woody; flowers yellow; leaves silky and grayish green; flowers borne singly in leaf axils. East. and West. Wash.; mostly in subalpine areas in the mountains. Summer.

145

NEWBERRY'S CINQUEFOIL (*Potentilla newberryi*) Flowers whitish to creamy white. East. Wash.; shores of vernal ponds in lowlands. Mid spring to mid summer.

BIENNIAL CINQUEFOIL (*Potentilla biennis*) Petals pale yellow, shorter than the calyx. East. Wash.; wastelands, moist meadows, and sandy places along water in the lowlands. Late spring and summer.

STREAMBANK CINQUEFOIL (*Potentilla rivalis*) Plants with slender, leafy stems to 20 inches with leafy clusters of flowers throughout. Leaves 3-cleft. East. Wash.; banks of streams and lakes. Late spring and summer. Flowers yellow.

SILVER-WEED CINQUEFOIL (*Potentilla anserina*) Plants with long stolons. Leaves silky-white above, all basal, and 9 or more in number. Flowers yellow. East. Wash.; wet meadows and stream and lake margins in lowlands. Late spring and summer.

PACIFIC CINQUEFOIL (*Potentilla pacifica*) Plants stemless, creeping by long stolons (runners). Basal leaves with numerous leaflets. Flowers single, yellow, and borne on long, slender stalks. West. Wash.; beaches and sand dunes, as well as marshes and creek banks near salt water. Late spring and summer.

CONVALLARIA CINQUEFOIL (*Potentilla arguta*) Plants tall, to 32 inches. Sepals relatively large, petals pale yellow, creamy white, or whitish, in very narrow inflorescence. East. Wash.; moist, grassy swales. Late spring to mid summer.

STICKY CINQUEFOIL (*Potentilla glandulosa*) Plants to 28 inches with reddish, sometimes greenish, glandular stems. Flowers yellow to whitish. East. and West. Wash.; moist places in grasslands and open woods. Late spring to mid summer.

SLENDER CINQUEFOIL (*Potentilla gracilis*) Plants tall, to 24 inches. Under-surface of leaves covered with silky white hairs; leaves cleft to 5-9 segments, each 1½-2½ inches long. Flowers yellow. East. and West. Wash.; variable, dry to moist habitats in lowlands (grass and sagebrush), as well as the forested and subalpine areas of mountains. Summer.

MOUNTAIN MEADOW CINQUEFOIL (*Potentilla diversifolia*) Plants to 18 inches, with downy foliage and leaves whitish-silky below which are cleft to 5-7 leaflets. Flowers yellow. East. and West. Wash.; middle to high elevations in the mountains, along streams and on meadows and rocky ridges. Summer.

DRUMMOND'S CINQUEFOIL (*Potentilla drummondii*) Plants to 24 inches and very leafy. Three distal leaflets usually partly fused at their bases. Teeth on leaves long and narrow. Flowers yellow. Cascades and Olympics; moist meadows in subalpine and alpine areas of high mountains. Summer.

RAINIER CINQUEFOIL (*Potentilla flabellifolia*) Plants to 14 inches. Leaflets usually 3 in number, spreading fan-like. Flowers yellow, similar in appearance to buttercups, but possessing green sepals and notched petals. East. and West. Wash.; wet habitats in subalpine meadows and streamsides, as well as drier places on ridges and rock slides in the higher mountains; common. Summer.

Chapter 24—The Pea Family (*Leguminosae*)

Members of this family are herbs, shrubs, or trees with alternate, compound leaves and perfect, but irregular flowers. Calyx or 4-5 sepals, sometimes 2-lipped. Petals 5, and unequal in size and shape. The upper petal is broad and called the *banner* or *standard,* the two lateral petals are the *wings,* and the lower or front petals are united to form the *keel.* Stamens 10; pistils 1. This large family contains many species of commercial or ornamental importance to man, but only native wildflower species are treated here. (Color Plates 26-29)

1. Fertile stamens 5 in number; flowers very small and not typically "legume-like". . . . . .WESTERN PRAIRIE-CLOVER
1. Fertile stamens usually 10 in number; flowers typically "legume-like". . .2

2. Stamens separate; leaves 3-foliate (in groups of 3's) and flowers yellow.
GOLDEN PEA
2. Stamens united; leaves variable, but if 3-foliate, then the flowers not yellow. 3

3. Leaves dotted with numerous small glands. 4
3. Leaves usually not thickly dotted with small glands. 5

4. Leaves numerous on a stem and pinnately arranged. . . . .WILD LICORICE
4. Leaves mostly 3-foliate. . . . . .PSORALEAS (*Psoralea*)

5. Leaves palmately compound, with leaflets numbering 3-17. 6
5. Leaves not palmately compound. 7

6. Flowers in long racemes. . . . . .LUPINES (*Lupinus*)
6. Flowers in heads or head-like spikes or racemes. . . .CLOVERS (*Trifolium*)

7. Keel usually as long as, or longer than, the wings.
SWEET-BROOMS (*Hedysarum*)
7. Keel usually shorter than the wings. 8

8. Leaves pinnate and even-numbered on a leaf-bearing stem (rachis). 9
8. Leaves pinnate and odd-numbered on rachis, there being a terminal leaflet. 10

9. Style flattened and hairy (or partly so) on the upper side. .PEAS (*Lathyrus*)
9. Style slender (not flattened) and hairy near the tip only. . .VETCHES (*Vicia*)

10. Flowers borne in axils or arranged in small heads or umbels.
LOTUSES (*Lotus*)
10. Flowers borne in spikes or racemes. 11

11. Stalks of flowers leafless, arising from plant base.
STEMLESS LOCOS (*Oxytropis*)
11. Stalks of flowers arising from leafy stems or branches.
LOCOWEEDS (*Astragalus*)

*　　*　　*

WESTERN PRAIRIE-CLOVER (*Petalostemon ornatum*) Plants to 24 inches with leaves containing 5-7 pinnately-arranged leaflets and tight, thick spikes of small, pinkish or reddish flowers. East. Wash.; dry, rocky, or sandy places in sagebrush. Late spring and early summer. (Color Plate 28)

GOLDEN PEA (*Thermopsis montana*) Plants slender and upright, to 3 feet, topped by long racemes of golden, pea-like flowers, about 3/4 inch long.

Figure 31.
Golden peas, *Thermopsis*. (Larrison)

Smooth, bright green foliage; leaves with 3 leaflets, clover-like. Plants spreading by underground stems. East. and West. Wash.; dry to moist, open places in lowlands, foothills, and intermediate montane areas, such as forest clearings and burns. Late spring and summer. (Color Plate 28) (Fig. 31)

WILD LICORICE (*Glycyrrhiza lepidota*) Plants tall, to 3 feet; leaves pinnately divided into 11-19 leaflets. Tiny, greenish-white flowers in dense, head-like raceme. Seed pods covered with hooked bristles. East. Wash.; waste, disturbed land and streambanks. Late spring and summer. In same genus as the true licorice. Northwest Indians used the wild plant—chewing it as well as eating the roots raw or roasted.

PSORALEAS (*Psoralea*)

Plants with slender, branching stems; upright or decumbent; leaves in 3 leaflets; flowers loose, shaggy heads of legume-type florets.

1. Flowers more than 3/8 inch long; leaflets oval-shaped...CALIFORNIA TEA
1. Flowers less than 3/8 inch long; leaflets long and narrow.
LANCE-LEAVED PSORALEA

*   *   *

CALIFORNIA TEA (*Psoralea physodes*) Leaves ovate-pointed. Banner yellowish; keel purple-tipped. West. Wash.; cut-over land and burns in forested areas. Late spring and early summer. Crushed leaves are aromatic.

LANCE-LEAVED PSORALEA (*Psoralea lanceolata*) Leaflets long and narrow. Flowers whitish; keel tipped with purple. East. Wash.; sandy places in sagebrush. Late spring and summer.

LUPINES (*Lupinus*) (Color Plate 27)

Plants with beautiful and distinctive leaves containing many leaflets radiating in a circle from the tip of a long petiole. Leaves mostly basal. Leaflets folded lengthwise in bud stage. Pea-like flowers in upright, terminal racemes.

1. Plants annual, with slender, weak taproot..........................2
1. Plants perennial with well-developed rootstocks....................5
2. Seeds 2 or 1..3
2. Seeds usually 4 or more.......................................4
3. Peduncles of flower racemes equaling length of leaf petioles.
RED-FLOWERED LUPINE
3. Peduncles of flower racemes shorter than leaf petioles.....LOW LUPINE
4. Keel slender, pointed, and sharply upturned........BICOLORED LUPINE
4. Keel blunt and not sharply upturned........SMALL-FLOWERED LUPINE
5. Banner hairy on the back, or the calyx with prominent dorsal spur above the pedicel...6
5. Banner not conspicuously hairy on the back; calyx not spurred.........9
6. Calyx spurred...................................SPURRED LUPINE
6. Calyx not spurred 7
7. Flowers borne in tightly-packed racemes; pedicels less than 3/16 inch long.....................................WOOLLY-LEAVED LUPINE
7. Flowers borne in open racemes; pedicels more than 3/16 inch long.....8

149

8. Flowers usually yellow; leaflets more than 2⅜ inches long.
SABINE'S LUPINE

8. Flowers usually blue (though sometimes yellow or white); leaflets less than 2⅜ inches long. . . . . .SILKY LUPINE

9. Banner reflexed (turned back) only at base. .SULFUR-FLOWERED LUPINE

9. Banner strongly reflexed. 10

10. Flowers usually yellow (rarely purplish). . . . . .SABINE'S LUPINE

10. Flowers usually not yellow. 11

11. Prostrate plants occurring entirely along saltwater beaches.
SEASHORE LUPINE

11. Plants not as above. 12

12. Stems commonly branched with floral racemes at tips of branches; leaves on main stems averaging 8 or more. 13

12. Stems usually unbranched; leaves on main stems averaging less than 8.15

13. Young leaves more or less silky. . . . . .RIVERBANK LUPINE

13. Young leaves thinly hairy, but not silky. 14

14. Banner and wings narrow; keel mostly exposed.SICKLE-KEELED LUPINE

14. Banner and wings broad; keel mostly hidden. . .BROAD-LEAVED LUPINE

15. Plants low and spreading; less than 12-14 inches tall. . . .PRAIRIE LUPINE

15. Plants taller, more than 12 inches tall. 16

16. Leaflets oblanceolate and rounded near the tip.STONY-GROUND LUPINE

16. Leaves lanceolate and tapering to tip. 17

17. Leaflets conspicuously hairy on upper surface. . . . . . . .WYETH'S LUPINE

17. Leaflets glabrous (smooth) on upper surface. . . .LARGE-LEAVED LUPINE

*   *   *

RED-FLOWERED LUPINE (*Lupinus microcarpus*) Plants to 16 inches with small leaves and large, yellow, pinkish, or reddish flowers. East. and West. Wash.; variable, moist to dry soils. Late spring to mid summer.

LOW LUPINE (*Lupinus pusillus*) Plants low (to 8 inches) with very hairy stems and light blue to deep bluish-purple flowers. East. Wash.; mostly on dunes and surrounding sandy areas. Late spring and early summer.

BICOLORED LUPINE (*Lupinus bicolor*) Plants hairy, to 16 inches. Flowers bluish, with white, purple-dotted center in the banners. West. Wash. and Columbia Gorge; open areas. Mid spring to mid summer.

SMALL-FLOWERED LUPINE (*Lupinus micranthus*) Plants to 16 inches with brownish-hairy foliage and small flowers that are bluish with white center in the banners. West. Wash. and Columbia Gorge; dry, rocky prairies. Spring.

SPURRED LUPINE (*Lupinus laxiflorus*) Plants to 20 inches with loose, spreading branches and flowers that may be whitish, pale bluish, pink, violet, reddish, or purple. Plants in our area mainly blue, violet, or purple. Best identified by the blunt spur on upper side of calyx. East. Wash.; sagebrush, grassland, and yellow pine woods. Spring and early summer.

WOOLLY-LEAVED LUPINE (*Lupinus leucophyllus*) Plants tall, to 36 inches, with grayish or rust-colored foliage. Flowers white, pale lavender, or lilac, in a tight, massed spike. East. Wash.; sagebrush, grasslands, and yellow pine woods. Summer.

SABINE'S LUPINE (*Lupinus sabinii*)   Leaflets and leaf petioles very long. Flowers yellow, in open raceme. Blue Mountains of East. Wash.; yellow pine woods. Late spring and early summer.

SILKY LUPINE (*Lupinus sericeus*)   Plants to 20 inches with silky, mostly silvery hairs. Flowers blue to lavender, though rarely yellow or white (the latter in Asotin County). East. Wash.; open areas. Late spring and summer.

SULFUR-FLOWERED LUPINE (*Lupinus sulphureus*)   Plants to 32 inches with sparse foliage. Leaves with very long petioles. Raceme of relatively few flowers which are mostly yellow in color, less commonly bluish or purplish. East. and Southwestern Wash.; open hillsides. Spring and early summer.

SEASHORE LUPINE (*Lupinus littoralis*)   Plants matted, with prostrate, branching stems and bluish or purplish flowers. West. Wash.; saltwater beaches. Late spring and summer.

RIVERBANK LUPINE (*Lupinus rivularis*)   Plants tall, to 40 inches, with erect stems arising from woody, decumbent bases. Flowers bluish. West. Wash. and Columbia Gorge; rocky prairies, open woodlands, and riverbanks in lowlands. Mid spring to mid summer.

SICKLE-KEELED LUPINE (*Lupinus albicaulis*)   Plants to 36 inches with somewhat sprawling lower stems. Flowers white to bluish-pink. West. Wash.; dry, open places. Summer. Calyx with prominent sickle-shaped keel.

BROAD-LEAVED LUPINE (*Lupinus latifolius*)   Plants to 40 inches with relatively broad, blunt-tipped leaves and bluish or lavender flowers. Cascades and West. Wash.; open, rocky places and open woods. Summer.

PRAIRIE LUPINE (*Lupinus lepidus*)   Plants to 14 inches, or more commonly mat-like in growth form. Foliage silky gray (sometimes rusty) with bluish flowers densely grouped in short racemes. East. and West. Wash.; dry prairies and ridges from lowlands to subalpine sections in the mountains. Summer.

STONY-GROUND LUPINE (*Lupinus saxosus*)   Plants to 10 inches with brownish-hairy foliage and relatively broad, short, blunt-tipped leaves. Flowers dark violet with yellow-centered banners. East. Wash.; dry, basaltic rimrock. Mid to late spring.

WYETH'S LUPINE (*Lupinus wyethii*)   Plants to 18 inches with deep violet to purple flowers with occasionally a yellowish or white-centered banner. East. Wash.; lowland sagebrush to montane and subalpine forests. Late spring and early summer.

LARGE-LEAVED LUPINE (*Lupinus polyphyllus*)   Plants tall, to 40-50 inches with numerous, large, smooth to hairy leaves. Flowers numerous, blue or violet, on tall spike. East. and West. Wash.; moist habitats in meadows, forests, and along streambanks from lowlands up into the mountains. Summer. The tallest and handsomest of the lupines and the species from which most of the cultivated varieties have been developed.

Figure 32.
Big-headed clover, a spring special of the dry country. (Yaich)

CLOVERS (*Trifolium*) (Color Plate 28) (Fig. 32)

Legumes characterized by leaves palmately divided into usually 3 leaflets and roundish, pleasantly-scented flower heads.

1. Plants annual, with slender taproots....................................2
1. Plants perennial, growing from prominent rootstocks................10

2. Prominent circle of fused bracts (involucre) at base of the flower cluster..3
2. Flowering heads without involucre...............................8

3. Involucre covered with long hairs...............................4
3. Involucre more or less smooth—non-hairy.........................5

4. Calyx hairy.....................................WOOLLY CLOVER
4. Calyx generally without hairs (i.e., glabrous).........THIMBLE CLOVER

5. Lower calyx teeth (lobes) 2- or 3-cleft.......WIDE-COLLARED CLOVER
5. Lower calyx teeth not cleft....................................6

6. Leaflets obovate, being widest near tip; only about twice as long as broad.
WHITE-TIPPED CLOVER
6. Leaflets lanceolate, several times longer than broad..................7

7. Flowering heads usually less than 3/8 inch wide; few flowers in head (less than 8) ....FEW-FLOWERED CLOVER
7. Flowering heads more than 3/8 inch wide; many flowers in head (more than 8) ....SAND CLOVER

8. Calyx covered with prominent hairs..............MACRAE'S CLOVER
8. Calyx not, or only partly, covered with prominent hairs...............9

9. Leaves obovate ....SLENDER CLOVER
9. Leaflets linear...................................PINOLE CLOVER

10. Prominent involucre at base of flowering head.WORMSKJOLD'S CLOVER
10. Flowering head without prominent involucre.......................11

11. Leaflets more than 3 in a cluster................BIG-HEADED CLOVER
11. Leaflets usually 3 in a cluster...................................12

12. Calyx very hairy...13
12. Calyx smooth (glabrous) or only slightly hairy.....................15

13. Corolla bending sharply downward at calyx to form a sharp angle with it.
WOOLLY-HEADED CLOVER
13. Corolla extending straight out from calyx and not forming an angle with it..14

14. Flowers usually purple; leaflets less than 3/4 inch long.
MULTIPEDUNCULATE CLOVER
14. Flowers usually yellowish; leaflets more than 3/4 inch long.
LONG-STALKED CLOVER

15. Flowering head noticeably longer than broad......DOUGLAS'S CLOVER
15. Flowering head roundish, about as broad as long.
LONG-STALKED CLOVER

*   *   *

WOOLLY CLOVER (*Trifolium microcephalum*) Plants prostrate to erect, with stems up to 2 feet long. Involucre hairy with spine-tipped lobes. Flowering

153

heads small, white to pinkish. East. and West. Wash.; moist meadows and streambanks, as well as dry slopes. Mid spring to mid summer.

THIMBLE CLOVER (*Trifolium microdon*) Basal part of stem prostrate, while terminal portion erect. Teeth on calyx lobes short, not spiny. Heads small, white or pale pink. West. Wash.; meadows and sandy areas. Spring and early summer.

WIDE-COLLARED CLOVER (*Trifolium cyathiferum*) Plants erect, to 20 inches. Leaflets blunt-tipped. Calyx broad, saucer-shaped, projecting beyond edges of flowering head. Flowers white, yellowish, or pinkish. East. Wash.; meadows and sandy areas. Late spring to mid summer.

WHITE-TIPPED CLOVER (*Trifolium variegatum*) Plants prostrate or erect with stems to 30 inches. Leaflets with spiny teeth. Flowers purple with white tips. West. (mostly) and East. Wash.; meadows, dry to moist. Mid spring to mid summer.

FEW-FLOWERED CLOVER (*Trifolium oliganthum*) Plants partially erect, to 8 inches. Leaflets elongate and sharply-toothed. Flowers few in head, lavender to purple, often with white tips. West. Wash.; moist to dry, rocky meadows. Early spring to mid summer.

SAND CLOVER (*Trifolium tridentatum*) Plants mostly erect, to 36 inches. Leaflets very narrow and toothed. Involucre with very long teeth. Flowers few in head, purple. West. Wash.; fields and grassy hillsides. Mid spring to mid summer.

MACRAE'S CLOVER (*Trifolium macraei*) Plants erect, to 12 inches. Flowering heads roundish to somewhat oblong; purple, pink, or whitish. West. Wash.; fields and grassy, weedy hillsides. Mid spring to early summer.

SLENDER CLOVER (*Trifolium gracilentum*) Plants upright, to 24 inches. Leaflets with terminal notch. Tip of peduncle often extending beyond flowering head which is white to purple. West. Wash.; grassy hillsides. Spring and early summer.

PINOLE CLOVER (*Trifolium bifidum*) Plants more or less erect, to 16 inches. Leaflets notched at tip. Calyx with sparsely-haired teeth. Flowers pink. Columbia Gorge and Southwestern Wash.; grassy hillsides. Mid spring to early summer.

WORMSKJOLD'S CLOVER (*Trifolium wormskjoldii*) Plants erect, to 12 inches. Flowering heads flattish and reddish purple, with often white tips. East. and West. Wash.; moist places along streams, in marshes, and on sand dunes along the sea coast. Late spring and summer.

BIG-HEADED CLOVER (*Trifolium macrocephalum*) Flower heads very large, white to pinkish. Leaflets varying in number, usually from 5 to 9. Plants tending to sprawl on ground. East. Wash.; open places in sagebrush and yellow pine woods in lowlands and in lower mountains. Mid spring to early summer.

WOOLLY-HEADED CLOVER (*Trifolium eriocephalum*) Plants to 24 inches. Leaflets long and narrow. Flower heads large, oblong, with hairy calyxes. Flowers yellowish, pinkish, or reddish. East. and West. Wash.; grassy hillsides and weedy fields. Late spring to mid summer.

MULTIPEDUNCULATE CLOVER (*Trifolium multipedunculatum*) Plants small, to 4 inches. Stems often rhizome-like with roots. Flowers red to purplish.

Central Cascades; subalpine ridges and dry, open slopes in the mountains. Summer.

LONG-STALKED CLOVER (*Trifolium longipes*) Plants often trailing with upright branches to 12 inches. Leaflets lanceolate with very small teeth. Flowers yellowish to purplish. East. and West. Wash.; moist places in lowlands and mountains. Summer.

DOUGLAS'S CLOVER (*Trifolium douglasii*) Plants erect to 32 inches, with long, narrow leaflets, and large reddish purple heads. East. Wash.; moist meadows and streamsides. Early to mid summer.

NOTE: In Swakane Canyon, which runs from the Columbia River up toward Entiat Ridge, there grows on the grassy hillsides below the yellow pine a very beautiful clover with rose-red to deep orchid flowers. This is Thompson's Clover (*Trifolium thompsonii*), named for John W. Thompson, long-time field student and photographer of Washington wildflowers and contributor of a number of photos to this guide.

SWEET-BROOMS (*Hedysarum*) (Color Plate 27)

Plants with several stems, 1 to 2 feet tall, growing from stout taproot. Flowers in long, upright racemes at tips of stems. Leaves pinnately divided, odd-numbered. The drooping pods are divided into rounded segments, with 1 seed each.

1. Leaflets oval-shaped, tapering abruptly to the tip.
                                          WESTERN SWEET-BROOM
1. Leaflets more elongate than ovate, tapering gradually to the tip.
                                          NORTHERN SWEET-BROOM

                    *   *   *

WESTERN SWEET-BROOM (*Hedysarum occidentale*) Flowers red to purple. East. and West. Wash.; subalpine areas of higher mountains. Summer.

NORTHERN SWEET-BROOM (*Hedysarum boreale*) Flowers pink to reddish purple. East. Wash.; open areas in the mountains. Summer.

PEAS (*Lathyrus*) (Color Plate 27)

Flowers and leaves very similar to those of the domestic peas. Somewhat similar to the vetches, but the flowers larger and fewer in the inflorescence. The beard in peas is the set of hairs along the upper side of the style from tip to base.

1. No coiling, twining tendrils at tips of stems or branches 2
1. Coiling, twining tendrils present at tips of stems and branches 5

2. Flowers usually single or not more than 2 in a cluster . . . . .TORREY'S PEA
2. Flowers usually more than 2 in a cluster (raceme) 3

3. Plants occurring on sand dunes along sea coast; foliage densely hairy; leaf stems flat . . . . .GRAY BEACH PEA
3. Plants not occurring on dunes along sea coast; nor very hairy; leaf stems not flat 4

4. Flowers more than 3/4 inch long . . . . .NEVADA PEA
4. Flowers less than 3/4 inch long .LANZWERT'S PEA

5. Plants occurring on coastal sand dunes or in salt marshes; stems winged or leaf stipules nearly as long as, or longer than, the leaflets 6
5. Plants usually not occurring on sand dunes along sea coast, or without winged stems or stipules approaching size of leaflets 7

6. Stems winged; stipules definitely shorter than the leaflets; leaflets usually 6 on a leaf . . . . .MARSH PEA
6. Stems not winged; stipules about same size as, or longer than, the leaflets; leaflets often more than 6 in number . . . . .JAPANESE BEACH PEA

7. Flowers blue or red 8
7. Flowers white 11

8. Leaflets 10-16 in a leaf; flowers in clusters (racemes) 5-13 in number.
LEAFY PEA
8. Leaflets seldom more than 10 in a leaf; flowers usually less than 5 in a cluster 9

9. Lower calyx tooth shorter than the calyx tube 10
9. Lower calyx tooth longer than calyx tube . . . . .FEW-FLOWERED PEA

10. Leaflets oval-shaped, about 2 times as long as wide . . . . . . .NEVADA PEA
10. Leaflets long and narrow (lanceolate) and several times longer than wide.
LANZWERT'S PEA

11. Lateral calyx lobes (teeth) very broad at base . . . . .NEVADA PEA
11. Lateral calyx lobes not very broad at base, but slightly constricted 12

12. Leaflets 6 in a leaf; occurring in Eastern Washington. . . .WOODLAND PEA
12. Leaflets 8-12 in a leaf; occurring in Western Washington.
COMMON PACIFIC PEA

*   *   *

TORREY'S PEA (*Lathyrus torreyi*)   Plants prostrate to erect; foliage softly hairy. Leaflets 10-16 in number. Inflorescences with only 1 or 2 flowers, which are lilac to bluish. West. Wash.; open places in the lowlands, such as prairies, meadows, and forest clearings. Late spring and early summer.

GRAY BEACH PEA (*Lathyrus littoralis*)   Plants prostrate to erect; foliage silky hairy. Leaflets 4-8 in number. Inflorescences with 2-10 flowers which are pink, red, purple, or white. West. Wash.; coastal sand dunes. Late spring and early summer.

NEVADA PEA (*Lathyrus nevadensis*)   Plants to 32 inches with sparsely-hairy foliage. 2-10 flowers per inflorescence; leaflets 4-10. Flowers blue, reddish, or white. East. and West. Wash.; clearings and open places in woods. Late spring and early summer.

LANZWERT'S PEA (*Lathyrus lanzwertii*)   Plants climbing or trailing; foliage sparsely hairy to smooth. Leaflets 4-12; flowers 2-8 per cluster: pale lavender to violet or white. East. Wash.; sagebrush and yellow pine woods. Late spring and early summer.

MARSH PEA (*Lathyrus palustris*)   Plants climbing; foliage smooth to densely hairy. Leaflets 6; flowers 2-5 in a cluster and pink to bluish purple or white. West. Wash.; dunes and tide flats and marshes along coastal salt water. Mid spring to mid summer.

JAPANESE BEACH PEA (*Lathyrus japonicus*)   Plants erect or climbing; smooth to hairy. Leaflets 6-12; flowers reddish purple to bluish and 2-8 in a raceme. West. Wash.; dunes and sandy areas along coastal beaches. Late spring and summer.

LEAFY PEA (*Lathyrus polyphyllus*)   Plants erect to climbing; mostly smooth. Leaflets 10-16; flowers purplish, bluish, or whitish and 5-13 in a raceme. West. Wash.; prairies and open woods; lowlands to foothills. Late spring and early summer.

FEW-FLOWERED PEA (*Lathyrus pauciflorus*)   Plants erect, to 24 inches. Leaves thick, leathery; leaflets 8-10. Flowers lilac or orchid, with whitish or bluish keel; 4-7 in raceme. East. Wash.; sagebrush, grasslands, and yellow pine and open fir woods; lowlands and lower montane areas. Mid spring to early summer.

WOODLAND PEA (*Lathyrus ochroleucus*)   Plants erect, to 32 inches; foliage smooth. Leaflets 6. Flowers white to yellowish white and 6-14 per raceme. East. Wash.; open woods. Late spring and early summer.

COMMON PACIFIC PEA (*Lathyrus vestitus*)   Plants erect to climbing with branches to 40 inches. Foliage smooth to slightly hairy. Leaflets 10. Flowers 5-20 in a raceme; cream colored, purple, or pinkish; banner and wings often of different colors. West. Wash.; open brush and woods. Mid spring to early summer.

VETCHES (*Vicia*) (Color Plate 29) (Fig. 33)

Trailing or climbing plants with numerous pinnately-arranged leaflets. The beard in vetches consists of a tuft of hairs at the tip of the style. Leaf tips with prominent tendrils.

1. Plants smaller, less than 30 inches tall; leaflets 8-20 in a leaf.
   AMERICAN VETCH
1. Plants larger, more than 40 inches tall; leaflets usually more than 20 in a leaf. . . . . .GIANT VETCH

*   *   *

AMERICAN VETCH (*Vicia americana*)   Flowers blue. East. and West. Wash.; roadsides, fields, and other open places. Late spring to mid summer.

GIANT VETCH (*Vicia gigantea*)   Flowers yellow or orange to light purple. West. Wash.; moist, open places in woods, as clearings and along water. Late spring and early summer.

NOTE: Various other vetches, all introduced, have escaped to a feral condition and may be encountered; the reader may find it desirable to identify vetches to the genus only.

LOTUSES (*Lotus*) (Color Plate 27)

Relatively small plants with a few pinnately-arranged leaflets and flowers often in small umbels, arising from leaf axils. Some variability in the genus, however. The axillary umbels make the best character for the genus.

1. Plants annual, with slender taproot; flowers solitary or in groups of 2 2
1. Plants perennial, with stout roots; flowers several and borne in umbels 4

Figure 33.
Vetch, *Vicia,* one of the most common weeds of the pea family. (Yaich)

158

2. Flowers more or less sessile (without peduncles) in axils of leaves.
MEADOW LOTUS
2. Flowers on definite peduncles as long as leaves......................3
3. Calyx teeth longer than the calyx tube.................PURSH'S LOTUS
3. Calyx teeth shorter than the calyx tube.......SMALL-FLOWERED LOTUS
4. All petals yellow...................................NEVADA LOTUS
4. All petals not yellow...5
5. Peduncle bract as a group of small leaflets located on peduncle well below
the flower cluster...............................THICK-LEAVED LOTUS
5. Peduncle bract small and, if present, located at or near base of flower
cluster 6
6. Flowers purplish or pinkish........................SEASIDE LOTUS
6. Flowers yellowish or whitish...........................BOG LOTUS

*   *   *

MEADOW LOTUS (*Lotus denticulatus*) Plants to 20 inches. Leaves with 2 terminal and 1-2 lateral leaflets, the latter usually on same side of petiole. Leaflets may be finely toothed. Flowers creamy, with purple-tipped banner. West. Wash. and Cascades; open, sandy places. Late spring and early summer.

PURSH'S LOTUS (*Lotus purshianus*) Plants hairy, with base of stem prostrate and distal part erect. Leaves with 3 leaflets. Flowers cream colored or pale yellow, tinged with reddish. East. and West. Wash.; sandy or rocky places in open or wooded areas in lowlands. Spring and summer.

SMALL-FLOWERED LOTUS (*Lotus micranthus*) Plants to 12 inches, with leaves having 3-6 leaflets. Flowers light yellow or pinkish, tinged with reddish, and borne singly on long stalks. West. Wash.; sandy areas from lowlands up into the mountains. Late spring and summer.

NEVADA LOTUS (*Lotus nevadensis*) Plants matted, with prostrate stems to 20 inches. Foliage grayish hairy, with 4-5 leaflets per leaf. Flowers few in an umbel; yellow, orange, or reddish. East. and West. Wash.; sandy, rocky places in lowlands. Late spring and summer.

THICK-LEAVED LOTUS (*Lotus crassifolius*) Plants prostrate to erect with stems as much as 36 inches long. Leaflets thick, oval, and 9-15 per leaf, and bright green in color. Flowers whitish or greenish yellow, tinged or spotted with purple. West. Wash. and Columbia Gorge; openings in moist woods and along streambanks. Late spring and early summer.

SEASIDE LOTUS (*Lotus formosissimus*) Plants mostly prostrate. Leaflets usually 5. Flowers purple, with yellow banners; borne in long-stalked umbels. West. Wash.; moist places in lowlands and foothills. Late spring and early summer.

BOG LOTUS (*Lotus pinnatus*) Plants to 16 inches with 5-9 leaflets. Flowers with banner and keel yellow and wings white or creamy; umbels borne on long stalks. East. and West. Wash.; moist places along streams and lakes. Late spring to mid summer.

159

STEMLESS LOCOS (*Oxytropis*) (Color Plate 28)

Plants similar to locoweeds but the leaves are mostly basal with the flowering stems only projecting above the ground. Leaves pinnately arranged; flowers in spikes or head-like racemes.

1. Flowers pale blue.....................DEFLEXED STEMLESS LOCO
1. Flowers not bluish..2
2. Flowers yellowish white; foliage grayish hairy, not glandular.
MEADOW STEMLESS LOCO
2. Flowers cream to reddish purple; foliage covered with warty, sticky glands.
STICKY STEMLESS LOCO

*   *   *

DEFLEXED STEMLESS LOCO (*Oxytropis deflexa*) Flowers pale blue. East. Wash.; moist areas along streams and in meadows in the foothills and mountains. Summer.

MEADOW STEMLESS LOCO (*Oxytropis campestris*) Flowers yellow or white. East. and West. Wash.; moist places in the mountains. Late spring and early summer.

STICKY STEMLESS LOCO (*Oxytropis viscida*) Flowers purple, except cream-colored in the Olympics. East. and West. Wash.; dry, rocky ridges in high mountains. Summer.

LOCOWEEDS (*Astragalus*) (Color Plate 26)

NOTE: This is a complex and difficult genus, and certain species in the following key will appear in several parts of it, due to their variability. Beginners may find it expedient to identify locoweeds to genus only.

1. Hairs on stems 2-branched.....................................2
1. Hairs on stem not 2-branched..................................3
2. Flowers larger; banner longer than 1/2 inch; keel blunt and more than 3/8 inch long...........................ASCENDING LOCOWEED
2. Flowers smaller; banner less than 1/2 inch; keel sharp-pointed and less than 3/8 inch long...........................STARVED LOCOWEED
3. Stipules opposite the lowermost nodes joined together and their common base surrounding the petiole.....................................4
3. Stipules opposite lowermost nodes not united by their bases..........19
4. Banner more than 5/8 inch long..................................5
4. Banner less than 5/8 inch long..................................8
5. Flowers erect, forming a tight flowering head........FIELD LOCOWEED
5. Flowers erect or spreading, but in a loose raceme..................6
6. Seed pod sessile or borne on a very short stalk (stipe).
LONG-LEAVED LOCOWEED
6. Seed pod borne on a noticeably long stalk (stipe)...................7
7. Pod borne erect on stem.....................LEIBERG'S LOCOWEED
7. Pod hanging downward from stem......THREAD-STALKED LOCOWEED
8. Banner more than 3/8 inch long..................................9
8. Banner less than 3/8 inch long..................................15

*   *   *

ASCENDING LOCOWEED (*Astragalus adsurgens*) Flowers white to purple.
East. Wash.; grasslands at low elevations and on foothills. Summer.

STARVED LOCOWEED (*Astragalus miser*) Flowers white to pale pink. East.
Wash.; moist grasslands and dry slopes from lowlands to subalpine. Late
spring to mid summer.

FIELD LOCOWEED (*Astragalus agrestis*)   Flowers purple to whitish. East. Wash.; moist areas from sagebrush to subalpine meadows. Summer.

LONG-LEAVED LOCOWEED (*Astragalus reventus*)   Flowers yellowish white to purplish. East. Wash.; sagebrush, rocky flats or scabland, grass slopes, and open yellow pine woods. Mid spring to early summer.

LEIBERG'S LOCOWEED (*Astragalus leibergii*)   Flowers whitish. East-central Cascades; rocky sagebrush to yellow pine woods of lowlands and foothills. Mid spring to early summer.

THREAD-STALKED LOCOWEED (*Astragalus filipes*)   Flowers creamy. East. Wash.; sagebrush in lowlands and foothills. Late spring and early summer.

COTTON'S LOCOWEED (*Astragalus cottonii*)   Flowers yellowish white with purplish keels. Olympic Mountains; high, rocky, alpine ridges. Summer.

WHITNEY'S LOCOWEED (*Astragalus whitneyi*)   Flowers yellowish white, tinged with lavender or purple. Eastern Cascades and East. Wash.; dry, open, rocky ridges. Late spring and summer.

LYALL'S LOCOWEED (*Astragalus lyalii*)   Flowers white to purplish. East. Wash.; sand dunes and sagebrush in lowlands. Late spring and early summer.

SMALL-POD LOCOWEED (*Astragalus microcystis*)   Flowers pink, lavender, to deep purple. East. Wash.; grassland and yellow pine woods of lowlands and foothills. Late spring to mid summer.

COLUMBIA LOCOWEED (*Astragalus succumbens*)   Flowers pink, with purple tinges. East. Wash.; sagebrush and sandy areas of lowlands and foothills. Mid spring to early summer.

BECKWITH'S LOCOWEED (*Astragalus beckwithii*)   Flowers creamy white to pale yellow. East. Wash.; grassy, rocky places in foothills. Mid spring to early summer.

TWEEDY'S LOCOWEED (*Astragalus tweedyi*)   Flowers yellowish white to white. East. Wash.; sagebrush of lowlands and foothills. Late spring and early summer.

HILLSIDE LOCOWEED (*Astragalus collinus*)   Flowers creamy white to yellowish. East. Wash.; sagebrush and rocky grasslands. Late spring and early summer.

CURVED-POD LOCOWEED (*Astragalus curvicarpus*)   Flowers yellowish white. East. Wash.; sagebrush. Late spring to mid summer.

PURSH'S LOCOWEED (*Astragalus purshii*)   Flowers yellowish to deep purple. East. Wash.; sagebrush and grasslands in foothills and lower mountains. Mid spring to early summer.

MOTTLED LOCOWEED (*Astragalus lentiginosus*)   Flowers white to pinkish, often purple tipped. East. Wash.; sagebrush and grasslands of lowlands to subalpine ridges of mountains. Late spring to mid summer.

HAIRY LOCOWEED (*Astragalus inflexus*)   Flowers reddish purple. East. Wash.; sagebrush and foothills. Mid spring to mid summer.

WOODY-POD LOCOWEED (*Astragalus sclerocarpus*)   Flowers white to greenish white; wings sometimes pale purple. East. Wash.; sand dunes along Columbia River. Mid spring to early summer.

Figure 34.
Flowers closely follow the snow in many areas. (Larrison)

HOWELL'S LOCOWEED (*Astragalus howellii*) Flowers pale yellow to whitish yellow. East. Wash.; sagebrush. Mid spring to early summer.

SNAKE RIVER LOCOWEED (*Astragalus riparius*) Flowers yellowish white to greenish white. Southeastern Wash.; breaks and slopes along the Snake River. Late spring and early summer.

PALOUSE LOCOWEED (*Astragalus arrectus*) Flowers yellow to white. East. Wash.; sagebrush and grasslands, as well as yellow pine woods, particularly in the Palouse country. Late spring and early summer.

COIL-POD LOCOWEED (*Astragalus speirocarpus*) Flowers white to lavender or bluish. East. Wash.; sagebrush, particularly near Columbia River. Spring.

Chapter 25—The Geranium Family (*Geraniaceae*)

Members of this family, as represented here, are herbs with perfect, regular flowers and lobed or divided leaves. Sepals and petals, 5; fertile stamens, 10. Fruits often characterized by very long beaks, hence, an alternate common name of "cranesbill." Leaves reminiscent of the deeply-dissected foliage of many of the horticultural species. (Color Plate 29)

1. Petals less than 1/2 inch long.................CAROLINA GERANIUM
1. Petals more than 1/2 inch long....................................2
2. Flowers white to pale pink; inside surface of petals hairy at least half of their length............................RICHARDSON'S GERANIUM
2. Flowers pink to purple; inside surface of petals hairy on lower 1/3 of their length only, or not at all hairy....................................3
3. Petals not hairy on inner surface; Western Washington.
OREGON GERANIUM
3. Petals hairy on part of inner surface; Eastern Washington.
STICKY GERANIUM

*   *   *

CAROLINA GERANIUM (*Geranium carolinianum*) Plants to 20 inches. Flowers pinkish to purplish; borne in tight clusters. East. and West. Wash.; wooded and waste areas, where often common. Spring to mid summer.

RICHARDSON'S GERANIUM (*Geranium richardsonii*) Plants to 30 inches. Leaves very large and smooth. Flowers white to pinkish and borne on long stalks. East. Wash.; woods in lowlands and mountains. Summer.

OREGON GERANIUM (*Geranium oreganum*) Plants to 30 inches. Foliage smooth or hairy. Flowers red to purple. Southwest. Wash.; common in moist, open meadows and woods. Late spring to mid summer.

STICKY GERANIUM (*Geranium viscosissimum*) Plants to 30 inches. Foliage glandular-hairy and sticky. Flowers pink, purple, or white. East. Wash.; meadows and open woods in lowlands and mountains. Late spring and summer.

Figure 35.
The deep woods habitat of the wood sorrel, *Oxalis*. (Larrison)

Chapter 26—The Wood Sorrel Family (*Oxalidaceae*)

Members of this family are smallish plants with alternate, palmately-compound, 3-lobed, clover-like leaves and perfect, regular flowers. Petals and sepals 5; stamens 10. Leaves obcordate (heart-shaped with point at leaf stalk) and with prominent central vein. Leaflets folded in bud stage and tending to fold up at night. Juice of plant is watery and acidic. Common in dense, moist woods, especially rainforests, where the plants may form a ground cover. (Color Plate 29)

1. Plants with prominent leafy stems; flowers yellow. .WEEDY WOOD SORREL
1. Plants with basal leaves—no stems; flowers not yellow. 2

2. Floral stem (peduncle) with single flower; flowers whitish or pale lavender.
OREGON WOOD SORREL
2. Floral stem (peduncle) with several flowers; flowers white.
GREAT WOOD SORREL

*   *   *

WEEDY WOOD SORREL (*Oxalis stricta*) Plants erect, to 20 inches. Flowers yellow. East. and West. Wash.; common as a weed in waste and open places, especially west of the Cascades. Spring, summer, and early fall.

OREGON WOOD SORREL (*Oxalis oregana*) Leaves basal; flowering stems to 6 inches. Flowers single on long petioles; about 1½ inches wide, white to pink with darker veins; yellow spot at base of each petal. West. Wash. and Cascades; moist, dense woods. Spring to early fall.

GREAT WOOD SORREL (*Oxalis trilliifolia*) Leaves basal; flowering stems to 10 inches. Flowers white, in clusters of 3-8; smaller than in *O. oregana*. Petals notched at tip. West. Wash.; moist woods and open, grassy places, sea level to subalpine. Late spring and summer.

Figure 36.
Sand dunes, a favorite habitat of the flax, *Linum.* (Larrison)

168

Chapter 27—The Flax Family (*Linaceae*)

Members of this family are slender, tall (to 30 inches) herbs with thin, tough, fibrous stems, and small, narrow leaves. Flowers are perfect and regular; petals, sepals, and stamens, 5 each. Numerous small, linear leaves, only about 1 inch long, alternating closely up the stems. Flowers often brightly colored and showy. Linen thread derived from a cultivated species of this genus. (Color Plate 29)

1. Flowers yellow . . . . NORTHWESTERN YELLOW FLAX
1. Flowers blue . . . . WESTERN BLUE FLAX

*　　*　　*

NORTHWESTERN YELLOW FLAX (*Linum digynum*)　Plants to 16 inches. Lower leaves in pairs. Flowers yellow. East. Wash.; open, grassy places. Late spring to mid summer.

WESTERN BLUE FLAX (*Linum perenne*)　Plants tall, to 30 inches. Stems leafy. Flowers blue. East. and West. Wash.; open, arid places in lowlands and mountains. Late spring to mid summer.

Jones, George N. 1936　*A Botanical Survey of the Olympic Peninsula.* University of Washington Press.

Jones, George N. 1938　*The Flowering Plants and Ferns of Mount Rainier.* University of Washington Press.

Munz, Philip A. 1964　*Shore Wildflowers of California, Oregon and Washington.* University of California Press.

Nelson, Ruth A. 1969　*Handbook of Rocky Mountain Plants.* Dale Stuart King, Tucson.

Peck, Morton E. 1961　*A Manual of the Higher Plants of Oregon.* 2nd ed. Binfords and Mort.

Rickett, Harold W. 1971　*Wild Flowers of the United States: The Northwestern States.* McGraw-Hill Book Company (2 very large volumes; most species in color).

Stewart, Charles 1972　*Wildflowers of the Olympics.* Olympic Natural History Association.

St. John, Harold 1963　*Flora of Southeastern Washington and of Adjacent Idaho.* Outdoor Pictures 3rd ed.

Figure 37.
Skyline Drive, a beautiful wildflower area on the Washington-Idaho border. (Larrison)

170

Chapter 28—The Spurge Family (*Euphorbiaceae*)

Members of this family, as treated here, are herbs with alternate or opposite leaves, very small flowers which may contain both or a single sex, and whorls of petal-like, green bracts below the tiny flowers. Stamens 1 to many. Sap often milky. (Color Plate 30)

1. Plants with erect stems; leaves alternate. . RETICULATE-SEEDED SPURGE
1. Plants prostrate and mat-forming; leaves opposite 2

2. Leaves linear-oblong (more or less same width throughout); leaf margins entire and thickened . . . . .RIDGE-SEEDED SPURGE
2. Leaves ovate-oblong (not the same width throughout); leaf margin near tip toothed and not thickened. . . . . .THYME-LEAVED SPURGE

*   *   *

RETICULATE-SEEDED SPURGE (*Euphorbia spathulata*) Plants to 18 inches with finely-toothed leaves. Flowers greenish yellow, borne in forked clusters. East. Wash.; dry hillsides. Late spring to mid summer.

RIDGE-SEEDED SPURGE (*Euphorbia glyptosperma*) Leaves oblong, rather than widest at or near tip. Plants to 16 inches, though often prostrate. Flowers pink and white. East. Wash.; dry, open plains and foothills. Summer.

THYME-LEAVED SPURGE (*Euphorbia serpyllifolia*) Stems usually prostrate, to 12 inches long. Flowers white. East. Wash.; dry, open plains and foothills. Late spring to early autumn.

———————

To many persons, especially those who have never actually set foot in it, the region above timberline seems a drab, forbidding area, devoid of life and the realm of perpetual frost and snow. Investigation will reveal that such is not exactly the case. While it is true that winters are long and severe and the nights, even in summer, are cold, such places can be among the most interesting of wildflower habitats. Cold, shearing winds and short growing seasons have forced alpine plants to a few inches in height, often growing in dense mats along with mosses, lichens, and grasses. These plants make up collectively the alpine tundra, related through a number of species and genera, as well as growth habit, to the tundra of the far North. Though the plants may be small, their flowers are often large, so that a tundra field in full flower may present an aspect of stunning beauty. To fully enjoy these flowers, one must often lie down, hence the name "belly plants" which botanists have often given them.

The tundra flowers and their habitats are discussed in detail in the book, *Land Above the Trees: A Guide to American Alpine Tundra,* by Ann H. Zwinger and Beatrice E. Willard and published in 1972 by Harper and Row.

Chapter 29—The Touch-Me-Not Family (*Balsaminaceae*)

Members of this family are fleshy herbs with alternate, simple leaves and irregular flowers with 2 lateral sepals and a larger posterior sepal that is often spurred. Petals 4, usually united into 2 pairs. Stamens 5. Upon ripening, capsule splits violently, throwing out the seeds.

1. Posterior sepal without spur...............SPUR-LESS JEWELL-WEED
1. Posterior sepal with spur.......................................2

2. Perianth orange-colored, unspotted...........ORANGE JEWELL-WEED
2. Perianth pale yellow, spotted with reddish, or unspotted..TOUCH-ME-NOT

*   *   *

SPUR-LESS JEWELL-WEED (*Impatiens ecalcarata*) Plants to 40 inches. Flowers deep yellow to orange. East. and West. Wash.; moist, shady woods. Late summer and early autumn.

ORANGE JEWELL-WEED (*Impatiens aurella*) Flowers with clear orange, unspotted petals. East. Wash.; moist, open woods and streambanks. Summer and early autumn.

TOUCH-ME-NOT (*Impatiens noli-tangere*) Plants to 24 inches. Flowers pale yellow, often spotted with reddish. East. and West. Wash.; moist, lowland woods. Mid summer to early autumn.

A particularly interesting phenomenon associated with wildflowers is *aspection,* the progressive seasonal change in the composition of a plant community. In other words, as the season moves from early spring to late fall, many flowers bloom at certain times, not much earlier or later. This results in a series of species complexes, each following the other.

Some examples may help. In the low, eastern parts of the state, often the first flower to bloom is the sagebrush buttercup, appearing on warm, south-facing slopes in February. Not long in following will be the rice-roots and cous. Eastern Washingtonians are also familiar with the striking aspects of blue-eyed grass and camas, each often so abundant in a meadow swale as to cause it to resemble the blue surface of a lake! Later in the season on exposed, rocky benches, onions or bitterroots may compete for our attention, while on moist slopes the ground may literally be covered with light blue lupines. In southeastern Washington, fields may be solid yellow with the blooming of the mule's ears. In the deep woods in early spring, we look for ladies'-slippers and calypsos, while in late summer and early fall we find the many composites.

All this means that the student of flowers has the whole growing season to enjoy his hobby, with each week or two bringing the possibility of something new.

Chapter 30—The Mallow Family (*Malvaceae*)

Members of this family usually have large, showy flowers with the stamens numerous and united in a tube around the pistil. Sepals are 5 and the petals broad and also in 5's. Flowers are usually perfect. (Color Plate 30)

1. Flowers yellow.....................................ALKALI MALLOW
1. Flowers not yellow 2
2. Stigma including the entire length of the style branches.
$\qquad$ OREGON SIDALCEA
2. Stigma including only the tips of the style branches...................3
3. Flowers large; petals measuring more than 3/4 inch in length; leaves large, resembling those of the grape................MOUNTAIN HOLLYHOCK
3. Flowers small; petals measuring less than 3/4 inch in length; leaves small and deeply lobed ....GLOBE MALLOW (*Sphaeralcea*)

* * *

ALKALI MALLOW (*Sida hederacea*) Flowers small and yellowish, borne in axils of leaves. Plants prostrate to erect, with stems to 16 inches. Foliage grayish; leaves almost round. East. Wash.; alkali areas. Summer.

OREGON SIDALCEA (*Sidalcea oregana*) Plants variable in height, to as much as 60 inches. Leaves roundish, deeply lobed, palmate, with lobes irregularly toothed. Stems straight, unbranched. Terminal raceme of pale, pink flowers with darker veins, about 3/4 inch in diameter. The leaves on the upper stalk smaller and with fewer and narrower lobes. East. Wash.; sagebrush and grassland plains or open, yellow pine forests. Late spring to mid summer. (Color Plate 30)

MOUNTAIN HOLLYHOCK (*Iliamna rivularis*) Plants in clumps of tall (to 6 feet), leafy stems. Leaves large, maple-like (up to 7 lobes), rough-textured. Flowers very attractive, pale pink to rose, 1-2 inches in diameter; fruit a circle of tightly-packed, round, flat-sided seeds. East. Wash.; usually found on banks of creeks and rivers. Summer. (Color Plate 30)

GLOBE MALLOWS (*Sphaeralcea*) (Color Plate 30) (Fig. 38)

1. Leaves lobed to less than halfway to midvein; flowers orange to reddish.
$\qquad$ WHITE-LEAVED GLOBE MALLOW
1. Leaves lobed almost to midvein; flowers reddish.
$\qquad$ CURRANT-LEAVED GLOBE MALLOW

* * *

WHITE-LEAVED GLOBE MALLOW (*Sphaeralcea munroana*) Plants to 32 inches. Leaves maple-shaped, to 2 inches long. Foliage and stems light gray-green, soft-hairy. Flowers orange to reddish. East. Wash.; open, desert areas, lowlands, and foothills. Summer.

CURRANT-LEAVED GLOBE MALLOW (*Sphaeralcea grossulariaefolia*) Stems 20-28 inches tall. Foliage grayish; leaves roundish, deeply-lobed. Flowers reddish. East. Wash.; open, desert areas, lowlands, and foothills. Early to mid summer.

173

Figure 38.
The globe mallow, *Sphaeralcea,* illustrating the characteristic broad flowers of the
mallow family, Malvaceae. (Patrick)

Figure 39.
The many-stamened flowers of the St. John's worts, *Hypericum.* (Yaich)

Chapter 31—The St. John's Wort Family (*Hypericaceae*)

Members of this family, as included here, are perennial or annual herbs with opposite, sessile leaves and sepals and petals in 5's. Stamens 5 to many, often grouped in 3's or 5's. (Color Plate 31) (Fig. 39)

1. Low plants, occurring in dense mat-like clumps...BOG ST. JOHN'S WORT
1. Taller, more erect plants, not occurring in dense mats.................2
2. Sepals long and narrow (3-5 times as long as broad).........GOATWEED
2. Sepals broader (less than 3 times as long as broad).
SLENDER ST. JOHN'S WORT

*   *   *

BOG ST. JOHN'S WORT (*Hypericum anagalloides*) Plants prostrate, mat-like. Leaves elliptic to roundish. Flowers orange-yellow, tiny (1/4 inch in diameter), and borne in a cyme. East. and West. Wash.; moist areas from sea level to subalpine. Summer.

GOATWEED (*Hypericum perforatum)* Tall, slender plants to 36 inches. Stiff stalks branched oppositely at top. Flowers deep yellow, terminally located at tips of branches to form a flat-topped mass of bloom. East. and West. Wash.; pastures, meadows, roadsides, and old fields; a serious and spreading pest. Summer. Also called Klamath weed.

SLENDER ST. JOHN'S WORT (*Hypericum formosum*) Stems erect (to 28 inches) with more or less clasping leaves. Leaf margins black-dotted. More informally branched at tops of stems than *H. perforatum* and not so flat-topped. East. and West. Wash.; moist places in lowlands and mountains. Summer and early autumn.

PLATE 1. Skunk cabbage, *Lysichitum,* Calla Lily Famly (Patrick); onion, *Allium,* Lily Family (Yaich); brodiaea, *Brodiaea,* Lily Family (Yaich); mariposa lily, *Calochortus,* Lily Family (Yaich). In this and following plates, order of the photos reads left to right, upper row, followed by left to right, lower row.

PLATE 2. avalanche lily, *Erythronium*, Lily Family (Clawson); queen's cup, *Clintonia*, Lily Family (Yaich); twisted-stalk, *Streptopus*, Lily Family (Yaich); Camas, *Camassia*, Lily Family (Patrick).

PLATE 3. Fritillary, *Fritillaria*, Lily Family (Yaich); lily, *Lilium*, Lily Family (Yaich); alp lily, *Lloydia*, Lily Family (Brindle); false lily-of-the-valley, *Maianthemum*, Lily Family (Yaich).

PLATE 4. False solomon's seal, *Smilacina*, Lily Family (Yaich); bronze bells, *Stenan-thium*, Lily Family (Yaich); twisted-stalk, *Streptopus*, Lily Family (Clawson); lamb's lily, *Tofieldia*, Lily Family (Brindle).

PLATE 5. Trillium, *Trillium,* Lily Family (Clawson); veratrum, *Veratrum,* Lily Family (Patrick); bear grass, *Xerophyllum,* Lily Family (Larrison); death camas, *Zigadenus,* Lily Family (Patrick).

PLATE 6. Iris, *Iris,* Iris Family (Yaich); blue-eyed grass, *Sisyrinchium,* Iris family (Yaich); calypso, *Calypso,* Orchid Family (Patrick); coralroot, *Corallorhiza,* Orchid Family (Yaich).

PLATE 7. Lady's-slipper, *Cypripedium,* Orchid Family (Yaich); phantom orchid, *Ebu-rophyton,* Orchid Family (Patrick); giant helleborine, *Epipactis,* Orchid Family (Thompson); evergreen orchid, *Goodyera,* Orchid Family (Thompson).

PLATE 8. Bog orchid, *Habenaria,* Orchid Family (Yaich); twayblade, *Listera,* Orchid Family (Yaich); ladies' tresses, *Spiranthes,* Orchid Family (Patrick); nettle, *Urtica,* Nettle Family (Larrison).

PLATE 9. Wild ginger, *Asarum*, Birthwort Family (Baker); buckwheat, *Eriogonum*, Polygonum Family (Yaich); mountain sorrel, *Oxyria*, Polygonum Family (Thompson); knotweed, *Polygonum*, Polygonum Family (Yaich).

PLATE 10. Dock, *Rumex*, Polygonum Family (Larrison); goosefoot, *Chenopodium*, Goosefoot Family (Patrick); winterfat, *Eurotia*, Goosefoot Family (Baker); saltbush, *Salicornia*, Goosefoot Family (Larrison).

PLATE 11. Sand verbena, *Abronia*, Four-o'clock Family (Larrison); red maids, *Calandrinia*, Purslane Family (Brindle); spring beauty, *Claytonia*, Purslane Family (Clawson); lewisia, *Lewisia*, Purslane Family (Yaich).

PLATE 12. Miner's lettuce, *Montia*, Purslane Family (Brindle); pussy-paws, *Spraguea*, Purslane Family (Thompson); sandwort, *Arenaria*, Pink Family (Yaich); field chick-weed, *Cerastium*, Pink Family (Thompson).

PLATE 13. Honkenya, *Honkenya*, Pink Family (Larrison); wild pink, *Silene*, Pink Family (Yaich); sand spurry, *Spergularia*, Pink Family (Thompson); common chickweed, *Stellaria*, Pink Family (Brindle).

PLATE 14. Water-shield, *Brasenia*, Water Lily Family (Larrison); yellow pond lily, *Nuphar*, Water Lily Family (Baker); peony, *Paeonia*, Peony Family (Yaich); monkshood, *Aconitum*, Buttercup Family (Patrick).

PLATE 15. Baneberry, *Actaea*, Buttercup Family (Baker); anemone, *Anemone*, Buttercup Family (Yaich); western anemone seed heads (Bauch); columbine, *Aquilegia*, Buttercup Family (Clawson).

PLATE 16. Marsh marigold, *Caltha*, Buttercup Family (Yaich); clematis, *Clematis*, Buttercup Family (Yaich); gold-thread in seed (note leaf design), *Coptis*, Buttercup Family (Brindle); larkspur, *Delphinium*, Buttercup Family (Clawson).

PLATE 17. Buttercup, *Ranunculus*, Buttercup Family (Yaich); meadow rue with spring beauty in foreground, *Thalictrum*, Buttercup Family (Baker); false bugbane, *Trautvetteria*, Buttercup Family (Patrick); vanilla-leaf, *Achlys*, Barberry Family (Yaich).

PLATE 18. Inside-out flower, *Vancouveria,* Barberry Family (Thompson); California poppy, *Eschscholzia,* Poppy Family (Yaich); dicentra, *Dicentra,* Fumitory Family (Yaich); rock cress, *Arabis,* Mustard Family (Patrick).

PLATE 19. Wintercress, *Barbarea*, Mustard Family (Yaich); tansy mustard, *Descurainea*, Mustard Family (Yaich); whitlow grass, *Draba*, Mustard Family (Yaich); wallflower, *Erysimum*, Mustard Family (Yaich).

PLATE 20. Peppergrass, *Lepidium,* Mustard Family (Baker); dagger-pod, *Phoenicaulis,* Mustard Family (Patrick); physaria, *Physaria,* Mustard Family (Thompson); smelow-skia, *Smelowskia,* Mustard Family (Thompson).

PLATE 21. Fringe-pod, *Thysanocarpus*, Mustard Family (Thompson); bee plant, *Cleome*, Caper Family (Thompson); sundew, *Drosera*, Sundew Family (Aller); stonecrop, *Sedum*, Stonecrop Family (Larrison).

PLATE 22. Boykinia, *Boykinia,* Saxifrage Family (Larrison); heuchera, *Heuchera,* Saxifrage Family (Patrick); prairie-star, *Lithophragma,* Saxifrage Family (Yaich); mitrewort, *Mitella,* Saxifrage Family (Brindle).

PLATE 23. Grass-of-parnassus, *Parnassia,* Saxifrage Family (Brindle); saxifrage, *Saxifraga,* Saxifrage Family (Yaich); suksdorfia, *Suksdorfia,* Saxifrage Family (Yaich); fringe-cup, *Tellima,* Saxifrage Family (Yaich).

PLATE 24. Foamflower, *Tiarella*, Saxifrage Family (Patrick); youth-on-age, *Tolmiea*, Saxifrage Family (Yaich); goatsbeard, *Aruncus*, Rose Family (Brindle); mountain avens, *Dryas*, Rose Family (Patrick).

PLATE 25. Strawberry, *Fragaria,* Rose Family (Brindle); geum, *Geum,* Rose Family (Patrick); horkelia, *Horkelia,* Rose Family (Thompson); partridge-foot, *Luetkia,* Rose Family (Yaich).

PLATE 26. Cinquefoil, *Potentilla*, Rose Family (Yaich); burnet, *Sanguisorba*, Rose Family (Baker); sibbaldia, *Sibbaldia*, Rose Family (Thompson); locoweed, *Astragalus*, Pea Family (Patrick).

PLATE 27. Sweet-broom, *Hedysarum,* Pea Family (Thompson); pea, *Lathryrus,* Pea Family (Larrison); lotus, *Lotus,* Pea Family (Thompson); lupine, *Lupinus,* Pea Family (Yaich).

PLATE 28. Stemless loco, *Oxytropis*, Pea Family (Thompson); prairie-clover, *Petalostemum*, Pea Family (Baker); yellow pea, *Thermopsis*, Pea Family (Yaich); Thompson's clover—prettiest of the clovers, *Trifolium*, Pea Family (Patrick).

PLATE 29. Vetch, *Vicia,* Pea Family (Yaich); geranium, *Geranium,* Geranium Family (Yaich); wood sorrel, *Oxalis,* Wood Sorrel Family (Yaich); flax, *Linum,* Flax Family (Larrison).

PLATE 30. Spurge, *Euphorbia*, Spurge Family (Aller); mountain hollyhock, *Iliamna*, Mallow Family (Yaich); sidalcea, *Sidalcea*, Mallow Family (Yaich); globe mallow, *Sphaeralcea*, Mallow Family (Patrick).

PLATE 31. St. John's wort, *Hypericum,* St. John's Wort Family, (Larrison); Flett's violet—prettiest of the violets, *Viola,* Violet Family (Clawson); blazing-star, *Mentzelia,* Blazing-star Family (Baker); prickly bear, *Opuntia,* Cactus Family (Brindle).

PLATE 32. Hedgehog cactus, *Pediocactus,* Cactus Family (Aller); loosestrife, *Lythrum,* Loosestrife Family (Larrison); clarkia, *Clarkia,* Evening Primrose Family (Thompson); willow-herb, *Epilobium,* Evening Primrose Family (Stopps).

PLATE 33. Gaura, *Gaura,* Evening Primrose Family (Thompson); evening primrose, *Oenothera,* Evening Primrose Family (Yaich); angelica, *Angelica,* Parsley Family (Yaich); water-hemlock, *Cicuta,* Parsley Family (Brindle).

PLATE 34. Indian Parsnip, *Cymopterus*, Parsley Family (Larrison); silver-top *Glehnia*, Parsley Family (Larrison); cow-parsnip, *Heracleum*, Parsley Family (Larrison); lovage, *Ligusticum*, Parsley Family (Larrison).

PLATE 35. Desert parsley, *Lomatium*, Parsley Family (Larrison); dogwood, *Cornus*, Dogwood Family (Yaich); candy stick, *Allotropa*, Heath Family (Yaich); prince's pine, *Chimaphila*, Heath Family (Patrick).

PLATE 36. Cone plant, *Hemitomes*, Heath Family (Thompson); many-flowered Indian pipe, *Hypopitys*, Heath Family (Yaich); single-flowered Indian pipe, *Monotropa*, Heath Family (Clawson); fringed pinesap, *Pleuricospora*, Heath Family (Yaich).

PLATE 37. Pine-drops, *Pterospora,* Heath Family (Larrison); wintergreen, *Pyrola,* Heath Family (Yaich); shooting-star, *Dodecatheon,* Primrose Family (Yaich); douglasia, *Douglasia,* Primrose Family (Clawson).

PLATE 38. Star-flower, *Trientalis*, Primrose Family (Patrick); beach thrift, *Armeria*, Plumbago Family (Thompson); frasera, *Frasera*, Gentian Family (Yaich); gentian, *Gentiana*, Gentian Family (Patrick).

PLATE 39. Swertia, *Swertia*, Gentian Family (Brindle); buckbean, *Menyanthes*, Buck-bean Family (Baker); dogbane, *Apocynum*, Dogbane Family (Larrison); milkweed, *Asclepias*, Milkweed Family (Yaich).

PLATE 40. Morning-glory, *Convolvulus,* Morning-glory Family (Clawson); collomia, *Collomia,* Phlox Family (Yaich); gilia, *Gilia,* Phlox Family (Yaich); linanthastrum, *Linan-thastrum,* Phlox Family (Baker).

PLATE 41. Linanthus, *Linanthus*, Phlox Family (Thompson); microsteris, *Microsteris*, Phlox Family (Baker); navarretia, *Navarretia*, Phlox Family (Brindle); showy phlox, *Phlox speciosus*, Phlox Family (Larrison).

PLATE 42. Microsteris, *Microsteris,* Phlox Family (Brindle); polemonium, *Polemonium,* Phlox Family (Yaich); hesperochiron, *Hesperochiron,* Waterleaf Family (Patrick); waterleaf, *Hydrophyllum,* Waterleaf Family (Yaich).

PLATE 43. Nama, *Nama*, Waterleaf Family (Thompson); nemophila, *Nemophila*, Waterleaf Family (Thompson); phacelia, *Phacelia*, Waterleaf Family (Yaich); romanzoffia,
Romanzoffia, Waterleaf Family (Thompson).

PLATE 44. Tarweed, *Amsinckia*, Borage Family (Yaich); cryptantha, *Cryptantha*, Borage Family (Larrison); hound's-tongue, *Cynoglossum*, Borage Family (Yaich); stickseed, *Hackelia*, Borage Family (Brindle).

PLATE 45. Gromwell, *Lithospermum,* Borage Family (Yaich); mertensia, *Mertensia,* Borage Family (Yaich); mouse-ears, *Myosotis,* Borage Family (Larrison); popcorn-flower, *Plagiobothrys,* Borage Family (Thompson).

PLATE 46. Giant hyssop, *Agastache*, Mint Family (Larrison); mint, *Mentha*, Mint Family (Larrison); balm, *Monardella*, Mint Family (Thompson); sage, *Salvia*, Mint Family (Thompson).

PLATE 47. Yerba buena, *Satureja,* Mint Family (Brindle); skull-caps, *Scutellaria,* Mint Family (Larrison); hedge nettle, *Stachys,* Mint Family (Yaich); blue curls, *Trichostema,* Mint Family (Baker).

PLATE 48. Bessya, *Bessya,* Figwort Family (Yaich); Indian paintbrush, *Castilleja,* Figwort Family (Yaich); collinsia, *Collinsia,* Figwort Family (Yaich); toadflax, *Linaria,* Figwort Family (Patrick).

PLATE 49. Monkey-flower, *Mimulus*, Figwort Family (Patrick); lousewort, *Pedicularis*, Figwort Family (Patrick); penstemon, *Penstemon*, Figwort Family (Yaich); figwort, Scrophularia, Figwort Family (Brindle).

PLATE 50. Synthyris, *Synthyris*, Figwort Family (Thompson); speedwell, *Veronica*, Figwort Family (Yaich); ground-cone, *Boschniakia*, Broomrape Family (Thompson); broomrape, *Orobanche*, Broomrape Family (Yaich).

PLATE 51. Butterwort, *Pinguicula*, Bladderwort Family (Clawson); bladderwort, *Utricularia*, Bladderwort Family (Brindle); bedstraw, *Galium*, Madder Family (Yaich; twinflower, *Linnaea*, Honeysuckle Family (Yaich).

PLATE 52. Columbine, *Aquilegia*, Buttercup Family (Yaich); corn-salad, *Plectritis*, Valerian Family (Thompson); valerian, *Valeriana*, Velarian Family (Larrison); wild cucumber, *Marah*, Cucumber Family (Yaich).

PLATE 53. Fruits of the wild cucumber (Patrick); bluebells, *Campanula,* Harebell Family (Patrick); downingia, *Downingia,* Harebell Family (Brindle); bluecups, *Githopsis,* Harebell Family (Thompson).

PLATE 54. Lobelia, *Lobelia*, Harebell Family (Larrison); saussurea, *Saussurea*, Sunflower Family (Thompson); blanketflower, *Gaillardia*, Sunflower Family; false sunfower,
Helianthella, Sunflower Family (Larrison).

PLATE 55. Woolly sunflower, *Eriophyllum*, Sunflower Family (Baker); hulsea, *Hulsea*, Sunflower Family (Yaich); tansy, *Tanacetum*, Sunflower Family (Brindle); gold-star, *Crocidium*, Sunflower Family (Brindle).

PLATE 56. Blepharipappus, *Blepharipappus,* Sunflower Family (Baker); yarrow, *Achillea,* Sunflower Family (Bauch); townsendia, *Townsendia,* Sunflower Family (Brindle); pearly everlasting, *Anaphalis,* Sunflower Family (Larrison).

PLATE 57. Hymenopappus, *Hymenopappus,* Sunflower Family (Thompson); Luina, *Luina,* Sunflower Family (Clawson); dandelion, *Taraxacum,* Sunflower Family (Patrick); hawkweed, *Hieracium,* Sunflower Family (Larrison).

PLATE 58. Hawksbeard, *Crepis*, Sunflower Family (Larrison); agoseris, *Agoseris*, Sunflower Family (Patrick); thistle, *Cirsium*, Sunflower Family (Yaich); wyethia, *Wyethia*, Sunflower Family (Yaich).

PLATE 59. Rudbeckia, *Rudbeckia*, Sunflower Family (Larrison); sunflower, *Helianthus*, Sunflower Family (Larrison); balsamroot, *Balsamorhiza*, Sunflower Family (Patrick); gum plant, *Grindelia*, Sunflower Family (Brindle).

PLATE 60. Tar-weed, *Madia,* Sunflower Family (Thompson); golden-weed, *Haplopappus,* Sunflower Family (Brindle); arnica, *Arnica,* Sunflower Family (Yaich); groundsel, *Senecio,* Sunflower Family (Brindle).

PLATE 61. Goldenrod, *Solidago,* Sunflower Family (Yaich); daisy, *Erigeron,* Sunflower Family (Yaich); golden-aster, *Chrysopsis,* Sunflower Family (Thompson); coltsfoot, *Petasites,* Sunflower Family (Patrick).

PLATE 62. Aster, *Aster*, Sunflower Family (Larrison); thoroughwort, *Brickellia*, Sunflower Family (Brindle); luina, *Luina*, Sunflower Family (Yaich); cudweed, *Gnaphalium*, Sunflower Family (Brindle).

PLATE 63. Pussy-toes, *Antennaria*, Sunflower Family (Patrick); poverty-weed, *Iva*, Sunflower Family (Baker); wormwood, *Artemisia*, Sunflower Family (Baker); lettuce, *Lactuca*, Sunflower Family (Baker).

PLATE 64. Skeleton-weed, *Lygodesmia,* Sunflower Family (Baker); three members of wildflower book committee, left to right: Hazel Wolf, Zella Schultz, and Earl J. Larrison, conferring in the rain on Hurricane Ridge in the Olympics (Patrick); south-facing slope just east of Chinook Pass on trail to Sheep Lake—an excellent place for wildflowers (Yaich); solid wildflowers on a slope near Wenatchee (Patrick).

Chapter 32—The Violet Family (*Violaceae*)

Members of this family are small, often ground-hugging, perennial herbs with alternate or basal leaves. Floral parts are in 5's. Corolla consisting of 2 upper petals, 2 lateral petals, and 1 lower petal (as in the domestic pansy); flowers otherwise perfect. Among the most appreciated of all wildflowers. (Color Plate 31)

1. Leaves deeply dissected to compound.........THREE-NERVED VIOLET
1. Leaves not as above..2

2. Flowers white, occasionally shaded with bluish or yellowish..........3
2. Flowers not white..4

3. Petals white with yellow bases; the lower 3 petals streaked with purplish, and all tinged with purplish on outside surface.........CANADA VIOLET
3. Petals white, the lower 3 streaked with purple; no yellow bases on petals.
SMALL WHITE VIOLET

4. Flowers partly or wholly yellow...................................5
4. Flowers bluish, purplish, or violet..............................11

5. Flowers borne on tips of erect leafy stems..........................6
5. Flowers not restricted to tips of erect stems.......................8

6. Flowers bluish, with yellow tinge at bases of petals......FLETT'S VIOLET
6. Flowers mostly yellowish or partly whitish; occasionally blue or brown on the back..7

7. Upper petals yellowish on back..........SMOOTH WOODLAND VIOLET
7. Upper petals bluish-red on back...................CANADA VIOLET

8. Leaves heart-shaped at base and as broad as long.................9
8. Leaves not heart-shaped; longer than broad......................10

9. Leaves finely dotted with purple and evergreen.....EVERGREEN VIOLET
9. Leaves not dotted with purple and not evergreen.
ROUND-LEAVED VIOLET

10. Leaves coarsely veined, smaller (usually less than 1½ inches long), and coarsely toothed or lobed...................PURPLE-TINGED VIOLET
10. Leaves not coarsely veined, larger (usually more than 1½ inches long), and not coarsely toothed or lobed.................NUTTALL'S VIOLET

11. Leaves and flowers arising from rootstocks; plants stoloniferous.
MARSH VIOLET
11. Leaves and flowers not arising from rootstocks; plants not stoloniferous, or if so, leafy stems present.....................................12

12. Plants occurring in Eastern Washington..........................13
12. Plants occurring in Western Washington..........................14

13. Head of style "bearded"...........WESTERN LONG-SPURRED VIOLET
13. Head of style not "bearded"................KIDNEY-LEAVED VIOLET

14. Head of style not "bearded"...................LANGSDORF'S VIOLET
14. Head of style "bearded"..15

15. Leaves strongly heart-shaped......WESTERN LONG-SPURRED VIOLET
15. Leaves not strongly heart-shaped.................HOWELL'S VIOLET

Figure 40.
Sun and woods—habitat of many violets. (Larrison)

THREE-NERVED VIOLET (*Viola trinervata*) Flowers bicolored and pansy-like, the upper petals reddish violet and the lower petals deep lilac, with yellowish bases. East. Wash.; sagebrush and rocky hillsides where soil is moist in spring. Early spring to early summer.

CANADA VIOLET (*Viola canadensis*) Leafy stems to 12 inches. Leaves ovate, basically heart-shaped and pointed at tip. Flowers mostly white with yellowish bases; upper petals blue-red on back. East. and West. Wash.; moist, shady woods. Late spring to mid summer.

SMALL WHITE VIOLET (*Viola macloskeyi*) Leaves roundish. Stolons arising from slender rootstocks. Flowers white (lower petals streaked with purple). East. and West. Wash.; boggy places in mountains. Late spring and summer.

FLETT'S VIOLET (*Viola flettii*) Leaves kidney-shaped. Flowers bluish, with yellow bases on petals. Olympics; rocky places in the open, alpine areas. Summer. Named for pioneer student of Mount Rainier plants and animals.

SMOOTH WOODLAND VIOLET (*Viola glabella*) Leaves bright green, pointed, and heart-shaped. Flowers yellowish with dark veins and center. East. and West. Wash.; moist woods and streambanks. Early spring to mid summer. Commonest yellow violet in the Cascades and Olympics.

EVERGREEN VIOLET (*Viola sempervirens*) Leathery, purple-dotted, evergreen leaves. Flowers yellowish. West. Wash.; moist woods, mountains and lowlands. Early spring to early summer. Plants with spreading, stoloniferous habit.

ROUND-LEAVED VIOLET (*Viola orbiculata*) Leaves round; heart-shaped at base. Flowers yellowish. East. and West. Wash.; moist, open upper montane areas of the Cascades and Olympics. Summer.

PURPLE-TINGED VIOLET (*Viola purpurea*) Flowers yellow, purplish on back, and with brownish lines on basal part of petals. East. Wash.; dry slopes from lowlands to upper parts of mountains. Late spring and summer.

NUTTALL'S VIOLET (*Viola nuttallii*) Leaves oval or lanceolate, tapering to petioles, and 2 inches or more. Flowers yellow; the lower 3 petals with purplish lines. East. and West. Wash.; dry places; variable, from sagebrush plains, arid mountain plateaus and ridges, to open yellow pine woods. Mid spring to mid summer.

MARSH VIOLET (*Viola palustris*) Plants with slender rhizomes and stolons. Leaves oval. Flowers lavender to pale violet. East. and West. Wash.; moist meadows, bogs, and streamsides; often under brush. Late spring to mid summer.

KIDNEY-LEAVED VIOLET (*Viola nephrophylla*) Leaves heart-shaped to kidney-shaped. Rootstocks stout. Flowers bluish violet. East. Wash.; moist meadows and streamsides. Late spring to early summer.

LANGSDORF'S VIOLET (*Viola langsdorfii*) Leaves kidney-shaped to ovate. Flowers violet, with white beards on side petals. Lower petals white at base. West. Wash.; wet meadows and bogs in lowlands. Mid spring to late summer.

WESTERN LONG-SPURRED VIOLET (*Viola adunca*) Leaves ovate-lanceolate. Flowers bluish or violet, with light center and prominent white beards on

Figure 41.
Growth habit of the prickly pear, *Opuntia.* (Larrison)

180

lateral petals. With prominent spur. East. and West. Wash.; variable; dry, open places and moist woods from sea level to subalpine areas. Mid spring and summer.

HOWELL'S VIOLET (*Viola howellii*) Leaves heart-shaped on long stalks. Flowers bluish violet with white bases on petals. West. Wash.; moist prairies and woods. Spring.

Chapter 33—The Blazing-Star Family (*Loasaceae*)

Members of this family, as included here, are herbs with elongate, deep-lobed, dandelion-like leaves with the flowers borne singly or in groups at the tips of the stems. Sepals and petals 5 each; stamens many, long, and thread-like. (Color Plate 31)

1. Petals larger, more than 3/4 inch long; plants perennial or biennial; flowers lemon yellow.................................GREAT BLAZING-STAR
1. Petals smaller, less than 3/4 inch; plants annual......................2
2. Flower heads coarse, not crowded; leaves deeply lobed; flowers yellow.
WHITE-STEMMED BLAZING-STAR
2. Flower heads crowded; leaves very weakly lobed; flowers yellow.
BUSHY BLAZING-STAR

*   *   *

GREAT BLAZING-STAR (*Mentzelia laevicaulis*) Plants tall, to 36 inches, with whitish stems and dandelion-like leaves. Flowers yellow, 2-3 inches long, and terminal. East. Wash.; dry areas in valleys and foothills. Summer and early autumn. Flowers open in evening, closing in sunshine till petals mature, then remain open.

WHITE-STEMMED BLAZING-STAR (*Mentzelia albicaulis*) Plants leafy, to 16 inches, with stems whitish and occasionally prostrate. Flowers yellow; petals less than 3/4 inch long; in terminal cymes. East. Wash.; dry, open valleys and foothills. Late spring to mid summer. Flowers open in sunshine.

BUSHY BLAZING-STAR (*Mentzelia dispersa*) Plants often single-stemmed, to 16 inches, with weakly-lobed leaves. Flowers yellow; small. East. Wash.; dry areas in valleys and foothills. Late spring to mid summer.

Figure 42.
The seabeach cactus of the northern Olympic Peninsula. (Clawson)

182

Chapter 34—The Cactus Family (*Cactaceae*)

Members of this family are characterized by their thick, fleshy stems, low-lying growth habit, and large sharp spines. The flowers are large, colorful, and showy, compared to the size of the plants, and regular and perfect in form. (Color Plate 31)

1. Stem jointed............................PRICKLY PEARS (*Opuntia*)
1. Stem not jointed; entire plant ball-like in shape.....HEDGEHOG CACTUS

*　　*　　*

HEDGEHOG CACTUS (*Pediocactus simpsonii*) Flowers light green to purple. East. Wash.; sagebrush plains and foothills, especially on exposed ridges and plateaus. Late spring to mid summer. (Color Plate 32)

PRICKLY PEARS (*Opuntia*) (Figs. 41, 42)

1. Joints of stem more or less round in cross-section, not strongly flattened.
BRITTLE PRICKLY PEAR
1. Joints of stem strongly flattened in cross-section.
MANY-SPINED PRICKLY PEAR

*　　*　　*

BRITTLE PRICKLY PEAR (*Opuntia fragilis*) Flowers yellow. East. and West. Wash.; dry, open ground in interior desert areas, as well as dry places on certain islands in northern Puget Sound and San Juan Islands region; beaches along northeastern part of Olympic Peninsula. Late spring to early summer.

MANY-SPINED PRICKLY PEAR (*Opuntia polyacantha*) Flowers yellowish, less commonly reddish. East. Wash.; dry desert areas in lowlands and foothills. Late spring and early summer.

Figure 43.
The promise of spring. (Larrison)

Chapter 35—The Loosestrife Family (*Lythraceae*)

Members of this family are annual or perennial herbs with opposite or alternate, simple leaves and perfect, usually regular, flowers which are borne either in the axils of leaves or in terminal spikes. Calyx lobes and petals 5-7. (Color Plate 32)

1. Plants small, less than 15 inches tall; leaves mostly alternate; flowers solitary . . . . HYSSOP LOOSESTRIFE
1. Plants large, more than 15 inches tall; leaves opposite; flowers crowded in terminal spikes . . . . PURPLE LOOSESTRIFE

*   *   *

HYSSOP LOOSESTRIFE (*Lythrum hyssopifolia*) Flowers white to light purple or deep pink. East. and (mostly) West. Wash.; wet, marshy places. Late spring to early autumn.

PURPLE LOOSESTRIFE (*Lythrum salicaria*) Flowers reddish purple. West. Wash.; lowland marshes in the Puget Sound region. Introduced from Europe and gives a beautiful aspect to lowland, west-side marshes in late summer and early fall.

———————

The names of many persons, botanists, explorers, scientists, etc., have been given to flowers. Here are a few of such names:

Austin, R. M.; 1823-1919 (American); *Eburophyton austiniae.*
Bessey, Charles E.; 1845-1915 (American); *Besseya.*
Boisduval, Jean A.; 1801-1879 (French); *Boisduvalia.*
Boykin, Samuel; 1786-1848 (American); *Boykinia.*
Brewer, William H.; 1828-1910 (American); *Cardamine breweri.*
Brickell, John; 1749-1809 (American); *Brickellia.*
Canby, William M.; 1831-1904 (American); *Lomatium canbyi.*
Chamisso, Ludwig A. von; 1781-1838 (German); *Montia chamissoi.*
Clark, William; 1770-1838 (American); *Clarkia.*
Clayton, John; 1685-1773 (American); *Claytonia.*
Clinton, DeWitt; 1769-1828 (American); *Clintonia.*
Collins, Zaccheus; 1764-1831 (American); *Collinsia.*
Dawson, Sir John; 1820-1899 (Canadian); *Angelica dawsonii.*
Descurain, Francois; 1658-1740 (French); *Descurainia.*
Douglas, David; 1798-1834 (British); *Douglasia.*
Downing, A. J.; 1815-1852 (American); *Downingia.*
Drummond, James F.; 1851-1921 (Scottish); *Anemone drummondii.*
Eaton, Daniel C.; 1834-1895 (American); *Erigeron eatonii.*
Eschscholtz, Johann F. von; 1793-1831 (Russian); *Eschscholzia.*
Fraser, John; 1750-1811 (British); *Frasera.*

(List continued in Chapter 37)

Figure 44.
Enchanter's nightshade, *Circaea*. (Yaich)

186

Chapter 36—The Evening Primrose Family (*Onagraceae*)

Members of this family are annual or perennial herbs (as included here) with simple, alternate or opposite leaves and with perfect flowers with floral parts in 2's or 4's. Ovary is inferior. (Color Plate 32)

1. Flower parts (sepals and petals) in 2's......ENCHANTER'S NIGHTSHADE
1. Flower parts (sepals and petals) in 4's.............................2

2. Plants with creeping or floating life form; leaves opposite.
WATER PURSLANE
2. Plants erect, not creeping or floating; leaves opposite or alternate.......3

3. Fruit not splitting open; nut-like.............SMALL-FLOWERED GAURA
3. Fruit a capsule and splitting open at maturity........................4

4. Leaves commonly opposite (alternate in *E. angustifolium)*; seeds with conspicuous tuft of long hairs at end; plants often growing in moist places.
WILLOW-HERBS (*Epilobium*)
4. Leaves mostly alternate; seeds not as above; plants growing in drier habitats 5

5. Calyx tube absent, with sepals free to the ovary.
GAYOPHYTUMS (*Gayophytum*)
5. Calyx tube present (formed by fusion of bases of sepals)..............6

6. Stamens with filaments attached to anthers near the middle of the anther.
EVENING PRIMROSES (*Oenothera*)
6. Stamens with filaments attached to anthers near the base of the anther...7

7. Calyx lobes erect.......................BOISDUVALIAS (*Boisduvalia*)
7. Calyx lobes turned sideways (at right angles to pedicel), or turned downward..CLARKIAS (*Clarkia*)

*   *   *

ENCHANTER'S NIGHTSHADE (*Circaea alpina*)   Plant erect,. to 12 inches. Leaves opposite, oval to heart-shaped and lightly toothed. Flowers white, small; stamens 2. East. and West. Wash.; cool, moist woods, especially in the mountains. Late spring and summer. (Fig. 44)

WATER PURSLANE (*Ludwigia palustris*) Leaves ovate to lanceolate; petals usually absent; greenish when present. East. and West. Wash.; often forming broad mats along the shores of ponds and pools in marshes and bogs; common. Mid summer to mid autumn.

SMALL-FLOWERED GAURA (*Gaura parviflora*) Plants to 60 inches, with tiny, pinkish flowers borne on long, drooping spikes. Plants leafy. East. Wash.; sandy, or rocky wasteland and old fields. Mid summer to mid autumn. (Color Plate 33)

WILLOW-HERBS (*Epilobium*) (Color Plate 32; Fig. 45)

These are tall plants with often showy flowers and usually with long, narrow, willow-like leaves (hence name). The seed pods are long and slender.

1. Flowers large, at least 1 inch in diameter; petals spreading or not........2
1. Flowers small, less than 1 inch in diameter; petals not spreading........4

Figure 45.
Fireweed, *Epilobium.* (Yaich)

188

2. Flowers yellow; petals more closed and not spreading; leaves opposite.
   YELLOW-FLOWERED WILLOW-HERB
2. Flowers purplish or rose-colored; petals open and spreading; leaves alternate 3
3. Flowers numerous on flowering stem; veins visible on under surface of leaves. .... FIREWEED
3. Flowers few on stem; veins invisible on under surface of leaves.
   BROAD-LEAVED WILLOW-HERB
4. Plants annual with slender taproot; skin on lower portion of stem shedding . 5
4. Plants perennial, arising from stout roots or rhizomes; skin on lower portions of stems not shedding. 6
5. Leaves mostly alternate; flowers borne in a loose panicle.
   TALL ANNUAL WILLOW-HERB
5. Leaves mostly opposite; flowers borne in axils of leaves or in a raceme.
   SMALL-FLOWERED WILLOW-HERB
6. Plants grayish-hairy; leaves linear, several times longer than wide.
   MARSH WILLOW-HERB
6. Plants not grayish-hairy; leaves not linear. 7
7. Bulb-like offsets or buds usually present at base of stem.
   COMMON WILLOW-HERB
7. Bulb-like offsets not present. 8
8. Plants smooth, not conspicuously hairy, though grayish colored.
   SMOOTH WILLOW-HERB
8. Plants hairy, but not grayish. 9
9. Plants smaller, usually less than 12 inches tall; montane or alpine.
   ALPINE WILLOW-HERB
9. Plants larger, usually more than 12 inches tall; plants of the lowlands and foothills .... WATSON'S WILLOW-HERB

*   *   *

YELLOW-FLOWERED WILLOW-HERB (*Epilobium luteum*) Plants to 16 inches, with 1-2 inch leaves bearing finely-toothed margins. Flowers single, creamy yellow and nodding on stems arising from leaf axils. Cascades and Olympics; moist habitats, such as streamsides, in the higher mountains. Mid summer to early autumn.

FIREWEED (*Epilobium angustifolium*) Plants to 48 inches; leaves lanceolate, 3-6 inches long. Flowers rose to purple; rarely white. East. and West. Wash.; common on old burns (where it is famous), as well as denuded soil, as shoulders of highways and railroad rights-of-way; lowland and mountainous areas. Summer and early autumn. An important necter source for honey bee farms in Western Washington.

BROAD-LEAVED WILLOW-HERB (*Epilobium latifolium*) Stems to 16 inches. Leaves broadly lanceolate. Flowers purplish, less commonly white; petals dark-veined; blooms large, 1½ inches wide. East. and West. Wash.; open, rocky or gravelly habitats in the mountains. Summer.

TALL ANNUAL WILLOW-HERB (*Epilobium paniculatum*) Plants to 36 inches. Leaves broad lanceolate with clusters of tiny leaves in axils of the larger leaves. Flowers rose to pale pinkish with notched petals, borne in terminal racemes or panicles. East. and West. Wash.; dry, open ground in woods, particularly in yellow pine forests of the eastern Cascades. Mid to late summer.

SMALL-FLOWERED WILLOW-HERB (*Epilobium minutum*) Plants to 16 inches, with branching stems and small, reddish-purple flowers. East. and West. Wash.; dry, rocky areas in lowlands and mountains. Late spring and summer.

MARSH WILLOW-HERB (*Epilobium palustre*) Plants to 16 inches with grayish-hairy foliage and tiny, white to pinkish flowers borne in a terminal, few-flowered cluster. Central and Northern Cascades and East. Wash.; wet, boggy places in the mountains. Summer.

COMMON WILLOW-HERB (*Epilobium glandulosum*) Plants to 36 inches with glandular-hairy stems and flower clusters. Leaves variable. Rootstocks often bearing leafy shoots. Flowers pink to purplish. East. and West. Wash.; moist places in the mountains. Summer.

SMOOTH WILLOW-HERB (*Epilobium glaberrimum*) Plants to 24 inches, grayish, with linear to lanceolate, opposite leaves. Stems often prostrate at base in mat-like clusters, then becoming erect. Stems leafy. Flowers reddish purple to pink. East. and West. Wash.; moist places in the mountains. Summer.

ALPINE WILLOW-HERB (*Epilobium alpinum*) Plants to 12 inches. Leaves 1-1½ inches long and finely toothed and oval to oval-elongate in shape. Flowers white, pink, or rosy. East. and West. Wash.; subalpine and alpine areas of the mountains. Summer and early autumn.

WATSON'S WILLOW-HERB (*Epilobium watsonii*) Plants to 40 inches with opposite, finely-toothed leaves bearing white, creamy, or reddish flowers in their axils. East. and West. Wash.; moist places in lowlands, foothills, and lower parts of mountains. Summer.

GAYOPHYTUMS (*Gayophytum*)

These are small, weedy plants with narrow leaves and very tiny flowers. Not usually making up a very conspicuous part of the floral community.

1. Most branches arising near base of plant; stems rather thickly leaved with the leaves generally longer than the internodes (distance on stem or branch between leaves) 2
1. Most branches arising above base of plant and occurring throughout height of plant; leaves often shorter than internodes. 3

2. Seeds within capsule lying parallel to the axis of the capsule; number of seeds 10 or less per capsule. . . . . .RACEMED GAYOPHYTUM
2. Seeds within a capsule lying at an angle to the axis of the capsule; number of seeds per capsule more than 10. . . . . .DWARF GAYOPHYTUM

3. Petals less than 1/25 inch in length; plant much branched.
                                        HAIR-STEMMED GAYOPHYTUM
3. Petals more than 1/25 inch in length; plant not much branched.
                                        NUTTALL'S GAYOPHYTUM

RACEMED GAYOPHYTUM (*Gayophytum racemosum*) Plants to 16 inches. Flowers white, turning pink. East. Wash.; open, vernally moist slopes in mountains. Summer.

DWARFED GAYOPHYTUM (*Gayophytum humile*) Plants small, to 6 inches. Leaves long and narrow. Flowers white, turning pink. East. Wash.; open slopes in foothills and lower parts of mountains. Summer. (Probably includes *G. nuttallii*.)

HAIR-STEMMED GAYOPHYTUM (*Gayophytum ramosissimum*) Plants to 20 inches, much branched, with very thin stems and long, narrow leaves. Flowers white, turning pink. East. Wash.; dry, open slopes on foothills and lower mountains. Early summer.

NUTTALL'S GAYOPHYTUM (*Gayophytum nuttallii*) Plants to 24 inches with branching restricted to upper parts of plant. Flowers white, turning pink. East. and West. Wash.; dry, rocky habitats at all elevations. Summer.

EVENING PRIMROSES (*Oenothera*) (Color Plate 33; Fig. 46)

Plants with large, showy flowers containing 4 broad yellow or white petals and 4 sepals. White flowers turn pink in age; yellow, to orange. Many species open their blooms in the evening and close them in the early morning, to wither the following day.

1. Plants with erect, leaf-bearing flowering stems. 2
1. Plants without erect, leaf-bearing flowering stems; flowers borne in rosette
   of basal leaves. 6
2. Petals white (aging to pink) and averaging more than 3/8 inch in length.
   WHITE-STEMMED EVENING PRIMROSE
2. Petals yellow or less than 3/8 inch long. 3
3. Flowers yellow; floral cup more than 3/4 inch deep. 4
3. Flowers white, pink (in age), or yellow; floral cup less than 3/4 inch deep. .5
4. Petals more than 1 inch long. . . . . .HOOKER'S EVENING PRIMROSE
4. Petals less than 1 inch long. . . . . .COMMON EVENING PRIMROSE
5. Lower leaves oval-shaped, less than twice as long as broad; flowers yellow.
   BOOTH'S EVENING PRIMROSE
5. Lower leaves several times longer than broad; flowers pale yellow to white,
   aging to pink. . . . . .SMALL-FLOWERED EVENING PRIMROSE
6. Flowers white, aging to pinkish or purple. . .DESERT EVENING PRIMROSE
6. Flowers yellow. 7
7. Leaves weakly, or not at all, lobed. . .LONG-LEAVED EVENING PRIMROSE
7. Leaves strongly lobed, in pinnate pattern.
   TANSY-LEAVED EVENING PRIMROSE

*   *   *

WHITE-STEMMED EVENING PRIMROSE (*Oenothera pallida*) Plants to 20 inches with leafy stems containing linear-lanceolate leaves possessing scattered blunt teeth. Flowers white, aging to pink. East. Wash.; sand dunes and other sandy or rocky places. Late spring to mid summer.

Figure 46.
Evening primrose, *Oenothera.* Compare these flowers with those in Figure 45.
Note similarity of the petals. (Larrison)

HOOKER'S EVENING PRIMROSE (*Oenothera hookeri*) Plants to 48 inches with reddish stems and crinkled, elongate leaves. Flowers yellow, aging to orange or reddish, and borne in a spike. East. Wash. and Columbia Gorge; dry, rocky places in river canyons. Summer.

COMMON EVENING PRIMROSE (*Oenothera biennis*) Plants to 36 inches with gray-hairy stems and yellow flowers borne in terminal spikes. East. (mostly) and West. Wash.; meadows, streamsides, etc., in lowlands and foothills. Summer.

BOOTH'S EVENING PRIMROSE (*Oenothera boothii*) Plants to 16 inches. Flowers white, aging to pinkish, borne in a dense spike, often drooping. East. Wash.; sagebrush and grasslands in lowlands and foothills. Early and mid summer.

SMALL-FLOWERED EVENING PRIMROSE (*Oenothera minor*) Plants to 10 inches with tiny, pale yellow or cream flowers which age to pinkish in color. East. Wash.; sandy or gravelly soil in sagebrush. Early and mid summer.

DESERT EVENING PRIMROSE (*Oenothera caespitosa*) Plants to 8-10 inches with long-petioled, weakly toothed, basal leaves and large flowers that are white, aging to pinkish. East. Wash.; rocky slopes and slides, as well as other open terrain, in desert country. Late spring and early summer. A very common and showy plant of the desert country.

LONG-LEAVED EVENING PRIMROSE (*Oenothera subacaulis*) Plants with basal leaves that are toothed near lower part of blade. Flowers yellow. East. Wash.; meadows and grassy streamside flats in lowlands (sagebrush) and foothills. Mid spring to mid summer.

TANSY-LEAVED EVENING PRIMROSE (*Oenothera tanacetifolia*) Plants with basal, deeply-lobed leaves, and yellow flowers. East. Wash.; moist spring swales in sagebrush, grassy streamside flats, and wet meadows in yellow pine woods. Summer.

BOISDUVALIAS (*Boisduvalia*)

Leafy plants with small, sessile flowers borne in axils of upper leaves. The petals, 4, characteristically 2-lobed. Foliage densely, but softly, hairy.

1. Leaves in inflorescence broader (in relation to length) than those of lower stem .... DENSELY-FLOWERED BOISDUVALIA
1. Leaves in inflorescence and those of lower stem of about same relative width 2
2. Leaves and stems smooth and greenish .... SMOOTH BOISDUVALIA
2. Leaves and stems hairy and grayish .... STIFF BOISDUVALIA

*   *   *

DENSELY-FLOWERED BOISDUVALIA (*Boisduvalia densiflora*) Plants to 40 inches with very hairy foliage. Flowers pale pink, reddish, or purplish. East. and West. Wash.; moist habitats and shores of vernal ponds, mostly in lowlands. Mid summer and early autumn.

SMOOTH BOISDUVALIA (*Boisduvalia glabella*) Leaves lanceolate to oval. Plants to 12 inches with mostly smooth foliage. Flowers rosy red. East. Wash.;

temporarily wet places in lowlands, such as muddy, spring swales. Early summer.

STIFF BOISDUVALIA (*Boisduvalia stricta*) Plants to 20 inches with gray-hairy foliage. Stems strictly upright. Leaves linear. Tiny pink to purple flowers. East. Wash.; moist places in lowlands. Early summer.

CLARKIAS (*Clarkia*) (Color Plate 32)

Plants with 4-petalled, purplish- or lavender-colored flowers; long, narrow leaves; and often oddly-lobed petals. Sepals or calyx lobes often bent downward.

1. Plants occurring in Western Washington.............................2
1. Plants occurring in Eastern Washington.............................3
2. Sepals turned downward; petals mostly less than 1/2 inch long; occasionally with dark purple spot on each petal.......FOUR-SPOTTED CLARKIA
2. Sepals not turned downward; petals mostly more than 1/2 inch long; occasionally a reddish spot on each petal............FAREWELL-TO-SPRING
3. Petals with 3 prominent lobes; fertile stamens 4.
LARGE-FLOWERED CLARKIA
3. Petals without prominent lobes; fertile stamens 8......COMMON CLARKIA

*   *   *

FOUR-SPOTTED CLARKIA (*Clarkia quadrivulnera*) Plants to 26 inches with funnel-shaped flowers of 4 unlobed petals. Sepals strongly reflexed. Flowers pinkish lavender to purple, occasionally with dark purplish spot on each petal. West. Wash. and Columbia Gorge; glacial outwash prairies and grassy slopes; not common. Late spring to mid summer.

FAREWELL-TO-SPRING (*Clarkia amoena*) Plants to 36 inches, with fan-shaped or oval, unlobed petals. Sepals not reflexed. Flowers pale pinkish to purplish with a reddish spot in center of petal. West. Wash.; open places in woods; not common. Summer.

LARGE-FLOWERED CLARKIA (*Clarkia pulchella*) Plants to 20 inches with lavender to reddish-purple flowers, the petals of which are prominently 3-lobed. East. Wash.; open, sandy or rocky places in lowlands, often in sagebrush or grassy areas. Late spring and early summer. Often very common.

COMMON CLARKIA (*Clarkia rhomboidea*) Plants to 40 inches with scattered, opposite leaves and reddish purple, paddle-shaped petals. East. Wash.; open, grassy places and yellow pine woods in lowlands and foothills. Early summer.

Chapter 37—The Water Milfoil Family (*Haloragaceae*)

Members of this family, as included here, are aquatic herbs with whorled leaves of 2 kinds: the submerged ones reduced to capillary filaments and the emergent leaves less divided or entire. Staminate flowers are located above the pistillate ones on the stem. Petals 4 or none. Calyx entire or 4-toothed or 4-lobed.

1. Upper leaves (bracts) larger (at least 3/8 inch long), long and narrow, and toothed (sometimes entire); stamens 4 . . . . WESTERN WATER MILFOIL
1. Upper leaves (bracts) tiny (less than 1/4 inch long) and not long and narrow; stamens 8 . . . . SPIKED WATER MILFOIL

*   *   *

WESTERN WATER MILFOIL (*Myriophyllum hippuroides*) Flowers yellowish white. West. Wash.; aquatic, occurring in ponds and slow-moving streams. Mid summer to mid fall.

SPIKED WATER MILFOIL (*Myriophyllum spicatum*) Petals shed immediately after formation. East. Wash.; aquatic, in ponds and slow-moving streams. Summer.

Fremont, John C.; 1813-1890 (American); *Senecio fremontii.*

Geyer, Carl A.; 1809-1853 (German); *Lomatium geyeri.*

Gmelin, Johann F.; 1748-1804 (German); Gmelin, Johann G.; 1709-1755 (German); *Ranunculus gmelinii.*

Goodyer, John; 1592-1664 (English); *Goodyera.*

Gray, Asa; 1810-1888 (American); *Grayia.*

Grindel, David; 1776-1838 (Russian); *Grindelia.*

Hackel, Joseph; 1783-1869 (Czech); *Hackelia.*

Henderson, Louis F.; 1853-1942 (American); *Dodecatheon hendersonii.*

Heucher, Johann H. von; 1677-1747 (German); *Heuchera.*

Honckeny, Gerhart A.; 1724-1805 (German); *Honkenya.*

Hooker, Sr. Joseph; 1817-1911 (British); *Disporum hookeri.*

Hooker, Sr. William J.; 1785-1865 (British); *Potentilla hookeriana.*

Horkel, Johann; 1769-1846 (German); *Horkelia.*

Howell, Thomas; 1842-1912; Howell, Joseph; 1830-1912 (American); *Howellia.*

Ives, Eli; 1779-1861 (American); *Ivesia.*

Kellogg, Albert; 1813-1887 (American); *Polygonum kelloggii.*

Koch, W. D. J.; 1771-1849 (German); *Kochia.*

Leichtlin, Max; 1831-1910 (German); *Camassia leichtlinii.*

Lesquereux, Leo; 1805-1889 (American); *Lesquerella.*

Lewis, Meriwether; 1774-1809 (American); *Lewisia.*

Lister, Martin; 1638-1712 (British); *Listera.*

Llwyd, Edward; 1660-1709 (Welsh); *Lloydia.*

(List continued in Chapter 41)

Chapter 38—The Mare's-Tail Family (*Hippuridaceae*)

Members of this family are more or less aquatic to semi-aquatic, perennial herbs with simple, erect stems and entire, whorled leaves; flowers tiny, usually perfect and borne in the leaf axils. Calyx without lobes; petals, none; stamen, 1; pistil, 1. Upright flower stems arising from creeping rhizomes.

1. More or less aquatic; leaves at least 1/2 inch long and 6-12 in a whorl.
COMMON MARE'S-TAIL
1. Mostly terrestrial; leaves less than 1/2 inch long and 5-8 in a whorl.
MOUNTAIN MARE'S-TAIL

*   *   *

COMMON MARE'S-TAIL (*Hippuris vulgaris*) West. Wash.; swampy margins of streams and ponds and in shallow fresh water in lowlands. Summer.
MOUNTAIN MARE'S-TAIL (*Huppuris montana*) Cascades and Olympics; wet meadows, marshy bogs, and streambanks in mountains, particularly in sub-alpine areas. Mid summer to early autumn.

One habitat—or ecologic niche—that is occupied by certain members of a number of different families is that of the aquatic environment. Some species may be entirely aquatic, living completely on or below the water surface. Others, such as the mare's-tails, are semi-aquatic, that is, growing in shallow water or at most in moist, wet places. Aquatics often show certain adaptations for their peculiar mode of existence. Some of these are of a rather technical nature, but others may easily be seen by the ordinary student. Examples would be the long anchoring stems that secure a floating plant firmly to the bottom. Fleshy leaves and bladder-like floats may enable other plants to maintain themselves on the water's surface. Still other species may have 2 kinds of leaves, a floating, typical leaf and a thread-like, much dissected submerged leaf, as in the case of some aquatic buttercups. The physiology and internal structure are such in aquatics that they can live in ground often saturated with water.

Perhaps the most important aspect of these plants is that the flower lover is assured of the fact that even swamps, bogs, ponds, or sloughs will have a community of plants, often of interesting and beautiful species. For further information on Washington aquatic flowers, the reader is referred to *Aquatic Plants of the Pacific Northwest With Vegetative Keys* by Albert N. Steward, LaRea Dennis, and Helen M. Gilkey, Oregon State College, 1960.

Chapter 39—The Ginseng Family (*Araliaceae*)

The single member of this family included here is a woody herb, or sub-shrub, with large, compound leaves and perfect, regular flowers with floral parts in 5's. Woody stems arising from sub-surface rhizomes.

WILD SARSAPARILLA (*Aralia nudicaulis*)   Flowers greenish white. Northeastern Wash.; moist, shady woods. Late spring and early summer. The aromatic juice from the rhizomes and roots of this genus have been used in medicine and in flavoring beverages.

––––––––––

Of the several systems for classifying vegetational patterns, perhaps one of the best known is the scheme of life zones proposed by Dr. C. Hart Merriam, first chief of the Bureau of Biological Survey (now known as the Bureau of Sport Fisheries and Wildlife). This plan, as slightly modified by C. V. Piper, envisages the state of Washington as covered by a number of zones identified by major vegetational types and controlled by a variety of environmental factors.

The lowlands of Western Washington, marked originally by great forests of Douglas fir and western red cedar and lying below about 1,000 feet elevation, were placed in the *Humid Transition Zone.* The counterpart of this zone in Eastern Washington, the *Arid Transition Zone,* is made up of two sections, an upper yellow pine belt (*Timbered Arid Transition*) and a lower grassland section (*Timberless Arid Transition*). Occurring immediately above the Transition Zones, are the broad montane forests, comprising the Merriam *Canadian Zone.* Formed mainly of lowland hemlock on the west side of the Cascades and in the Olympics, this zone in the eastern part of the state includes a variety of firs, pines, and larches.

At the upper boundary of the Canadian Zone, the forests begin to open up and to be composed more and more of true firs, particularly subalpine fir. The trees themselves assume a spire-like shape and group together in small groves, interspersed with meadows of lush grasses, sedges, and wildflowers. This is the *Hudsonian Zone.* On some of the higher peaks in the state, the subalpine forests and meadows give way to barren fields and slopes of rocks and scattered mosses, and perhaps even permanent areas of snow and ice. This latter region is the *Arctic-Alpine Zone.*

The semi-desert areas of Eastern Washington, formerly largely covered with sagebrush, make up the *Upper Sonoran Zone.*

Other systems of classification are perhaps more detailed and more sensitive to minor variations, but the Merriam life zone system is a convenient one for the layman to use in identifying the broad bands of vegetation in Washington.

Figure 47.
Cow-parsnip, *Heracleum.* (Larrison)

Chapter 40—The Parsley Family (*Umbelliferae*)

Members of this family are commonly hollow-stemmed herbs with flowers conspicuously arranged in umbels. Leaves are usually compound and the umbels may be simple or compound. Calyx tube is united with the ovary, and the calyx teeth ("sepals") are very small or missing. Petals (usually long-clawed) and stamens, 5 each per flower. Ovary inferior; pistils 2, united at their base. Stems and foliage usually strong-smelling. (Color Plate 33) *Note:* This family contains several very difficult genera and the beginner may find the going hard at first.

1. Leaves simple and entire.....................WESTERN LILAEOPSIS
1. Leaves compound, or at least deeply cleft...........................2

2. Most leaves on plant compound with well-developed leaflets...........3
2. Most leaves on plant dissected into small, narrow segments, but not divided into well-defined leaflets.................................14

3. Leaflets 3 in number and large, averaging at least 4 inches in width.
COW-PARSNIP
3. Leaflets more than 3 in number and usually less than 4 inches wide.....4

4. Plants perennial, arising from fleshy, thickened, and divided roots; lacking taproot or upright rootstock.......................................5
4. Plants annual, biennial, or perennial, arising from taproot or vertical rhizome, or rarely with fibrous roots.................................7

5. Leaves palmately lobed or compound.............SANICLES (*Sanicula*)
5. Leaves pinnately compound.......................................6

6. Plants erect; calyx teeth tiny or lacking; lateral veins of leaflets not extending to meet the teeth....................HEMLOCK WATER-PARSNIP
6. Plants semi-prostrate or scrambling; calyx teeth well developed; lateral veins of leaflets extending to meet the teeth...........WATER PARSLEY

7. Plants less than 8 inches tall and not occurring along the seashore; flowering stems mostly not leafy................................8
7. Plants mostly more than 8 inches tall or occurring along seashore; stems usually leafy 9

8. Leaflets toothed or lobed..............DESERT PARSLEYS (*Lomatium*)
8. Leaflets entire ....TAUSCHIAS (*Tauschia*)

9. Plants annual or biennial with slender taproots; tending to be weedy.
WESTERN HEDGE-PARSLEY
9. Plants perennial with stout roots or rhizomes, tending not to be weedy..10

10. Umbels with a series of tight, head-like flower clusters; flowers sessile.
BEACH SILVER-TOP
10. Umbels not with a series of tight, head-like flower clusters; flowers on stalks (pedicels) 11

11. Fruits dorsally flattened.......................................12
11. Fruits roundish in cross-section or flattened laterally (not dorsally)....13

12. Flowers white or pinkish.....................ANGELICAS (*Angelica*)
12. Flowers yellow.......................DESERT PARSLEYS (*Lomatium*)

13. Leaves with well-defined leaflets.........SWEET CICELIES (*Osmorhiza*)
13. Leaflets not always well-defined (separated to base).
LOVAGES (*Ligusticum*)

14. Plant an annual or biennial with weak taproot and white or pinkish flowers.
WESTERN HEDGE-PARSLEY
14. Plants perennial, usually with stout taproots or fibrous roots...........15

15. Plants occurring along the seashore......PACIFIC HEMLOCK-PARSLEY
15. Plants not occurring along the seashore..........................16

16. Plants with a stout, elongated taproot...........................17
16. Plants with fibrous or fleshy roots.............................20

17. Leaves sparse and cleft into a few segments.
NARROW-LEAVED TURKEY PEA
17. Leaves numerous and cleft into a number of segments.............18

18. Fruits not flattened dorsally...................LOVAGES (*Ligusticum*)
18. Fruits flattened dorsally 19

19. Fruits with all the ribs winged...........NORTHERN INDIAN PARSNIP
19. Fruits with only some of the ribs winged..DESERT PARSLEYS (*Lomatium*)

20. Bulblets present in axils of upper leaves............WATER-HEMLOCK
20. Bulblets not occurring in axils of leaves.........................21

21. Fruits strongly flattened dorsally; flowers white or yellow.
DESERT PARSLEYS (*Lomatium*)
21. Fruits flattened laterally; flowers white or pink.....................22

22. Fruits long and narrow...............DESERT PARSLEYS (*Lomatium*)
22. Fruits not long and narrow....................................23

23. Plants more than 8 inches tall.................YAMPAHS (*Perideridia*)
23. Plants less than 8 inches tall..................................24

24. Fruits longer than broad......................TAUSCHIAS (*Tauschia*)
24. Fruits more or less roundish...........NARROW-LEAVED TURKEY PEA

*　　*　　*

WESTERN LILAEOPSIS (*Lilaeopsis occidentalis*) Leaves long (to 6 inches), tubular, and hollow. Flowers very small, white, and borne in umbel-like cluster on short flower stalks. West. Wash.; salt marshes and beaches. Early and mid summer.

COW-PARSNIP (*Heracleum lanatum*) Plants tall, to 6-10 feet. Leaves very large, cleft into 3 lobed and toothed parts. Flowers whitish, creamy, or pale greenish and borne in immense, flat umbels. East. and West. Wash.; moist swales and streambanks from lowlands to well up in the mountains. Summer. (Color Plate 34; Fig. 47)

HEMLOCK WATER-PARSNIP (*Sium suave*) Plants to 48 inches with pinnately compound leaves. Submerged leaves are filamentous. East. and West. Wash.; swamps and shallow, inshore waters of ponds in lowlands and foothills. Flowers white. Summer.

WATER PARSLEY (*Oenanthe sarmentosa*) Stems to 48 inches, often trailing or climbing. Leaves twice-pinnate. Flowers white, in loose umbels. West.

Wash. and Columbia Gorge; wet places near standing or running water in lowlands; sometimes in the water. Summer.

WESTERN HEDGE-PARSLEY (*Caucalis microcarpa*) Plants to 16 inches with slender, delicate stems and very finely-divided leaves. Flowers white, but petals few; the inflorescence consisting primarily of leaf-life bracts. East. and West. Wash.; moist streambanks and wet canyon sides. Mid spring to early summer.

BEACH SILVER-TOP (*Glehnia leiocarpa*) Plants low, to 4 inches with broad, dark-greenish, 3-part leaves and whitish, woolly-rayed flowers. Flowers very hard to see. West. Wash.; sand dunes and beaches along the ocean coast. Summer. (Color Plate 34)

PACIFIC HEMLOCK-PARSLEY (*Conioselinum pacificum*) Plants to 48 inches with delicate, finely-divided leaves, the leaflets of which are prominently toothed and cleft. The whitish flowers in umbels containing long bracts projecting downward. West. Wash.; beaches and sandy bluffs along the seashore. Mid to late summer.

NARROW-LEAVED TURKEY PEA (*Orogenia linearifolia*) Plants to 6 inches with fleshy roots and long, narrow, 3-lobed leaves. Flower clusters white and very small. Southeast. Wash.; hillsides and ridges, especially on wet slopes covered into the spring by snowbanks and cornices. Early to late spring. One of the earliest of the wildflowers.

NORTHERN INDIAN PARSNIP (*Cymopterus terebinthinus*) Plants to 24 inches with finely-divided, basal leaves and yellowish flowers in umbels on long stems. Often 1 leaf on a flowering stem. East. Wash.; dry, open, rocky or sandy habitats; lowlands and lower montane areas. Mid spring to mid summer. (Color Plate 34)

WATER-HEMLOCK (*Cicuta douglasii*) Plants tall, to 6 or more feet, with pinnately-compound leaves bearing lanceolate, sharp-toothed leaflets, white flowers in large, compound umbels. Veins in leaflets running to notches between teeth. Base of stem thickened, hollow and giving rise to numerous, tuberous roots. East. and West. Wash.; marshes and other wet habitats in lowlands and foothills. Summer. This is an extremely poisonous plant. (Color Plate 33)

SANICLES (*Sanicula*)

Plants with usually toothed and cleft basal leaves, small flower heads, and often with spine-covered fruits.

1. Plants occurring along the seashore with prostrate life form.
                                                                BEACH SANICLE
1. Plants not occurring along the seashore and with erect life form. 2

2. Lower leaves roundish and palmately lobed or cleft. . .WESTERN SANICLE
2. Lower leaves longer than broad and ternately or somewhat pinnately lobed
   or cleft . . . . .SIERRA SANICLE

*   *   *

BEACH SANICLE (*Sanicula arctopoides*) Tips of leaves long and narrow. Plants are spreading and mat-like. Flowers yellow. Floral clusters fringed with

Figure 48.
Sweet cicely, *Osmorhiza*. (Larrison)

202

long, basal bracts. West. Wash.; open, exposed bluffs along coastal salt-water; not common. Spring.

WESTERN SANICLE (*Sanicula crassicaulis*) Plants erect, to 4 feet. Leaves large, lobed, and toothed: the teeth tipped with bristles. Flowers yellow or purplish, in small, tight heads. West. Wash. and Columbia Gorge; woods and some open places. Late spring and early summer.

SIERRA SANICLE (*Sanicula graveolens*) Plants to 20 inches with small, palmately-cleft leaves, the terminal leaflet with a long stalk. Flowers very small and greenish white. East. and West. Wash.; open woods in lowlands and foothills. Early summer.

DESERT PARSLEYS (*Lomatium*) (Color Plate 35; Fig. 49)

Attractive plants with showy umbels of small flowers and finely-divided leaves usually found growing in dry places in generally semi-desert areas. Flowers most commonly yellow.

1. Terminal segments of leaves large, 3/8 inch or more in length. 2
1. Terminal segments of leaves small, less than 3/8 inch long. 15

2. Terminal parts of leaves forming definite leaflets. 3
2. Terminal parts of leaves narrow and not leaflet-like in form. 5

3. Leaflets strongly lobed or cleft. . . . . . . .FEW-FRUITED DESERT PARSLEY
3. Leaflets entire or weakly toothed. 4

4. Leaflets larger, more than 3/8 inch wide. . . . . . .NAKED DESERT PARSLEY
4. Leaflets smaller, less than 1/4 inch wide.
                                    BRANDEGE'S DESERT PARSLEY

5. Fruits narrowly oblong 6
5. Fruits broader, not narrowly oblong. 7

6. Secondary umbel (involucel) not present. . . . .SWALE DESERT PARSLEY
6. Secondary umbel (involucel) present.
                                    NARROW-LEAVED DESERT PARSLEY

7. Bractlets of secondary umbels broad and roundish near tip. . . . . . . .COUS
7. Bractlets of secondary umbels narrow near tip, or missing. 8

8. Flowers usually white 9
8. Flowers mostly yellowish (uncommonly purplish). 11

9. Pedicels of fruits more than 1/4 inch long.
                                    COEUR D'ALENE DESERT PARSLEY
9. Pedicels of fruits less than 1/4 inch long. 10

10. Plants small, usually less than 6 inches tall.
                                    GORMAN'S DESERT PARSLEY
10. Plants larger, usually more than 6 inches tall.
                                    GEYER'S DESERT PARSLEY

11. Plants with 1 or a few stems arising from simple rootcrowns.
                                    NARROW-LEAVED DESERT PARSLEY
11. Plants with several to many stems arising from a large, woody root. 12

12. Fruits with thick wings. 13
12. Fruits with thin wings. 14

13. Plants large, usually more than 24 inches tall; flowers yellow or purple.
FERN-LEAVED DESERT PARSLEY
13. Plants smaller, usually less than 24 inches tall; flowers purple.
COLUMBIA DESERT PARSLEY
14. Plants larger, usually more than 24 inches tall.
THOMPSON'S DESERT PARSLEY
14. Plants smaller, usually less than 24 inches tall.
BRANDEGE'S DESERT PARSLEY
15. Bractlets of secondary umbels (involucels) broad or toothed at tip.....16
15. Bractlets of secondary umbels narrow at tip or missing..............18
16. Plants occurring west of the Cascades; leaves very finely divided.
FINE-LEAVED DESERT PARSLEY
16. Plants occurring east of the Cascades; leaves not so finely divided.....17
17. Bractlets of secondary umbels fused at base.
WATSON'S DESERT PARSLEY
17. Bractlets of secondary umbels distinct at base..................COUS
18. Wings of fruits thickened.......................................19
18. Wings of fruits thin..22
19. Surface of leaves rough; plants larger, usually more than 24 inches tall.
FERN-LEAVED DESERT PARSLEY
19. Surface of leaves smooth; plants smaller, usually less than 24 inches
tall 20
20. Flowers salmon-yellow in color. SALMON-FLOWERED DESERT PARSLEY
20. Flowers purple..21
21. Plants occurring in Yakima County southward; leaves finely divided, very
long and narrow.....................COLUMBIA DESERT PARSLEY
21. Plants occurring in the Wenatchee Mountains; leaves toothed, not finely
divided and very narrow.............WENATCHEE DESERT PARSLEY
22. Plants occurring in Cascade and Olympic Mountains.
FEW-FRUITED DESERT PARSLEY
22. Plants not occurring as above..................................23
23. Plants with thickened, bulbous roots, not stalked, or with low life form
(usually less than 12 inches tall).................................24
23. Plants without thickened, bulbous roots, or stalked, or more than 12 inches
tall 26
24. Pedicels short, less than 1/8 to 1/4 inch long.....................25
24. Pedicels more than 1/4 inch long..........CANBY'S DESERT PARSLEY
25. Fruits less than 1/4 inch long; plants less than 6 inches tall.
GORMAN'S DESERT PARSLEY
25. Fruits more than 1/4 inch long; plants more than 6 inches tall.
GEYER'S DESERT PARSLEY
26. Ovaries and fruits hairy...27
26. Ovaries and fruits smooth, not hairy.............................28
27. Flowers white or purplish, rarely yellow........GRAY DESERT PARSLEY
27. Flowers yellow....................THOMPSON'S DESERT PARSLEY

28. Flowers white or purplish, rarely yellow..........................29
28. Flowers yellow 30
29. Leaves hairy...............................GRAY DESERT PARSLEY
29. Leaves smooth, not hairy.................GEYER'S DESERT PARSLEY
30. Stems single or few; root with single, often unbranched crown.
                                       SWALE DESERT PARSLEY
30. Stems several to many; root with a branched crown.
                                       GRAY'S DESERT PARSLEY

*   *   *

FEW-FRUITED DESERT PARSLEY (*Lomatium martindalei*)   Flowers white, yellowish-white, or yellow. West. Wash., including the Cascades and Olympics; dry, rocky slopes and meadows in the subalpine zone. Late spring and summer.

NAKED DESERT PARSLEY (*Lomatium nudicaule*) Flowers yellow. East. and West. Wash.; open places and woods in lowlands and mountains; common in sagebrush and yellow pine forests. Mid spring to early summer. The only desert parsley with broad, rather than finely-divided leaves.

BRANDEGE'S DESERT PARSLEY (*Lomatium brandegei*)   Flowers yellow. East. Wash.; open, grassy slopes and yellow pine woods in foothills and mountains. Late spring and early summer.

SWALE DESERT PARSLEY (*Lomatium ambiguum*)   Flowers yellow. East. Wash. and east slopes of Cascades; open, rocky flats and hillsides in lowlands and mountains. Late spring and early summer.

NARROW-LEAVED DESERTC PARSLEY (*Lomatium triternatum*)   Flowers yellow. East. Wash.; mostly in dry, open meadows and hillsides in lowlands and foothills. Late spring and early summer.

COUS (*Lomatium cous*) Flowers yellow. Southeast. Wash.; dry, open, rocky slopes, sagebrush flats, and subalpine meadows and ridges. Mid spring to mid summer. The famous food plant of the Indians.

COEUR D'ALENE DESERT PARSLEY (*Lomatium farinosum*)   Flowers white. East. Wash.; rocky slopes and flats in lowlands and foothills. Mid to late spring.

GORMAN'S DESERT PARSLEY (*Lomatium gormanii*)   Flowers white, rarely purple, with purplish-black anthers. East. Wash.; sagebrush slopes and flats, as well as rocky scabland areas, from lowlands to subalpine areas. Early spring. Often considered the earliest spring flower in Eastern Washington.

GEYER'S DESERT PARSLEY (*Lomatium geyeri*) Flowers white. East. Wash.; open, sagebrush and grasslands in lowlands, foothills, and lower mountains. Spring.

FERN-LEAVED DESERT PARSLEY (*Lomatium dissectum*)   Flowers yellow or purple. East. Wash.; meadows and open, rocky slopes and slides, in foothills and mountains. Mid spring to early summer.

COLUMBIA DESERT PARSLEY (*Lomatium columbianum*)   Flowers purple to (rarely) yellow. Columbia Gorge and south-central Wash.; open, rocky slopes, mostly along the Columbia River. Early spring.

Figure 49.
Lomatium nudicaule, an unusal desert parsley. (Yaich)

206

THOMPSON'S DESERT PARSLEY (*Lomatium thompsonii*) Flowers yellow. Chelan County; open, yellow pine woods and grassy slopes. Early summer.

FINE-LEAVED DESERT PARSLEY (*Lomatium utriculatum*) Flowers yellow. West. Wash.; open prairies and rocky slopes in lowlands. Mid spring to early summer.

WATSON'S DESERT PARSLEY (*Lomatium watsonii*) Flowers yellow. East. Wash.; sagebrush slopes. Late spring.

SALMON-FLOWERED DESERT PARSLEY (*Lomatium salmoniflorum*) Flowers salmon-red to salmon-yellow. East. Wash.; dry, rocky places. Early spring.

WENATCHEE DESERT PARSLEY (*Lomatium cuspidatum*) Flowers purple. Wenatchee Mountains; open, rocky slopes. Late spring and early summer.

CANBY'S DESERT PARSLEY (*Lomatium canbyi*) Flowers white, with purple anthers. East. Wash.; rocky, sagebrush slopes. Early spring.

GRAY DESERT PARSLEY (*Lomatium macrocarpum*) Flowers white, purplish, or rarely yellow. East. Wash.; open, rocky places in lowlands and foothills. Early to late spring.

GRAY'S DESERT PARSLEY (*Lomatium grayi*) Flowers yellow. East. Wash. and east slopes of Cascades; dry, rocky places in lowlands, foothills, and lower parts of mountains. Spring.

TAUSCHIAS (*Tauschia*)

Small plants a few inches tall arising from bulbous or thickened roots and with very small, compound umbels. Leaves mostly basal; pinnately or ternately compound.

1. Leaf blades very long and narrow; occurring in sagebrush areas in Yakima County . . . . HOOVER'S TAUSCHIA
1. Leaf blades ovate to lanceolate, but never long and narrow; occurs on Mount Rainier . . . . STRICKLAND'S TAUSCHIA

*   *   *

HOOVER'S TAUSCHIA (*Tauschia hooveri*) Flowers white, with purple anthers. Root round and bulbous. Yakima County; sagebrush areas. Early to mid spring.

STRICKLAND'S TAUSCHIA (*Tauschia stricklandii*) Flowers yellow. Root long and thick. Mount Rainier; moist, subalpine meadows. Late summer.

ANGELICAS (*Angelica*) (Plate 33)

Tall plants with compound leaves and very large, compound umbels. The leaves are usually 3-cleft, with each of the subdivisions pinnately divided into large, toothed segments.

1. Plants occurring along the seashore; involucral bracts absent 2
1. Plants not occurring along the seashore; involucral bracts present or absent 3
2. Underside of leaves densely woolly . . . . SEACOAST ANGELICA
2. Underside of leaves smooth . . . . SEA-WATCH

3. Leaf-bearing portion of leaf stem bending downward.KNEELING ANGELICA
3. Leaf-bearing portion of leaf stem not bending downward...............4
4. Leaflets long and narrow (several times longer than wide); leaflets usually less than 2 inches long........................CANBY'S ANGELICA
4. Leaflets not long and narrow (1½ to 2 times longer than wide); leaflets usually more than 2 inches long.................SHINING ANGELICA

*　　*　　*

SEACOAST ANGELICA (*Angelica hendersonii*) Plants to 60 inches with white, woolly hairs on undersides of leaves. Flowers white. Southwest. Wash.; bluffs and sand dunes along the sea beach. Summer.

SEA-WATCH (*Angelica lucida*) Plants to 48 inches with leaves having smooth undersides. Flowers white. Sea coast of West. Wash.; bluffs and sand dunes along the sea beach. Summer.

KNEELING ANGELICA (*Angelica genuflexa*) Leaf stalk bending downward at point of attachment of first pair of segments. Flowers white or pinkish. West. Wash.; moist places, especially swamps. Summer.

CANBY'S ANGELICA (*Angelica canbyi*) Plants to 48 inches with relatively small leaflets. Flowers white. East. Wash.; moist habitats, such as streambanks; lowlands and Cascade foothills. Mid summer to early autumn.

SHINING ANGELICA (*Angelica arguta*) Plants to 7 feet with immense leaves often reaching 18-24 inches in length. Leaflets sharply toothed and occasionally lobed. Flowers white. East. (mostly) and West. Wash.; moist habitats, such as bogs, marshes, streamsides, and wet meadows, in lowlands and up into the mountains. Summer.

SWEET CICELIES (*Osmorhiza*) (Fig. 48)

Plants with sweet, licorice-like odor to crushed stems, several-cleft leaves, and few-flowered umbels.

1. Base of fruits not bristly, but smooth; flowers yellow.
WESTERN SWEET CICELY
1. Base of fruits bristly; flowers whitish or purplish......................2
2. Flowers whitish or greenish white...........MOUNTAIN SWEET CICELY
2. Flowers usually purple.....................PURPLISH SWEET CICELY

*　　*　　*

WESTERN SWEET CICELY (*Osmorhiza occidentalis*) Plants to 48 inches, with aromatic foliage, usually 12-rayed, yellow-flowered umbels. East. and West. Wash.; dry woods, brush, and rocky banks. Mid spring to mid summer.

MOUNTAIN SWEET CICELY (*Osmorhiza chilensis*) Plants to 40 inches with greenish-white to white flowers bearing 3-8 rays. East. and West. Wash.; woods; common. Mid spring to early summer.

PURPLISH SWEET CICELY (*Osmorhiza purpurea*) Plants to 24 inches, with 6-rayed purplish flowers. East. and West. Wash.; moist, open habitats in mountains. Early and mid summer.

LOVAGES (*Ligusticum*) (Color Plate 34)

Relatively small umbellifers with finely-divided leaves and rather flat-topped umbels. Flowers usually all basal, except for 1 or 2 on stem. Most characters of genus rather technical. Rely on generic key.

1. Plants occurring west of Cascade Mountains. . PARSLEY-LEAVED LOVAGE
1. Plants occurring in and east of the Cascade Mountains. 2

2. Plants usually more than 28 inches tall; stalks (rays) of terminal umbel numerous (usually more than 15). . . . . CANBY'S LOVAGE
2. Plants usually less than 28 inches tall; stalks (rays) of terminal umbel few (usually less than 15). . . . . GRAY'S LOVAGE

*　　*　　*

PARSLEY-LEAVED LOVAGE (*Ligusticum apiifolium*) Stems leafy, to 5 feet. Flowers white. West. Wash.; open to semi-open places in the lowlands. Late spring to mid summer.

CANBY'S LOVAGE (*Ligusticum canbyi*) Plants to 48 inches with 1 or more leaves on the stem. Flowers white. Cascades and East. Wash.; wet habitats in mountains, such as streamsides, boggy seepage slopes, and moist meadows. Late spring and summer.

GRAY'S LOVAGE (*Ligusticum grayi*) Plants to 24 inches with all leaves basal, long stemmed, and finely dissected. Resembles the valerians, but the leaves of the lovage are different. Flowers white. Cascades and East. Wash.; open woods and dry to semi-moist slopes and meadows in mountains. Mid summer to early autumn. Flowers occasionally purplish tipped.

YAMPAHS (*Perideridea*)

Sparse, thin-stemmed umbellifers with flower clusters at or near tips of long stems and with few, long, narrow leaves. Roots tuberous.

1. Fruits roundish, about as wide as long. . . . . WESTERN YAMPAH
1. Fruits oblong, about twice as long as broad. . . . . OREGON YAMPAH

*　　*　　*

WESTERN YAMPAH (*Perideridia gairdneri*) Plants to 5 feet; leaves very narrow. Flowers white. East. and West. Wash.; dry to moist meadows and woods in lowlands and foothills. Summer.

OREGON YAMPAH (*Perideridia oregana*) Plants to 36 inches; leaves slightly broader than in above species. Flowers white. Cascades and West. Wash.; open habitats, such as meadows and slopes, in lowlands, foothills, and lower mountains. Summer.

Chapter 41—The Dogwood Family (*Cornaceae*)

Members of this family are trees, shrubs, or herbs with opposite or whorled (rarely alternate) leaves. Flowers small and regular. Sepals, petals, and stamens usually 4. Ovary inferior. One herbaceous species included as a wildflower in this guide. (Color Plate 35)

BUNCHBERRY (*Cornus canadensis*) Plants to 12 inches. A false whorl of 6 leaves at tip of stem from which projects a tight head of small, yellowish flowers surrounded in turn by 4 large white sepals (the apparent "flower"). Flowers followed by conspicuous, tight clusters of bright red, berry-like fruits. East. and West. Wash.; common and widely distributed in dense to semi-open coniferous woods. A great favorite of forest travelers. Also called "Canada dogwood" or "dwarf cornel."

Luetkea, Count F. P.; 1797-1882 (Russian); *Luetkea.*
Lyall, David; 1817-1895 (Scottish); *Saxifraga lyallii.*
Menzies, Archibald; 1754-1842 (Scottish); *Menziesia.*
Mertens, F. C.; 1764-1831 (German); *Mertensia.*
Michaux, Andre; 1746-1802 (French); *Artemisia michauxiana.*
Monti, Guiseppe; 1682-1760 (Italian); *Montia.*
Muhlenberg, Gotthilf H. E.; 1753-1815 (American); *Centaurium muhlenbergii.*
Munro, William; 1818-1889 (British); *Sphaeralcea munroana.*
Navarrete, Fernandez; 1610-1689 (Spanish); *Navarretia.*
Nuttall, Thomas; 1786-1859 (American); *Polygonum nuttallii.*
Parry, Charles C.; 1823-1890 (American); *Campanula parryi.*
Piper, Charles V.; 1867-1926 (American); *Anemone piperi.*
Pursh, Frederick; 1774-1820 (German-American); *Purshia.*
Richardson, Sir John, 1787-1865 (Scottish); *Penstemon richardsonii.*
Rumiantzev, Nikolai; 1754-1826 (Russian); *Spiranthes romanzoffia.*
Rudbeck, Olaf (father and son); 1630-1702, 1660-1740 (Swedish); *Rudbeckia.*
Rydberg, Per A.; 1860-1931 (American); *Penstemon rydbergii.*
Sabine, Sir Edward; 1788-1883 (British); *Lupinus sabinii.*
Saussure, Horace B. de; 1740-1799 (Swiss); *Saussurea.*
Schreber, Johann C. D. von; 1739-1810 (German); *Brasenia schreberi.*
Scouler, John; 1804-1871 (Scottish); *Corydalis scouleri.*
Shepherd, John; 1764-1836 (British); *Shepherdia.*
Smelowsky, Timotheus; 1770-1815 (Russian); *Smelowskia.*
Smith, Sir J. E.; 1759-1828 (British); *Disporum smithii.*
Sprague, Isaac; 1811-1895 (American); *Spraguea.*
Stanley, Edward; 1775-1851 (British); *Stanleya.*
Suksdorf, Wilhelm N.; 1850-1932 (American); *Suksdorfia.*
Tofield, Thomas; 1730-1779 (British); *Tofieldia.*
Tolmie, William F.; 1812-1888 (Scottish); *Tolmiea.*
Torrey, John; 1796-1873 (American); *Lathyrus torreyi.*
Townsend, David; 1787-1858 (American); *Townsendia.*
Trautvetter, Ernst R. von; 1809-1889 (Russian); *Trautvetteria.*
Vancouver, George; 1757-1798 (British); *Vancouveria.*
Wyeth, Nathanial; 1802-1856 (American); *Wyethia.*

Chapter 42—The Heath Family (*Ericaceae*)

Members of this family, as here included, are perennial herbs with simple, alternate, often evergreen leaves which are occasionally scale-like. Flowers perfect and usually regular. Floral parts in 4's or 5's. Petals are usually united. Some species are saprophytes or parasites, living on decaying or living tissues of other plants, respectively. (Color Plate 35)

1. Plants with green leaves. 2
1. Plants without green leaves. 3

2. Leaves located along the stem, not basal. . .PRINCE'S PINES (*Chimaphila*)
2. Leaves basal. . . . . .WINTERGREENS (*Pyrola*)

3. Flowering stems less than 8 inches tall; styles long, projecting from flowers.
    LEAFLESS WINTERGREEN
3. Flowering stems more than 8 inches tall; styles short, not projecting beyond flowers 4

4. Petals united, forming a tubular corolla. 5
4. Petals individual, not united to form tubular corolla; or petals absent. 6

5. Plant whitish; anthers without awns. . . . . .CONE PLANT
5. Plant reddish purple; anthers with awns. . . . . .PINE-DROPS

6. Flowers arranged in a dense spike on flowering stem. 7
6. Flowers arranged as solitary on flowering stem or in 1-sided racemes. . . .8

7. Flowers with petals; plant whitish. . . . . .FRINGED PINESAP
7. Flowers without petals; plant striped dark reddish. . . . . .CANDYSTICK

8. Flowers solitary and drooping at end of flowering stem; plant whitish.
    SINGLE-FLOWERED INDIAN PIPE
8. Flowers several, in 1-sided raceme on flowering stem; plant reddish to yellowish. . . . . .MANY-FLOWERED INDIAN PIPE

*   *   *

LEAFLESS WINTERGREEN (*Pyrola aphylla*)   Described under wintergreens (below).

CONE PLANT (*Hemitomes congestum*)   Plants to 8 inches with stocky stem crowded with pinkish, urn-shaped flowers. Leaves scale-like. West. Wash.; dense coniferous woods in Olympics and Cascades. Summer. (Color Plate 36)

PINE-DROPS (*Pterospora andromedea*)   Plants to 36 inches with single, reddish stems; red to white, urn-shaped, nodding flowers. East. and West. Wash.; deep humus soils in coniferous woods, where parasitic on roots of living plants. Summer. (Color Plate 37)

FRINGED PINESAP (*Pleuricospora fimbriolata*)   Stocky, stubby stems (to 8 inches) with cluster of yellowish flowers in a dense spike at tip. Leaves scale-like and fringed. Floral bracts also fringed. West. Wash.; deep, moist, coniferous woods, scarcely projecting above ground surface; mostly in the mountains. Summer. (Color Plate 36)

CANDYSTICK (*Allotropa virgata*)   Plants to 20 inches with stout, erect stem with striped red and white markings; flowers urn-shaped, in dense, erect, spike-like racemes; leaves scale-like. Flowers striped white or pinkish. West.

Figure 50.
Candystick, *Allotropa,* a denizen of the deep woods. (Yaich)

Wash., including east slope of Cascades; deep humus of coniferous forests. Summer. (Color Plate 35; Fig. 50)

SINGLE-FLOWERED INDIAN PIPE (*Monotropa uniflora*) Plants to 12 inches with waxy white to pinkish or yellowish coloration. A single, down-turned, bell-shaped, white flower at tip of stem. Plant turns black when picked. East. and West. Wash.; deep, moist, shaded, coniferous forests. Summer. (Color Plate 36)

MANY-FLOWERED INDIAN PIPE (*Hypopitys monotropa*) Plants to 10 inches with clusters of white, pinkish, or yellowish bell-shaped flowers at tips of stems. East. and West. Wash.; moist, shaded, coniferous woods. Late spring to mid summer. Also commonly called "Pinesap." (Color Plate 36)

PRINCE'S PINES (*Chimaphila*) (Color Plate 35)

Attractive woodland plants with whorled, evergreen leaves from which project more or less leafless stalks bearing 1 or a few nodding, flattish, waxy white or pinkish flowers. The stigma is basal without style and stamens are prominently displayed.

1. Leaves oblanceolate, much longer than wide, and toothed near the outer end and not at base........................WESTERN PRINCE'S PINE
1. Leaves oval or elliptical, toothed along the entire edge or not toothed at all.
LITTLE PRINCE'S PINE

*   *   *

WESTERN PRINCE'S PINE (*Chimaphila umbellata*) Plants to 12 inches. Anthers purplish. Leaves widest in outer half and dark greenish. Flowers pinkish red and often more than 3-8 in cluster. East. and West. Wash.; coniferous woods. Summer.

LITTLE PRINCE'S PINE (*Chimaphila menziesii*) Plants to 6 inches. Anthers yellow. Leaves widest in basal half and white-streaked. Flowers white or pinkish and 3 or less. East. and West. Wash.; coniferous woods, more in the mountains. Summer.

WINTERGREENS (*Pyrola*) (Color Plate 37)

Perennial, evergreen flowers with mostly basal leaves. Flowers nodding and single or in few-flowered racemes; pinkish, whitish, or greenish with 5 waxy petals. Small, but widely distributed, forest flowers.

1. Flowers single, at ends of flowering stems.
SINGLE-FLOWERED WINTERGREEN
1. Flowers 2 or more in racemes at ends of flowering stems...............2

2. Flowers less than 3/8 inch broad; style straight.......................3
2. Flowers more than 3/8 inch broad; style bent to 1 side.................4

3. Petals white, more than 1/8 inch long; style more than 1/8 inch long.
ONE-SIDED WINTERGREEN
3. Petals pinkish, 1/8 inch or less long; style less than 1/8 inch long.
LESSER WINTERGREEN

4. Plants without green leaves, or rarely 1 or 2 leaves on sterile branches.
LEAFLESS WINTERGREEN
4. Plants with 1 or more green leaves on all stems or branches............5

5. Leaves deep green, mottled with pale streaks along larger veins.
                              WHITE-VEINED WINTERGREEN
5. Leaves not mottled. 6
6. Leaves tapering gradually to narrow base. . . . . . TOOTHED WINTERGREEN
6. Leaves not tapering gradually to narrow base. 7
7. Petals pinkish to purplish. . . . . PINK WINTERGREEN
7. Petals pale yellowish to greenish white.
                         GREENISH-FLOWERED WINTERGREEN

                           *   *   *

SINGLE-FLOWERED WINTERGREEN (*Pyrola uniflora*)   Plants to 5 inches.
Leaves finely toothed and rounded at tip. A single, flat, star-shaped, white or
pinkish, waxy flower with drooping habit on each plant. East. and West. Wash.;
on rotting wood in mossy, coniferous forests from sea level up into the mountains. Early summer. One of the most attractive of the rainforest flowers; also
called "wood nymph."

ONE-SIDED WINTERGREEN (*Pyrola secunda*)   Plants to 6 inches. Leaves
ovate, not basal, but mostly growing on stem close to ground, shiny green and
scalloped or toothed. Flowers located on 1 side of flowering stem. Style
straight. Petals greenish white. East. and West. Wash.; coniferous woods,
where often common. Summer.

LESSER WINTERGREEN (*Pyrola minor*)   Small, basal leaves; straight style.
Flowers pink to reddish, small, and on 1 side of stem. East. and West. Wash.;
coniferous woods, especially shady, mossy places. Summer.

LEAFLESS WINTERGREEN (*Pyrola aphylla*)   Leaves absent or present as
small, basal greenish blades. Flowers greenish white, cream colored, or pink.
East. and West. Wash.; coniferous woods. Summer. Not a true species, but the
leafless forms of other species of wintergreens.

WHITE-VEINED WINTERGREEN (*Pyrola picta*)   Plants to 10 inches. Leaves
dark green with prominent white veining. Flowers greenish white, cream
colored, or pinkish. Style curved. East. and West. Wash.; coniferous woods.
Summer.

TOOTHED WINTERGREEN (*Pyrola dentata*)   Leaves bluish green, lanceolate
to oblanceolate; toothed. Flowers cream colored to greenish white. East. and
West. Wash.; dry forests in the lowlands, particularly yellow pine woods.
Summer.

PINK WINTERGREEN (*Pyrola asarifolia*) Plants to 16 inches with large, green
oval leaves. Flowers pinkish or reddish; style hook-shaped. East. and West.
Wash.; moist coniferous woods of lowlands and mountains. Summer to early
autumn.

GREENISH-FLOWERED WINTERGREEN (*Pyrola chlorantha*)   Leaves small,
round, and thick. Flowers pale yellow to greenish white. East. and West. Wash.;
moist to semi-dry coniferous forests. Summer.

Chapter 43—The Primrose Family (*Primulaceae*)

Members of this family are herbs with perfect, regular flowers and simple leaves. Floral parts usually in 5's, though sepals and corolla lobes may number 4-9 in some species. Sepals united at base or united throughout. Stamens attached to the corolla tube. (Color Plate 37)

1. Leaves basal 2
1. Leaves not basal. 4

2. Flowers very small, less than 1/4 inch long. . . . . .ANDROSACHE
2. Flowers more than 1/4 inch long. 3

3. Calyx and lobes of corolla turned sharply backward in the flower.
SHOOTING-STARS (*Dodecatheon*)
3. Calyx and lobes of corolla not turned backward in the flower, but spreading.
DOUGLASIAS (*Douglasia*)

4. Leaves opposite 5
4. Leaves in whorl at the top of the stem; a few scales or leaves lower on stem . . . . .STAR-FLOWERS (*Trientalis*)

5. Seacoast plants with fleshy leaves; flower consisting of calyx only.
SALTWORT
5. Not as above; flowers with corollas.YELLOW LOOSESTRIFES (*Lysimachia*)

*   *   *

ANDROSACHE (*Androsache septentrionalis*) Plant small and tufted with hairy, slightly toothed leaves. Flowers white, borne in umbels. East. and West. Wash.; dry, rocky places in higher mountainous areas. Late spring and summer.

SALTWORT (*Glaux maritima*) Flowers tiny, pink or whitish, and borne singly in leaf axils. East. and West. Wash.; tidal flats and marshes near salt water, as well as saline soils in the interior. Late spring to mid summer.

SHOOTING-STARS (*Dodecatheon*) (Color Plate 37; Fig. 51)

Perennial herbs with basal leaves and flowers 1 to several, nodding, and located at tips of long flowering stems. Petals and sepals strongly turned back to resemble rays of a shooting star or comet.

1. Leaves broad *and* toothed; flowers white. . . . . .WHITE SHOOTING-STAR
1. Leaves not broad *and* toothed. 2

2. Stigma with conspicuous cap, at least twice as broad as style.
JEFFREY'S SHOOTING-STAR
2. Stigma not conspicuously capped, or if so, the cap less than twice as thick as the style. 3

3. Leaves broad. . . . . .HENDERSON'S SHOOTING-STAR
3. Leaves more or less lanceolate, tapering gradually to the petiole. 4

4. Filaments of stamens scarcely united at base. . .DESERT SHOOTING-STAR
4. Filaments of stamens united at base into a tube for almost half their length.5

5. Filament tube yellowish. . . . . .FEW-FLOWERED SHOOTING-STAR
5. Filament tube purplish. . . . . .NARCISSUS SHOOTING-STAR

Figure 51.
Shooting star, *Dodecatheon*; best known member of the family
in the Washington wilds. (Larrison)

WHITE SHOOTING-STAR (*Dodecatheon dentatum*) Plants to 16 inches with toothed or scalloped leaves and white flowers. East. Wash., including east slope of Cascades and Columbia Gorge; moist, shaded woods and streambanks. Late spring to mid summer.

JEFFREY'S SHOOTING-STAR (*Dodecatheon jeffreyi*) Plants to 24 inches with leaves simple or toothed or scalloped. Colors variable, mostly pink to purple, but even whitish or yellowish. East. and West. Wash.; wet places, such as mountain parks and subalpine meadows and streambanks. Summer.

HENDERSON'S SHOOTING-STAR (*Dodecatheon hendersonii*) Plants to 18 inches with broad oval or triangular leaves and light orchid to deep magenta flowers. West. Wash.; open prairies, as well as woodlands of the lowlands. Early to late spring.

DESERT SHOOTING-STAR (*Dodecatheon conjugens*) Plants to 10 inches with mostly smooth and entire leaves. Flowers white to magenta. East. Wash.; moist places in sagebrush and foothill grasslands and montane meadows. Late spring and early summer.

FEW-FLOWERED SHOOTING-STAR (*Dodecatheon pulchellum*) Plants to 20 inches with mostly smooth foliage. Leaves oblanceolate. Flowers purple to lavender, rarely white. East. and West. Wash.; variable, open grasslands, prairies, alkaline marshes, mountain streambanks, and subalpine meadows. Mid spring and summer.

NARCISSUS SHOOTING-STAR (*Dodecatheon poeticum*) Plants to 6 inches with glandular hairy foliage and toothed leaves. Flowers pink to orchid. East. Wash.; principally the southeastern Cascades; moist areas. Spring.

DOUGLASIAS (*Douglasia*) (Color Plate 37)

Low, matted plants with somewhat woody stems and small, crowded leaves. Flowers somewhat bell-shaped and borne singly or in umbel-shaped inflorescences.

1. Leaves grayish and hairy (pubescent)..............SNOW DOUGLASIA
1. Leaves more or less smooth (glabrous) and not pubescent.
                                    SMOOTH-LEAVED DOUGLASIA
                        *   *   *

SNOW DOUGLASIA (*Douglasia nivalis*) Plants matted with grayish foliage. Flowers red or purple. East. Wash., including the northeastern Cascades; open barren or rocky areas, including sagebrush hillsides and alpine ridges. Mid spring to late summer.

SMOOTH-LEAVED DOUGLASIA (*Douglasia laevigata*) Mat-like plants with reddish flowers grouped several to a stem tip. Leaves 1/2 inch or less. West. Wash.; rocky cliffs and slopes from sea level to alpine areas. Spring and summer.

YELLOW LOOSESTRIFES (*Lysimachia*)

Plants with yellow flowers in which the filaments of the stamens are joined together, making a tube or sleeve around the ovary.

1. Plants with solitary, axillary flowers; leaves oval-shaped.
                                    FRINGED LOOSESTRIFE
1. Plants with flowers in racemes; leaves lanceolate.....................2

2. Floral racemes in axils of leaves . . . . TUFTED LOOSESTRIFE
2. Floral racemes terminal—at tips of stems . . . . BOG LOOSESTRIFE

*   *   *

FRINGED LOOSESTRIFE (*Lysimachia ciliata*) Plants to 40 inches with more or less smooth foliage; long, slender stems; and oblong-ovate or oval leaves. Flowers yellow and axillary. East. Wash.; mostly in the Columbia Gorge; wet meadows and similar places near water. Summer.

TUFTED LOOSESTRIFE (*Lysimachia thyrsiflora*) Plants to 32 inches with smooth foliage and erect stems. Leaves opposite and lanceolate. Flowers yellowish, in short, dense, axillary racemes. East. and West. Wash.; wet habitats, such as shores and swamps. Late spring to mid summer.

BOG LOOSESTRIFE (*Lysimachia terrestris*) Plants to 36 inches with narrow, lanceolate leaves and yellow flowers borne in spike-like racemes. West. Wash.; wet, swampy areas; introduced into cranberry bogs. Summer.

STAR-FLOWERS (*Trientalis*) (Color Plate 38)

Smallish plants with a rosette or crowded group of leaves mostly near the tip of the stem from which project 1 or more star-shaped, white flowers.

1. Leaves sharp-pointed and all located in whorl at tip of stem.
BROAD-LEAVED STAR-FLOWER
1. Leaves not sharp-pointed; more or less scattered along the stem, in addition to the terminal whorl . . . . NORTHERN STAR-FLOWER

*   *   *

BROAD-LEAVED STAR-FLOWER (*Trientalis latifolia*) Flowers pink to reddish. East. and West. Wash.; woods and prairies, but mostly in the mountains in East. Wash. Mid spring to mid summer.

NORTHERN STAR-FLOWER (*Trientalis arctica*) Flowers white. East. and West. Wash.; wet places, such as bogs and swamps. Late spring and summer.

Chapter 44—The Plumbago Family (*Plumbaginaceae*)

Members of this family are seashore herbs with basal leaves and perfect, regular flowers; all floral parts in 5's. Sepals are united as are the petals at their bases. Flowers are pink. One species in our area. (Color Plate 38)

BEACH THRIFT (*Armeria maritima*) Flowers pink, in tight roundish heads at the tips of long stalks. West. Wash.; sandy bluffs and banks along saltwater, and on some inland prairies. Early spring to mid summer.

The Indians of the Pacific Northwest were well acquainted with a number of wildflowers. The extent of their knowledge and the uses they put many species indicate dramatically the keenness of their observational powers and the necessities of taking advantage of natural resources in an economy based primarily on a literal living off the land.

A detailed source of information on Indian uses of plants is Dr. Erna Gunther's ETHNOBOTANY OF WESTERN WASHINGTON published by the University of Washington Press at $2.45. Written by a long-time student of Northwest Indians, this book is a gold mine of Indian plant lore. A few items are mentioned here, derived mainly from this source.

Various species of plants were used for construction materials, food, medicines, dyes, etc. Obviously, the various tree species figured prominently in house and canoe manufacture, but one of the most famous of the wildflowers, the bear grass, has been widely used in the making of baskets. What to many of us seems a lowly plant, the skunk cabbage, was highly appreciated. The roots and flowers were variously cooked for food, while the leaves were used for wrapping materials and drinking cups. The roots, properly prepared, served as a diuretic or poultice. The leaves featured also as materials for treating sores and rheumatism. They were widely used for wrapping foods in the barbecuing process of cooking. There is even a reported use of the plant in a sealer's canoe as a charm to cause the seals to lie still in the water, thus permitting their easier capture.

The leaves of that common flower of the rain forest, the wood sorrel, were eaten as a "pick-up" food by hunters or as "wilted lettuce" cooked in grease. Medicinally, the juice from the leaves served as an eye wash.

The Skagits used the bleeding heart as a toothache medicine, by which name it was known to them. They also used the plant as a vermifuge and hair tonic.

The water lily was commonly used to supply a liniment for rheumatism.

While most of us avoid the nettles if at all possible, these plants supplied a number of values to the Indians. Strips of bark were woven into a cord or twine, often for nets. Medicinally, the foliage or extracted juices were used as a liniment, poultice, general tonic, muscle relaxant for childbirth, specific for colds as well as nosebleed and headaches, and many more. Obviously, it functioned well as a counter irritant!

Figure 52.
Flower photography can be exciting. (Larrison)

Chapter 45—The Gentian Family (*Gentianaceae*)

Members of this family are smooth-foliaged herbs with opposite, non-petioled, simple, entire leaves on a 4- or 5-toothed calyx and a 4- or 5-lobed corolla. Stamens same number as corolla lobes. Petals fused for much of their length to form the tube-like corolla with only the distal lobes separate. (Color Plate 38)

1. Corolla long, slender, and tubular; corolla lobes spreading like spokes on a wheel . . . . CENTAURIES (*Centaurium*)
1. Corolla and lobes not as above. 2

2. Corolla bell-shaped. . . . . GENTIANS (*Gentiana*)
2. Corolla not bell-shaped. 3

3. Flower parts in 5's. . . . . SWERTIA
3. Flower parts in 4's. . . . . FRASERAS (*Frasera*)

*　　*　　*

SWERTIA (*Swertia perennis*) Erect, often moderately tall, plants with greenish white or bluish flowers in loose, terminal cymose panicle. Basal leaves large; stem leaves small. East. and West. Wash.; meadows, bogs, and streambanks in montane and subalpine areas. Summer. (Color Plate 39)

CENTAURIES (*Centaurium*)

Medium-sized plants with opposite leaves and flowers in loose, terminal inflorescences. Corolla tube long and slender with prominently-spreading distal lobes.

1. Flowers all borne on long pedicels (at least 1/8 inch long).
WESTERN CENTAURY
1. Flowers on short pedicels (less than 1/8 inch long).
MUHLENBERG'S CENTAURY

*　　*　　*

WESTERN CENTAURY (*Centaurium exaltatum*) Flowers light red to whitish. Plants to 12 inches. East. Wash.; moist shores of alkaline lakes and ponds. Summer.

MUHLENBERG'S CENTAURY (*Centaurium muhlenbergii*) Plants to 12 inches with white or pink flowers. East. Wash. and the Columbia Gorge; moist soil in open regions. Summer.

GENTIANS (*Gentiana*) (Color Plate 38)

Plants with usually bluish flowers in the form of large, funnel-shaped tubes with terminal lobes. Lobes of cup-like calyx with prominent teeth.

1. Flowers smaller (corollas less than 3/4 inch long). . .NORTHERN GENTIAN
1. Flowers larger (corollas more than 1 inch long). 2

2. Plants less than 12 inches tall. . . . . MOUNTAIN BOG GENTIAN
2. Plants more than 12 inches tall. 3

3. Leaves more or less oval-shaped and sharply narrowing at base.
OBLONG-LEAVED GENTIAN

3. Leaves oblong-lanceolate (considerably longer than wide and not sharply
   narrowing at base). . . . . .STIFF GENTIAN

*   *   *

NORTHERN GENTIAN (*Gentiana amarella*) Plants to 20 inches. Leaves broad lanceolate. Flowers numerous, small, bluish, purplish, lavender, or yellowish and terminal and axillary. East. and West. Wash.; moist meadows and woods. Summer.

MOUNTAIN BOG GENTIAN (*Gentiana calycosa*) Plants to 12 inches, clustered. Flowers large, bluish (rarely yellow), and one to several at tips of stems. Several long, fringe-like teeth between corolla lobes. East. and West. Wash.; moist meadows and streambanks, primarily in the subalpine and alpine areas of the higher mountains. Mid summer to fall. First collected by William Fraser Tolmie on Mount Rainier in 1833.

OBLONG-LEAVED GENTIAN (*Gentiana affinis*) Plants leafy, to 18 inches with showy, dark blue flowers in terminal groups. Teeth between corolla lobes short. East. Wash.; moist areas, such as meadows and grasslands in lowlands and mountains. Mid summer to early autumn.

STIFF GENTIAN (*Gentiana sceptrum*) Plants often tall (to 48 inches). Flowers blue, few, and terminal. No fringed teeth between corolla lobes. Upper leaves larger than lower ones. West. Wash.; bogs and wet meadows in lowlands. Mid summer to autumn.

FRASERAS (*Frasera*) (Color Plate 38)

Medium-sized to sometimes tall plants with large, terminal clusters or spikes of flowers. Corolla lobes with distinct fringed glands at their bases. Some species with a circle of hair-like scales surrounding the stamens. These plants are often a prominent part of the community in which they occur.

1. Plants with paired, opposite leaves on stems. . . . . SHINING FRASERA
1. Plants with stem leaves in whorls of 3-5. 2

2. Flowers greenish yellow with purple spots. . . . . GIANT FRASERA
2. Flowers light bluish . . . . .CLUSTERED FRASERA

*   *   *

SHINING FRASERA (*Frasera albicaulis*) Plants to 30 inches. Leaves long and narrow, with white margins and 3 prominent veins. Flowers bluish to white. East. Wash.; open, grassy slopes of plains and foothills. Late spring to mid summer.

GIANT FRASERA (*Frasera speciosa*) Plants to 6 or more feet. Flowers greenish yellow, spotted with purplish, and in elongated, terminal group. East. Wash.; grassy areas in valleys and foothills, as well as open yellow pine woods. Summer.

CLUSTERED FRASERA (*Frasera fastigiata*) Plants to 48 inches. Stem leaves sessile, elliptic to lanceolate. Flowers light blue, borne in short (but elongate), dense, terminal cluster. Blue Mountains and border areas of East. Wash.; moist swales in meadows and yellow pine woods. Late spring to mid summer.

222

Chapter 46—The Buckbean Family (*Menyanthaceae*)

Members of this family are perennial herbs with simple or compound leaves with long petioles and perfect, regular flowers borne in racemes or cymes. Leaves and flowering stems arising from horizontal rhizomes. Stamens 5. Semi-aquatic to aquatic plants. (Color Plate 39)

1. Leaves compound with 3 leaflets........................BUCKBEAN
1. Leaves simple, not compound......................DEER-CABBAGE

*   *   *

BUCKBEAN (*Menyanthes trifoliata*) Flowers white to pinkish in terminal clusters on stout, upright stems. Mostly West. Wash.; but also in extreme northeastern part of state; bogs and shallow lakes, where it is usually found with the stems submerged and only the leaves and flowers emerging above the water's surface. Late spring and summer.

DEER-CABBAGE (*Nephrophyllidium cristi-galli*)   Flowers white. Olympic Peninsula; bogs, swamps, and wet meadows. Summer.

The trials and tribulations of the early plant collectors can hardly be over-emphasized. They were truly heroic men. A very exhaustive treatment of these botanical pioneers is given in Susan Delano McKelvey's *Botanical Exploration of the Trans-Mississippi West* published in 1955 by the Arnold Arboretum of Harvard University. Though out of print, this fascinating volume can probably be found in some city libraries.

Following are some quotations selected from the journals of David Douglas who, during the 1820's and 30's almost single-handedly explored the plants of many areas of the Pacific Northwest.

*   *   *

I laboured under very great disadvantage by the almost continual rain; many of my specimens I lost, and although I had several oilcloths, I was unable to keep my plants and my blanket dry or to preserve a single bird. . . . Only two nights were dry . . . before I could lie down to sleep my blanket drying generally occupied an hour. . . .

Last night I was much annoyed by a herd of rats, which devoured every particle of seed I had collected, bit a bundle of dry plants almost right through, carried off my razor and soap-brush. One . . . was in the act of depriving me of my inkstand, which I had been using before I lay down . . . I lifted my gun . . . and gave him the contents. I found it a very strange species, body 10 inches, tail 7. . . .

When my people in England are made acquainted with my travels, they may perhaps think I have told them nothing but my miseries. That may be very correct, but I know that such objects as I am in quest of are not obtained without a share of labour, anxiety of mind, and sometimes risk of personal safety. . . .

(Douglas' journal continued in Chapter 48)

Figure 53.
A bog in Mount Rainier National Park completely choked with buckbean,
Menyanthes. (Larrison)

224

Chapter 47—The Dogbane Family (*Apocynaceae*)

Members of this family are perennial herbs with milky juice and simple, opposite leaves. Flowers are perfect and regular, with the floral parts in 5's. Pistils 2. Flowers are numerous and small. (Color Plate 39)

1. Flowers 1/4 inch long or more and pinkish; leaves drooping or spreading out horizontally 2
1. Flowers less than 1/4 inch long and whitish or greenish white; leaves pointing upward 3
2. Corolla twice as long as calyx; leaves spreading.
                                        INTERMEDIATE DOGBANE
2. Corolla almost three times as long as the calyx; leaves drooping.
                                        SPREADING DOGBANE

3. Leaves with distinct petioles and tapering gradually to base. . INDIAN HEMP
3. Leaves without distinct petioles and broad, not gradually tapering, at base.
                                        CLASPING-LEAVED DOGBANE

                        *   *   *

INTERMEDIATE DOGBANE (*Apocynum medium*) Plants branching, to 20 inches. Leaves variable in shape. Flowers pinkish, in terminal or axillary panicles. East. and West. Wash.; open ground in lowlands and foothills. Summer and early autumn. Apparently a hybrid between 2 other dogbane species.

SPREADING DOGBANE (*Apocynum androsaemifolium*) Plants erect, branched, to 20 inches. Foliage smooth, with elliptic to oblong leaves. Flowers bell-shaped, pink, in terminal or axillary panicles. Corolla lobes recurved. East. and West. Wash.; dry, somewhat shaded places in lowlands, foothills, and lower mountains. Summer and early autumn.

INDIAN HEMP (*Apocynum cannabinum*) Plants to 20 inches, with smooth, oblong to almost lanceolate leaves. Flowers white or greenish white, in tight, terminal panicles. Corolla lobes erect. East. and West. Wash.; dry to moist, open places in lowlands and lower mountain areas. Summer and early autumn.

CLASPING-LEAVED DOGBANE (*Apocynum sibiricum*) Similar to above species, but upper leaves mostly without petioles. Flowers white, in small, close, terminal panicles. East. and West. Wash.; waste and cultivated lowlands. Summer and early autumn.

Chapter 48—The Milkweed Family (Asclepiadaceae)

Members of this family are perennial herbs with milky juice, opposite (or whorled) leaves, and perfect, regular flowers. Flower parts in 5's. Stigma and stamens arranged as a trap for insects which, if they succeed in escaping, carry with them large masses of pollen to cross-fertilize other milkweeds. (Color Plate 39)

1. Stem leaves mostly in whorls; flower stalks (pedicels) not woolly.
   NARROW-LEAVED MILKWEED
1. Stem leaves paired and opposite and not in whorls; flower stalks very woolly. . . . . SHOWY MILKWEED

*   *   *

NARROW-LEAVED MILKWEED (*Asclepias fascicularis*)   Flowers greenish white, tinged with purple. East. Wash.; dry to moist places in sagebrush, grasslands, and open yellow pine woods. Summer.

SHOWY MILKWEED (*Asclepias speciosa*)   Flowers greenish, tinged with red. Plants 2-4 feet, with thick, woolly leaves. Flowers in axillary and terminal umbels. East. Wash.; sandy, gravelly places, often near water. Summer.

Continuation of David Douglas' journal:

The luxury of a night's sleep on a bed of pine branches can only be appreciated by those who have experienced a route over a barren plain, scorched by the sun, or fatigued by groping through a thick forest, crossing gullies, dead wood, lakes, stones, etc. Indeed so much worn was I three times by fatigue and hunger that twice I crawled, for I could hardly walk, to a small abandoned hut. I killed two partridges . . . which I placed in my little kettle to boil for supper. . . . I awoke at daybreak and beheld my supper burned to ashes and three holes in the bottom of my kettle. . . . I had to make a little tea. . . . This I did by scouring out the lid of my tinder-box and boiling water in it!

I have a tent, but generally am so much fatigued that the labour of pitching it is too great. Here it could not be done for want of wood, and tent-poles cannot be carried. . . .

I laid myself down early on the floor of the Indian Hall, but was very shortly afterwards roused from my slumber by an indescribable herd of fleas, and had to sleep out among the bushes; the annoyance of two species of ants, one very large, black, 3/4 of an inch long, and a small red one, rendered it worse, so this night I did not sleep and gladly hailed the returning day. . . .

My store of clothes is very low, nearly reduced to what I have on my back —one pair of shoes, no stockings, two shirts, two handkerchiefs, my blanket and cloak; thus I adapt my costume to that of the country, as I could not carry more, without reducing myself to an inadequate supply of paper and such articles of Natural History. . . .

(Douglas' journal continued in Chapter 49)

Chapter 49—The Morning-Glory Family (*Convolvulaceae*)

Members of this family are twining or trailing herbs with alternate leaves. Flowers regular. Sepals and stamens 5. The petals are joined to produce a funnel-shaped corolla. A large family, containing some famous weeds. (Color Plate 40)

1. Leaves round, not pointed, and fleshy . . . . BEACH MORNING-GLORY
1. Leaves triangular, sharply pointed, and not fleshy.
HEDGE MORNING-GLORY

*   *   *

BEACH MORNING-GLORY (*Convolvulus soldanella*) Flowers red to purple. West. Wash.; sandy beaches and dunes along salt water. Mid spring to early autumn.

HEDGE MORNING-GLORY (*Convolvulus sepium*) Flowers white or pink. Two large, pointed bracts about the calyx. West. Wash.; waste areas in moist lowlands. Late spring to fall. A pernicious weed in many localities. Twines and climbs over fences and shrubbery.

Note: Very similar to this species is the field bindweed (*Convolvulus arvensis*), a very common weed from Europe. Plant is similar to *C. sepium* but is a very much smaller plant with smaller flowers. A vine trailing over the ground in fields and along roadsides. Flowers about 1 inch in diameter and 1 inch long, ranging in color from white to pink.

Continuation of David Douglas' journal:

I am now here, and God knows where I may be the next. In all probability, if a change does not take place, I will shortly be consigned to the tomb. I can die satisfied with myself. I never have given cause for remonstrance or pain to an individual on earth. I am in my twenty-seventh year.

My outfit is five pounds of tea, and the same quantity of coffee, twenty-five pounds of sugar, fifteen pounds of rice, and fifty pounds of biscuit; a gallon of wine, ten pounds of powder and as much of balls, a little shot, a small silk fishing-net, and some angling tackle, a tent, two blankets, two cotton and two flannel shirts, a handkerchief, vest, coat, and a pair of deer-skin trousers . . . two pairs of shoes, one of stockings, twelve pairs of mocassins, and a straw hat. These constitute the whole of my personal effects; also a ream and a half of paper, and instruments of various kinds; my faithful servants, several Indians, ten or twelve horses, and my old terrier . . . who has guarded me throughout all my journies, and whom . . . I mean certainly to pension off, on four pennyworth of cat's meat per day!

*   *   *

In the last quotation, Douglas was obviously better off than on previous trips!

Figure 54.
White gilias on a Palouse hillside. (Larrison)

228

Chapter 50—The Phlox Family (*Polemoniaceae*)

Members of this family are annual or perennial herbs with alternate or opposite, entire leaves and perfect, regular flowers. Floral parts in 5's. Petals often partly united to form a bell-shaped corolla. Plant form varies from erect, leafy stems to moss-like cushions. (Color Plate 40)

1. Lower leaves opposite and entire; lower part of corolla long and tubular. . .2
1. Lower leaves not all opposite or entire; lower part of corolla not long and tubular 3

2. Flowers large; plants perennial. . . . . .PHLOX (*Phlox*)
2. Flowers small; plants annual. . . . . .PINK MICROSTERIS

3. Leaves palmate and sharply divided. 4
3. Leaves not all palmately divided. 6

4. Plants annual and very slender. . . . . .LINANTHUSES (*Linanthus*)
4. Plants perennial and strongly branched. 5

5. Leaves soft and not prickly; plants woody at base.
NUTTALL'S LINANTHASTRUM
5. Leaves stiff and prickly; plants shrubby with woody stems.
GRANITE LEPTODACTYLON

6. Leaves definitely pinnately compound. . . . . . .POLEMONIUMS (*Polemonium*)
6. Leaves not definitely pinnately compound. 7

7. Lobes of calyx unequal and needle-pointed. . . .NAVARRETIAS (*Navarretia*)
7. Lobes of calyx equal and not needle-pointed. 8

8. Calyx not split by developing capsule. . . . . .GILIAS (*Gilia*)
8. Calyx split by developing capsule. . . . . .COLLOMIAS (*Collomia*)

*   *   *

PINK MICROSTERIS (*Microsteris gracilis*) Plants low, to 8 inches, with numerous spreading branches and sessile, lanceolate leaves. Corolla tube yellowish with pink lobes. Flowers axillary on slender stems. East. and West. Wash.; moist grasslands and open woods in lowlands and foothills. Early spring to early summer. (Color Plate 41)

NUTTALL'S LINANTHASTRUM (*Linanthastrum nuttallii*) Small plant, usually less than 8 inches tall. Leaves linear in whorl-like clusters on stems. Flowers clustered and terminal, with yellow corolla tubes and whitish lobes. Anthers orange. Cascades and East. Wash.; open, rocky or semi-wooded slopes in montane and alpine areas. Summer. (Color Plate 40)

GRANITE LEPTODACTYLON (*Leptodactylon pungens*) Low, shrubby plant to 20 inches. Foliage dense and spine-like. Flowers white, yellowish, or pinkish, with spreading corolla lobes. East. Wash.; open, rocky or sandy habitats in the arid desert regions and foothills. Spring to mid summer.

PHLOX (*Phlox*) (Color Plates 41, 42)

Low-growing, usually matted (there are exceptions) or cushion-like plants with masses of flat-lobed flowers with prominently spreading lobes. Flowers may be single or in terminal cymes. Leaves dense and often needle-like.

1. Plants erect with some leaves larger than 1¼ inches.................2
1. Plants more or less mat-like.......................................4
2. Style about same length as stamens....................SHOWY PHLOX
2. Style considerably longer than stamens............................3
3. Those parts of calyx between ribs with noticeable keels.
                                                    LONG-LEAVED PHLOX
3. Those parts of calyx between ribs without noticeable keels.
                                                       STICKY PHLOX
4. Leaves very stiff, with dense cobwebby hairs.............GRAY PHLOX
4. Leaves soft, without dense cobwebby hairs........................5
5. Stems somewhat erect (2 or more inches tall); leaves somewhat stiff and
   very narrow....................................CLUSTERED PHLOX
5. Stems less erect, plants more matted; leaves softer and not so narrow....6
6. Flowers with styles less than 1/8 inch long........HENDERSON'S PHLOX
6. Flowers with styles more than 1/8 inch long........SPREADING PHLOX

                        *   *   *

SHOWY PHLOX (*Phlox speciosa*) Plants to 16 inches with narrow-lanceolate leaves and white or pink flowers in dense, leafy cymes. East. Wash.; sagebrush, grassland, and open yellow pine woods. Mid spring to early summer.

LONG-LEAVED PHLOX (*Phlox longifolia*) Plants to 20 inches, often very woolly below. Leaves very narrow, to 4 inches long in upper parts of plant. Flowers pink or white in open, many-flowered cymes. East. Wash.; dry, rocky places in open areas from lowlands to foothills and subalpine sites. Mid spring to mid summer.

STICKY PHLOX (*Phlox viscida*) Plants to 12 inches with linear-lanceolate leaves and lavender or white flowers in single to few-flowered terminal clusters. Blue Mountains; open, rocky habitats. Late spring and early summer.

GRAY PHLOX (*Phlox hoodii*) Plants mat-like with firm, pungent foliage. Flowers blue, pink, or white and terminal and mostly single. East. Wash.; sagebrush and higher grasslands. Mid spring to early summer.

CLUSTERED PHLOX (*Phlox caespitosa*) Plants with abundance of closely-clustered stems. Leaves linear, somewhat stiff and pungent. Flowers bluish. East. Wash.; open yellow pine woods and sagebrush slopes. Mid spring to early summer.

HENDERSON'S PHLOX (*Phlox hendersonii*) Dwarfed, densely-clustered plants with long, narrow, glandular-hairy leaves and bluish flowers that are solitary at ends of stems. Eastern Cascades; open, rocky areas in the high mountains. Summer.

SPREADING PHLOX (*Phlox diffusa*) Plants in form of loose mats of massed flowers and needle-like leaves. Stems somewhat woody; leaves yellowish green. Flowers white, pink, or lilac. East. and West. Wash.; dry, open, rocky places, as well as open woods, at moderate to high elevations in the mountainous areas, lowering to suitable habitats in lowlands and foothills in the northeastern part of the state. Late spring (lower elevations) to late summer (higher elevations).

LINANTHUSES (*Linanthus*) (Color Plate 41)

Plants with tall, single stems with scattered whorl-like clusters of very narrow leaves. Flowers bell-shaped or with long corolla tubes.

1. Corolla tube at least 4 times as long as the corolla lobes.
                                    BICOLORED LINANTHUS
1. Corolla tube not 4 times as long as corolla lobes.....................2
2. Corolla about 1/8 inch or less long; higher elevations.
                                    NORTHERN LINANTHUS
2. Corolla more than 1/4 inch long; lowlands.
                              THREAD-STEMMED LINANTHUS

                    *   *   *

BICOLORED LINANTHUS (*Linanthus bicolor*) Plants to 6 inches. Corolla tube yellow with pink, purplish, or white lobes. West. Wash. and Columbia Gorge; open areas in lowlands and foothills. Mid spring to early summer.

NORTHERN LINANTHUS (*Linanthus septentrionalis*) Plants to 12 inches. Corolla light blue or white with yellow throat. East. Wash.; grasslands and open yellow pine woods in foothills and lower mountainous areas. Late spring to mid summer.

THREAD-STEMMED LINANTHUS (*Linanthus pharnaceoides*) Plants to 12 inches and with many branches. Corolla lobes more spreading. Flowers bluish. East. Wash.; sagebrush, grasslands, and open yellow pine woods. Late spring to mid summer.

POLEMONIUMS (*Polemonium*) (Color Plate 42)

Plants with long, pinnately-divided leaves. The leaflets together resemble rungs on a ladder, hence the often commonly used name of "Jacob's ladder" for this genus. Flowers usually bunched in terminal clusters.

1. Flowers inconspicuous; corolla same size as, or shorter than, calyx.
                                    ANNUAL POLEMONIUM
1. Flowers conspicuous; corolla noticeably longer than calyx.............2
2. Flowering stems solitary and erect...........WESTERN POLEMONIUM
2. Flowering stems clustered and more or less erect....................3
3. Calyx more than 1/4 inch long..................GIANT POLEMONIUM
3. Calyx less than 1/4 inch long......................................4
4. Plants less than 4 inches high; leaves less than 3/8 inch long.
                                    SLENDER POLEMONIUM
4. Plants more than 4 inches high; leaves more than 3/8 inch long.
                                    SHOWY POLEMONIUM

                    *   *   *

ANNUAL POLEMONIUM (*Polemonium micranthum*) Plants slender and delicate, to 12 inches. Flowers very small, white or bluish. East. Wash.; dry, open places, such as sagebrush and grasslands. Spring.

WESTERN POLEMONIUM (*Polemonium occidentale*) Plants tall, to 40 inches. Upper flowering stems glandular-downy. Leaflets numerous, often 20 or more. Flowers blue, in narrow, terminal clusters. East. Wash.; wet meadows and streambanks. Summer.

GIANT POLEMONIUM (*Polemonium carneum*) Plants tall, to 40 inches. Leaflets less numerous, usually less than 20. Flowers few per cluster, large, and variable in color (pink, lavender, light red, purple, white, or blue). West. Wash.; moist, semi-open to open habitats in lowlands and middle montane areas. Late spring to mid summer.

SLENDER POLEMONIUM (*Polemonium elegans*) Plants tufted, 2-4 inches tall. Leaves compound with numerous, tightly-fitting, tiny leaflets. Foliage very pungent. Flowers blue. Cascades; rocky places in the highest alpine areas of the mountains. Mid to late summer. Another species first discovered on Mount Rainier (Charles Vancouver Piper, 1895).

SHOWY POLEMONIUM (*Polemonium pulcherrimum*) Loosely tufted plants, to 16 inches. Compound leaves with 15-21 leaflets, 1/2 inch or more long. Flowers blue, with yellow or white "eyes," funnel-shaped and borne in open cymes. East. and West. Wash.; open to partly-open places in subalpine and alpine areas in the higher mountains. Late spring and summer. Foliage with skunk-like odor. A smaller alpine variety is 2-4 inches tall.

NAVARRETIAS (*Navarretia*) (Color Plate 41)

Small plants with spiny foliage and small flowers clustered into leafy, pincushion-like heads.

1. Flowers yellow....................YELLOW-FLOWERED NAVARRETIA
1. Flowers not yellow 2
2. Plants dark green, sticky, and with pronounced skunk-like odor.
SKUNK-WEED
2. Plants white-hairy, not sticky, and without skunk-like odor.
NEEDLE-LEAVED NAVARRETIA

*   *   *

YELLOW-FLOWERED NAVARRETIA (*Navarretia breweri*) Plants to 5 inches. Flowers yellow, to 1/4 inch long. East. Wash.; dry, open meadows. Late spring to mid summer.

SKUNK-WEED (*Navarretia squarrosa*) Plants to 20 inches. Foliage downy, sticky, and with skunk-like odor. Flowers blue, to 1/2 inch long. East. and West. Wash.; open places in the lowlands and foothills. Summer.

NEEDLE-LEAVED NAVARRETIA (*Navarretia intertexta*) Plants to 8 inches. Foliage with downward-pointing hairs. Flowers to 1/3 inch long and white to pale blue in color. East. and West. Wash.; mostly moist, open habitats from lowlands up into the mountains. Summer.

GILIAS (*Gilia*) (Color Plate 40)

Plants variable, but leaves usually pinnately divided. Flowers showy and usually funnel-shaped.

1. Flowers large (corolla tube at least 5/8 inch long) and usually bright red.
SCARLET GILIA
1. Flowers small (corolla tube less than 3/8 inch long) and not bright red...2
2. Flowers in 1 to several dense clusters at end of stem...BLUE FIELD GILIA
2. Flowers not in dense clusters.......................................3

3. Leaves restricted to base of plant and more or less toothed or lobed.....4
3. Leaves not restricted to base and leaves more or less entire............5
4. Leaves and lower part of plant hairy...................OBSCURE GILIA
4. Leaves and lower part of plant not hairy.........NAKED-STEMMED GILIA
5. Some, particularly lower, leaves 3-parted; dry lowlands.
MINUTE-FLOWERED GILIA
5. None of the leaves 3-parted; foothills and mountainous areas.
SMOOTH-LEAVED GILIA

*   *   *

SCARLET GILIA (*Gilia aggregata*) Plants tall, to 40 inches. Leaves numerous, cleft, and along length of stem. Flowers scarlet red to occasionally white. East. Wash.; drier habitats in grasslands, open clearings, and yellow pine and sub-alpine woods from lowlands to above timberline. Late spring and summer.

BLUE FIELD GILIA (*Gilia capitata*) Plants to 30 inches with loosely branched stems and pinnately cleft leaves. Flowers light bluish to white. East. and (mostly) West. Wash.; dry, open places in lowlands. Summer.

OBSCURE GILIA (*Gilia sinuata*) Plants to 12 inches, branched from base. Leaves mostly basal, fleshy, and cleft 2/3rds to center. Flowers bluish. East. Wash.; dry, open places in lowlands and foothills. Late spring to mid summer.

NAKED-STEMMED GILIA (*Gilia leptomeria*) Plants to 12 inches, branched from base. Foliage glandular hairy with leaves mostly in basal rosette. Flowers numerous, pinkish to lavender to white. East. Wash.; dry, open places in lowlands. Late spring to mid summer.

MINUTE-FLOWERED GILIA (*Gilia minutiflora*) Plants to 16 inches, much branched, and with pale green foliage. Lower leaves 3-parted; upper leaves entire. Flowers small (1/5 inch long) and white or bluish; in leafy, loose panicle. East. Wash.; dry, open, sandy places in sagebrush lowlands. Summer.

SMOOTH-LEAVED GILIA (*Gilia capillaris*) Plants to 16 inches with often smooth foliage. Leaves linear and mostly entire. Flowers pinkish lavender, bluish, or whitish. East. Wash.; open and semi-wooded places in lowlands and mountains, such as grasslands and yellow pine woods. Summer.

COLLOMIAS (*Collomia*) (Color Plate 40)

Plants similar to gilias (with which they are sometimes included). Flowers in heads, each bloom with a leaf-like bract. Calyx trumpet-shaped, as is corolla (with spreading lobes). Leaves alternate. Calyx splits as capsule develops. Flowers funnel-shaped with teeth of calyx connected by whitish membranes. Flowers usually borne in compact heads at tips of branches or stems.

1. Plants perennial with horizontally spreading stems.....ALPINE COLLOMIA
1. Plants annual; mostly with single, erect stems.......................2
2. Lower leaves more or less pinnately divided..VARIED-LEAVED COLLOMIA
2. Lower leaves entire, not divided...................................3
3. Flowers large, corollas about 1 inch long..LARGE-FLOWERED COLLOMIA
3. Flowers small, corollas 1/2 inch or less long........................4

233

4. Plants with single, unbranched stems......NARROW-LEAVED COLLOMIA
4. Plants with branched stems..5
5. Flowers mostly borne singly; corolla small, less than 1/4 inch long.
DIFFUSE COLLOMIA
5. Flowers mostly borne in clusters; corolla large, more than 1/4 inch long.
YELLOW-STAINING COLLOMIA

* * *

ALPINE COLLOMIA (*Collomia debilis*) Plants prostrate and mat forming. Leaves various, crowded, and mostly terminal; blades palmately divided into 3-7 lobes. Flowers white, blue, lavender, or pink. East. and West. Wash.; rockslides and pumice slopes in the highest parts of the mountains. Summer.

VARIED-LEAVED COLLOMIA (*Collomia heterophylla*) Plants to 6 inches with alternate, pinnately-cleft leaves. Flowers white, pink, or lavender; in leafy cluster at stem tip. West. Wash.; moist woods, clearings, and streambanks in lowlands and foothills. Summer.

LARGE-FLOWERED COLLOMIA (*Collomia grandiflora*) Plants tall, to 40 inches and sparsely branched. Leaves long (to 2 inches) and linear. Flowers with long funnels; salmon pink, light reddish, yellow, or white. East. and West. Wash.; dry, open or semi-wooded areas in lowlands and lower mountainous locations. Late spring and summer.

NARROW-LEAVED COLLOMIA (*Collomia linearis*) Plants branched, to 24 inches. Leaves long (to 3 inches) and lanceolate. Flowers white, pink, or purple. East. (mostly) and West. Wash.; variable in distribution, occurring in dry to moist habitats, open or partly-shaded, in lowlands and montane areas. Late spring and summer.

DIFFUSE COLLOMIA (*Collomia tenella*) Plants diffusely branched with branches up to 6 inches. Leaves entire, numerous, and linear-oblanceolate. Flowers axillary and lavender, pink, or white in color. East. Wash.; sagebrush and grasslands in the lowlands and foothills. Early summer.

YELLOW-STAINING COLLOMIA (*Collomia tinctoria*) Plants to 6 inches with very sticky foliage. Leaves lanceolate. Flowers pinkish, lavender, or white; in loose, sparse clusters. East. Wash.; dry, open, rocky habitats in foothills and higher mountains. Summer.

Chapter 51—The Waterleaf Family (*Hydrophyllaceae*)

Members of this family are herbs or shrubs with opposite or alternate leaves and perfect, regular flowers. The corolla is fused (no separate petals), but 5-lobed. Sepals and stamens 5 each. (Color Plate 42)

1. Flowers borne singly or few in loose, irregular terminal inflorescence.....2
1. Flowers not borne singly, but in a tight, many-flowered inflorescence.....4

2. Leaves toothed to lobed...................NEMOPHILAS (*Nemophila*)
2. Leaves entire, not toothed or lobed................................3

3. Plants with leaf-bearing stems.......................NAMAS (*Nama*)
3. Plants without leaf-bearing stems....HESPEROCHIRONS (*Hesperochiron*)

4. Leaves mostly basal; style entire, not lobed; flowers in racemes.
ROMANZOFFIAS (*Romanzoffia*)
4. Leaves usually not basal; style lobed; flowers not in racemes...........5

5. Flowers in tight, head-like clusters........WATERLEAVES (*Hydrophyllum*)
5. Flowers not in tight, head-like clusters, but often in inturned cymes.
PHACELIAS (*Phacelia*)

NEMOPHILAS (*Nemophila*) (Color Plate 43)

These are small plants growing close to the ground with opposite or alternate leaves and attractive flowers borne singly in the leaf axils. Flowers often bell-like. Flowers sometimes opposite single leaves. Leaves toothed or lobed.

1. Leaves alternate; corolla shorter than calyx.
SHORT-FLOWERED NEMOPHILA
1. Leaves mostly opposite; corolla equal to or longer than calyx.
SMALL-FLOWERED NEMOPHILA

*   *   *

SHORT-FLOWERED NEMOPHILA (*Nemophila breviflora*) Flowers lavender. East. Wash.; semi-open woods and brushy areas in foothills and lower parts of mountains. Mid spring to mid summer.

SMALL-FLOWERED NEMOPHILA (*Nemophila parviflora*) Flowers lavender. East. and West. Wash.; shaded woods and lower parts of mountains. Mid spring to mid summer.

NAMAS (*Nama*) (Color Plate 43)

Plants with usually entire leaves; borne singly. Flowers in axils of leaves or in terminal, leafy cymes. Flowers funnel-shaped.

1. Corolla long (more than 1/4 inch), projecting noticeably above hairy base.
PURPLE NAMA
1. Corolla short (less than 1/4 inch), scarcely projecting above hairy base.
MATTED NAMA

*   *   *

PURPLE NAMA (*Nama aretioides*) Corolla yellow with pink lobes. East. Wash.; sagebrush areas, usually in sandy places. Late spring and early summer.

MATTED NAMA (*Nama densum*) Flowers white or lavender. East. Wash.; sandy or sagebrush areas in driest part of Columbia Basin. Late spring and early summer.

235

Figure 55.
Phacelia, in a rockslide habitat. (Larrison)

236

HESPEROCHIRONS (*Hesperochiron*) (Color Plate 42)

Plants with basal rosettes of stalked, entire leaves and bell-shaped or flat flowers.

1. Corolla flat, with lobes spreading at right angles to the peduncle.
                                    DWARF HESPEROCHIRON
1. Corolla bell-like, with lobes scarcely spreading.
                                    CALIFORNIA HESPEROCHIRON

                    *   *   *

DWARF HESPEROCHIRON (*Hesperochiron pumilus*)   Flowers white. East. Wash.; open meadows and slopes from lowlands to higher parts of the mountains. Mid spring to early summer.

CALIFORNIA HESPEROCHIRON (*Hesperochiron californicus*)   Flowers white, lavender, or purple. East. Wash.; alkali flats and meadows in lowlands and foothill swales. Mid spring to early summer.

ROMANZOFFIAS (*Romanzoffia*) (Color Plate 43)

Small plants with mostly basal, long-stalked leaves with roundish shape and broadly-scalloped margins. Flowers in loose, open racemes.

1. Plants with well-developed, woolly tubers at base.
                                    TRACY'S ROMANZOFFIA
1. Plants lacking tubers at base (bases of petioles may be bulbous).
                                    CLIFF ROMANZOFFIA

                    *   *   *

TRACY'S ROMANZOFFIA (*Romanzoffia tracyi*)   Flowers white. West. Wash.; on moist bluffs and cliffs along salt water. Spring.

CLIFF ROMANZOFFIA (*Romanzoffia sitchensis*)   Flowers white. East. and West. Wash.; moist cliffs and steep, rocky slopes in the higher mountains. Summer.

WATERLEAVES (*Hydrophyllum*) (Color Plate 42)

Tall, leafy plants with flowers in terminal, head-like clusters, and prominently-lobed leaves. Usually found in moist, often shady places. Long, projecting stamens.

1. Leaflets entire or lobed......................BALL-HEAD WATERLEAF
1. Leaflets strongly and numerously toothed or lobed....................2
2. Leaves broader than long, or mostly so...........SLENDER WATERLEAF
2. Leaves obviously much longer than broad.......FENDLER'S WATERLEAF

                    *   *   *

BALL-HEAD WATERLEAF (*Hydrophyllum capitatum*) Plants to 12 inches with spreading stems and hairy foliage. Flowers lavender, bluish, or white in a terminal, globe-shaped cluster, resembling soft, furry, blue ball. Mostly East. Wash.; moist woods and wet, open seepage slopes. Spring and early summer.

SLENDER WATERLEAF (*Hydrophyllum tenuipes*) Similar to the following species, but with the flowers greenish white or bluish. West. Wash.; moist woods in lowlands. Late spring and early summer.

FENDLER'S WATERLEAF (*Hydrophyllum fendleri*) Plants to 16 inches with pinnately compound leaves. Flowers white, lavender, or purple in clusters at tips of long stalks. East. and West. Wash.; moist, open or semi-open places in lowlands and mountains. Late spring and summer.

PHACELIAS (*Phacelia*) (Color Plate 43; Fig. 55)

Flowers clustered or scattered in 2 rows on one side of a coiled stem. Many other characters of the genus varying from species to species.

1. Leaves entire, not toothed (may be sparsely or weakly lobed)...........2
1. Leaves toothed or pinnately (and often abundantly) lobed..............5
2. Plants annual; leaves linear or with a few lobes. Flowers violet or blue.
   NARROW-LEAVED PHACELIA
2. Plants perennial or biennial; leaves not linear. Flowers whitish..........3
3. Leaves seldom with more than 1 pair of basal leaflets.................4
3. Leaves often with more than 1 pair of leaflets.....WOODLAND PHACELIA
4. Each plant with single, erect stem...........VARIED-LEAVED PHACELIA
4. Each plant branching, with several stems...........COMMON PHACELIA
5. Stamens shorter than corolla..................GLANDULAR PHACELIA
5. Stamens as long as, or longer than, corolla........................6
6. Flowers in tight, elongate inflorescences; leaves silvery and silky.
   GRAY PHACELIA
6. Flowers not in tight, elongate inflorescences; leaves not silvery or silky...7
7. Leaves coarsely lobed and scarcely or not at all toothed...TALL PHACELIA
7. Leaves not coarsely lobed, but numerously and pinnately so; margins strongly toothed.......................LONG-BRANCHED PHACELIA

* * *

NARROW-LEAVED PHACELIA (*Phacelia linearis*) Plants to 12 inches, with erect or spreading stems. Leaves numerous and linear-lanceolate. Flowers blue or lavender, relatively large, and bell-shaped. Stamens protruding beyond corolla. East. (mostly) and West. Wash.; open, arid habitats in lowlands and foothills. Spring and early summer.

WOODLAND PHACELIA (*Phacelia nemoralis*) Plants tall, to 6 feet, with bristly foliage. Leaves dull green and divided. Flowers yellowish or greenish, in dense clusters. Stamens exceeding petals. West. Wash.; moist, shaded woods in lowlands and lower mountain slopes; often along dry trails and roadsides. Spring to mid summer.

VARIED-LEAVED PHACELIA (*Phacelia heterophylla*) Plants to 48 inches with grayish green leaves. Flowers white or rarely purple. East. and West. Wash.; open, arid places in lowlands and foothills. Late spring to mid summer.

COMMON PHACELIA (*Phacelia hastata*) Plants to 24 inches. Foliage silvery and fine-hairy. Leaves entire or with pair of small, basal, lateral leaflets. Flowers whitish, lavender, or purple. Cascades and East. Wash.; arid, open situations from lowlands to high in the mountains. Late spring and summer.

238

GLANDULAR PHACELIA (*Phacelia glandulifera*) Plants to 10 inches with glandular, strong-smelling foliage. Stems reddish. Flowers with yellowish corollas and blue or lavender lobes. East. Wash.; sandy, sage-covered places in lowlands and hills. Early summer.

GRAY PHACELIA (*Phacelia sericea*) Plants 2-6 inches tall with dense, head-like clusters of white to bluish-purple flowers. Leaves and stems covered with silky hairs. Leaves grayish in color. East. and West. Wash.; a plant of open, rocky or gravelly subalpine or alpine areas in the Cascades and Olympics. Summer.

TALL PHACELIA (*Phacelia procera*) Plants tall, to 60 inches with downy, glandular foliage. Flowers greenish white, in dense clusters at tips of branches. Cascades; moist meadows and open woods. Summer.

LONG-BRANCHED PHACELIA (*Phacelia ramosissima*) Plants to 48 inches with sticky-hairy foliage. Stems much branched. Flowers white to lavender and in small clusters at tips of branches. East. Wash.; arid places and foothills, especially on rocky cliffs and slides. Summer.

It doesn't take a beginning flower student long to realize that considerable variability exists in our native species of flowers. Perhaps the most striking variation is that of size. Individual plants growing in well-watered or well-drained and sunny or protected places (depending on the needs of the species) will be larger, with more leaves and flowers, than will be individuals occurring in less favored sites. Plants that are growing on warm, sunny, south-facing exposures may leaf out earlier in the spring and bloom considerably before their cousins on cold, north-facing slopes. Differences in the mineral constitution of the soil may be reflected in marked differences in the growth and vigor of plants, as well as the particular floral community composition of a locality.

Other than these site variations, there may be numerous genetic aberrations as well. We have seen large fields of blue gentians spotted here and there with a few mutant white-flowering plants. Other mutations may occur in the form of departure from the normal in the size and growth form of the plant, shape of the leaves, etc. Such a genetic variation may become fixed in a population and eventually characterize that population so that scientists will recognize it and give it some kind of infraspecific name to identify it. For this and other reasons, we occasionally find subspecific or variety names added to the technical names of certain species. These have not been referred to in this guide, as the authors have felt that persons using the book would be mainly interested in learning the species' identifications. The descriptions, sizes, and other characterizations of plants in WASHINGTON WILDFLOWERS deal with the flowers treated in their average appearances. Forms, varieties, subspecies, etc., are more properly the province of the plant systematist who has the means and understanding to recognize and evaluate them.

Figure 56.
Delicate flowers of the gromwell, *Lithospermum*. (Yaich)

240

Chapter 52—The Borage Family (*Boraginaceae*)

Members of this family are herbs (as included here) with rough, hairy surfaces, usually alternate leaves which are mostly simple and entire. Flowers are perfect and regular. Calyx with 5 sepals; petals fused, but corolla lobed. Stamens 5; ovary superior. A considerable variety of plant and flower types in this family. Usually 4 nutlets. (Color Plate 44)

1. Style conspicuously 2-branched; plants entirely prostrate on ground surface.
ANNUAL COLDENIA
1. Style not conspicuously 2-branched; plants not entirely prostrate on ground surface 2

2. Corolla tube (below the lobes) 1/2 inch long or longer 3
2. Corolla tube less than 1/2 inch long 5

3. Flowers with prominent hairs along margins of leaves; plants rough hairy.
TARWEEDS (*Amsinckia*)
3. Flowers without prominent hairs along margins of leaves; plants not rough hairy 4

4. Lower leaves without petioles . . . . .WESTERN GROMWELL
4. Lower leaves with prominent petioles . . . . .MERTENSIAS (*Mertensia*)

5. Leaves large and tongue-like, usually more than 2 inches wide.
GREAT HOUND'S-TONGUE
5. Leaves not as above 6

6. Nutlets covered with bristles or prickles or with a prominent wing 7
6. Nutlets without bristles or prickles 9

7. Nutlets widely spreading in fruit . . . . .PECTOCARYAS (*Pectocarya*)
7. Nutlets not widely spreading in fruit (erect, incurved, or slightly spreading) .8

8. Flowers minute; singly distributed along flower stem.
MOUSE-EARS (*Myosotis*)
8. Flowers large; more or less bunched along upper part of flowering stem.
STICKSEEDS (*Hackelia*)

9. Surface of nutlets more or less smooth or very slightly wrinkled; surface covered with sharp hairs . . . . .CRYPTANTHAS (*Cryptantha*)
9. Surface of nutlets strongly wrinkled and not sharp-haired.
POPCORN-FLOWERS (*Plagiobothrys*)

*   *   *

ANNUAL COLDENIA (*Coldenia nuttallii*) Stems mostly prostrate and up to 8 inches long. Foliage finely hairy; leaves elliptic to oval; often in star-like, radiating clusters. Flowers purplish. East. Wash.; sandy habitats in the arid desert interior. Late spring and summer.

WESTERN GROMWELL (*Lithospermum ruderale*) Plants to 20 inches. Foliage rough hairy with stems erect, becoming prostrate. Leaves narrow-lanceolate. Leaves and stems closely clustered. Flowers pale yellow. Seeds amazingly "tooth-like." East. (mostly) and West. Wash.; dry, open places in lowlands, foothills, and lower reaches of the mountains. Mid spring and early summer. (Color Plate 45; Fig. 56)

GREAT HOUND'S-TONGUE (*Cynoglossum grande*) Plants to 36 inches. Leaves oval, to 6 inches, on very long petioles. Foliage mostly smooth. Flowers blue or violet, in irregular panicle. West. Wash. and Columbia Gorge; wooded areas in lowlands. Spring. (Color Plate 44)

TARWEEDS (*Amsinckia*) (Color Plate 44)

Flowers arranged in curled "spikes," hence another common name of "fiddle-necks." Flowers usually reddish or orange-yellow. Foliage with long dense bristles.

1. Seashore plants occurring along coastal saltwater; leaves spiny-toothed.
   SEASIDE TARWEED
1. Plants not occurring along coastal saltwater; leaves not spiny-toothed....2
2. Sepals variable in width and reduced from 5 by fusion of 2 or more; fused sepals lobed at tip..........................TESSELLATE TARWEED
2. Sepals 5 in number and of equal width and not lobed at tips............3
3. Stamens attached below middle of corolla tube; tufts of hair in throat of tube...BUGLOSS TARWEED
3. Stamens attached above the middle of the carolla tube; no hairy structures in throat of tube...4
4. Corolla orange to deep orange-yellow; with light red in throat.
   RIGID TARWEED
4. Corolla pale yellow...........................MENZIES' TARWEED

*   *   *

SEASIDE TARWEED (*Amsinckia spectabilis*) Stems to 32 inches, erect or spreading. Leaves somewhat fleshy and sparsely bristled; lanceolate. Flowers orange, in curled spikes. West. Wash.; sandy beaches and bluffs along salt-water. Early summer.

TESSELLATE TARWEED (*Amsinckia tessellata*) Plants to 40 inches with narrow to oval, hairy leaves. Long hairs on foliage distinctive. Flowers yellow or orange with red markings in throat of corolla tube. East. (mostly) and West. Wash.; open, often barren or weedy places. Spring and early summer.

BUGLOSS TARWEED (*Amsinckia lycopsoides*) Stems to 40 inches, erect or prostrate. Leaves bristly-hairy. Mouth of corolla tube with 5 hairy swellings. Flowers orange-yellow or yellow, with red markings in throat of corolla tube. East. (mostly) and West. Wash.; dry, open places in lowlands and foothills; often in disturbed, weedy areas. Spring and early summer.

RIGID TARWEED (*Amsinckia retrorsa*) Plants to 40 inches with erect, bristly stems. Upper leaves lanceolate, hairy. Flowers orange with red markings in throat of corolla tube and borne in dense racemes. East. (mostly) and West. Wash.; dry, open places such as old fields and roadsides. Spring and early summer.

MENZIE'S TARWEED (*Amsinckia menziesii*) Plants to 28 inches with thin, lanceolate leaves. Foliage hairy. Flowers pale yellow. East. and West. Wash.; open, brushy places, either dry or moist. Late spring and summer.

242

MERTENSIAS (*Mertensia*) (Color Plate 45)

Perennial plants with lush, green foliage and limp, bluish, bell-shaped flowers. Often found in moist habitats. Flowers pink in bud, changing to blue when mature.

1. Plants large, usually more than 16 inches tall, and blooming in late spring and summer in moist meadows and streambanks......................2
1. Plants small, usually less than 16 inches tall, and blooming as soon as melting snow permits on subalpine ridges, partially wooded slopes, and arid plains 3
2. Occurring in lowlands of southern Puget Sound region.
WESTERN MERTENSIA
2. Occurring in Eastern Washington and the Olympic Mountains of Western Washington......................................TALL MERTENSIA
3. Stems 1 or 2, arising from a shallow tuber-like root, and usually without basal leaves.........................LONG-FLOWERED MERTENSIA
3. Stems several, arising as a cluster from a thick, but non-tuber-like root, and usually with well-developed basal leaves............LEAFY MERTENSIA

*   *   *

WESTERN MERTENSIA (*Mertensia platyphylla*)   Plants to 40 inches. Leaves numerous, oval or elliptic. West. and Northeast. Wash.; creek margins and moist woods in the lowlands. Late spring to mid summer. Flowers blue.

TALL MERTENSIA (*Mertensia paniculata*)   Plants as much as 60 inches, in clustered clumps. Leaves lance-ovate to ovate and sharp-pointed. Flowers blue. East. Wash., Cascades, and Olympic Mountains; damp, wet habitats, such as thickets along streams, boggy meadows, seepage slopes and cliffs, and the margins of streams and ponds, mostly in the mountains. Late spring and summer. Leaves fleshy, with blue-gray "bloom."

LONG-FLOWERED MERTENSIA (*Mertensia longiflora*)   Plants to 8 inches, with stems single or at most a few from a base. Flowers blue. East. Wash.; sagebrush plains and yellow pine woods in lowlands, foothills, and lower mountain areas. Spring.

LEAFY MERTENSIA (*Mertensia oblongifolia*)   Plants to 12 inches in clusters of old and new leaves, which may reach 3 inches in length on very long petioles. Flowers blue, numerous, and in dense to open, leafy panicles. East. Wash.; sagebrush and grassy plains in lowlands and foothills. Spring and early summer.

PECTOCARYAS (*Pectocarya*)

Low, often prostrate plants with small, simple, entire leaves and small, white flowers.

1. Plants with more or less prostrate growth form; leaves so narrow as to be thread-like.................................SLENDER PECTOCARYA
1. Plants usually ascending in growth form; leaves narrow, but not thread-like 2
2. Plants bushy, with several branches; leaves larger (to 3/4 inch long by 1/16 inch wide); leaves noticeably bristly.............BRISTLY PECTOCARYA

2. Plants tall and slender with stem single or once-or twice-branched; leaves smaller and narrower (to 5/8 inch long by 1/16 inch wide); leaves not noticeably bristly.............................LITTLE PECTOCARYA

* * *

SLENDER PECTOCARYA (*Pectocarya linearis*) Flowers white. East. Wash.; dry places in sand dunes and sagebrush. Spring and early summer.

BRISTLY PECTOCARYA (*Pectocarya setosa*) Flowers white. East. Wash.; sagebrush plains; not common. Late spring to early summer.

LITTLE PECTOCARYA (*Pectocarya pusilla*) Flowers white. East. Wash.; sagebrush plains in lowlands. Late spring.

MOUSE-EARS (*Myosotis*) (Color Plate 45)

Small, often nodding plants with tiny, blue or white flowers with yellow centers. Leaves long and narrow. Commonly known also as "forget-me-nots."

1. Leaves mostly not hairy; stems lax and not directly upright; calyx with short, appressed hairs...............................SMALL MOUSE-EARS
1. Leaves distinctly hairy with appressed hairs; stems directly upright; calyx with thick, spreading hairs....................SPRING MOUSE-EARS

* * *

SMALL MOUSE-EARS (*Myosotis laxa*) Flowers blue. Cascades and West. Wash.; wet places in lowlands. Summer.

SPRING MOUSE-EARS (*Myosotis verna*) East. (mostly) and West. Wash.; open, moist or dry places in lowlands and foothills. Late spring to mid summer.

STICKSEEDS (*Hackelia*) (Color Plate 44)

Plants with elongate leaves and smallish flowers with 5 knob-like appendages in the center of each flower. The fruits (nutlets) bear barbed bristles.

1. Flowers white, yellowish white, or somewhat greenish.................2
1. Flowers blue 5
2. Corolla yellowish white or greenish................ROUGH STICKSEED
2. Corolla white with a yellow eye...................................3
3. Leaves rather strongly hairy.......................GRAY STICKSEED
3. Leaves not strongly hairy...4
4. Leaves long and narrow (usually less than 3/8 inch wide); flowers numerous on generally leafless branches; plants slender and not bushy.
SAGEBRUSH STICKSEED
4. Leaves broader (usually more than 3/8 inch wide); flowers 1 to several on leafy branches; plants bushy.................SPREADING STICKSEED
5. Leaves narrow, 3/8 inch or less wide...........OKANOGAN STICKSEED
5. Leaves broader, usually more than 3/8 inch wide..JESSICA'S STICKSEED

ROUGH STICKSEED (*Hackelia hispida*) Plants to 20 inches. Leaves linear-lanceolate and covered with short, harsh hairs. Flowers yellowish white or pale greenish. East. Wash.; rock slides and cliffs in deep canyons. Late spring to mid summer.

GRAY STICKSEED (*Hackelia cinerea*) Plants to 32 inches. Leaves long and narrow; densely hairy. Flowers white with a yellow eye. East. Wash.; yellow pine and open fir woods, in rocky places and along streams. Late spring to mid summer.

SAGEBRUSH STICKSEED (*Hackelia arida*) Plants to 32 inches. Leaves very long and narrow. Flowers white with yellow eyes and borne on long, often curved, 1-sided spikes. East. Wash.; sagebrush and yellow pine woods in lowlands and foothills. Late spring and early summer.

SPREADING STICKSEED (*Hackelia diffusa*) Plants to 24 inches. Leaves lance-shaped and thin. Flowers white (rarely pale blue) with yellow eyes, in loose, spreading inflorescence. Columbia Gorge and East. Wash.; rocky habitats, such as cliffs and slides, mostly along the Columbia River. Summer.

OKANOGAN STICKSEED (*Hackelia ciliata*) Plants to 36 inches. Foliage coarsely hairy. Flowers blue with yellow eyes. East. Wash.; sagebrush and yellow pine woods in lowlands and foothills. Late spring and early summer.

JESSICA'S STICKSEED (*Hackelia micrantha*) Plants to 40 inches. Stems bunched, hairy, and with long, narrow leaves. Flowers blue with yellow or white eyes and borne in open, terminal clusters. Cascades and East. Wash.; open habitats (meadows, streambanks), dry or moist, on foothills and mountains. Summer.

CRYPTANTHAS (*Cryptantha*) (Color Plate 44)

Plants with very bristly foliage and flowers in raceme-like clusters with often coiled tips. Flowers are white. A difficult group of closely similar species which here are keyed only without species descriptions.

1. Plants perennial with a cluster of stems arising from a sturdy taproot; numerous basal leaves forming a definite tuft; flowers in tight, crowded, elongate head . . . . GRAY CRYPTANTHA
1. Plants annual with one or a few stems arising from a slender taproot; without tuft or cluster of basal leaves; flowers not always in crowded head 2

2. Plants with mat-or cushion-forming life style; flowers borne singly in upper axils of stem branches . . . . MATTED CRYPTANTHA
2. Plants not mat- or cushion-forming; flowers borne in spikes 3

3. Flowers large, as much as 1/3 inch across . . . . . . COMMON CRYPTANTHA
3. Flowers small, less than 1/8 inch across 4

4. Nutlets smooth-surfaced 5
4. Nutlets rough-surfaced, with distinct tubercles or spines 8

5. Hairs on calyx hooked . . . . WEAK-STEMMED CRYPTANTHA
5. Hairs on calyx straight 6

6. Groove on ventral surface of nutlet centrally located 7
6. Groove on ventral side of nutlet not central, but located to 1 side.
SLENDER CRYPTANTHA

7. Restricted to dunes in Franklin County........FENDLER'S CRYPTANTHA
7. Common in open or semi-open country in Eastern Washington.
                                         TORREY'S CRYPTANTHA
8. Majority of nutlets with prominent wings on margin. WINGED CRYPTANTHA
8. Nutlets without wings on margin....................................9
9. Plants often with several branches arising from taproot; leaves and stems covered with spreading hairs.................OBSCURE CRYPTANTHA
9. Plants usually with single stem (which may branch) arising from the taproot; leaves and stems not covered with spreading hairs.
                                         PINE WOODS CRYPTANTHA

                          *   *   *

GRAY CRYPTANTHA (*Cryptantha leucophaea*) Flowers white. East. Wash.; sandy areas along the Columbia River. Late spring and early summer.

MATTED CRYPTANTHA (*Cryptantha circumscissa*) Flowers white. East. Wash.; sandy places in lowlands. Mid spring to mid summer.

COMMON CRYPTANTHA (*Cryptantha intermedia*) Flowers white. East. and West. Wash.; dry, open places in lowlands. Late spring to early autumn.

WEAK-STEMMED CRYPTANTHA (*Cryptantha flaccida*) Flowers white. East. Wash;. dry, open places in lowlands. Late spring and early summer.

SLENDER CRYPTANTHA (*Cryptantha affinis*) Flowers white. East. Wash.; open slopes and yellow pine woods of foothills and lower parts of mountains. Early summer.

FENDLER'S CRYPTANTHA (*Cryptantha fendleri*) Flowers white. Franklin County, in Wash.; sand dunes. Late spring to mid summer.

TORREY'S CRYPTANTHA (*Cryptantha torreyana*) Flowers white. Northern Cascades and East. Wash.; dry, open, or semi-wooded places in lowlands, foothills, and lower parts of mountains. Late spring to mid summer.

WINGED CRYPTANTHA (*Cryptantha pterocarya*) Flowers white. East. Wash.; dry, open areas in lowlands. Spring and early summer.

OBSCURE CRYPTANTHA (*Cryptantha ambigua*) Flowers white. East. Wash.; dry, open areas in lowlands and up into the mountains. Summer.

PINE WOODS CRYPTANTHA (*Cryptantha simulans*) Flowers white. East. Wash.; yellow pine woods. Summer.

POPCORN-FLOWERS (*Plagiobothrys*) (Color Plate 45)

Slender, annual herbs with simple, opposite leaves. Flowers in tight, terminal heads with corollas gibbous (swollen) or spurred at base. Stamens 3 in number. These are small, delicate plants with hairy foliage and mostly basal leaves. Flowers are small and are borne in terminal, raceme-like groups.

1. Plants with a cluster of basal leaves; stem leaves few.
                                         SLENDER POPCORN-FLOWER
1. Plants without cluster of basal leaves; leaves on stems numerous........2

2. Flowers large (1/4 to 3/8 inch wide); occurring in Western Washington.
FRAGRANT POPCORN-FLOWER
2. Flowers small (less than 1/4 inch wide); occurring in Eastern Washington.
SCOULER'S POPCORN-FLOWER
*   *   *

SLENDER POPCORN-FLOWER (*Plagiobothrys tenellus*) Plants to 12 inches. Leaves broad-lanceolate, in basal rosette, and soft-hairy. Flowers white, with basal bracts to inflorescence. East. (mostly) Wash.; dry, open areas in lowlands. Mid spring to early summer.

FRAGRANT POPCORN-FLOWER (*Plagiobothrys figuratus*) Plants to 18 inches. Leaves narrow-linear with appressed hairs. Flowers large, fragrant, white with a yellow eye. West. Wash.; meadows and fields in lowlands. Late spring and early summer.

SCOULER'S POPCORN-FLOWER (*Plagiobothrys scouleri*) Plants to 12 inches with narrow leaves that are hairy only below. Flowers white and extended along stems with basal bracts. East-side plants often prostrate. East. and West. Wash.; moist places in lowlands and lower reaches of mountains. Late spring and summer.

Chapter 53—The Verbena Family (*Verbenaceae*)

Members of this family, as included here, are herbs with opposite or whorled leaves; perfect, regular or irregular flowers, and 4 stamens. Ovary superior. A large, tropical family, but poorly represented in our area.

1. Plants prostrate on ground; leaves deeply lobed.....BRACTED VERBENA
1. Plants erect, not prostrate on the ground; leaves not deeply lobed.......2
2. Leaves with prominent free petioles; inflorescence as a panicle of spikes at top of stem...................................BLUE VERBENA
2. Leaves without prominent, free petioles (petioles, if present, are extremely short and hardly free); inflorescence as few or single terminal spikes.
ERECT VERBENA
*   *   *

BRACTED VERBENA (*Verbena bracteata*) Plants with prostrate stems often reaching 20 inches in length. Flowers blue, pink, or white and often partly hidden by the bracts of the inflorescence. East. and West. Wash.; disturbed or waste ground. Late spring to early fall.

BLUE VERBENA (*Verbena hastata*) Plants to 60 inches with coarsely-toothed lanceolate (upper) or hastate (lower) leaves. Flowers blue or violet, in several spikes at tip of stem. East. and West. Wash.; disturbed or waste ground. Summer and early autumn.

ERECT VERBENA (*Verbena stricta*) Plants to 48 inches. Foliage hairy. Leaves oval, coarsely toothed. Flowers blue or purple, in 1 to several spikes at tips of stems. East. Wash.; dry, open, often waste, habitats. Summer and early autumn.

247

Figure 57.
Hedge nettle, *Stachys*. (Larrison)

248

Chapter 54—The Mint Family (*Labiatae*)

Members of this family, as treated here, are aromatic herbs with distinctly 4-angled stems and simple, opposite leaves. Flowers are perfect and irregular, being more or less 2-lipped (upper lip of corolla 2-lobed or entire; lower lip 3-lobed). Stamens 4; sepals 5; upper leaves sometimes bract-like. Many species prefer moist places. Several exotic weeds belong to this family and some exist in Washington but do not qualify for inclusion here as native wild-flowers. (Color Plate 46)

1. Corolla appears 1-lipped, or 2-lipped with upper lip cleft to base and these lobes moved to sides of lower lip 2
1. Corolla definitely 2-lipped or nearly regular; not as above 3

2. Lower lip less than twice as long as other lobes of corolla.
DOWNY BLUE CURLS
2. Lower lip more than twice as long as other lobes of corolla . . WOOD SAGE

3. Corolla more or less regular (corolla lobes all about same size) 4
3. Corolla definitely 2-lipped 6

4. Stamens 4 in number; plants aromatic 5
4. Stamens 2; plants not aromatic, but odorless.
WATER HOREHOUNDS (*Lycopus*)

5. Flowers in dense, terminal, head-like clusters . . . . WESTERN BALM
5. Flowers in axillary clusters or elongated terminal spikes . . . . . . FIELD MINT

6. Stamens 2 in number . . . . DORR'S SAGE
6. Stamens 4, where present 7

7. Calyx 2-lobed, with definite crest on upper lobes.
SKULL-CAPS (*Scutellaria*)
7. Calyx 2-lobed or regular, but without definite crest on upper lobe 8

8. Flowers axillary . . . . YERBA BUENA
8. Flowers terminal 9

9. Stamens much longer than corolla . . . . GIANT HYSSOPS (*Agostache*)
9. Stamens not as long as corolla lobes 10

10. Flowers borne in terminal racemes . . . . NUTTALL'S DRAGON'S-HEAD
10. Flowers borne in circular whorls (in an often interrupted spike or terminal inflorescence) 11

11. Filaments of lower stamens longer than those of upper stamens.
HEDGE NETTLES (*Stachys*)
11. Filaments of lower stamens shorter than those of upper stamens.
SMALL-FLOWERED MOLDAVICA

*   *   *

DOWNY BLUE CURLS (*Trichostema oblongum*) Plants to 18 inches with soft, hairy foliage and violet flowers in small clusters borne in axils. Long, curled, bluish stamens distinctive. East. Wash. and the Columbia Gorge; moist, open habitats, especially where soil surface has been broken. Summer. (Color Plate 47)

WOOD SAGE (*Teucrium canadense*) Plants to 40 inches with soft, hairy foliage. Flowers purple, in dense racemes. East. and West. Wash.; moist bottoms and streamsides; not common. Summer.

Figure 58.
Self-heal, *Prunella*. A very common weed of the mint family. (Yaich)

WESTERN BALM (*Monardella odoratissima*) Small, tufted plants to 15 inches. Leaves small, ovate. Flowers purple or white, in dense, terminal clusters surrounded by reddish-purple bracts. East. Wash.; dry, rocky slopes from lowlands up into the mountains. Late spring and summer. (Color Plate 46)

FIELD MINT (*Mentha arvensis*) Plants to 30 inches. White, pink, or purple flowers in dense clusters in axils of stem leaves. East. and West. Wash.; moist, open places, often near water. Summer and early autumn. (Color Plate 46)

DORR'S SAGE (*Salvia dorrii*) Plants to 24 inches. Foliage scurfy and grayish. Flowers bluish or (rarely) white, in dense clusters near tips of stems. Stamens projecting well beyond corollas. East. Wash.; dry, sagebrush-covered plains and hills. Late spring and early summer. (Color Plate 46)

YERBA BUENA (*Satureja douglasii*) A slender, trailing, evergreen vine with pleasantly aromatic odor. Flowers white or purple and borne singly in leaf axils. East. and (mostly) West. Wash.; open, coniferous woods. Summer. Many kitchen herbs (basil, savory, etc.) belong to this genus. (Color Plate 47)

NUTTALL'S DRAGON'S-HEAD (*Dracocephalum nuttallii*) Plants to 20 inches. Leaves coarsely toothed. Flowers purple, in terminal spikes. East. Wash. and Columbia Gorge; marshes and stream and lake shores in lowlands and foothills. Late summer and early fall.

SMALL-FLOWERED MOLDAVICA (*Moldavica parviflora*) Plants to 32 inches. Leaves sharply toothed with purple flowers in dense, terminal spike. East. Wash.; moist, open places in foothills and mountains. Summer.

WATER HOREHOUNDS (*Lycopus*)

Tall plants with usually toothed leaves, tiny white flowers growing in clusters circling the stem at each pair of leaves, and 2 functional stamens.

1. Roots not swollen and tuber-like; leaves strongly toothed to lobed.
   CUT-LEAVED WATER HOREHOUND
1. Roots swollen and tuber-like; leaves not strongly toothed.............2
2. Upper leaves tapering basally to short petioles...........BUGLE-WEED
2. Upper leaves not tapering basally to short petioles (which are absent).
   PACIFIC WATER HOREHOUND

*   *   *

CUT-LEAVED WATER HOREHOUND (*Lycopus americanus*) Plants to 32 inches with smooth foliage and short-petioled, lanceolate, toothed leaves. Flowers white in axillary clusters. East. and West. Wash.; moist habitats in lowlands and foothills. Summer.

BUGLE-WEED (*Lycopus uniflorus*) Plants to 16 inches with coarsely-toothed, lanceolate, short-petioled leaves. Flowers white to pink, in axillary clusters. West. Wash.; bogs, marshes, and streamsides; lowlands and mountains. Mid summer and early autumn.

PACIFIC WATER HOREHOUND (*Lycopus asper*) Plants to 28 inches. Foliage slightly hairy with very short petioled, coarsely-toothed leaves. Flowers white, in axillary clusters. Leaves long and narrow. East. Wash.; wet places near water, marshes, etc. Summer.

SKULL-CAPS (*Scutellaria*) (Color Plate 47)

Plants characterized by tube-like corollas arising from 2-lipped calyxes, the upper lip of which has a hump or bulge.

1. Flowers in spike-like racemes which are often borne in axils of leaves.
MAD-DOG SKULL-CAP
1. Flowers borne singly in axils of leaves..............................2
2. Bases of leaves squarish or truncate where joining petiole; lower leaves more than 1 inch long..........................MARSH SKULL-CAP
2. Bases of leaves not truncate, but tapering gradually to petiole; larger leaves usually less than 1 inch long.............NARROW-LEAVED SKULL-CAP

*   *   *

MAD-DOG SKULL-CAP (*Scutellaria lateriflora*) Plants to 36 inches. Petioles more than 1/4 inch long. Leaves oval to long-ovate. Flowers blue, in axillary racemes. East. and West. Wash.; moist places in lowlands. Summer.

MARSH SKULL-CAP (*Scutellaria galericulata*) Petioles less than 1/4 inch long; leaves lanceolate. Flowers solitary in leaf axils; corolla violet with white tube. Plants to 32 inches. East. and West. Wash.; wet habitats, especially meadows, in lowlands. Summer.

NARROW-LEAVED SKULL-CAP (*Scutellaria angustifolia*) Plants to 20 inches, erect or spreading. Flowers bluish violet. East. Wash.; open, often rocky places, in lowlands and foothills. Late spring and early summer.

GIANT HYSSOPS (*Agastache*) (Color Plate 46)

Plants with toothed, often triangular leaves, and flowers in large, dense, terminal spikes. Plants with anise or licorice odor to crushed leaves.

1. Under surface of leaves finely and densely haired.
WESTERN GIANT HYSSOP
1. Under surface of leaves either smooth or with scattered hairs.
NETTLE-LEAVED GIANT HYSSOP

*   *   *

WESTERN GIANT HYSSOP (*Agastache occidentalis*) Flowers violet. East. slopes of Cascades; dry, rocky slopes. Summer.

NETTLE-LEAVED GIANT HYSSOP (*Agastache urticifolia*) Flowers white or pinkish. East. Wash.; dry, open slopes and brush in foothills and mountains. Summer.

HEDGE NETTLES (*Stachys*) (Color Plate 47; Fig. 57)

Plants with nettle-like leaves and flowers in often dense, interrupted spikes (interrupted, that is, by leaves). Corolla 2-lipped, the lower lip bent strongly downward.

1. Upper leaves without petioles.................SWAMP HEDGE NETTLE
1. Upper leaves with conspicuous petioles............................2
2. Flowers 3/4 inch long or longer.............COOLEY'S HEDGE NETTLE
2. Flowers less than 3/4 inch long..............MEXICAN HEDGE NETTLE

SWAMP HEDGE NETTLE (*Stachys palustris*) Plants to 36 inches. Leaves triangular. Flowers purple with white spots. East. and West. Wash.; wet meadows and shores of lakes and streams. Summer.

COOLEY'S HEDGE NETTLE (*Stachys cooleyae*) Plants tall, to 60 inches. Leaves ovate and hairy. Flowers reddish purple. Cascades and West. Wash.; moist habitats, swamps, etc. Summer.

MEXICAN HEDGE NETTLE (*Stachys mexicana*) Plants to 36 inches. Flowers pink. West. Wash.; moist woods and swamps in coastal lowlands. Summer.

Moisture-laden masses of marine air often concentrate at the mouths of river valleys and on the lower slopes of the windward faces of the Olympic and Cascade mountains to produce areas of tremendous rainfall, often averaging well above 100 inches. Not only is the precipitation copious but it is well distributed throughout the year so that few, if any, prolonged or even modest periods of drought occur. This situation is particularly well marked along the ocean coast where definite storms may be spelled off by fogs and low stratus drizzles which, accompanied by mild temperatures and high humidities, produce an almost jungle-like climate.

Indeed, such a climate is reflected in a near jungle-like vegetation that is unique in the state. The forests are dominated by immense cedars, hemlocks, and spruces whose great size blocks out much of the sunshine, allowing only a dim, foliage-filtered, greenish light to reach the ground. The latter, however, is completely covered by a thick carpet of mosses, ferns, and such wildflowers as wood sorrels, foamflowers, and trail plants. Certain members of the heath family are abundant and most delicate and winsome of all is the lovely wood nymph. Flowers crowd in dense masses along the margins of rainforest streams and brooks, where those species with tall stems and abundant foliage predominate. Far from being devoid of wildflowers, the rainforest is a rich and unique habitat for the botany student to explore and enjoy.

A striking feature of the rainforest is the *nurse log*. More than just a dead log, some great cedar or spruce laid low by a winter storm, these prostrate giants harbor on their decaying, moss-encrusted upper surfaces a culturing and protective substrate for the germination and establishment of numerous ferns, trees, and herbs. Besides providing the rainforest with natural "planters," it seems that the nurse logs are vitally necessary for the establishment of young trees above the competition on the forest floor.

When next you visit the ocean side of the Olympic National Park, spend a few hours strolling through the cathedral aisles of the rainforest—a never to be forgotten experience!

Figure 59.
Owl's clover, *Orthocarpus*. The seabeach form on an appropriate page of the
Washington Wildflowers manuscript. (Larrison)

254

Chapter 55—The Figwort Family (*Scrophulariaceae*)

Members of this family are annual or perennial herbs with perfect, complete, and irregular flowers, and calyxes of 5 or 4 sepals. Petals fused into an often 2-lipped or nearly regular corolla. Stamens usually 4 (less commonly 5 or 2). Ovary superior. A massive family contributing a number of tame garden flowers. (Color Plate 48)

1. Upper lip of corolla forming a hood inclosing the anthers.............2
1. Upper lip of corolla not forming a hood, or corolla absent (*Besseya*)....5

2. Leaves toothed or strongly dissected and basal as well as located on stems ....LOUSEWORTS (*Pedicularis*)
2. Leaves not toothed or strongly dissected; not basal.................3

3. Plants perennial; upper corolla lip much larger than lower lip.
INDIAN PAINTBRUSHES (*Castilleja*)
3. Plants annual; upper corolla lip about same size as lower lip..........4

4. Calyx lobes separate to base to form upper and lower segments; flower clusters with 5 or fewer flowers............CLUSTERED BIRD'S-BEAKS
4. Calyx lobes not cleft to base; flower clusters with many flowers.
OWL'S-CLOVERS (*Orthocarpus*)

5. Filaments 5 in number, though 1 may be sterile (not bearing an anther)..6
5. Filaments 2-4 in number..7

6. Sterile filaments long and well-developed; leaves basal as well as on stem ....PENSTEMONS (*Penstemon*)
6. Sterile filament merely a projecting knob on upper lip, not long and well-developed ....FIGWORTS (*Scrophularia*)

7. Anthers 2 in number...8
7. Anthers 4 in number..10

8. Leaves opposite and located entirely on the stem; no basal leaves.
SPEEDWELLS (*Veronica*)
8. Leaves mostly basal; those on stem small and mostly alternate.........9

9. Corolla present; sepals entirely distinct........SYNTHYRISES (*Synthyris*)
9. Corolla absent or almost so; sepals fused as base........RED BESSEYA

10. Sepals separate (distinct) to base...................BLUE TOADFLAX
10. Sepals fused at base..11

11. Central lobe of lower lip of corolla pouch- or sack-like and inclosing the stamens ....COLLINSIAS (*Collinsia*)
11. Central lobe of lower lip of corolla not pouch- or sack-like............12

12. Corolla with short, poorly-developed tube and only slightly 2-lipped.
TONELLAS (*Tonella*)
12. Corolla with well-developed tube and lips........................13

13. Calyx with 5 prominent angles...........MONKEY-FLOWERS (*Mimulus*)
13. Calyx without prominent angles................DOWNY MIMETANTHE

* * *

CLUSTERED BIRD'S-BEAK (*Cordylanthus capitatus*) Flowers purple. East. Wash.; sagebrush and yellow pine woods in lowlands, foothills, and lower parts of mountains. Summer.

RED BESSEYA (*Besseya rubra*) Flowers dark red. East. Wash.; open meadows and grasslands in lowlands and foothills. Spring. (Color Plate 48)

BLUE TOADFLAX (*Linaria canadensis*) Flowers light blue. East. and West. Wash.; moist, sandy areas. Spring and early summer. (Color Plate 48)

DOWNY MIMETANTHE (*Mimetanthe pilosa*) Flowers yellow with reddish dots. East. Wash.; moist habitats, such as streambanks and wet swales in dry lowlands. Summer.

LOUSEWORTS (*Pedicularis*) (Color Plate 49)

Plants with usually finely-divided, basal or cauline (on stem) leaves. Flowers 2-lipped and borne in often tall racemes or spikes. Stems in clusters and the larger species often in conspicuous patches.

1. Leaves simple and toothed; lobes of calyx 2 in number.
   LEAFY LOUSEWORT
1. Leaves mostly pinnately compound; calyx lobes 5 in number...........2
2. Plants leafy throughout with leaves near base about the same size as those on stem....................................BRACTED LOUSEWORT
2. Plants with most leaves at base of stem; stem leaves, when present, small and few in number...3
3. Upper corolla lip helmet-shaped but without a prominent beak-like projection ....RAINIER LOUSEWORT
3. Upper corolla lip helmet-shaped and with a prominent beak-like projection...4
4. Beak straight and 1/8 inch long or less.......BIRD'S-BEAK LOUSEWORT
4. Beak strongly curved and usually more than 1/8 inch long..............5
5. Beak strongly down-curved ....COILED LOUSEWORT
5. Beak strongly upcurved ....ELEPHANT'S-HEAD

*   *   *

LEAFY LOUSEWORT (*Pedicularis racemosa*) Plants to 12-14 inches. Leaves and stems often reddish. Leaves not dissected, but toothed. Beak with single curve. Flowers pink. East. and West. Wash.; mostly montane coniferous forests. Summer.

BRACTED LOUSEWORT (*Pedicularis bracteosa*) Plants tall, to 48 inches. Stems with large, fern-like, basal leaves. Beak very short. Flowers greenish yellow, tinged with reddish or brownish. East. and West. Wash.; moist habitats in woods and meadows of the mountains. Summer.

RAINIER LOUSEWORT (*Pedicularis rainierensis*) Plants small, 7 to 12 inches tall. Basal and stem leaves present. Beak absent. Flowers yellow to yellowish white. Mount Rainier; moist meadows and subalpine groves. Mid and late summer.

BIRD'S-BEAK LOUSEWORT (*Pedicularis ornithorhyncha*) Plants small, to 6 inches. Beak straight. Flowers purple and clustered at tip of stem. Central and Northern Cascades; dry, subalpine and alpine meadows. Mid summer to early autumn.

COILED LOUSEWORT (*Pedicularis contorta*) Plants to 24 inches. Leaves strongly dissected. Curled beak coiled up within petal-like lip of white or yellowish white flower. East. and West. Wash.; meadows and woods in higher parts of mountains. Summer.

ELEPHANT'S-HEAD (*Pedicularis groenlandica*) Plants to 24 inches. Flowers pink to red and resembling the head and trunk of an elephant. East. and West. Wash.; wet meadows and stream margins. Summer.

INDIAN PAINTBRUSHES (*Castilleja*) (Color Plate 48; Fig. 60)

Medium-sized plants with often brightly-colored heads comprised of tiny flowers and larger bracts at tops of often clustered stems. Generally plants of the mountains where they may be common enough to form aspects in the meadows.

1. Plants annual with slender taproot and single stem arising therefrom.
   ANNUAL INDIAN PAINTBRUSH
1. Plants perennial with well-developed roots from which arise a cluster of several stems 2

2. Species occurring in Western Washington, including the Cascades (except eastern slope of that range). 5
2. Species occurring in Eastern Washington, including the east slope of the Cascades. 8

3. Bracts yellow. . . . . .GOLDEN INDIAN PAINTBRUSH
3. Bracts not yellow 4

4. Flowers yellow; bracts purplish; restricted to Mount Rainier.
   MOUNT RAINIER INDIAN PAINTBRUSH
4. Flowers and upper bracts reddish or purple. 5

5. Leaves and bracts entire, not cleft into lobes.
   COMMON INDIAN PAINTBRUSH
5. Leaves and bracts cleft into linear lobes. 6

6. Flowers and upper bracts rose-purple.
   SMALL-FLOWERED INDIAN PAINTBRUSH
6. Flowers and upper bracts scarlet. 7

7. Plants usually less than 8 inches tall; upper lip of the corolla much larger than the tube. . . . . .CLIFF INDIAN PAINTBRUSH
7. Plants usually more than 8 inches tall; upper lip of corolla same length as tube. . . . . .HARSH INDIAN PAINTBRUSH

8. Leaves and bracts mostly divided into linear lobes. 9
8. Leaves and bracts entire or mostly so (except for a few of the upper leaves) 13

9. Flowers and bracts red to scarlet. . . . . .HARSH INDIAN PAINTBRUSH
9. Flowers and bracts not red or scarlet. 10

10. Upper bracts white or pinkish (rose-colored at Harts Pass).
    SMALL-FLOWERED INDIAN PAINTBRUSH
10. Flowers yellowish, not as above. 11

11. Leaves and lobes all very narrow; occurs in Northeastern Washington.
    DEER INDIAN PAINTBRUSH

257

Figure 60.
Indian paintbrush, *Castilleja;* beloved of wildflower students. (Yaich)

11. Leaves and lobes not very narrow; occurring elsewhere than entirely in Northeastern Washington. 12

12. Usually found in very dry (sagebrush) habitats.
THOMPSON'S INDIAN PAINTBRUSH
12. Usually found in more or less moist (meadow) habitats.
CUSICK'S INDIAN PAINTBRUSH

13. Upper bracts with yellow band below red tips.
SUKSDORF'S INDIAN PAINTBRUSH
13. Upper bracts not as above. 14

14. Usually occurring at or below lower timberline on mountains. 15
14. Usually occurring at or above upper timberline on mountains. 16

15. Flowers and upper bracts yellowish. . .YELLOWISH INDIAN PAINTBRUSH
15. Flowers and upper bracts red or crimson. COMMON INDIAN PAINTBRUSH

16. Upper parts of plant very hairy; upper bracts entire.
ELMER'S INDIAN PAINTBRUSH
16. Upper parts of plant not very hairy; upper bracts commonly lobed.
ROSY INDIAN PAINTBRUSH

                    *   *   *

ANNUAL INDIAN PAINTBRUSH (*Castilleja exilis*) Plants to 32 inches with slender stems and very narrow, entire leaves. Upper bracts tipped with scarlet; flowers yellowish. East. Wash.; moist, alkaline flats and meadows in lowlands. Summer and early autumn.

GOLDEN INDIAN PAINTBRUSH (*Castilleja levisecta*) Plants to 12 inches. Leaves cleft into 2-6 narrow lobes. Foliage glandular-hairy. Bracts golden yellow. West. Wash.; meadows and grassy prairies in lowlands. Mid spring to early autumn.

MOUNT RAINIER INDIAN PAINTBRUSH (*Castilleja cryptantha*) Plants small, to 6 inches. Foliage glandular-hairy. Lower lip of flower longer than upper lip. Bracts purple; flowers yellow. Mount Rainier; subalpine meadows. Mid to late summer.

COMMON INDIAN PAINTBRUSH (*Castilleja miniata*) Plants 12-24 inches tall with lanceolate, entire leaves. Flower bracts are 3-5 cleft and red-scarlet, or crimson. East. and West. Wash.; meadows and open, grassy slopes in mountains; common. Late spring to early autumn.

SMALL-FLOWERED INDIAN PAINTBRUSH (*Castilleja parviflora*) Stems tufted, to 12 inches. Leaves cleft to middle into 3-5 segments. Bracts rose-purple, though whitish in northeastern Cascades; rarely white elsewhere. Cascade and Olympic Mountains; moist, subalpine meadows. Very common. Summer and early autumn.

CLIFF INDIAN PAINTBRUSH (*Castilleja rupicola*) Plants densely tufted, to 8 inches, and with densely hairy foliage. Leaves deeply cleft into 3-7 lobes. Bracts scarlet or crimson. Cascades; cliffs and rocky slopes. Summer.

HARSH INDIAN PAINTBRUSH *(Castilleja hispida)* Plants to 14 inches tall, with hairy foliage. Leaves cleft to middle into 3-5 narrow lobes. Bracts broad with scarlet tips. East. and West. Wash.; grassy slopes and clearings in lowlands and lower reaches of mountains. Mid spring to late summer.

259

DEER INDIAN PAINTBRUSH (*Castilleja cervina*) Plants to 24 inches with clustered stems. Bracts broader than leaves and yellowish. Northeastern Wash.; grassy slopes and yellow pine woods in lowlands and foothills. Early to mid summer.

THOMPSON'S INDIAN PAINTBRUSH (*Castilleja thompsonii*) Plants to 16 inches with clustered stems with hairy foliage. Bracts 3-5 cleft and yellowish. East. Wash.; sagebrush, arid grasslands, and open slopes of mountains from lowlands to subalpine areas. Late spring and summer.

CUSICK'S INDIAN PAINTBRUSH (*Castilleja cusickii*) Plants to 24 inches with sticky-hairy foliage. Bracts entire or with short lobes; yellow, rarely purplish. East. Wash.; montane and subalpine meadows. Late spring and summer.

SUKSDORF'S INDIAN PAINTBRUSH (*Castilleja suksdorfii*) Plants with solitary stems to 20 inches. Leaves smooth to sparsely hairy; entire or lobed. Bracts with yellow band below red tips. Southern Cascades; moist, subalpine meadows. Summer and early autumn. Named after the well-known student of southern Washington flowers, Wilhelm Nikolaus Suksdorf, who spent much time investigating the floras of Mount Adams and the Columbia Gorge.

YELLOWISH INDIAN PAINTBRUSH (*Castilleja lutescens*) Plants to 24 inches with clustered stems. Leaves mostly entire and linear. Bracts yellowish. East. Wash.; grassy slopes and yellow pine woods. Late spring and summer.

ELMER'S INDIAN PAINTBRUSH (*Castilleja elmeri*) Plants to 12 inches, with clustered stems, and sticky-hairy, usually entire, linear leaves. Bracts crimson to scarlet, rarely yellow. Northeastern Cascades; subalpine meadows. Summer.

ROSY INDIAN PAINTBRUSH (*Castilleja rhexifolia*) Plants to 12 inches with usually entire leaves. Bracts crimson to scarlet, and less commonly yellow. Northeastern Cascades; subalpine meadows and high, open ridges. Summer.

OWL'S-CLOVERS (*Orthocarpus*) (Fig. 59)

Somewhat similar in gross aspect to Indian paintbrushes, but usually smaller in stature and with upper and lower corolla lips about the same size. Lower lip often sack-like.

1. Corolla small, 1/4 inch or less long . . . . DWARF OWL'S-CLOVER
1. Corolla large, 3/8 inch or more long 2

2. Lower lip of corolla expanded as a single lobe 3
2. Lip of corolla expanded into 3 lobes 7

3. Upper leaves sharply differentiated from bracts in size 4
3. Upper leaves not sharply differentiated in size from bracts 6

4. Leaves entire, not lobed . . . . MOUNTAIN OWL'S-CLOVER
4. Leaves lobed 5

5. Upper bracts with pinkish-purple tips . . . . . . THIN-LEAVED OWL'S-CLOVER
5. Upper bracts greenish or yellow-green and not pink-tipped.
BEARDED OWL'S-CLOVER

6. Flowers yellow . . . . YELLOW OWL'S-CLOVER
6. Flowers pinkish, purplish, or white . . . . BRACTED OWL'S-CLOVER

7. Bracts entirely green.........................HAIRY OWL'S-CLOVER
7. Bracts tipped with yellow, white, or purple..........................8
8. Leaves very long and narrow; not occurring in salt marshes.
NARROW-LEAVED OWL'S-CLOVER
8. Leaves not long and narrow; occurring in salt marshes.
PAINTBRUSH OWL'S-CLOVER

*   *   *

DWARF OWL'S-CLOVER (*Orthocarpus pusillus*) Plants to 8 inches, with purple-tinged foliage and long branches with thread-like lobes on leaves. Flowers reddish purple to yellow and scattered along branches. West. Wash.; moist, lowland habitats. Spring and early summer.

MOUNTAIN OWL'S-CLOVER (*Orthocarpus imbricatus*) Plants to 14 inches with entire, lanceolate leaves, pink-tipped bracts. Flower purplish. Similar in appearance to some alpine paintbrushes but the stem is shorter. Olympic Mountains where common. Mid summer to early autumn.

THIN-LEAVED OWL'S-CLOVER (*Orthocarpus tenuifolius*) Plants to 14 inches with long, narrow-lobed leaves, and flowers yellow with purple tips to corolla. East. Wash.; open places in lowlands and lower parts of mountains. Late spring and summer.

YELLOW OWL'S-CLOVER (*Orthocarpus luteus*) Plants to 16 inches, with hairy stems and yellow flowers in spike-like inflorescence at tip of stem. East. Wash.; lowland meadows. Mid and late summer.

BEARDED OWL'S-CLOVER (*Orthocarpus barbatus*) Plants to 10 inches with conspicuously hairy leaves. Leaf blades broad, but with long narrow lobes. Bracts and corolla yellow to greenish yellow. East. Wash.; sagebrush areas. Early summer.

BRACTED OWL'S-CLOVER (*Orthocarpus bracteosus*) Plants to 16 inches, with 3-lobed leaves and bracts. Upper bracts and corolla purple or white. West. Wash.; lowland meadows. Summer.

HAIRY OWL'S-CLOVER (*Orthocarpus hispidus*) Plants to 16 inches, with hairy foliage, and very narrow leaves and leaf-lobes. Flowers white or yellowish white. East. (mostly) and West. Wash.; moist meadows and swales. Late spring and summer.

NARROW-LEAVED OWL'S-CLOVER (*Orthocarpus attenuatus*) Plants to 14 inches, with tall, delicate stems bearing very long, narrow leaves, the upper ones lobed. Inflorescence long, narrow, and tight, with white or pale pinkish corollas and bracts. West. Wash.; meadows in lowlands. Spring and early summer.

PAINTBRUSH OWL'S-CLOVER (*Orthocarpus castillejoides*) Plants to 14 inches, with broad, short-lobed leaves and upper bracts. Foliage hairy and slightly sticky. Floral bracts white, yellow, or purple; corollas yellow with purple markings. West. Wash.; salt marshes along Puget Sound and ocean coast. Summer.

Figure 61.
The penstemons are widespread throughout the state of Washington and present many challenges to the flower photographer. (Yaich)

PENSTEMONS (*Penstemon*) (Color Plate 49; Fig. 61)

These are tall, showy plants with tall, colorful flowers and tube-like corollas. One sterile and 4 fertile stamens are usually present, the sterile stamen often hairy, hence the name "beard-tongues" which has been applied to this genus. Many penstemons have 2 lips, the upper with 2 lobes and the lower with 3. A large and somewhat difficult group to identify to species.

1. Stamens with noticeably very hairy or woolly anthers.................2
1. Stamens either without hairy anthers or the hairs mostly inconspicuous..5

2. Plants large (usually more than 16 inches tall) and with herbaceous, not woody stems; no basal leaves; largest leaves over 2 to 2½ inches long.
WOODLAND PENSTEMON
2. Plants smaller (usually less than 16 inches tall) and with woody lower stem; basal as well as stem leaves present. Largest leaves not over 2 to 2½ inches long 3

3. Plants with erect, not mat-like growth form, and with bracts and basal leaves above the ground....................SHRUBBY PENSTEMON
3. Plants mat-like in growth form.....................................4

4. Flowers deep pink or rose in color................ROCK PENSTEMON
4. Flowers bluish lavender or purplish violet.....DAVIDSON'S PENSTEMON

5. Anthers horseshoe-shaped with long, downward-pointing lower extremities...6
5. Anthers not horseshoe-shaped................................10

6. Plants with glandular, sticky flowers..............................7
6. Plants without glandular, sticky flowers..........................9

7. Leaves and stems glandular and sticky; leaves basal as well as on stem.
GLANDULAR PENSTEMON
7. Leaves and stems not glandular and sticky; stem leaves only..........8

8. Flowers smaller, less than 3/4 inch long; upper lip divided to more than half its length............................WHORLED PENSTEMON
8. Flowers larger, more than 7/8 inch long; upper lip divided less than half its length.............................CUT-LEAVED PENSTEMON

9. Flowers large, usually more than 1 inch long; lobes of corolla edged with hairs.....................................ELEGANT PENSTEMON
9. Flowers smaller, usually less than 1 inch in length; lobes of corolla not edged with hairs.........................SPREADING PENSTEMON

10. Plants shrubby in lower parts and flowers white.SCORCHED PENSTEMON
10. Plants not shrubby in lower parts and flowers generally not white......11

11. Leaves mostly not toothed; plants usually not glandular and sticky.....12
11. Plants, especially flowers, glandular and sticky, or if not, leaves toothed.17

12. Plants with creeping life form; flowers rather small with corolla less than 5/8 inch long...13
12. Plants erect, not creeping; flowers usually larger with corolla near or more than 3/4 inch long...15

13. Flowers yellow to yellowish white..............YELLOW PENSTEMON
13. Flowers bluish or purple...14

263

14. Flowers very small, corolla less than 3/8 inch long; mouth of corolla not expanded ....TALL PENSTEMON
14. Flowers larger, corolla more than 3/8 inch long; mouth of corolla tube expanded ....RYDBERG'S PENSTEMON

15. Plants with grayish foliage..............SHARP-LEAVED PENSTEMON
15. Plants with foliage not gray.....................................16

16. Leaves relatively narrow, less than 1 inch wide and more than 4 times as long as broad...............................SHOWY PENSTEMON
16. Leaves relatively broad, more than 1 inch wide; less than 5 times as long as broad.................................PENNELL'S PENSTEMON

17. Corolla more than 3/4 inch long and mouth of tube expanded.
                                    CRESTED-TONGUED PENSTEMON
17. Corolla less than 3/8 inch long and mouth of tube not expanded.......18

18. Most leaves more or less toothed...............................19
18. Most leaves not toothed (that is, entire)..........................21

19. Flowers relatively large with corolla tube more than 5/8 inch long.
                                        BROAD-LEAVED PENSTEMON
19. Flowers relatively small with corolla tube less than 5/8 inch long......20

20. Leaves prominently toothed...................KITTITAS PENSTEMON
20. Leaves sparsely and inconspicuously toothed.
                                            SUBSERRATE PENSTEMON

21. Most leaves not hairy...22
21. Most leaves hairy..23

22. Flowers smaller, corolla less than 1/2 inch long.
                                        WASHINGTON PENSTEMON
22. Flowers larger, corolla more than 1/2 inch long.
                                        TAPER-LEAVED PENSTEMON

23. Many leaves alternate and their bases separated from stem.
                                            GAIRDNER'S PENSTEMON
23. Most leaves opposite and their bases often surrounding stem.
                                                LOWLY PENSTEMON

                        *   *   *

WOODLAND PENSTEMON (*Penstemon nemorosus*)   Plants to 24 inches. Leaves toothed and 2-3 inches long. Flowers pinkish purple, 1 inch long, and in narrow panicles of 2-5 flowers at end of each stem. Cascades and West. Wash.; moist woods and rocky slopes, mostly in the mountains. Mid and late summer. Recently designated *Nothochelone nemorosa*.

SHRUBBY PENSTEMON (*Penstemon fruticosus*)   Plants to 12 inches, but freely spreading. Foliage shrubby. Leaves sharply pointed. Flowers 1-1½ inches long. Anthers very hairy. Flowers bluish lavender to pale purple. Cascade crest eastward; rocky, open or wooded habitats in the mountains, often in shallow soil. Late spring and summer.

ROCK PENSTEMON (*Penstemon rupicola*)   Plants 3-6 inches tall. Leaves grayish. Flowers rose to scarlet or lavender and 1-1½ inches long. Cascades and Columbia Gorge; rocky cliffs, mostly in the mountains. Summer.

DAVIDSON'S PENSTEMON (*Penstemon davidsonii*) Plants to 4 inches in dense, creeping mats. Round, leathery, evergreen leaves. Flowers 1 inch long and bluish lavender to violet. Cascades and Olympics; rocky cliffs and slides; common. Summer.

GLANDULAR PENSTEMON (*Penstemon glandulosus*) Plants to 40 inches. Foliage soft-hairy. Leaves sharply toothed. Flowers bright bluish lavender; 1-1¾ inches long. East. Wash.; open, rocky places in lowlands, foothills, and mountains. Late spring to mid summer.

WHORLED PENSTEMON (*Penstemon triphyllus*) Plants to 20 inches. Leaves linear-lanceolate, sessile, and toothed. Flowers lavender to purplish violet, in loose group. Southwestern Wash.; dry, rocky cliffs and slopes. Late spring to mid summer.

CUT-LEAVED PENSTEMON (*Penstemon richardsonii*) Plants to 30 inches. Leaves sharply toothed or cleft. Stems numerous, brittle. Flowers lavender; 1 inch long. East. Wash. and Columbia Gorge; dry, open, rocky places in the lowlands. Late spring and summer.

ELEGANT PENSTEMON (*Penstemon venustus*) Plants to 28 inches. Foliage smooth and grayish. Leaves lanceolate to lanceolate-oblong, toothed. Flowers bright bluish lavender or purplish violet; 1-1¼ inches long. Southeastern Wash.; open, rocky places in lowlands, foothills, and lower parts of mountains. Late spring and summer.

SPREADING PENSTEMON (*Penstemon serrulatus*) Plants to 24 inches. Leaves oblong, sharp-pointed, and toothed. Flowers dark bluish or dark purplish; 3/4 inch long. Cascades and West. Wash.; moist habitats from lowlands to subalpine areas in mountains. Summer.

SCORCHED PENSTEMON (*Penstemon deustus*) Plants to 24 inches. Stems branching and woody. Flowers whitish to yellowish white; 1/2 to 3/4 inch long. East. Wash.; dry, open, rocky places from lowlands to high mountains. Late spring to mid summer.

YELLOW PENSTEMON (*Penstemon confertus*) Plants to 16 inches. Flowers yellowish and less than 1/2 inch long, in dense, terminal clusters. East. Wash. from Cascade crest eastward; moist meadows, woods, and streambanks from lowlands up into the mountains. Late spring and summer.

TALL PENSTEMON (*Penstemon procerus*) Plants to 24 inches. Upper leaves toothed. Flowers dark bluish purple to rarely yellowish, 1/2 inch or less long, and in 1-2 massed whorls per stem. East. and West. Wash.; dry ridges and meadows and open woods from foothills to the subalpine. Summer. A small, 2-5 inch alpine variety exists also.

RYDBERG'S PENSTEMON (*Penstemon rydbergii*) Plants to 28 inches. Leaves oblanceolate and often basal where forming rosettes. Flowers bluish purple, spreading from stem. East. Wash. and Columbia Gorge; grassy slopes and sagebrush in foothills and lower mountains. Late spring and early summer.

SHARP-LEAVED PENSTEMON (*Penstemon accuminatus*) Plants to 16 inches. Leaves thick, leathery, and entire. Flowers bright blue to pink; 3/4 to 1 inch long. East. Wash.; sandy areas, such as dunes, in arid lowlands; also dry, hot canyons. Spring and early summer.

SHOWY PENSTEMON (*Penstemon speciosus*) Plants to 32 inches. Foliage smooth and greenish. Leaves lanceolate, leathery, and entire. Flowers blue to pale lavender, 1 to 1½ inches long. East. Wash.; sagebrush and yellow pine woods, in lowlands and foothills. Late spring to mid summer.

PENNELL'S PENSTEMON (*Penstemon pennellianus*) Plants to 20 inches. Foliage smooth; leaves entire. Flowers blue, 1 inch long. Southeastern Wash.; open, rocky areas in the Blue Mountains. Late spring and early summer.

CRESTED-TONGUED PENSTEMON (*Penstemon eriantherus*) Plants to 16 inches. Leaves entire or toothed. Flowers light blue, lavender, reddish, or purplish; 1 to 1½ inches long. East. Wash.; arid, open slopes in lowlands, foothills, and lower parts of mountains. Late spring to mid summer.

BROAD-LEAVED PENSTEMON (*Penstemon ovatus*) Plants 6-12 inches. Leaves oval and toothed. Flowers blue, 1/2 to 3/4 inches long. West. Wash.; open woods in lowlands and lower parts of mountains. Late spring to mid summer.

KITTITAS PENSTEMON (*Penstemon pruinosus*) Plants to 16 inches. Leaves toothed or entire. Flowers bluish to lavender; 1/2 to 5/8 inch long. East. Wash.; open, rocky habitats. Late spring to mid summer.

SUBSERRATE PENSTEMON (*Penstemon subserratus*) Plants to 32 inches. Leaves narrowly oval and toothed. Flowers blue to purple; 3/4 inch long. East. Wash. and Columbia Gorge; open woods in lowlands. Late spring and early summer.

WASHINGTON PENSTEMON (*Penstemon washingtonensis*) Plants to 20 inches; tufted. Leaves entire and mostly basal in rosettes. Flowers blue; rarely yellowish white; 1/2 inch long. Northeastern Cascades; open areas in middle elevations in mountains. Mid to late summer.

TAPER-LEAVED PENSTEMON (*Penstemon attenuatus*) Plants to 28 inches; tufted. Leaves entire and dark green. Flowers blue, purple, yellow, or white; 1/2 to 3/4 inch long. East. Wash.; grassy slopes and open yellow pine and fir woods of foothills and lower montane areas. Summer.

GAIRDNER'S PENSTEMON (*Penstemon gairdneri*) Plants to 16 inches; matted. Leaves linear and entire. Flowers rose purple; 3/4 inch long. Northeastern Wash.; dry, open, rocky places in lowlands and foothills. Late spring and early summer.

LOWLY PENSTEMON (*Penstemon humilis*) Plants to 12 inches with densely-clustered stems. Leaves entire, thick, lanceolate, and mostly basal. Flowers bluish purple; 1/2 inch long. East. Wash.; dry, rocky, sagebrush areas in lowlands, foothills, and mountains. Late spring to mid summer.

FIGWORTS (*Scrophularia*) (Color Plate 49)

1. Flowers deep reddish to reddish brown . . . . CALIFORNIA FIGWORT
1. Flowers greenish or greenish brown . . . . LANCE-LEAVED FIGWORT

* * *

CALIFORNIA FIGWORT (*Scrophularia californica*) Plants to 5 feet. Leaves large, triangular. Flowers dark red to reddish brown; 1/2 inch long. East. Wash.; moist habitats in lowlands. Summer.

LANCE-LEAVED FIGWORT (*Scrophularia lanceolata*) Plants to 48 inches. Leaves variable. Flowers greenish to greenish brown; 1/3 to 1/2 inch long. East. and West. Wash.; moist habitats in lowlands and lower mountain areas. Summer.

SPEEDWELLS (*Veronica*) (Color Plate 50)

Small, bright blue flowers with usually upright stems and paired leaves. Petals 4 in number, but 1 of which is smaller than the other 3. Stamens 2 in number.

1. Plants usually growing in water; flowers in axillary racemes 2
1. Plants usually not growing in water; flowers in terminal racemes or occurring singly in axils of leaves 4

2. Leaves more or less oval-shaped, definitely not long and narrow.
AMERICAN SPEEDWELL
2. Leaves not oval-shaped, but long and narrow 3

3. Leaves very narrow, many times longer than wide and usually not tapering at base . . . . MARSH SPEEDWELL
3. Leaves moderately narrow, several times longer than wide, and tapering at base . . . . BROAD-FRUITED SPEEDWELL

4. Flowers solitary in axils of leaves . . . . PURSLANE SPEEDWELL
4. Flowers grouped in terminal racemes 5

5. Lower leaves with definite petioles . . . . THYME-LEAVED SPEEDWELL
5. Lower leaves without petioles 6

6. Leaves oval-shaped and crowded on stem . . . . CUSICK'S SPEEDWELL
6. Leaves oblong, not oval-shaped, and not crowded on stem.
ALPINE SPEEDWELL

*   *   *

AMERICAN SPEEDWELL (*Veronica americana*) Leaves fleshy, on creeping stems turning upward at tips. Leaves lanceolate and toothed. Tiny, blue flowers. East. and West. Wash.; common in slow-moving streams in lowlands and lower parts of mountains. Late spring to mid summer.

MARSH SPEEDWELL (*Veronica scutellata*) Mostly entire, very narrow leaves on creeping stems. Flowers bluish to lilac. East. and West. Wash.; slow-moving streams in lowlands and mountains. Late spring to early autumn.

BROAD-FRUITED SPEEDWELL (*Veronica catenata*) Leaves long and narrow. Flowers white, pink, or pale blue. East. and West. Wash.; slow-moving streams; not common. Summer.

PURSLANE SPEEDWELL (*Veronica peregrina*) Leaves fleshy, blunt, and entire. White or blue flowers borne singly in leaf axils. East. and West. Wash.; wet meadows and stream sides. Mid spring to early autumn.

THYME-LEAVED SPEEDWELL (*Veronica serpyllifolia*) Stems creeping, turning upward at tips. Flowers pale blue to whitish, borne in racemes at tips of stems. East. and West. Wash.; moist meadows and fields. Late spring and summer.

CUSICK'S SPEEDWELL (*Veronica cusickii*) Leaves fleshy, oval, and opposite. Plants often clustered. Flowers dark blue, with yellow centers, about 3/8 inch wide. East. and West. Wash.; moist meadows, rockslides, and streambanks in subalpine areas; common. Mid and late summer. Mt. Pilchuck specimens lavender blue, dark striped, and without yellow centers.

ALPINE SPEEDWELL (*Veronica wormskjoldii*) Plants small, to 6 inches. Leaves occasionally toothed. Flowers light blue to bluish violet. East. and West. Wash.; streambanks, bogs, and moist meadows in upper parts of mountains. Late summer.

SYNTHYRISES (*Synthyris*) (Color Plate 50)

Plants with mostly basal leaves, flowers in racemes, and petals and sepals in 4's.

1. Leaves deeply and pinnately cleft . . . . PINNATE SYNTHYRIS
1. Leaves toothed, not deeply or pinnately cleft 2
2. Flowers bell-shaped with the corolla lobes shorter than the corolla tube.
ROUND-LEAVED SYNTHYRIS
2. Flowers not bell-shaped with the corolla lobes much longer than the tube . . 3
3. Occurring east of the Cascades and in the Columbia Gorge.
WESTERN MOUNTAIN SYNTHYRIS
3. Occurring in Cascades and mountains of Western Washington.
FRINGED SYNTHYRIS

*   *   *

PINNATE SYNTHYRIS (*Synthyris pinnatifida*) Plants to 8 inches. Flowers blue. Olympic Mountains; high, rocky areas in mountains. Summer.

ROUND-LEAVED SYNTHYRIS (*Synthyris reniformis*) Leaves rather kidney-shaped and weakly lobed. Stems to 6 inches, with blue flowers. West. Wash. and Columbia Gorge; coniferous woods in the lowlands. Spring.

WESTERN MOUNTAIN SYNTHYRIS (*Synthyris missurica*) Plants to 12 inches. Flowers bluish. East. Wash. and Columbia Gorge; moist habitats in foothills and mountains. Mid spring to mid summer.

FRINGED SYNTHYRIS (*Synthyris schizantha*) Plants to 12 inches with blue flowers in dense, clustered racemes. Olympic and Cascade Mountains; moist, shaded cliffs. Late spring and summer.

COLLINSIAS (*Collinsia*) (Color Plate 48)

Plants with almost legume-like flowers (upper lip of 2 corolla lobes, and lower lip of 3).

1. Corolla tube at least twice as long as calyx.
LARGE-FLOWERED COLLINSIA
1. Corolla tube not much longer than calyx 2
2. Flowers bluish purple, with white base on upper lip.
FEW-FLOWERED COLLINSIA
2. Upper lip white, tipped with violet; lower lip violet.
SMALL-FLOWERED COLLINSIA

LARGE-FLOWERED COLLINSIA (*Collinsia grandiflora*) Upper lip white or purple; lower lip bluish violet. West. Wash. from Cascade crest westward; open flats and slopes in lowlands and mountains. Spring and early summer.

FEW-FLOWERED COLLINSIA (*Collinsia sparsiflora*) Plants to 12 inches. Flowers bluish purple with white base on upper lip. Southeastern Wash.; open slopes and flats. Spring.

SMALL-FLOWERED COLLINSIA (*Collinsia parviflora*) Plants to 8 inches; commonly bunched at base and spreading. Flowers with upper lip white, tipped with violet; lower lip violet. East. and West. Wash.; open places in lowlands and mountains. Spring.

TONELLAS (*Tonella*)

1. Flowers large, corolla at least 1/4 inch wide. LARGE-FLOWERED TONELLA
1. Flowers small, corolla less than 1/4 inch wide. SMALL-FLOWERED TONELLA

* * *

LARGE-FLOWERED TONELLA (*Tonella floribunda*) Flowers blue. Southeastern Wash.; rocky areas in river canyons. Spring and early summer.

SMALL-FLOWERED TONELLA (*Tonella tenella*) Columbia Gorge; moist, shaded habitats in woods, often in mossy substrates. Flowers pale bluish or whitish, with violet tips. Spring.

MONKEY-FLOWERS (*Mimulus*) (Color Plate 49)

Plants common in wet places, particularly in the mountains, and characterized by a 2-lipped or tube-shaped corolla. Flowers usually borne singly in the axils of paired leaves. Plants usually growing in dense clusters. Some have a grinning "monkey face."

1. Plants perennial, growing from rootstocks or runners.................2
1. Plants annual, growing from slender tap roots......................7

2. Flowers mainly pinkish or rose, marked with yellow (rarely yellow or white).
   LEWIS'S MONKEY-FLOWER
2. Flowers mainly yellow...3

3. Calyx lobes not all similar in size, the upper one larger than the others...4
3. Calyx lobes more or less all the same size.......................5

4. Low alpine plants, commonly less than 8 inches tall; flowers often less than
   5 in number...........................TILING'S MONKEY-FLOWER
4. Taller, more lowland plants, commonly more than 8 inches tall; flowers
   usually more than 5 in number..........COMMON MONKEY-FLOWER

5. Plants with mat-like growth form, with leaves mostly basal and flowers
   borne on single, upright pedicels........PRIMROSE MONKEY-FLOWER
5. Plants not mat-like and with leaves along the stems; the flowers axillary..6

6. Plants distinctly slimy and musky-smelling....MUSKY MONKEY-FLOWER
6. Plants not distinctly slimy or musky-smelling..COAST MONKEY-FLOWER

7. Flowers yellow, often marked with reddish........................8
7. Flowers red or purple, sometimes marked with yellow or white........11

269

8. Corolla distinctly 2-lipped, the lower lip much longer than the upper one.9
8. Corolla not distinctly 2-lipped, the lower lip only slightly longer than the upper 10
9. Upper calyx lobe larger than others of the calyx.
                                        COMMON MONKEY-FLOWER
9. Upper calyx lobe not longer than the others.
                                     CHICKWEED MONKEY-FLOWER
10. Base of leaf tapering gradually to the petiole.
                               SHORT-FLOWERED MONKEY-FLOWER
10. Base of leaf not tapering gradually to the petiole, but blunt.
                                FREE-FLOWERING MONKEY-FLOWER
11. Flowers large (more than 3/8 inch long) and projecting well beyond the calyx . . . . .DWARF MONKEY-FLOWER
11. Flowers small (less than 3/8 inch) and scarcely projecting beyond the calyx. . . . . .BREWER'S MONKEY-FLOWER

                    *   *   *

LEWIS'S MONKEY-FLOWER (*Mimulus lewisii*) Plants in dense clusters, often 12-20 inches tall. Leaves numerously toothed. Flowers 1-1½ inches long; pink to rose, marked with yellow; less commonly yellow or white. East. and West. Wash.; moist places along streams and seepage slopes at middle to high altitudes. Summer.

TILING'S MONKEY-FLOWER (*Mimulus tilingii*) Plants to 4 inches, often mat forming. Flowers yellow, 3/4 to 1 inch, and borne singly on each stem. East. and West. Wash.; along streams and brooks at high elevations in mountains; often common. Late summer and early autumn.

COMMON MONKEY-FLOWER (*Mimulus guttatus*) Plants tall, to 24 inches. Leaves oval. Flowers yellow, dotted with reddish, and borne in terminal racemes. East. and West. Wash.; wet habitats in mountains; common. Mid spring to early autumn.

PRIMROSE MONKEY-FLOWER (*Mimulus primuloides*) Flowers yellow, dotted with reddish; single, and very small, and growing from tips of 2-4 inch stems. Cascades and East. Wash.; moist, open places in mountains. Summer.

MUSKY MONKEY-FLOWER (*Mimulus moschatus*) Plants to 16 inches with hairy, sticky stems, and musky odor. Leaves finely toothed, 1-2 inches long. Flowers yellow, marked with reddish lines or dots. East. and West. Wash.; moist habitats in lowlands and up into the mountains. Late spring and summer.

COAST MONKEY-FLOWER (*Mimulus dentatus*) Plants to 16 inches. Leaves ovate to long-ovate and sharply toothed. Flowers yellow, often dotted or washed with reddish. West. Wash.; mainly in the Olympics; moist places along streams and in dense-damp woods. Late spring and summer.

CHICKWEED MONKEY-FLOWER (*Mimulus alsinoides*) Plants to 12 inches. Flowers small, less than 1/2 inch long, and yellow with dark reddish blotch at base of lower lip. Leaves oval. Cascades and West. Wash.; moist, mossy places in shaded woods in lowlands. Spring and early summer.

SHORT-FLOWERED MONKEY-FLOWER (*Mimulus breviflorus*) Plants to 6 inches. Flowers pale yellow. East. Wash.; moist habitats in open lowlands. Spring and early summer.

FREE-FLOWERING MONKEY-FLOWER (*Mimulus floribundus*) Plants to 20 inches. Foliage sticky-hairy. Flowers yellow, sometimes dotted with red. East. Wash.; moist, open habitats in lowlands and foothills. Late spring to early fall.

DWARF MONKEY-FLOWER (*Mimulus nanus*) Plants small, to 5 inches, often growing in mats or patches. Flowers magenta, marked with yellow. East. Wash.; sandy or gravelly habitats in lowlands and foothills. Late spring and summer.

BREWER'S MONKEY-FLOWER (*Mimulus breweri*) Plants small, to 6 inches. Leaves entire, lanceolate. Flowers purplish to reddish, sometimes marked with yellow. Cascades and East. Wash.; dry meadows and slopes in lower to middle parts of mountains. Summer.

Southeast of Connell and north of the Snake River in southern Franklin County, Washington, lies an area of some 100 square miles of sand dunes and scattered junipers, known locally as "The Juniper Forest." The northern part of this complex, containing the largest dunes and the principal juniper groves and comprising some 8½ square miles, has been set aside by the U.S. Bureau of Land Management as a natural preserve and protected from vehicular travel and commercial exploitation.

The important features of the preserve are the large sand dunes (the biggest in the state), the 6 groves of western junipers (the largest grove of which covers some 300 acres), and the populations of desert wildflowers and small mammals and birds that inhabit the various sites. The area has been intensively studied for the past several years by Earl Larrison and several of his students who have found a number of interesting birds and mammals, as well as plants.

Desert floras are a variable commodity, their periods and intensity of flowering depending on winter and spring rainfall, temperatures, and winds. Thus, each year may exhibit a slightly different assemblage of flowers compared with previous and succeeding years.

In March, one may usually look for fritillaries and drabas, while April and early May often bring a variety of species such as balsamroots, phlox, clarkias, evening primroses, lomatiums, sego lilies, wallflowers, and many others. The best blooming takes place in the spring, but a number of species continue to appear on through the summer and well into the fall. The best time to visit the Juniper Forest for flowers is in late April or early May. The area cannot be driven into, so you must hike. Take a hat, colored glasses, this guide, a compass, and water canteen, and start early in the morning.

271

Chapter 56—The Broomrape Family (*Orobanchaceae*)

Members of this family are root parasites without chlorophyll-bearing foliage. Leaves are reduced to alternate scales. Flowers are irregular, with 4-5 sepals; tubular, more or less 2-lipped corolla; 4 stamens, and superior ovary. Not especially showy plants. (Color Plate 50)

1. Stamens hairy at base.....................HOOKER'S GROUND-CONE
1. Stamens not hairy at base.................BROOMRAPES (*Orobanche*)

*   *   *

HOOKER'S GROUND-CONE (*Boschniakia hookeri*) Stem thick and fleshy, 4-6 inches tall, reddish or yellowish. Tiny flowers protrude between scale-like leaves on upper portion of the "cone." Flowers 2-lipped. Flowers whitish. West. Wash.; parasitic on salal in lowlands near salt water. Early summer. (Color Plate 50)

BROOMRAPES (*Orobanche*) (Color Plate 50)

These plants are chlorophyll-lacking, root parasites with unbranched stems bearing small scale-like leaves and 1 or more flowers at the stem tips.

1. Flowers borne on definite pedicels not possessing small bracts.........2
1. Flowers not borne on pedicels or, if so, the pedicels with small bracts....3
2. Flower-bearing pedicels numerous (4 or more) and usually shorter than stem; lobes of calyx same length as, or shorter than, tube.
CLUSTERED BROOMRAPE
2. Flower-bearing pedicels few (3 or less) and longer than stem; lobes of calyx longer than calyx tube.....................NAKED BROOMRAPE
3. Plants parasitic on coniferous trees.................PINE BROOMRAPE
3. Plants not as above..4
4. Flowers more or less sessile—without pedicels....DESERT BROOMRAPE
4. Flowers (at least some) with definite pedicels.......................5
5. Lower lip of corolla spreading and turned downward.STOUT BROOMRAPE
5. Lower lip of corolla not spreading and erect (not turning downward).
CALIFORNIA BROOMRAPE

*   *   *

CLUSTERED BROOMRAPE (*Orobanche fasciculata*) Plants small, to 6 inches, with glandular, downy or hairy foliage with 4-10 flowers on clustered stalks. Flowers purple or yellow. East. and West. Wash.; open places in lowlands and foothills, parasitizing a variety of species, especially sagebrush. Late spring and early summer.

NAKED BROOMRAPE (*Orobanche uniflora*) Plants tiny, to 4 inches, with 1 to several, long-stalked flowers at tip of stem. Most plants we have found were single-flowered. Flowers purple. East. and West. Wash.; open or semi-open habitats, including open woods, from lowlands to (rarely) subalpine zone; not common. Mid spring and summer.

PINE BROOMRAPE (*Orobanche pinorum*) Plants glandular-downy, to 12 inches. Stem thick, with branching inflorescence. Flowers yellow, with 2 bracts beneath calyx. East. and West. Wash.; coniferous woods; rare. Mid and late summer.

DESERT BROOMRAPE (*Orobanche ludoviciana*)   Plants to 8 inches with glandular foliage and spike-like inflorescence. Flowers purple or pink, striped with white. East. Wash.; open habitats in lowlands and foothills; parasitic on composites, especially sages. Mid summer and early autumn.

STOUT BROOMRAPE (*Orobanche grayana*) Plants to 12 inches with thick, glandular-downy stems bearing dense inflorescences. Flowers purple or whitish with dark lines. East. and West. Wash.; open habitats; parasitic on species of composites. Summer. Recently considered a variety of the following.

CALIFORNIA BROOMRAPE (*Orobanche californica*) Plants small, to 5 inches with glandular-downy stems; dense flower groups at stem tips. Flowers purple. East. Wash.; open desert areas where parasitic on sagebrush. Summer.

Chapter 57—The Bladderwort Family (*Lentibulariaceae*)

Members of this family are small herbs living in shallow, aquatic or moist habitats with 2-lipped flowers and spurred corollas. Stamens 2. The plants are insectivorous, capturing the insects either on their sticky leaves or in small bladders which are modified leaves. The insects are digested for nourishment. (Color Plate 51)

1. Submerged plants, with leaves dissected into needle-like lobes bearing bladder-like swellings . . . . BLADDERWORTS (*Utricularia*)
1. Plants not submerged, but growing in wet places; leaves not as above.
                                                                     BUTTERWORT

*   *   *

BUTTERWORT (*Pinguicula vulgaris*) Plants to 4 inches with greasy-looking, yellow-green leaves lying flat on the ground. Flowers single on individual stems and nodding. Conical purple to white flowers with spurs. East. and West. Wash.; bogs, streambanks, and wet meadows in the mountains. Summer. (Color Plate 51)

BLADDERWORTS (*Utricularia*) (Color Plate 51)

1. Flowers large, lower lip more than 3/8 inch long; lobes of leaves round; bladders numerous. . . . . COMMON BLADDERWORT
1. Flowers small, lower lip less than 3/8 inch long; lobes of leaves flat; bladders irregular on leaf stalks. 2
2. Bladders borne on ordinary leaves; spur much shorter than lower lip.
                                                              LESSER BLADDERWORT
2. Bladders borne on separate, non-leaf-bearing branches; spur almost as long as lower lip. . . . . MOUNTAIN BLADDERWORT

*   *   *

COMMON BLADDERWORT (*Utricularia vulgaris*) Flowers yellow. East. and West. Wash.; standing water (ponds and lakes), sluggish streams, marshes, as well as moist banks and rocks; common. Summer.

Figure 62.
How the color picture of the bedstraw, *Galium,* was made by Jim Yaich.
Both photos made in the rain. (Larrison)

274

LESSER BLADDERWORT (*Utricularia minor*) Flowers yellow. East. and West. Wash.; standing or slow-moving water. Summer.

MOUNTAIN BLADDERWORT (*Utricularia intermedia*) Flowers yellow, with lower lip twice as long as upper. East. and West. Wash.; standing or slow-moving water. Summer.

Chapter 58—The Madder Family (*Rubiaceae*)

Members of this family are herbs (ours) with entire, opposite or whorled leaves; flower parts in 4's; and perfect, regular flowers. Petals joined into lobed corolla. Stamens same number as corolla lobes. Ovary inferior. (Color Plate 51)

1. Leaves opposite.......................................KELLOGGIA
1. Leaves appearing whorled.....................BEDSTRAWS (*Galium*)

*   *   *

KELLOGGIA (*Kelloggia galioides*) Plants to 24 inches with paired, lanceolate leaves on slender stems. The pink or white flowers are borne in open groups at tips of stems. East. Wash.; open areas or woods, often on streambanks or in rocks.

BEDSTRAWS (*Galium*) (Color Plate 51)

Plants with square stems, bristly surfaces, and leaves in circles or whorls. Flowers tiny, star-like.

1. Plants annual with a short taproot.........LOW MOUNTAIN BEDSTRAW
1. Plants perennial with a well-developed, creeping rootstock (rhizome).....2

2. Leaves mostly in whorls of 4......................................3
2. Leaves mostly in whorls of 5-8...................................6

3. Leaves 1-veined from the base...................SMALL BEDSTRAW
3. Leaves 3-veined from the base....................................4

4. Flowers white.............................NORTHERN BEDSTRAW
4. Flowers yellowish 5

5. Plants occurring in Eastern Washington....MANY-FLOWERED BEDSTRAW
5. Plants occurring in Western Washington...........OREGON BEDSTRAW

6. Fruits without hooked spines.....................PACIFIC BEDSTRAW
6. Fruits with hooked spines..7

7. Flowers borne in 3's on axillary peduncles.......FRAGRANT BEDSTRAW
7. Flowers borne in groups at ends of stems or branches.
                                           TALL ROUGH BEDSTRAW

*   *   *

LOW MOUNTAIN BEDSTRAW (*Galium bifolium*) Plants low, to 8 inches. Upper leaves paired; lower leaves in whorls of 4's or 5's. Flowers white, borne singly in axils of leaves. East. (mostly) and West. Wash.; moist habitats in mountains. Late spring and summer.

SMALL BEDSTRAW (*Galium trifidum*) Plants with slender reclining or supported branches reaching 20-26 inches. Leaves oblanceolate to linear. Flowers white, mostly borne singly in axils. East. and West. Wash.; moist habitats in mountains. Summer and early autumn.

NORTHERN BEDSTRAW (*Galium boreale*) Plants to 24 inches. Leaves lance-shaped. Flowers small, white and borne in large groups at tips of stems. East. and West. Wash.; moist places from lowlands up into the mountains. Summer.

MANY-FLOWERED BEDSTRAW (*Galium multiflorum*) Stems stiff, to 12 inches, and clustered. Leaves oblong-lanceolate to ovate, in whorls of 4's. Flowers greenish yellow, numerous, and borne in small axillary clusters. East. Wash.; dry, open, rocky places. Late spring and summer.

OREGON BEDSTRAW (*Galium oreganum*) Plants to 16 inches with 5 or more whorls of elliptic leaves. Flowers greenish yellow, borne in upper axils of terminal groups. West. Wash.; moist places in meadows and woods. Summer.

PACIFIC BEDSTRAW (*Galium cymosum*) Plants tall, to 24-30 inches. Leaves oblanceolate, in 4's to 6's. Flowers white, abundant, and borne in small cymes at tips of branches. West. Wash.; moist places in lowlands. Summer.

FRAGRANT BEDSTRAW (*Galium triflorum*) Plants tall, to 36 inches. Leaves more or less lanceolate and usually in whorls of 6. Flowers white to greenish, fragrant, and borne in 3's at the tips of branched stalks from axils. East. and West. Wash.; moist woods in lowlands and up into the mountains. Summer.

TALL ROUGH BEDSTRAW (*Galium asperrimum*) Plants to 30 inches with erect or supported branches which are noticeably very bristly. Leaves lance-olate or lanceolate-linear in whorls of 6-8. Flowers white, in leafy, terminal groups. East. Wash.; woods in foothills and mountains. Summer.

Chapter 59—The Honeysuckle Family (*Caprifoliaceae*)

Members of this family, as treated here, are perennial herbs and trailing or twining, shrubby vines with opposite leaves and perfect flowers. Petals are fused, often into tube-like corollas with the lobes sometimes irregular. Calyx 3-5 lobed. Stamens 5 or 4. Ovary inferior. Our species have strong trailing or twining habits. (Color Plate 51)

1. Stamens 5; fruits fleshy....................HONEYSUCKLES (*Lonicera*)
1. Stamens 4; fruits a dry capsule.......................TWIN-FLOWER

*   *   *

TWIN-FLOWER (*Linnaea borealis*) A delicate, creeping plant with small, shiny, oval, evergreen leaves and paired, pale pink, nodding, fragrant flowers. East. and West. Wash.; in coniferous forests, open or dense, throughout the state, showing some preference for ground receiving some sunshine; common. Summer. A great favorite of wildflower lovers and outdoor enthusiasts in general. Named in honor of Karl von Linne, father of modern systematic botany who considered this species his favorite of all flowers. (Color Plate 51)

HONEYSUCKLES (*Lonicera*) (Color Plate 52)

1. Corolla slightly, if at all, 2-lipped; tube long, 3 to 4 times as long as the lips; flowers large, 1 inch or more long; stems smooth.ORANGE HONEYSUCKLE
1. Corolla strongly 2-lipped; tube shorter than or equally the lips; flowers smaller, 3/4 inch long; stems hairy..............HAIRY HONEYSUCKLE

*   *   *

ORANGE HONEYSUCKLE (*Lonicera ciliosa*) Flowers orange, red, or orange yellow. Leaves smooth, with whitish bloom beneath. East. and (mostly) West. Wash.; open woods and edges of clearings. Late spring to mid summer.

HAIRY HONEYSUCKLE (*Lonicera hispidula*) Flowers pink or yellowish pink. Leaves and stems slightly hairy. West. Wash.; dry, often rocky, though occasionally moist habitats in open woods. Summer.

Figure 63.
The valerian, *Valeriana,* a favorite food of the pika. (Yaich)

278

Chapter 60—The Valerian Family (*Valerianaceae*)

Members of this family are annual or perennial herbs with branched stems, opposite simple or pinnately-divided leaves, and perfect flowers. Petals fused to form 5-lobed, often irregular, corolla tube. Stamens 1 to 4. Ovary inferior. (Color Plate 52)

1. Plants annual; calyx segments absent; leaves simple.
CORN-SALADS (Plectritis)

1. Plants perennial; calyx segments of numerous plume-like bristles; some leaves on stems compound................VALERIANS (*Valeriana*)

CORN-SALADS (*Plectritis*) (Color Plate 52)

1. Spreading (gibbous) lip of corolla larger than tube; spur short and thick.
ROSY CORN-SALAD

1. Spreading (gibbous) lip of corolla shorter than tube; spur well developed and relatively long...2

2. Corolla hardly 2-lipped (almost equally 5-lobed); flowers white or pale pinkish ....DESERT CORN-SALAD

2. Corolla definitely 2-lipped; flowers deep pink with red dots at base of lower lip...............................LONG-SPURRED CORN-SALAD

*   *   *

ROSY CORN-SALAD (*Plectritis congesta*) Flowers pink or white. West. Wash. and Cascades; meadows and spring seepage slopes. Mid spring to early summer.

DESERT CORN-SALAD (*Plectritis macrocera*) East. and West. Wash.; moist meadows and spring seepage slopes. Flowers white to pale pink. Late spring and early summer.

LONG-SPURRED CORN-SALAD (*Plectritis ciliosa*) Flowers deep pink with red dots on base of lower lip. Klickitat County and Columbia Gorge; moist meadows and seepage slopes. Spring.

VALERIANS (*Valeriana*) (Color Plate 52; Fig. 63)

Perennial herbs with strong odors and mostly basal (sometimes opposite) leaves. Flowers in panicle-like cymes. Calyx teeth bristle-like and in-rolled. Corolla funnel-shaped and swollen near base. Stamens 3.

1. Basal leaves long and narrow, and tapering gradually to the petioles; flowers in loose panicle, not round or flat cluster; taproot stout and short.
TOBACCO-ROOT

1. Basal leaves oval-shaped (at least not long and narrow) and with blade and petiole sharply differentiated; flowers tending to be in round or flat clusters; with stout rhizome and numerous fiber-like roots....................2

2. Corolla small and short (1/8 inch or less long); corolla lobes same length as tube...3

2. Corolla larger and longer (more than 1/8 inch long); corolla lobes shorter than tube 4

279

3. Plants small, less than 15 inches; stems with few leaves.
                                                    WOODS VALERIAN
3. Plants large, more than 15 inches; stem leafy.......WESTERN VALERIAN
4. Stamens not projecting noticeably beyond lobes of corolla.
                                                    COLUMBIAN VALERIAN
4. Stamens projecting noticeably beyond lobes of corolla.................5
5. Stem leaves equal to or smaller than basal leaves; leaflets more or less
   entire.......................................SCOULER'S VALERIAN
5. Stem leaves usually larger than basal leaves; leaflets coarsely toothed.
                                                    SITKA VALERIAN

                        *   *   *

TOBACCO-ROOT (*Valeriana edulis*)   Plants smooth, to 24 inches. Basal leaves thick, oblanceolate, and entire. Flowers white to pinkish. East. Wash.; moist, open habitats, such as meadows, in foothills and mountains. Summer.

WOODS VALERIAN (*Valeriana dioica*)   Plants tall, to 24 inches. Flowers white, small (less than 1/5 inch long), and borne in compact clusters on short stalks. Stem leaves deeply pinnately cleft. Northwestern Wash.; moist meadows and similar habitats in mountains. Late spring to mid summer.

WESTERN VALERIAN (*Valeriana occidentalis*)   Plants large, to 30-36 inches. Basal leaves oval-shaped and a number entire. Flowers white, in compact heads. East. Wash.; moist places in meadows or woods in foothills or mountains. Late spring to mid summer.

COLUMBIAN VALERIAN (*Valeriana columbiana*)   Plants to 20 inches. Basal leaves crenulate to lobed. Flowers white, larger than in other valerians and in more open heads. Central and Northern Cascades; open, moist slopes. Late spring to mid summer.

SCOULER'S VALERIAN (*Valeriana scouleri*)   Plants 18-36 inches. Leaves not toothed. Flowers white to pinkish in compact heads. West. Wash.; moist woods from lowlands to intermediate elevations in mountains; also commonly found in meadows and on moist cliffs. Common. Mid spring to mid summer.

SITKA VALERIAN (*Valeriana sitchensis*)   Plants tall, to 40 inches. Leaflets large and coarsely toothed. Flowers white, in flattish heads. East. and West. Wash.; moist meadows and woods in intermediate and subalpine parts of the mountains. Common in the Cascades where a favorite food of the pikas. Summer.

Chapter 61—The Cucumber Family (*Cucurbitaceae*)

Members of this family are climbing or trailing herbs with palmately-lobed leaves and male and female flowers (male flowers in racemes or loose clusters; female flowers solitary). Stamens 3; calyx and corolla 5- to 7-lobed. Ovary inferior. The family contains the domestic cucumbers, squashes, gourds, and melons. One species in our area. (Color Plates 52, 53)

WILD CUCUMBER (*Marah oreganus*)   Flowers white. West. Wash.; open habitats, such as fields and moist bottoms, in lowlands and foothills. Spring and early summer.

———————

Many visitors to the wild scene have long had an interest in natural foods. The earlier residents of the continent depended to a considerable extent on wild plants, especially when hunting, camping, or travelling through the forests or over the prairies. Today, with supermarkets, TV dinners, and convenience foods of all kinds, we seldom give thought to nature's storehouse, nor are we ordinarily dependent on it. The pursuit of knowledge on natural foods has become more of a fetish of the food cultists or a theoretical consideration indulged in by popular nature writers.

There is more to this business of natural foods than appears on the surface, however. While we would hardly recommend the wholesale harvesting of such foods and, indeed, there is really very little need to do so, the growing numbers of persons visiting the wildlands on recreational jaunts increases the chance of some getting lost and running out of food. Some knowledge of what may be utilized in the local region for emergency rations is evidently desirable. We remember the case of one elderly school teacher who mislaid the trail while out berry picking and subsisted satisfactorily on berries and nectar-rich flowers for several days, turning up in better shape than some of those searching for her. She had put common sense and some knowledge of natural foods to work.

The survival value of natural foods cannot be over-estimated. While perhaps not as tasty as our familiar larder items, you would be surprised at what is available. Did you know that the dainty violet, both leaves and flowers, can be used in a variety of ways? Miner's lettuce has long been valued for cooked or raw greens. The lowly dandelion has many uses, varying from salads to wines. The roots and bulbs of many species may be eaten.

Since certain species are more valuable than others and a few are poisonous, it is well to know what plants you are gathering. A number of books have been prepared on natural foods. The following are convenient, low-priced, and informative.

The Edible Wild: A Complete Cookbook and Guide to Edible Wild Plants in Canada and North America by Berndt Berglund and Clare E. Bolsby. 1971. Scribners.

Western Edible Wild Plants by H. D. Harrington. 1972. U. New Mexico Press.

Wild Edible and Useful Plants of the West by Donald R. Kirk. 1970. Naturegraph.

Figure 64.
Bluebells, *Campanula,* in the rain. (Yaich)

Chapter 62—The Harebell Family (*Campanulaceae*)

Members of this family are annual or perennial herbs with alternate leaves, milky juice, and perfect, regular or irregular flowers. Calyx and corolla usually 5-lobed. Corolla sometimes with 2 lips. Ovary inferior. Flowers often bell- or tube-like. (Color Plate 53)

1. Corolla irregular (2-lipped) or absent; stamens united into a tube-like structure or ring about the style....................................2
1. Corolla regular and usually present; stamens not united as above.......4

2. Flowers without pedicels, being borne sessile in the axils of leaves or leaf-like bracts; semi-aquatic to aquatic..............ELEGANT DOWNINGIA
2. Flowers borne on pedicels of varying length; not necessarily aquatic or semi-aquatic, though some Howellias may be.......................3

3. Corolla relatively large, at least 1/4 inch long........LOBELIAS (*Lobelia*)
3. Corolla very small, less than 1/8 inch long, or absent; mostly aquatic.
HOWELLIAS

4. Plants perennial with well-developed roots; flowers with distinct pedicels.
CAMPANULAS (*Campanula*)
4. Plants annual with small, poorly-developed roots; flowers without distinct pedicels..5

5. Flowers single and mostly terminal (at ends of stems and stem branches).
BLUECUPS
5. Flowers not as above but scattered along the stems and stem branches, or as interrupted spikes...6

6. Corolla deeply lobed (divided for more than half of length of corolla).
VENUS'S LOOKING-GLASS
6. Corolla not deeply lobed (to less than half the length of the corolla).
HETEROCODON

*   *   *

ELEGANT DOWNINGIA (*Downingia elegans*) Plants to 20 inches. Leaves 1 inch long and lance-shaped. Flowers blue to violet with yellow or white center and dark veins. East. Wash.; temporary pools, pond and lake margins, and wet meadows. Summer. (Color Plate 53)

HOWELLIA (*Howellia aquatilis*) Floating branches to 24 inches. Leaves thread-like, to 1½ inches. Flowers white, with corollas very small or missing. West. and possibly East. Wash.; aquatic habitats, as ponds and lakes; not common. Late spring and early summer.

BLUECUPS (*Githopsis specularioides*) Plants small, to 6 inches, grayish and bristly. Leaves oval or wedge-shaped, 1/4 inch long, and sparsely toothed. Flowers blue with white throat. East. and West. Wash.; open, arid habitats in lowlands and foothills. Late spring and early summer. (Color Plate 53)

VENUS'S LOOKING-GLASS (*Triodanis perfoliata*) Plants to 30 inches. Leaves oval-shaped, scalloped, and margined with hairs. Flowers purple or lavender. East. and West. Wash.; mostly open places, often in disturbed soil, in lowlands and lower parts of mountains. Late spring and summer.

HETEROCODON (*Heterocodon rariflorum*) Plants to 12 inches, bristly, with small, oval, toothed leaves. Flowers borne in axils and blue in color. East. and West. Wash.; open, wet, often gravelly places in lowlands and foothills. Summer.

LOBELIAS (*Lobelia*) (Color Plate 54)

1. Leaves flat; basal as well as distributed along stem......KALM'S LOBELIA
1. Leaves round in cross-section, hollow, and basal........WATER LOBELIA

*   *   *

KALM'S LOBELIA (*Lobelia kalmii*) Flowers blue or white. Northeastern Wash.; peat bogs and aquatic margins. Summer.

WATER LOBELIA (*Lobelia dortmanna*) Flowers bluish to white. East. and West. Wash.; shallow water near shores of lakes and ponds. Summer.

BLUEBELLS (*Campanula*) (Color Plate 53; Fig. 64)

Small, annual or perennial herbs with usually characteristic bluish, bell-shaped flowers. Leaves alternate and flower parts in 5's.

1. Pistil much longer than corolla; lobes of corolla spreading and often recurved...................................SCOULER'S BLUEBELL
1. Pistil not extending beyond outer edge of corolla; corolla lobes scarcely spreading...2
2. Flowers in fruit strongly down-turned ("nodding"); basal leaves roundish and slightly, if at all, crenately toothed. Plant growth form larger, to 14 inches tall (though some individuals may be dwarfed alpines).
ROUND-LEAVED BLUEBELL
2. Flowers in fruit not strongly down-turned; leaves not roundish, but much longer than broad; leaves often strongly toothed; plant growth form dwarfed, seldom more than 6 inches tall.....................................3
3. Corolla large, more than 3/4 inch long; lobes much shorter than corolla tube.......................................ALASKA BLUEBELL
3. Corolla small, less than 3/4 inch long; corolla lobes longer or shorter than the tube 4
4. Plants occurring in the Olympic Mountains..........PIPER'S BLUEBELL
4. Plants not occurring as above...................................5
5. Plants delicate, with single terminal flowers; leaf surfaces smooth.
PARRY'S BLUEBELL
5. Plants more stocky, with flowers along stem; leaf surfaces minutely hairy.
ROUGH BLUEBELL

*   *   *

SCOULER'S BLUEBELL (*Campanula scouleri*) Plants to 12 inches with branching stems. Leaves strongly toothed and pointed at tip. Flowers pale blue, 1/4 to 1/2 inch long; sometimes bluish white. Cascades and West. Wash.; woods, either open or dense; occasionally in rocky places. Lowlands to middle elevations in mountains. Summer.

ROUND-LEAVED BLUEBELL (*Campanula rotundifolia*) Stems not branched, to 14 inches. Basal leaves blunt at tip; rounded and weakly toothed. Stem leaves linear. Flowers blue, 3/4 inch long. East. and West. Wash.; occurs in variety of habitats from lowlands to subalpine; common. Summer and early autumn. The famous "Bluebells of Scotland" are of this species.

ALASKA BLUEBELL (*Campanula lasiocarpa*) Leaves mostly basal and sharply toothed. Flowers blue. Northern Cascades; alpine habitats. Summer.

PIPER'S BLUEBELL (*Campanula piperi*) Plants low (to 4 inches) and weakly matted. Leaves toothed and widest near tip. Flowers blue to whitish, star-shaped, and 1 inch wide. Olympic Mountains; rocky habitats in subalpine and alpine areas. Summer.

PARRY'S BLUEBELL (*Campanula parryi*) Plants low, to 10 inches. Leaves mostly entire. Flowers bluish. Central and Northern Cascades; subalpine meadows. Summer.

ROUGH BLUEBELL (*Campanula scabrella*) Plants small, to 5 inches; downy; clustered. Leaves basal, entire, and widest near tip. Flowers blue. Cascades; rocky habitats, such as talus slopes and outcroppings. Summer.

In recent years, the annual Audubon campout over Memorial Day weekend at Wenas Park has become as much a wildflower foray as an event devoted to birds. While the avifauna of Wenas and surrounding areas is spectacular, so are the native wildflowers. Within a relatively short distance of the campsite at the Boise Cascade campground are dense fir and pine forests, open yellow pine woods, brushy stream bottoms, sagebrush slopes, moist meadows, high open grasslands, mountain parks, and subalpine ridges. Campout time in late May often finds the flowers at their height of blooming.

Particularly attractive are the high open ridges, such as Manastash and Umptanum, where the ground is literally covered with a profusion of composites, Indian painbrushes, lupines, penstemons, onions, lilies, and bitter-roots. The yellow pine flats may be carpeted with a solid mass of sky-blue lupines, while the drier wooded slopes may contain big-headed clover in a solid aspect. Moist meadows along streams are clothed with camas, while here and there the wild peony may be found. The Rocky Prairies in the southern part of the Wenas area often present a variety of mountain park flowers. At the other extreme, the state game farm area lower down the valley has a number of sagebrush and wet meadow and thicket species.

A recent feature of the campout has been an exhibit in the headquarters area of several dozen of the more common Wenas wildflowers. Whether you are interested in birds, flowers, butterflies, or good fresh air, the annual Audubon Wenas campout is a delightful experience.

Figure 65.
False sunflower, *Helianthella,* showing typical ray and disk flowers in a
composite head. (Larrison)

Chapter 63—The Sunflower Family (*Compositae*)

Members of this family are called "composites" because what seems to be a separate flower is actually a complex or composite of many flowers joined together into a head, supported on a common receptacle and surrounded by an involucre of bracts or what appears to be the sepals for the flower head. Heads are:

(1) *disk-shaped* (discoid), when all the flowers have the petals fused into tubular corollas (no ray flowers),

(2) *ligulate,* when the corollas are all strap-shaped (i.e., all ray flowers), or

(3) *radiate,* when the outer corollas are strap-shaped (ray flowers) and the inner ones are tubular (disk flowers).

The receptacle, at the end of the stem, which supports the flower head, is often covered with bracts or scales known as *chaff.* Surrounding each flower may be a tuft of bristle-like structures constituting the calyx and called the *pappus*; stamens, when present, 5, usually united into a tube; ovary inferior, fruit called an *achene.* Pappus scaly, spiny, hair-like or none. (Color Plate 54)
Note: This family is both the largest of the Washington wildflower groups and the most difficult. Do not be discouraged if it takes you a while to learn the composites!

1. Head composed entirely of ligulate, perfect flowers; sap milky 2
1. Head composed of not all ligulate flowers; the ligulate, or ray, flowers (when present) marginal, and with or without pistils; sap not milky 14

2. Bristles of the pappus hair-like 3
2. Bristles of the pappus feathery, scale-like, or missing 11

3. Achenes strongly flattened . . . . LETTUCE (*Lactuca*)
3. Achenes round or angular in cross-section 4

4. Achenes spiny . . . . DANDELIONS (*Taraxacum*)
4. Achenes not spiny, but smooth 5

5. Flowers pink, purplish, or white 6
5. Flowers yellow, orange, or red (except white in *Hieracium albiflorum*) 7

6. Stem leaves large and more than 3/8 inch wide.
　　　　　　　　　　　　　　　　　　WESTERN RATTLESNAKE-ROOT
6. Stem leaves very narrow, less than 3/8 inch wide . . . . . . SKELETON-WEED

7. Bristles of pappus fused at base . . . . APARGIDIUM
7. Bristles of pappus separate to base and individually distinct 8

8. Plants perennial, growing from rhizomes with numerous fibrous roots; no single taproot, pappus brownish . . . . HAWKWEEDS (*Hieracium*)
8. Plants perennial, annual, or biennial, developing from 1 or several taproots, but not from a rhizome, pappus usually white 9

9. Stems with leaves and several heads to a stem . . HAWKSBEARDS (*Crepis*)
9. Stems usually without leaves and with single head per stem 10

10. Achenes with elongated, narrow neck or filament (beak) between seed and pappus . . . . AGOSERISES (*Agoseris*)
10. Achenes without elongated, narrow neck or filament (beak) between seed and pappus . . . . MICROSERISES (*Microseris*)

11. Flowers pink or white . . . . RUSH PINKS (*Stephanomeria*)
11. Flowers yellow, orange, or rarely purple 12

12. Pappus consisting of scales, occasionally with a terminal awn or bristle.
MICROSERISES (*Microseris*)
12. Pappus consisting of feathery bristles 13

13. Leaves with spiny margins . . . . THISTLES (*Cirsium*)
13. Leaves without spiny margins . . . . AMERICAN SAUSSUREA

14. Heads with ray flowers 15
14. Heads without ray flowers and disk-shaped 49

15. Rays yellow to orange, occasionally purple or reddish at base 16
15. Rays not yellow or orange, but white, red, pink, purple, or blue 39

16. Pappus chaffy, or spiny, or lacking, but not hairy 17
16. Pappus with hair-like or feathery bristles; receptacle naked 32

17. Receptacle covered with chaff or bristles 18
17. Receptacle either naked or with a single row of chaff between rays and disk 24

18. Involucral bracts in two dissimilar series (one circle of bracts shorter than the other) . . . . BEGGAR-TICKS (*Bidens*)
18. Involucral bracts in one or more similar series 19

19. Receptacle covered with bristles. GREAT-FLOWERED BLANKET-FLOWER
19. Receptacle covered with chaff and with sepal-like bracts 20

20. Plants with definite leafy stems 21
20. Plants with more or less leafless stems; leaves mostly basal.
BALSAMROOTS (*Balsamorhiza*)

21. All the leaves on the stems alternate 22
21. Leaves on lower stem opposite 23

22. Receptacle flat or nearly so; ray flowers fertile . . . . . . WYETHIAS (*Wyethia*)
22. Receptacle more or less cone-shaped; ray flowers infertile (without reproductive organs) . . . . RUDBECKIAS (*Rudbeckia*)

23. Achenes of the disk strongly flattened.
SINGLE-FLOWERED FALSE SUNFLOWER
23. Achenes of the disk slightly flattened . . . . SUNFLOWERS (*Helianthus*)

24. Rays longer (more than 1/4 inch long); receptacle naked 25
24. Rays shorter (less than 1/4 inch long); row of bracts sometimes present between rays and disk 27

25. Pappus spiny; involucre sticky or gummy . . . . . . GUM-PLANTS (*Grindelia*)
25. Pappus not spiny; involucre not sticky or gummy 26

26. Involucral bracts less than 15 . . . . COMMON WOOLLY SUNFLOWER
26. Involucral bracts more than 20 . . . . DWARF HULSEA

27. Leaves strongly dissected . . . . WESTERN TANSY
27. Leaves entire or toothed, but not strongly dissected 28

28. Involucral bracts nested in several series . . . . FLESHY JAUMEA
28. Involucral bracts in a single series 29

29. Involucral bracts fused into a lobed or toothed cup.
LASTHENIAS (*Lasthenia*)
29. Involucral bracts more or less separate and distinct 30

288

Figure 66.
A characteristic dry-slope habitat for composites. In this photo, the
woolly sunflower, *Eriophyllum*. (Yaich)

292

*　　　*　　　*

WESTERN RATTLESNAKE-ROOT (*Prenanthes alata*)　Lower leaves triangular-shaped and toothed, on long (12-24 inches) leafy stems. Flowers white, in raceme-like arrangement. Upper leaves lance-shaped. West. Wash.; moist, shady woods, along streamsides, etc. Mid summer to autumn.

SKELETON-WEED (*Lygodesmia juncea*)　Basal leaves in rosette; upper leaves small. Flowering heads pink, rarely white, on long nearly leafless branches. East. Wash.; open, sandy places, often in desert or semi-desert areas. Summer. (Color Plate 64)

APARGIDIUM (*Apargidium boreale*)　Flowering heads yellow, on leafless, long, unbranched stems. West. Wash.; sphagnum bogs, wet mountain meadows, and other moist places. Summer.

AMERICAN SAUSSUREA (*Saussurea americana*)　Erect leafy stems (12-48 inches) topped with dense clusters of small, violet to purple flower heads. Leaves sharply-toothed. Ray flowers absent. East. and West. Wash.; moist places, such as meadows and wet-rocky slopes fed by snowbanks in the upper montane and subalpine country of the mountains. Mid to late summer. (Color Plate 54)

GREAT-FLOWERED BLANKET-FLOWER (*Gaillardia aristata*)　Heads solitary on long stems. Disk flowers purplish; rays yellow, often purple at base. East. (mostly) and West. Wash.; dry prairies and meadows in lowlands and foothills. Late spring to early autumn. (Color Plate 54)

SINGLE-FLOWERED FALSE SUNFLOWER (*Helianthella uniflora*)　Plants low, stems 1-3 feet tall, and growing in clusters. Leaves and stems rough or harsh. Flowers yellow. East. Wash.; grassy slopes and yellow pine woods. Late spring and summer (Color Plate 54; Fig. 65)

COMMON WOOLLY SUNFLOWER (*Eriophyllum lanatum*)　Size variable, though usually 8-24 inches tall. Leaves pinnately divided and deeply lobed. Flowers yellow. East. and West. Wash.; dry, open habitats in lowlands and foothills as well as subalpine meadows. Late spring and summer. (Color Plate 55; Fig. 66)

DWARF HULSEA (*Hulsea nana*)　Leaves basal, white woolly, and deeply toothed or lobed. Large, yellow flower heads singly located at tips of stems which are 4-12 inches long. Mount Rainier and southward in the Cascades; high, barren gravel, cinder, or pumice areas; mostly in subalpine and alpine zones. Mid to late summer. (Color Plate 55)

WESTERN TANSY (*Tanacetum douglasii*) Aromatic plants with leaves twice (and finely) divided; more or less fleshy. Flowering heads yellow and button-like with ray flowers 1/8 inch or less long. West. Wash.; coastal sand dunes. Summer and early autumn. (Color Plate 55)

FLESHY JAUMEA (*Jaumea carnosa*) Leaves narrow, in pairs, and fleshy. Heads yellow with 6-10 irregularly-spaced, 3-toothed rays. West. Wash.; tidal marshes and flats along salt water. Mid summer to early autumn.

BRISTLE-HEAD (*Rigiopappus leptocladus*) Slim, wiry plant with short, narrow leaves. Flower heads yellowish or reddish and borne singly at ends of branches. Rays 5-15. East. Wash.; sagebrush and grasslands in lowlands. Spring and early summer.

SLENDER RABBIT-LEAVES (*Lagophylla ramosissima*) Plants white-downy. Lower leaves shedding before blooming. Rays short (1/4 inch or less) and turning reddish on underside with age. Leaves narrow, hairy, and borne in pairs. East. Wash.; open, arid places in lowlands and foothills. Late spring and early summer.

GOLD-STAR (*Crocidium multicaule*) Small plants (to 6-8 inches) with fleshy leaves. Heads yellow and single at the tips of leafless branches. Rays 8-13 and less than 1/2 inch long. East. and West. Wash.; sandy areas, as well as rocky cliffs, in open places; often common in East. Wash. Spring. (Color Plate 55)

BLEPHARIPAPPUS (*Blepharipappus scaber*) Stems upright (4-12 inches) with numerous grassblade-like leaves. Flowers white, with 2-7 broad, 3-lobed rays, which have purple veins on underside. East. Wash.; grassy habitats in low-lands and foothills. Spring and early summer. (Color Plate 56)

YARROW (*Achillea millefolium*) Leaves aromatic and very finely divided. Flowering heads white; flowers small, and in flat-topped clusters. East. and West. Wash.; common in open habitats, especially waste areas, in lowlands and foothills. Spring, summer, and fall. A familiar, strongly aromatic, and abundant species (though apparently a complex of several taxa). Occasionally to 10,000 feet in mountains. (Color Plate 56)

SHOWY TOWNSENDIA (*Townsendia florifer*) Low, branching plant with hoary, spatulate leaves. Flowering heads numerous and pale blue or purplish; rela-tively large and showy. East. Wash.; arid, open habitats in lowlands and foot-hills. Late spring to mid summer. (Color Plate 56; Fig. 67)

WHITE LAYIA (*Layia glandulosa*) Basal leaves lobed or toothed and bristly. Flowering heads with yellow disks and numerous white rays. Plants low, 4-12 inches tall. East. Wash.; open, sandy habitats in lowlands and foothills. Spring and early summer.

PEARLY EVERLASTING (*Anaphalis margaritacea*) Plants erect and tall (to 36 inches) with very narrow, long leaves and numerous small, button-like flower heads borne at tips of stems. Foliage white woolly. East. and West. Wash.; open places, such as roadsides, meadows, and pastures, from lowlands up into the mountains; abundant and widespread. The white flowers dry with little change and remain on the stalks well into the fall. Mid summer to fall. (Color Plate 56)

TRAIL PLANT (*Adenocaulon bicolor*) Large triangular leaves that are green above and grayish white below. Flower heads white, small, and at tips of branches. Large bicolored leaves distinctive. East. and West. Wash.; deep, moist woods in lowlands and up to intermediate elevations in the mountains. A characteristic plant of the rain forest. Summer. (Fig. 68)

LOW-TUFTED HYMENOPAPPUS (*Hymenopappus filifolius*) Stems erect from woody base and bearing a few woolly, pinnately cleft leaves. Flowering heads pale yellow to pink, few in number, and scattered. East. Wash.; dry, sandy or gravelly places in lowlands and foothills. Late spring to mid summer. (Color Plate 57)

SILVER-LEAF (*Chaenactis douglasii*) Plants low (to 12 inches tall) with one to several red stems. Leaves mostly basal and pinnately and finely cleft. Flowering heads with pinkish or creamy white flowers, often with red tips. Bracts long, to 1/2 inch. East. Wash.; dry, sandy or gravelly areas in lowlands and foothills. Late spring and summer. (Color Plate 57)

LETTUCE (*Lactuca*) (Color Plate 63)

1. Flowering heads large and showy; plants usually less than 36 inches tall; lower leaves not deeply cleft; upper leaves often entire. . . . BLUE LETTUCE
1. Flowering heads small and not so showy; plants usually more than 36 inches tall; lower leaves deeply cleft; upper leaves less deeply cleft.

*   *   *   TALL BLUE LETTUCE

BLUE LETTUCE (*Lactuca pulchella*) Flowers blue. East. and West. Wash.; moist, open places such as meadows and pastures. Summer and early autumn.

TALL BLUE LETTUCE (*Lactuca biennis*) Flowers blue, white, or yellow. East. and West. Wash.; moist meadows, fields, and pastures. Mid to late summer.

DANDELIONS (*Taraxacum*) (Color Plate 57)

Biennial or perennial herbs with milky juice and strongly toothed to pinnatifid, basal leaves. Heads solitary and terminal on hollow stems. Flowers yellow.

1. Leaves deeply cleft; primarily a plant of the lowlands, especially in waste places, lawns, etc.; weedy. . . . . COMMON DANDELION
1. Leaves not deeply cleft; primarily plants of the mountainous regions; not weedy. 2
2. Achenes brownish; leaves with large, sharp-pointed, often backward-directed teeth . . . . BROWN-SEEDED DANDELION
2. Achenes reddish; leaves with blunt teeth, not so backward-directed.

*   *   *   RED-SEEDED DANDELION

COMMON DANDELION (*Taraxacum officinale*) Flowers yellow. East. and West. Wash.; widespread and common in lowland waste places, lawns, and pastures. Early spring to fall. A very common weed.

BROWN-SEEDED DANDELION (*Taraxacum ceratophorum*) Flowers yellow. East. and West. Wash.; moist meadows and flats in the mountains. Mid to late summer.

Figure 67.
Townsendias, often a bright patch on a hot-dry hillside in Eastern Washington. (Yaich)

RED-SEEDED DANDELION (*Taraxacum eriophorum*) Flowers yellow. East. and West. Wash.; moist meadows and flats in the mountains. Summer.

HAWKWEEDS (*Hieracium*) (Color Plate 57)

Biennial plants with milky juice and alternate and basal leaves which may be entire or toothed. Flower heads small and in panicles or cymes. Flowers all ligulate (strap-shaped). Leaves and stems often densely hairy.

1. Basal leaves smaller than those of middle portion of stem.
CANADA HAWKWEED
1. Basal leaves larger than those higher on stem........................2
2. Flowers white.......................WHITE-FLOWERED HAWKWEED
2. Flowers yellow...3
3. Leaves more or less smooth, without long hairs..LOW ALPINE HAWKWEED
3. Leaves not smooth, but hairy.......................................4
4. Leaves sparsely hairy and grayish above; occurring mainly in Cascade Mountains.................................SCOULER'S HAWKWEED
4. Leaves strongly hairy and not grayish above; occurring mainly east of the Cascades...5
5. Most leaves very slender for basal 1/3 of their length, often tapering abruptly from widest point of their length; involucre strongly glandular.
HOUND'S-TONGUE HAWKWEED
5. Most leaves not so slender for lower 1/3 of their length, but tapering gradually from widest point to base; involucre not strongly glandular.
WESTERN HAWKWEED

*   *   *

CANADA HAWKWEED (*Hieracium canadense*) Plants to 40 inches. Leaves numerous, lanceolate, and mostly smooth. Flat-topped clusters and yellow flowers. East. Wash.; moist woods and meadows. Mid summer to early fall.

WHITE-FLOWERED HAWKWEED (*Hieracium albiflorum*) Plants 12-30 inches tall. Only species of hawkweed in our area with white flowers. Cascades and West. Wash.; woods, meadows, and slopes in lowlands up to intermediate elevations in the mountains. Summer.

LOW ALPINE HAWKWEED (*Hieracium gracile*) Leaves basal, oblong, entire, and with broad petioles. Stems slender with few to no leaves. Yellow heads borne singly at stem tips or in raceme-like clusters. East. and West. Wash.; dry, subalpine and alpine meadows. Mid to late summer.

SCOULER'S HAWKWEED (*Hieracium scouleri*) Medium-sized plant (12-30 inches tall). Basal leaves long (to 10 inches) and mostly entire, though bristly. Flowers yellow. Cascades and West. Wash.; dry places in open woods, as well as slopes and meadows from lowlands well up into the mountains. Summer.

HOUND'S-TONGUE HAWKWEED (*Hieracium cynoglossoides*) Leaves lanceolate, sharp-pointed, entire or with low teeth, and usually densely hairy. Flower cluster elongated and of yellow flowers. Cascades and East. Wash.; open, arid habitats in foothills and lower mountainous areas. Summer.

WESTERN HAWKWEED (*Hieracium albertinum*) Stems solitary. Lower and basal leaves strongly hairy. Petioles often winged. Flowers yellow. East. Wash.; open, arid prairies in lowlands and foothills. Mid to late summer.

HAWKSBEARDS (*Crepis*) (Color Plate 58)

Note: Extensive hybridization and other genetic irregularities commonly occur in this genus. The species included here represent recognizable high points in the group, but some specimens of *Crepis* may be found that cannot be satisfactorily keyed. The Intermediate Hawksbeard (*"Crepis intermedia"*) has occasionally been used to include some of these anomalies. In general, these are annual or biennial plants with milky juice, alternate and basal toothed or pinnatifid leaves. Flower heads in branching inflorescences. Leaves often dandelion-like. Flowers yellow or orange.

1. Leaves and stems smooth (not so hairy, but may contain bristles) 2
1. Leaves and stems covered with soft hairs 3

2. Flowers numerous, 20-50 in a head . . . . MEADOW HAWKSBEARD
2. Flowers not so numerous, usually numbering less than 15 in a head.
DWARF HAWKSBEARD

3. Involucres and/or lower stems hairy 4
3. Involucres and lower stems more or less not hairy 5

4. Plants large, mostly more than 12 inches tall and with more than 10 flowering heads . . . . BEARDED HAWKSBEARD
4. Plants smaller, mostly less than 12 inches tall and with less than 10 flowering heads . . . . LOW HAWKSBEARD

5. Heads with less than 10 flowers and the flowers with less than 8 inner involucral bracts . . . . LONG-LEAVED HAWKSBEARD
5. Heads with more than 10 flowers and the flowers with more than 8 inner involucral bracts 6

6. Lobes of leaves long and very narrow and not toothed.
SLENDER HAWKSBEARD
6. Lobes of leaves not long and very narrow and occasionally toothed 7

7. Leaves grayish . . . . WESTERN HAWKSBEARD
7. Leaves not grayish, but green . . . . BAKER'S HAWKSBEARD

*　　*　　*

MEADOW HAWKSBEARD (*Crepis runcinata*) Leaves mostly basal, green, and oblanceolate. Stem leaves reduced. Flower yellow. East. Wash.; moist meadows and flats in lowlands, foothills, and mountains. Late spring to mid summer.

DWARF HAWKSBEARD (*Crepis nana*) Small, tufted plants less than 3 inches high. Leaves numerous and roundish. Flowering heads yellow and borne on short stalks among the leaves. East. and West. Wash.; rock slides, outcroppings, and gravelly habitats, mostly in the high mountains. Mid to late summer.

BEARDED HAWKSBEARD (*Crepis barbigera*) Inflorescence strongly hairy. Flowers yellow. East. and West. Wash.; open, arid habitats in lowlands and foothills. Late spring and summer.

298

LOW HAWKSBEARD (*Crepis modocensis*)   Stems slender and branching. Basal leaves bipinnately cleft. Flowers yellow. East. Wash.; open, arid habitats in lowlands and foothills. Late spring and summer.

LONG-LEAVED HAWKSBEARD (*Crepis acuminata*)   Leaves long (6-20 inches), more or less lanceolate, and strongly pinnatifid. Inflorescence large and diffuse. Flowers yellow. East. Wash.; open, arid habitats in foothills and lower montane areas. Late spring and early summer.

SLENDER HAWKSBEARD (*Crepis atrabarba*)   Stems one to several and slender. Basal leaves broadly lanceolate, with few lobes—the distal 1/3 of the leaf entire and very narrow. Flower heads yellow and in open cyme. East. Wash.; open, arid habitats in lowlands and mountains. Late spring and early summer.

WESTERN HAWKSBEARD (*Crepis occidentalis*)   Basal leaves long (to 12 inches) and irregularly lobed or toothed. Flower heads yellow and often numerous on a stem. East. Wash.; arid, open habitats in lowlands and foothills. Late spring and early summer.

BAKER'S HAWKSBEARD (*Crepis bakeri*)   Low plants (4-12 inches tall) with reddish stems and hairy, lobed (with teeth) leaves. Usually not more than 12 flowering heads (yellow) on a stem. East. Wash.; open, arid habitats. Spring.

AGOSERISES (*Agoseris*) (Color Plate 58)

Mostly perennial plants with milky juice and sessile, basal leaves. Flowering heads single on leafless, hollow stems. Leaves entire to pinnately lobed or divided. Taproot long and blackish.

1. Flowers orange in color, turning purple when dry . . . . . . ALPINE AGOSERIS
1. Flowers yellow, turning pink when dry 2

2. Plants annual, with weak taproot . . . . ANNUAL AGOSERIS
2. Plants perennial, with stout taproots 3

3. Beak of the achene about half as long as the seed . . . . PALE AGOSERIS
3. Beak of the achene longer than the seed 4

4. Beak less than twice as long as seed 5
4. Beak more than twice as long as seed 6

5. Plants occurring along salt water; leaves short, mostly less than 4 inches long . . . . SEASIDE AGOSERIS
5. Plants not occurring along salt water; leaves long, mostly more than 4 inches long . . . . TALL AGOSERIS

6. Lobes on leaves pointing strongly backward . . . SPEAR-LEAVED AGOSERIS
6. Lobes on leaves not pointing strongly backward.
                                          LARGE-FLOWERED AGOSERIS

*   *   *

ALPINE AGOSERIS (*Agoseris aurantiaca*)   Leaves 4-14 inches long, entire, and widest above the middle. Flowers orange, turning purple on drying. East. and West. Wash.; meadows and open, subalpine woods in the upper parts of the mountains. Summer.

ANNUAL AGOSERIS (*Agoseris heterophylla*)   Plants small (to 15 inches). Leaves to 6 inches and toothed or lobed. Flowers yellow, turning pink. East.

Figure 68.
Trailplant, *Adenocaulon;* a common species of the rainforest. (Larrison)

Wash.; open, arid habitats in lowlands and foothills. Late spring and early summer.

PALE AGOSERIS (*Agoseris glauca*) Plants small to medium (4-30 inches). Leaves varying in length from 2-14 inches, narrowly lanceolate, sparsely toothed or entire, and grayish. Flowers yellow, drying to pink. East. and West. Wash.; open places, such as meadowlands, from lowlands to alpine areas. Late spring and summer.

SEASIDE AGOSERIS (*Agoseris apargioides*) Plants small, to 8-10 inches. Foliage smooth to densely hairy. Leaves small (to 4 inches), entire or lobed. Flowers yellow. West. Wash.; sandy beaches, dunes, and bluffs along the ocean coast. Summer.

TALL AGOSERIS (*Agoseris elata*) Tall plants (to 24 inches). Foliage somewhat grayish. Flowers yellow, drying to pink. West. Wash.; meadows and clearings in forests, from lowlands up into the mountains. Early summer.

SPEAR-LEAVED AGOSERIS (*Agoseris retrorsa*) Leaves 4-8 inches long; lanceolate, sharp-pointed, and deeply lobed. Upper lobes on leaf turned backwards. Flowers yellow, drying to pink. East. Wash.; yellow pine woods, mostly in foothills. Late spring and early summer.

LARGE-FLOWERED AGOSERIS (*Agoseris grandiflora*) Plants hairy when young, becoming less so in age. Leaves (4-10 inches) elliptical, broadest near tip. Flower head large, yellow in color, but drying to pink. East. and West. Wash.; meadows and prairies in lowlands and foothills. Early and mid summer.

MICROSERISES (*Microseris*)

Perennial plants with pale, fleshy roots. Some species are fibrous-rooted annuals. Leaves mostly basal, entire to pinnatifid. Heads nodding as buds, borne singly on leafless stems. Flowers yellow and all strap-shaped.

1. Plants annual, with weak taproots. 2
1. Plants perennial, with stout taproots. 3

2. Pappus scales notched at tip with awn arising in the notch; seeds black.
LINEAR-LEAVED MICROSERIS
2. Pappus scales on achenes not notched but tapering gradually to the awn;
   seeds brown . . . . COAST MICROSERIS

3. Leaves present on flowering stems. 4
3. Leaves usually not present on flowering stems. 5

4. Awns of pappus feather-like. . . . . NODDING MICROSERIS
4. Awns of pappus not feather-like, but filamentous. . . CUTLEAF MICROSERIS

5. Margins of leaves crenate. . . . . SUKSDORF'S MICROSERIS
5. Margins of leaves not crenate, but with a few conspicuous, pointed lobes.
ALPINE MICROSERIS

*   *   *

LINEAR-LEAVED MICROSERIS (*Microseris lindleyi*) Leaves linear, entire or with a few lobes. Flower yellow. East. Wash.; open, arid places in the lowlands and foothills. Spring and early summer.

COAST MICROSERIS (*Microseris bigelovii*) Plants with tufted leaves which may be entire, or toothed or lobed. Flowers yellow or orange, borne in heads on leaflets, fleshy stems. Pappus silvery. West. Wash.; open, wet places along the ocean coast. Late spring and early summer.

NODDING MICROSERIS (*Microseris nutans*) Leaves large (to 12 inches) and various, cleft or entire. Buds strongly nodding. East. Wash.; open, moist habitats in lowlands and mountains. Spring and early summer. Flowers yellow.

CUTLEAF MICROSERIS (*Microseris laciniata*) Plants often large (to 48 inches). Leaves large (10-20 inches long), usually basal, and narrow. May be entire or pinnately cleft. Heads large with sometimes 200-250 flowers, which are yellow. Cascades and West. Wash.; open habitats in lowlands and foothills. Late spring and early summer.

SUKSDORF'S MICROSERIS (*Microseris troximoides*) Leaves 4-8 inches long, margins entire or slightly scalloped. Heads with 20-30 flowers, yellow, and the pappus scales without awns. East. Wash.; open, arid habitats in lowlands and foothills. Spring and early summer.

ALPINE MICROSERIS (*Microseris alpestris*) Small plants (to 8-10 inches). Leaves basal, widest beyond the middle, and toothed or lobed in basal half. Flowering heads yellow and borne on leafless stalks. Cascades; open habitats, particularly meadows and grassy slopes in subalpine and alpine areas. Summer.

RUSH PINKS (*Stephanomeria*)

1. Plants annual with weak taproots; pappus brownish.
                                          STIFF-BRANCHED RUSH PINK
1. Plants perennial, arising from stout, creeping roots; pappus white.
                                          WHITE-PLUMED RUSH PINK

*   *   *

STIFF-BRANCHED RUSH PINK (*Stephanomeria paniculata*) Flowers pink. East. Wash.; open, arid habitats in lowlands and foothills. Mid summer to early autumn.

WHITE-PLUMED RUSH PINK (*Stephanomeria tenuifolia*) Stems slender, smooth, and clustered; occasionally prostrate on ground. Leaves thread-like. Heads small, with only a few pink flowers at tips of branches that arise from a zig-zag stem. East. Wash.; dry, rocky places in lowlands and foothills. Summer.

THISTLES (*Cirsium*) (Color Plate 58)

Mostly perennial plants with alternate, prickly leaves. Flowering heads large and containing all tubular flowers. Foliage "thistle-like."

1. Bracts of the involucre with a conspicuous, thickened, sticky ridge near the tip. 2
1. Bracts of the involucre without a conspicuous, thickened, sticky ridge near the tip. 3
2. Flowers white to creamy white. .PALOUSE THISTLE
2. Flowers purple to pink. . . . . .WAVY-LEAVED THISTLE
3. Bracts of involucre broad at base (tapering abruptly to tip) with little or no hairs on margin. . . . . .DWARF THISTLE
3. Bracts of involucre narrow at base, tapering gradually to tip and usually hairy on the margins. 4

302

4. Flowers usually creamy white........................WEAK THISTLE
4. Flowers usually purple...5
5. Style shorter than corolla, or barely extending beyond it...INDIAN THISTLE
5. Style extending conspicuously beyond the corolla.......:EDIBLE THISTLE

*   *   *

PALOUSE THISTLE (*Cirsium brevifolium*) Leaves green, smooth above, and pinnatifid. Flowers white to creamy or yellowish white. East. Wash.; open, grassy areas, pastures, and roadsides. Summer and fall.

WAVY-LEAVED THISTLE (*Cirsium undulatum*) Leaves white-hairy above with undulating margins and weak spines. Flowers pinkish purple. East. Wash.; dry, open places. Summer and early autumn.

DWARF THISTLE (*Cirsium scariosum*) Plants small, stems to 12 inches. Leaves deeply pinnatifid and with weak spines. Flowers white, pink, or purple. East. Wash.; moist meadows, mostly in foothills and mountains. Summer.

WEAK THISTLE (*Cirsium remotifolium*) Stems cobwebby-hairy but leaves more or less smooth, narrow, and toothed or pinnately cleft. Heads creamy white and single to few at ends of leafless branches. Cascades and West. Wash.; moist, open and partly-wooded areas in the lowlands and lower valleys. Summer and early autumn.

INDIAN THISTLE (*Cirsium brevistylum*) Leaves crisply hairy on upper surface and woolly on undersurface; toothed or lobed. Flowering heads (purplish red) often buried in leaves. Cascades and West. Wash.; moist meadows and slopes in lowlands and lower montane areas. Summer.

EDIBLE THISTLE (*Cirsium edule*) Stems stout and often to 6-7 feet tall. Heads pinkish purple and single or in tight clusters at tips of stems. Cascades and West. Wash.; moist meadows and open woods in lowlands and mountains. Mid summer to early autumn.

BEGGAR-TICKS (*Bidens*)

Annual or perennial plants with opposite, toothed or lobed leaves and large, yellow, many-flowered heads. Species usually growing on moist ground or in water.

1. Leaves simple; flowers nodding..............NODDING BEGGAR-TICK
1. Leaves compound; flowers not nodding...........................2
2. Flowers orange ....STICKTIGHT
2. Flowers pale yellow.......................WESTERN BEGGAR-TICK

*   *   *

NODDING BEGGAR-TICK (*Bidens cernua*) Leaves toothed or entire. Flowering heads pale yellow and turning downward at tips of stems or even drooping. East. and West. Wash.; moist habitats in lowlands, especially river bottoms. Mid summer to early autumn.

STICKTIGHT (*Bidens frondosa*) Flowering heads orange, without rays, and the small disks (1/2 inch or less) conspicuously surrounded by leafy bracts.

303

Figure 69
Balsamroot, *Balsamorhiza;* an abundant spring flower on
Eastern Washington slopes. (Yaich)

Leaves opposite, 3-5 lobed. Plants to 28 inches and many-branched. East. and West. Wash.; open, often wet, waste areas in lowlands. Summer and fall.

WESTERN BEGGAR-TICK (*Bidens vulgata*) Flowering heads yellow to pale yellow with numerous bracts. East. and West. Wash.; open, mostly moist, places in lowlands. Mid summer to early fall.

BALSAMROOTS (*Balsamorhiza*) (Color Plate 59; Fig. 69)

Large, perennial plants with large, mostly basal leaves. One to several large flower heads on a long stem. Stem leaves small, almost bract-like. Heads with both ray and disk flowers. Sunflower-like.

1. Leaves broad, entire (though may be slightly crenulate), and not lobed or sharply toothed 2
1. Leaves cleft into leaflets or lobes, or sharply toothed 4
2. Plants densely covered with soft hairs; leaves silvery.
ARROW-LEAVED BALSAMROOT
2. Plants not densely—but sparsely—covered with soft hairs; leaves green. .3
3. Rays falling shortly after appearing; occurs west of Cascades.
NORTHWEST BALSAMROOT
3. Rays remaining on heads on drying; occurs east of Cascades.
CAREY'S BALSAMROOT
4. Leaves and stems covered with long, soft, silk hairs.
WOOLLY BALSAMROOT
4. Leaves and stems sometimes hairy, but not covered with long, soft, silky hairs 5
5. All leaves strongly cleft into pinnate series of lobes.
HOOKER'S BALSAMROOT
5. All leaves not cleft into lobes, some merely sharply toothed.
SERRATED BALSAMROOT

*   *   *

ARROW-LEAVED BALSAMROOT (*Balsamorhiza sagittata*) Basal leaves arrowhead-shaped and up to 12 inches in length; entire and silvery-velvety on underside. Heads single at tips of mostly leafless stems. Flowers yellow. East. and West. Wash.; open habitats and hill slopes in lowlands and foothills; often common east of Cascades where commonly called the "wild sunflower." Mid spring to mid summer.

NORTHWEST BALSAMROOT (*Balsamorhiza deltoidea*) Basal leaves triangular to oval in shape with long petioles. Heads single or few per plant. Flowers yellow. West. Wash.; open habitats in lowlands. Spring and early summer.

CAREY'S BALSAMROOT (*Balsamorhiza careyana*) Basal leaves heart-shaped to hastate; greenish. Heads 1 to a few; yellow. East. Wash.; dry, open habitats in lowlands, as well as foothills and mountains. Early spring to mid summer.

WOOLLY BALSAMROOT (*Balsamorhiza incana*) Foliage covered with white woolly hairs. Flowers yellow. East. Wash.; moist, as well as dry, open habitats in foothills and lower montane areas. Late spring to mid summer.

HOOKER'S BALSAMROOT (*Balsamorhiza hookeri*) Basal leaves pinnately divided, smooth, and up to 20 inches long. The yellow flowering heads are borne singly. East. wash.; dry, rocky areas in desert lowlands and foothills. Spring and early summer.

SERRATED BALSAMROOT (*Balsamorhiza serrata*) Leaves ovate-lanceolate and sharply toothed. Flowers yellow. East. Wash.; dry, rocky, exposed places in desert country. Spring and early summer.

WYETHIAS (*Wyethia*) (Color Plate 58)

1. Leaves smooth, without hairs.........................MULE'S EARS
1. Leaves hairy..........................NARROW-LEAVED WYETHIA

*   *   *

MULE'S EARS (*Wyethia amplexicaulis*) Flowers yellow. East. Wash.; dry, open meadows and slopes in foothills and lower montane areas. Late spring and early summer.

NARROW-LEAVED WYETHIA (*Wyethia angustifolia*) Flowers yellow. Southern Wash.; mostly in Columbia Gorge; moist meadows and open slopes in foothills and lower mountains. Late spring and early summer.

RUDBECKIAS (*Rudbeckia*) (Color Plate 59)

1. Disk long and finger-like (2 inches long or more when mature), without spreading rays..............................WESTERN RUDBECKIA
1. Disk not long and finger-like (but button-like), and with spreading rays.
BLACK-EYED SUSAN

*   *   *

WESTERN RUDBECKIA (*Rudbeckia occidentalis*) East. and West. Wash.; moist habitats, such as streambanks and wet slopes, sometimes wooded; often in mountains. Disk black or dark brown. Summer.

BLACK-EYED SUSAN (*Rudbeckia hirta*) East and West. Wash.; open meadows in lowlands and foothills. Flowers with yellow rays. Mid summer to early autumn.

SUNFLOWERS (*Helianthus*) (Color Plate 59)

1. Plants annual with weak taproot; leaves broad, some almost as wide as long; bracts of involucre very broad.................COMMON SUNFLOWER
1. Plants perennial with stout taproot; leaves narrow, at least several times longer than wide; bracts of involucre very narrow..CUSICK'S SUNFLOWER

*   *   *

COMMON SUNFLOWER (*Helianthus annuus*) Flowers yellow. East. and West. Wash.; open, waste or disturbed places in lowlands and foothills. Summer and early autumn.

CUSICK'S SUNFLOWER (*Helianthus cusickii*) East. Wash.; dry, open places in lowlands and foothills. Spring and summer. As in all the sunflowers, with the exception of a few reddish species not in our area, the blooms are the familiar yellow.

306

GUM PLANTS (*Grindelia*) (Color Plate 59)

Perennial plants with basal leaves and single, yellow heads at tips of branches in corymbose cymes. Heads typically gummy or sticky. Both ray and disk flowers usually present in head.

1. Flowering head consisting of disk only; no rays present.
                                                COLUMBIA GUM PLANT
1. Flowering head consisting of both disk and rays......................2
2. Tips of involucral bracts not curled backward; leaves usually hairy.
                                                BROAD-LEAVED GUM PLANT
2. Tips of involucral bracts curled backward; leaves smooth, not hairy......3
3. Rays numerous, usually more than 25 in number...........RESIN-WEED
3. Rays few, usually less than 25 in number. SMALL-FLOWERED GUM PLANT

*   *   *

COLUMBIA GUM PLANT (*Grindelia columbiana*) Leaves short, usually less than 4 inches and entire. Flower heads 1/2 inch wide, without rays, yellow, and strongly resinous. East. Wash. and Columbia Gorge; gravelly or sandy habitats, particularly along streams and rivers. Summer.

BROAD-LEAVED GUM PLANT (*Grindelia integrifolia*) Plants moderately large (6-30 inches tall), hairy, with basal leaves large (to 16 inches) and widest between middle and tip. Flowers heads flat, yellow, and moderately sticky. West. Wash.; lowlands of the Puget Sound region and in salt marshes and on rocky areas along the ocean coast. Summer.

RESIN-WEED (*Grindelia squarrosa*) Stem branched and smooth. Leaves oval to oblong, dark bluish green. Heads numerous and yellow. East. Wash.; dry, open habitats, particularly along roadsides. Mid summer to early autumn.

SMALL-FLOWERED GUM PLANT (*Grindelia nana*) Stems branched. Lower leaves to 6 inches and toothed or entire. Heads large and yellow. East. Wash.; open places, such as rocky flats, streamsides, grasslands, and sandy banks in the lowlands. Summer and fall.

LASTHENIAS (*Lasthenia*)

Annual or perennial plants with opposite leaves and terminal heads containing both ray and disk flowers. Leaves may be thin and linear or dark green and fleshy.

1. Leaves entire, not toothed near tip; involucre fused to form a lobed cup concealing the rays...........................SMOOTH LASTHENIA
1. Leaves not entire, but toothed near the tip; involucre not fused—the rays conspicuously showing ....GOLD-FIELDS

*   *   *

SMOOTH LASTHENIA (*Lasthenia glaberrima*) Flowers yellow. West. Wash.; wet, often muddy, places. Early to mid summer.

GOLD-FIELDS (*Lasthenia minor*) Flowers yellow. West. Wash.; low ground near salt water. Mid summer to early autumn.

TAR-WEEDS (*Madia*) (Color Plate 60)

Annual or perennial flowers with mostly alternate, sticky, glandular leaves and strongly-scented heads containing both ray and disk flowers. Conspicuous circle of bracts between the ray and disk flowers.

1. Flowering heads small; involucre less than 3/16 inch high; rays tiny.....2
1. Flowering heads larger; involucre more than 3/16 inch high; rays conspicuous 3

2. Leaves mostly opposite...........................LEAST TAR-WEED
2. Leaves mostly alternate..........................LITTLE TAR-WEED

3. Disk flowers fertile (with pistil and stamens)........................4
3. Disk flowers sterile, lacking pistils and stamens......................5

4. Flowering heads long and narrow................STINKING TAR-WEED
4. Flowering heads more or less roundish..........MOUNTAIN TAR-WEED

5. Disk flowers with circle of chaff (the pappus) at base of corolla.
WOODLAND TAR-WEED
5. Disk flowers without circle of chaff (pappus) at base of corolla..........6

6. Rays more than 3/8 inch long; not lemon-smelling....SHOWY TAR-WEED
6. Rays less than 3/8 inch long; strong lemon odor......LEMON TAR-WEED

*   *   *

LEAST TAR-WEED (*Madia minima*) Plants small (to 6 inches) and bushy. Foliage with numerous stalked glands. Heads yellow, borne singly or in tight clusters. East. (mostly) and West. Wash.; grasslands or yellow pine woodlands. Late spring to mid summer.

LITTLE TAR-WEED (*Madia exigua*) Plants medium (to 12 inches). Leaves narrow, with stalked glands. Heads yellow, tightly clustered, and borne on thread-like stalks. East. and West. Wash.; dry, open habitats in lowlands and lower montane areas. Late spring to mid summer.

STINKING TAR-WEED (*Madia glomerata*) Plants taller (to 30 inches). Stems very hairy with yellowish, stalked glands. Rays few or none and very small. Flowers yellow. East. and West. Wash.; roadsides and other dry, open habitats in lowlands and foothills. Mid summer to early autumn.

MOUNTAIN TAR-WEED (*Madia gracilis*) Plants taller (to 40 inches). Foliage roughly hairy. Involucre crowded with glandular hairs. Flowers yellow. East. and West. Wash.; roadsides and other open places in lowlands and foothills. Summer.

WOODLAND TAR-WEED (*Madia madioides*) Plants medium (to 24 inches). Leaves lanceolate, narrow, and often toothed. Heads yellow, few in number, and borne in raceme-like groups. West. Wash.; open, sunlit woods. Early to mid summer.

SHOWY TAR-WEED (*Madia elegans*) Plants taller (to 48 inches). Leaves narrowly lanceolate. Flowering heads in branched inflorescence and yellow; rays often with reddish base forming circle of red around yellow eye. West. Wash.; roadsides and other dry, open waste habitats. Mid summer to early autumn.

LEMON TAR-WEED (*Madia citriodora*) Plants with blackish, stalked glands. Tips of stamens black. Flowers yellow with prominent lemon odor. East. Wash.; open slopes of foothills, especially in Blue Mountains. Late spring and early summer.

GOLDENWEEDS (*Haplopappus*) (Color Plate 60)

Herbs with alternate leaves and many-flowered, single, or clustered heads containing both ray and disk flowers, although the rays sometimes absent. Pappus bristly, hair-like, and reddish or brownish.

Note: Only the non-shrubby species, i.e., the truly herbaceous wildflowers, of the genus are described. A difficult group to identify.

1. Rays absent . . . . LARGE-FLOWERED GOLDENWEED
1. Rays present 2
2. Plants forming dense mats; flowering stems usually with only 1 head per stem 3
2. Plants not forming dense mats; flowering stems with 1 or more heads per stem 5
3. Stems leafy, the leaves almost as large as the basal ones.
LYALL'S GOLDENWEED
3. Stems with few or no leaves, and those leaves present are small and bract-like 4
4. Leaves stiff, not woolly . . . . NARROW-LEAVED GOLDENWEED
4. Leaves soft and woolly . . . . WOOLLY GOLDENWEED
5. Flowering heads small, usually less than 5/8 inch high; rays large and prominent . . . . PALOUSE GOLDENWEED
5. Flowering heads large, usually more than 5/8 inch high; rays small and not prominent . . . . LARGE-FLOWERED GOLDENWEED

* * *

LARGE-FLOWERED GOLDENWEED (*Haplopappus carthamoides*) Basal leaves broad; upper leaves smaller and without petioles; all leaves entire. Flower heads yellow, without rays, and large. East. Wash.; open meadows and slopes in lowlands and foothills. Summer.

LYALL'S GOLDENWEED (*Haplopappus lyallii*) Plants small (4-8 inches tall) and leafy. Leaves small (1-2 inches), alternate, and oblong. Flowers yellow, borne singly at tips of stems. East. and West. Wash.; rock slides and outcroppings in alpine areas of the high mountains. Mid summer to early fall.

NARROW-LEAVED GOLDENWEED (*Haplopappus stenophyllus*) Leaves numerous, narrowly oblanceolate, without petioles, and often lasting for several years. Heads broad, yellow and solitary. East. Wash.; dry, rocky places in sagebrush areas in lowlands and foothills. Late spring to mid summer.

WOOLLY GOLDENWEED (*Haplopappus lanuginosus*) Plants densely grayish hairy. Leaves numerous, borne on short, basal stalks. Heads broad, yellow, and solitary. East. Wash.; open, arid, rocky habitats in lowlands and foothills. Late spring and summer.

PALOUSE GOLDENWEED (*Haplopappus liatriformis*) Plants softly hairy. Leaves oblanceolate with petioles. Flowers yellow. Palouse region of East. Wash.; grassy habitats. Mid to late summer.

Figure 70.
Arnica, common flower of the forest edge. (Larrison)

310

ARNICAS (*Arnica*) (Color Plate 60; Fig. 70)

Perennial plants with mostly opposite, entire or toothed leaves and large, yellow flowers borne singly or in small groups. Heads often fragrant, containing both ray and disk flowers and borne on peduncles often slightly nodding.

1. Stems with usually more than 4 pairs of leaves.........................2
1. Stems with usually 4 pairs of leaves or less...........................4

2. Involucral bracts with tuft of long hairs at tip...........MEADOW ARNICA
2. Involucral bracts without tufts of hairs at tip.........................3

3. Leaves toothed..................................CLASPING ARNICA
3. Leaves not toothed...........................LONG-LEAVED ARNICA

4. Rays absent......................................PARRY'S ARNICA
4. Rays present 5

5. Pappus brownish ....SOFT-LEAVED ARNICA
5. Pappus whitish 6

6. Leaves narrow, 3 times or more as long as wide.....................7
6. Leaves broad, usually less than 3 times as long as wide.................9

7. Heads small, with 10 or fewer rays................RYDBERG'S ARNICA
7. Heads large, with more than 10 rays...............................8

8. Base of stem swollen and densely covered with brownish woolly hairs.
                                                    SHINING ARNICA
8. Base of stem not as above.............................TWIN ARNICA

9. Leaves definitely heart-shaped................HEART-LEAVED ARNICA
9. Leaves not heart-shaped.....................BROAD-LEAVED ARNICA

                     *   *   *

MEADOW ARNICA (*Arnica chamissonis*) Plants with 5-10 pairs of lanceolate, stalkless leaves. Several flower heads per stem. East. and West. Wash.; moist meadows in the high mountains. Flowers yellow. Early and mid summer.

CLASPING ARNICA (*Arnica amplexicaulis*) Leaves toothed, sessile, and tightly clasping the stem. Flowers yellow. East. and West. Wash.; moist, open woods and streamsides in the mountains. Summer.

LONG-LEAVED ARNICA (*Arnica longifolia*) 5-12 pairs of leaves per stem. Plants growing to several feet, with leaves up to 5 inches. Leaves lanceolate and usually entire. Flowers yellow. East. and West. Wash.; rocky places near water in the higher parts of the mountains. Mid summer to early autumn.

PARRY'S ARNICA (*Arnica parryi*) Ray flowers absent; flowering heads yellow. Stems glandular. Leaves lanceolate to ovate. East. and West. Wash.; variable, occurring in open woods as well as meadows and hillsides in foothills and lower montane areas. Mid to late summer.

SOFT-LEAVED ARNICA (*Arnica mollis*) Foliage covered with soft, white hairs. Leaves mostly sessile. Flowers yellow. Moist meadows in subalpine and alpine areas of the mountains. Summer and early autumn.

RYDBERG'S ARNICA (*Arnica rydbergii*) Basal leaves stalked; others sessile. Heads per stem single to several. Flowers yellow. East. and West. Wash.; open meadows and slopes in the alpine country of the mountains. Mid to late summer.

SHINING ARNICA (*Arnica fulgens*) Foliage sticky hairy. Lower leaves petioled; upper leaves sessile. Leaves oblanceolate. Flowers yellow. East. Wash.; open, grassy areas in lowlands and foothills. Late spring to mid summer.

TWIN ARNICA (*Arnica sororia*) Leaves elliptic, entire, and tapering to short stalks. Heads 1 or 3-7 in a cyme. Flowers yellow. East. Wash.; dry meadows and slopes in foothills and lower montane areas. Late spring to mid summer.

HEART-LEAVED ARNICA (*Arnica cordifolia*) 2-4 pairs of heart-shaped leaves. East. (mostly) and West. (rarely) Wash.; woods in foothills and mountains; a smaller variety in open, alpine areas. Flowers yellow. Spring and early summer, though later at higher elevations.

BROAD-LEAVED ARNICA (*Arnica latifolia*) Plants 12-24 inches tall. Leaves oval and coarsely-toothed. Flowers yellow and large and showy. East. and West. Wash.; moist woods, meadows, and open, rocky places in the mountains; often very common. Early to mid summer.

GROUNDSELS (*Senecio*) (Color Plate 60)

Herbs (ours) with alternate leaves and many-flowered heads arranged singly or in cymes. Heads yellow, usually radiate and often with small bracts at base of involucre.

1. Leaves on stem approximately the same size throughout its length, or only slightly smaller near upper part of stem; basal leaves not arranged as a cluster or tuft. 2
1. Leaves on stem becoming noticeably smaller toward upper part of stem; basal leaves often in form of cluster or tuft. 4
2. Plants small, usually less than 8 inches tall; leaves less than 1½ inches long . . . . .FREMONT'S GROUNDSEL
2. Plants larger, usually more than 8 inches tall; leaves more than 1½ inches long 3
3. Leaves triangular. . . . . .SPEAR-HEADED GROUNDSEL
3. Leaves not triangular. . . . . .SERRATED GROUNDSEL
4. Plants hairy when mature. 5
4. Plants not hairy when mature. 10
5. Flowering heads large; disk more than 5/8 inch wide.
 WEBSTER'S GROUNDSEL
5. Flowering heads smaller; disk less than 5/8 inch wide. 6
6. Plants with many fibrous roots. . . . . .TALL WESTERN GROUNDSEL
6. Plants with a single, woody rhizome. 7
7. Leaves sharply toothed. 8
7. Leaves very slightly toothed, or entire. 9
8. Plants with several stems arising from base. . . . . . .ELMER'S GROUNDSEL
8. Plants with a single stem arising from base. .BLACK-TIPPED GROUNDSEL
9. Plants occurring east of the Cascades. . . . . .GRAY GROUNDSEL
9. Plants occurring west of the Cascades. . . . . . . .MACOUN'S GROUNDSEL
10. Leaves entire or definitely toothed, but not lobed or crenate. 11
10. Leaves crenate or lobed, but not entire or toothed. 12

*   *   *

FREMONT'S GROUNDSEL (*Senecio fremontii*) Plants low, 4-8 inches tall and often tufted. Leaves 3/4-2 inches long, toothed; flowers yellow, 1/4-1/2 inch wide, and often in terminal clusters. East. and West. Wash.; rocky places in subalpine and alpine areas of the mountains. Mid summer to early autumn.

SPEAR-HEADED GROUNDSEL (*Senecio triangularis*) 12-36 inches tall. Stems leafy throughout; leaves 2-6 inches long, triangular, and toothed. Flower heads yellow and in compact, terminal corymbs. East. and West. Wash.; sphagnum bogs, streamsides, and wet meadows in lowlands and mountains. Often common. Summer and early autumn.

SERRATED GROUNDSEL (*Senecio serra*) Stems smooth and leafy. Leaves sharply toothed; narrowly lanceolate. Flowers yellow. East. Wash.; meadows and open slopes in foothills and lower montane areas. Summer.

WEBSTER'S GROUNDSEL (*Senecio neowebsteri*) Foliage cobwebby-hairy. Leaves roundish; toothed; and stalked. Heads yellow, usually single, and nodding. Olympics; rockslides in subalpine and alpine areas. Late summer and early autumn.

TALL WESTERN GROUNDSEL (*Senecio integerrimus*) Leaves oval to lanceolate (to 5 inches), toothed or entire, and tapering to petiole. Flowers white to yellow, borne in few to many heads, and rays few per head (5-12). East. and West. Wash.; variable, found in dry to moist, open or wooded habitats, in lowlands and mountains; common. Late spring to mid summer.

ELMER'S GROUNDSEL (*Senecio elmeri*) Plants low and small. Flowers yellow. Cascades; rocky habitats in alpine areas of mountains. Mid to late summer.

BLACK-TIPPED GROUNDSEL (*Senecio lugens*) Leaves finely toothed. Heads yellow; numerous in compact cluster. Bracts with conspicuous black tips. Olympics; subalpine and alpine meadows. Mid to late summer.

GRAY GROUNDSEL (*Senecio canus*) Stems and undersides of leaves white woolly. Leaves entire. Heads yellow, in flat cluster, and with 5-8 rays per head. East. and West. Wash.; dry, rocky habitats from lowlands to high mountains. Late spring and summer.

MACOUN'S GROUNDSEL (*Senecio macounii*) Leaves narrow (to 6 inches). Heads large and yellow. Bracts not black-tipped. West. Wash.; meadows and open woods in lowlands. Summer.

GREAT SWAMP GROUNDSEL (*Senecio hydrophilus*) Stems and leaves smooth and somewhat fleshy. Leaves mostly entire. Heads yellow, many and crowded in a cluster. Rays few or none. East. and West. Wash.; moist meadows, streambanks, and swamps in lowlands and foothills. Summer and early autumn.

FETID GROUNDSEL (*Senecio foetidus*) Foliage smooth; leaves toothed. Flowers yellow. East. Wash.; moist meadows in foothills and mountains. Late spring to mid summer.

FEW-FLOWERED GROUNDSEL (*Senecio pauciflorus*) Leaf bases not tapering to petiole, but distinct. Heads several in tight cluster. Flowers dark orange to red; bracts purplish. East. and West. Wash.; meadows and moist slopes in the subalpine and alpine areas of the higher mountains. Mid to late summer.

DWARF ARCTIC GROUNDSEL (*Senecio resedifolius*) Plants low. Flowers yellow to orange. Cascades and East. Wash.; rocky places in high, alpine areas. Mid summer to early autumn.

FEW-LEAVED GROUNDSEL (*Senecio cymbalarioides*) Leaves few, fleshy, and long-stalked (to 1½ inches and round or elliptic); tapering to petiole and toothed or entire. Flowers yellow. East. and West. Wash.; moist woods and meadows to subalpine slopes in mountains. Summer and early autumn.

FLETT'S GROUNDSEL (*Senecio flettii*) Leaves deeply cleft. Rays short and pale yellow. Cascades and Olympics; rockslides and outcroppings in foothills and mountains. Summer.

GOLDEN GROUNDSEL (*Senecio pseudaureus*) Leaves indented at base. Heads yellow and several in a tight cluster. East. and West. Wash.; moist habitats in meadows and woods. Summer.

GOLDENRODS (*Solidago*) (Color Plate 61)

Perennial, often large, plants with alternate, simple leaves and small, numerous, yellow-flowered heads in racemes or corymbs. Disk and ray flowers present, though the latter small and inconspicuous. The dense, but delicate, terminal clusters of flowers very characteristic.

1. Inflorescence distributed on a number of branches arising along the main stem, rather than concentrated in a single cluster or spike.
WESTERN GOLDENROD
1. Inflorescence not distributed on a number of branches, but restricted to a head-like cluster or spike at tip of main stem 2

2. Flowering stems arising from creeping rhizomes. 3
2. Flowering stems not arising from creeping rhizomes. 5

3. Stems and leaves covered with fine, short hairs. . . . CANADA GOLDENROD
3. Stems (below the flowers) and leaves glabrous. 4

4. Rays usually 8 in number. . . . . MISSOURI GOLDENROD
4. Rays usually more than 8 in number. . . . . GIANT GOLDENROD

5. Rays 8 in number.............................DUNE GOLDENROD
5. Rays 13 in number........................NORTHERN GOLDENROD

*   *   *

WESTERN GOLDENROD (*Solidago occidentalis*) Plants tall (to 7 feet). Leaves long (2-4 inches) and narrow and smooth. Flowers yellow, in tight clusters mixed with leaves, and at ends of long branches. East. and West. Wash.; meadows and streamsides in lowlands. Mid summer to fall.

CANADA GOLDENROD (*Solidago canadensis*) Plants medium-tall (to 34 inches). Leaves lanceolate and toothed. Flower heads yellow, numerous, and in dense panicles. East. and West. Wash.; meadows and open woods in low-lands. Late summer and fall.

MISSOURI GOLDENROD (*Solidago missouriensis*) Foliage more or less smooth. Basal leaves to 8 inches, tapering to stalk, and occasionally toothed. Stem leaves very narrow and entire. Heads yellow, tightly bunched, and borne on slightly curved, upright branches. East. and West. Wash.; dry, open habitats in lowlands and mountains. Summer and autumn.

GIANT GOLDENROD (*Solidago gigantea*) Foliage smooth; whitish bloom on stems. Flowers yellow. East. (mostly) and West. Wash.; moist, open habitats in lowlands. Mid summer to early autumn.

DUNE GOLDENROD (*Solidago spathulata*) Plants relatively small (to 24 inches). Leaves toothed or scalloped and widest beyond the middle. Rays short and few (7-9). Flowers yellow. East. and West. Wash.; occurring variably from coastal sand dunes to subalpine and alpine areas of the high mountains. Summer and early autumn.

NORTHERN GOLDENROD (*Solidago multiradiata*) Plants tufted with basal leaves; stems 6-12 inches tall. Numerous, small yellow heads in dense termi-nal panicles. East. and West. Wash.; open habitats in subalpine and alpine areas of mountains. Mid to late summer.

DAISIES (*Erigeron*) (Color Plate 61)

1. Pistil-bearing corollas very numerous in a flowering head and almost thread-like 2
1. Pistil-bearing corollas few to many, but neither "very numerous" nor "thread-like" 3
2. Row of rayless pistillate flowers between disk and rays.....BITTER DAISY
2. Row of rayless pistillate flowers between disk and rays absent.
LOW MEADOW DAISY
3. Pappus of disk flowers composed of row of larger inner bristles and a row of shorter, outer bristles, while pappus of the ray flowers is without bristles.
SWEET SCABRIOUS DAISY
3. Pappuses of ray and disk flowers similar...........................4
4. Leaves numerous along stem, close together, and similar in size from top to bottom of stem.....................CALIFORNIA RAYLESS DAISY
4. Leaves not as above...5
5. Plants mostly tall and not spreading; stem leaves well developed.......6
5. Plants low and spreading; stem leaves much smaller than basal leaves...7

315

6. Disk flowers short, less than 1/8 inch long.................FLEABANE
6. Disk flowers longer, more than 1/8 inch long............SHOWY DAISY

7. All or some leaves noticeably lobed or strongly toothed.
                                        DWARF MOUNTAIN DAISY
7. All leaves usually entire, or some slightly toothed or lobed.............8

8. Flowering heads very woolly....................................9
8. Flowering heads not woolly...................................10

9. Ray flowers yellow.................................GOLDEN DAISY
9. Ray flowers not yellow.............................FLETT'S DAISY

10. Ray flowers yellow, or absent.................................11
10. Ray flowers not yellow, but present...........................16

11. Rays present, obvious, and yellow.............................12
11. Rays very small when present, or absent........................14

12. Hairs on leaves very fine and pressed closely to leaf or stem surface.
                                          LINEAR-LEAVED DAISY
12. Hairs on leaves coarser and projecting from leaf or stem surface......13

13. Leaves flexible...................................PIPER'S DAISY
13. Leaves stiff.............................DWARF YELLOW DAISY

14. Pistil-bearing flowers absent.....................SCABLAND DAISY
14. Pistil-bearing flowers present................................15

15. Achenes covered with numerous long hairs..........CUSHION DAISY
15. Achenes not covered with numerous long hairs, but only sparsely hairy.
                                          DWARF YELLOW DAISY

16. Stem leaves well developed and often relatively broad..............17
16. Stem leaves not well developed and usually relatively narrow........18

17. Plants occurring in Cascades and Western Washington.LEIBERG'S DAISY
17. Plants occurring east of the Cascades...................GRAY DAISY

18. Hairs on stem closely appressed to stem surface..................19
18. Hairs on stem spreading, not appressed..........................20

19. Basal leaves long and narrow......................EATON'S DAISY
19. Basal leaves more or less oval-shaped...............COMMON DAISY

20. Plants with numerous branches...................SPREADING DAISY
20. Plants with few or no branches................................21

21. Basal leaves with 3 prominent nerves...........................22
21. Basal leaves without 3 prominent nerves........................23

22. Basal leaves pointed at tip....................LONG-LEAVED DAISY
22. Basal leaves blunt at tip...............................GRAY DAISY

23. Achenes covered with numerous long hairs...........CUSHION DAISY
23. Achenes not covered (or only sparingly so) with numerous long hairs.
                                                HAIRY DAISY

*   *   *

BITTER DAISY (*Erigeron acris*) Plants low (4-8 inches). Basal leaves spatulate-lanceolate. Flowers single or in terminal clusters; rays very narrow. East. and West. Wash.; rocky habitats in high mountains. Flowers white, pink, or purple. Summer and early autumn.

LOW MEADOW DAISY (*Erigeron lonchophyllus*) Basal leaves narrow, to 6 inches. Foliage hairy to nearly smooth. Flowers white to (rarely) pink; rays numerous and small. Mountains in Cascade Range and East. Wash.; moist meadows in mountains. Mid to late summer.

SWEET SCABRIOUS DAISY (*Erigeron annuus*) Plants tall (2-5 feet). Leaves hairy and toothed; basal leaves to 4 inches. Heads white and in leafy cluster. East. Wash.; moist, waste habitats in lowlands. A common introduced weed. Summer.

CALIFORNIA RAYLESS DAISY (*Erigeron inornatus*) Plants low to medium sized (to 36 inches). Leaves numerous and fringed, varying from plant to plant in size and shape. Flowers yellow; heads without rays. East. Wash.; dry, rocky places in lowlands and foothills. Mid to late summer.

FLEABANE (*Erigeron philadelphicus*) Foliage hairy. Basal leaves toothed, tapering to long petioles. Upper leaves clasping. Heads pink to white, single to many on a stem. Rays very numerous. East. and West. Wash.; moist, often waste or disturbed areas in lowlands and foothills. Late spring and summer.

SHOWY DAISY (*Erigeron speciosus*) Plants 12-24 inches tall. Stems leafy to top. Leaves lanceolate, 2-6 inches. Several flowers (blue or white) per stem; rays many (to 100) and hair-like. East. and West. Wash.; open woods and clearings in foothills and mountains. Summer.

DWARF MOUNTAIN DAISY (*Erigeron compositus*) Plants tufted, with numerous 3-clefted basal leaves. Flower heads white, pink, or blue and single on 2-4 inch stems. East. and West. Wash.; sandy or gravelly habitats, mostly in lowlands; rare in alpine areas. Late spring and summer.

GOLDEN DAISY (*Erigeron aureus*) Plants low (1-6 inches). Basal leaves stalked and elliptic; foliage downy-hairy. Involucre woolly-hairy. Flower heads single per stem and yellow. Cascades; rocky habitats in subalpine and alpine areas of the mountains; common. Mid to late summer. The "yellow aster" of the high country.

FLETT'S DAISY (*Erigeron flettii*) Plants low (to 6 inches). Rays 25-50 in number. Flowers white. Olympic Mountains; rocky habitats in alpine zone. Mid to late summer.

LINEAR-LEAVED DAISY (*Erigeron linearis*) Plants low (to 12 inches) grayish, and covered with fine hairs. Leaves very narrow and to 4 inches; yellow at base. Flower heads yellow, one to several per stem. East. Wash.; dry, open places on rocky slopes and sagebrush plains in lowlands and foothills. Late spring to mid summer.

PIPER'S DAISY (*Erigeron piperianus*) Flowers yellow. East. Wash.; sagebrush plains. Late spring and early summer.

DWARF YELLOW DAISY (*Erigeron chrysopsidis*) Plants covered with harsh hairs and stems tufted. Leaves numerous and more or less basal. Heads single per stem and yellow. East. Wash.; open sagebrush areas in lowlands and foothills. Late spring and summer.

SCABLAND DAISY (*Erigeron bloomeri*) Plants covered with fine, white hairs. Leaves very narrow. Heads yellow; rays absent. East. Wash.; arid, rocky habitats in foothills and mountains. Summer.

Figure 71.
Coltsfoot, *Petasites*, showing the peculiar leaves. (Patrick)

318

CUSHION DAISY (*Erigeron poliospermus*) Plants tufted and often spreading to form cushions. Foliage bristly-hairy. Leaves spatulate. Heads solitary and pink, purple, or violet. East. Wash.; sagebrush areas in lowlands and foothills. Mid spring to early summer.

LEIBERG'S DAISY (*Erigeron leibergii*) Plants low. Flowers blue, pink, or white. East. slope of Cascades; rocky habitats in upper parts of mountains. Summer.

GRAY DAISY (*Erigeron caespitosus*) Plants low (to 12 inches); stems spreading, then erect; mat-like. Lower leaves spatulate. Heads blue, white or pink and one to several per stem. East. Wash.; rocky habitats in lowlands and foothills. Summer.

EATON'S DAISY (*Erigeron eatonii*) Stems hairy, reddish basally, spreading and then erect. Basal leaves narrow and long (to 6 inches). Heads white and several per stem. East. Wash.; dry, rocky places in foothills and mountains. Summer.

COMMON DAISY (*Erigeron peregrinus*) Plants 12-24 inches tall. Stems slender and erect, with flowers usually borne singly at tips. Flowers white, reddish, or purple. East. and West. Wash.; moist habitats, such as meadows and streambanks in the mountains; numerous and widely distributed. Mid to late summer.

SPREADING DAISY (*Erigeron divergens*) Plants low to medium (to 30 inches). Foliage hairy. Leaves short (1 inch) and very narrow. Flowers blue, pink, or white. Often growing in thick mats. East. and West. Wash.; dry, open places in lowlands and foothills. Late spring and summer.

LONG-LEAVED DAISY (*Erigeron corymbosus*) Plants grayish and clustered with short, harsh hairs. Stems to 20 inches with 1 to several blue or pink heads. East. Wash.; mostly in sagebrush. Early summer.

HAIRY DAISY (*Erigeron pumilus*) Plants tufted. Leaves linear-oblanceolate. Heads blue, pink, or white and in loose cyme with few to many heads. Bracts densely hairy. East. Wash.; sagebrush and grassland areas in lowlands and foothills. Late spring and early summer.

GOLDEN-ASTERS (*Chrysopsis*) (Color Plate 61)

1. Heads with disk flowers only . . . . OREGON GOLDEN-ASTER
1. Heads with both disk and ray flowers . . . . HAIRY GOLDEN-ASTER

*   *   *

OREGON GOLDEN-ASTER (*Chrysopsis oregona*) East. and West. Wash.; sand and gravel bars along river banks. Flowers yellow. Summer and early autumn.

HAIRY GOLDEN-ASTER (*Chrysopsis villosa*) Flowers yellow. East. and West. Wash.; sandy or gravelly places, often along water courses in lowlands and foothills. Summer and early autumn.

COLTSFEET (*Petasites*) (Color Plate 61; Fig. 71)

1. Leaves strongly lobed............................SWEET COLTSFOOT
1. Leaves toothed, not lobed.................ARROW-HEAD COLTSFOOT

*   *   *

SWEET COLTSFOOT (*Petasites frigidus*) Cascades and West. Wash.; moist meadows and woods. Commonly in abundance along roadsides. Flower white. Early spring to mid summer. A small, alpine variety exists, in addition to the larger, lower altitude form.

ARROW-HEAD COLTSFOOT (*Petasites sagittatus*) Flowers white. East. Wash.; wet habitats in swamps and meadows. Mid spring to early summer.

ASTERS (*Aster*) (Color Plate 62)

Note: It is not always easy to distinguish asters from daisies. As a rule, daisies flower earlier in the year than do asters, but there are exceptions and overlaps. Most species of daisies have an involucre composed of bracts nearly equal in length and arranged in a single row, but some have involucres resembling those of the asters. The rays of daisy flowering heads are usually more numerous and narrower. The bracts of daisies are comparatively long and narrow, usually without green tips. The stalks supporting flowering heads of asters often have leaves, unlike the situation in most daisies. Asters are taller, more leafy, and have more flowering heads per stem.

1. Rays poorly developed (less than 1/8 inch long) or absent...........2
1. Rays well developed and usually more than 1/8 inch long.............3

2. Rays absent.............................RAYLESS ALKALI ASTER
2. Rays present ....ALKALI ASTER

3. Plants with usually a single, stout taproot...........................4
3. Plants without taproots, but with fibrous roots or rhizomes............5

4. Leaves entire; heads 1 to a stem.....................ALPINE ASTER
4. Leaves toothed; heads more than 1 to a stem............HOARY ASTER

5. Rays fewer than 8 per head and white-colored.....................6
5. Rays more than 8 per head or not white, or both....................7

6. Rays less than 4 to a head and shorter than 1/8 inch.
WHITE-TIPPED ASTER
6. Rays 4 or more to a head and longer than 1/8 inch......OREGON ASTER

7. Plants with 5, 8, 13, or 21 rays; keeled bracts; and without creeping rhizomes 8
7. Plants not entirely as above.....................................10

8. Leaves usually more than 5/8 inch wide.........ENGELMANN'S ASTER
8. Leaves usually less than 5/8 inch wide.............................9

9. Flowers white; occurring in the Olympics.............OLYMPIC ASTER
9. Flowers lavender-purple; occurring in the Cascades...CASCADE ASTER

10. Involucral bracts covered with glandular hairs......................11
10. Involucral bracts not covered with glandular hairs..................14

11. Leaves sharply toothed............................SHOWY ASTER
11. Leaves either not sharply toothed or entire........................12

320

*   *   *

RAYLESS ALKALI ASTER (*Aster brachyactis*) Ray absent. East. Wash.; moist habitats, often along shores of alkaline ponds. Late summer and autumn.

ALKALI ASTER (*Aster frondosus*) Plants annual. Leaves fleshy, more or less smooth, and linear to linear-lanceolate. Heads many, in narrow panicles. Rays very small, narrow, and pinkish. East. Wash.; shores of alkaline ponds and moist swales. Late summer and fall.

ALPINE ASTER (*Aster alpigenus*) Plants small (usually less than 12-15 inches). Leaves 1-3 inches in basal tufts. Flowering stems usually 2-6 inches with single, large flower at tip. Flowers violet to lavender. East. and West. Wash.; subalpine or alpine areas in mountains. Mid to late summer.

HOARY ASTER (*Aster canescens*) Foliage gray-hairy. Stems and leaves stiff. Basal leaves oblanceolate, toothed to nearly entire. Upper parts of plant glandular, especially the involucres. Rays 8-15, bright bluish purple. East. Wash.; open, arid areas in lowlands and foothills. Mid summer to early fall. One of the latest blooming wildflowers in the Columbia Basin. Recently designated as *Machaeranthera canescens*.

WHITE-TIPPED ASTER (*Aster curtus*) Plants slender, unbranched, with up-right stems bearing a few flower heads which possess usually two very small pale yellow or whitish rays. West. Wash.; open prairies. Mid to late summer.

OREGON ASTER (*Aster oregonensis*) Stems slender and erect, to 24 inches, and branched. Leaves entire and smooth. Basal leaves oblanceolate. Heads white, numerous. West. Wash.; open woods. Late summer and early autumn.

ENGELMANN'S ASTER (*Aster engelmannii*) Stems tall (to 5 feet) and thinly hairy. Leaves lanceolate to elliptic (2-4 inches), and mostly smooth. Heads large, with white rays, and arranged in raceme-like clusters. Cascades and East. Wash.; open places in forests in foothills and mountains. Mid summer and early autumn.

OLYMPIC ASTER (*Aster paucicapitatus*) Leaves numerous, narrow, and without petioles. Plants small (10-20 inches). Leaves 1-2 inches. Heads large, as much as 1 inch for disk width. Rays usually 13 in number (1/2 inch long) and white. Olympics; open areas in subalpine and alpine zones. Late summer and autumn.

CASCADE ASTER (*Aster ledophyllus*) Stems tall (12-30 inches) and leafy. Leaves lanceolate (3/4 to 2 inches), dark green above and gray-green below. Flowers lavender purple and large with several heads to a stem tip. Cascades and Northeastern Wash.; open places in the subalpine and alpine zones. Mid summer to early autumn.

SHOWY ASTER (*Aster conspicuus*) Plants to 24 inches. Leaves lanceolate to oval; coarsely toothed. Inflorescence of numerous (10-40) blue or violet heads in flat-topped tight cluster. East. Wash.; open pine woods. Mid summer to early autumn.

ENTIRE-LEAVED ASTER (*Aster integrifolius*) Stems stout and rigid, to 20 inches. Basal and lower leaves lance-shaped, more or less entire. Upper leaves clasping. Heads violet to purple and few in a cluster. East. Wash.; grasslands and open yellow pine woods in foothills and lower montane areas. Mid and late summer.

WESTERN MEADOW ASTER (*Aster campestris*) Stems erect or leaning, to 16 inches. Leaves linear or lanceolate (to 1/2 inch wide in some), entire, and sessile or partly clasping. Heads violet to purple and solitary, few, or numerous. East. Wash.; open, dry habitats in lowlands and foothills. Mid summer to fall.

NORTHERN ASTER (*Aster modestus*) Stems erect and leafy (to 24-30 inches). Leaves non-petioled, lanceolate, and toothed (leaves sometimes entire). Flowers purple to violet, and large and showy. East. and West. Wash.; woods, especially along moist streambanks. Mid to late summer.

ARCTIC ASTER (*Aster sibiricus*) Plants low, to 4 inches. Leaves 1-3 inches long. Flower heads with purple rays. East. and West. Wash.; open, rocky habitats in the subalpine and alpine reaches of the mountains. Mid and late summer.

ROUGH-LEAVED ASTER (*Aster radulinus*) Stems to 24 inches. Leaves variable; harshly hairy. Rays white to pale violet or purple. Cascades and West. Wash.; woods and open forests in fairly dry places. Mid summer to early autumn.

HEATH-LIKE ASTER (*Aster pansus*) Flower heads with white rays. East. Wash.; open habitats in lowlands. Mid and late summer.

SMOOTH ASTER (*Aster laevis*) Foliage grayish. Stems tall, to 48 inches. Leaves mostly smooth, thick, and lance-shaped. Heads numerous and blue to purple. East. Wash.; open habitats in lowlands and foothills. Mid summer to early autumn.

DOUGLAS'S ASTER (*Aster subspicatus*) Stems clustered, to 50 inches tall. Leaves lance-shaped, mostly clasping, and toothed. Flower heads violet, purple, or blue and few to many in open, leafy clusters. East. and West. Wash.; moist habitats along streams and salt water and in woods in lowlands. Mid summer to fall. The common aster of the Puget Sound region.

EATON'S ASTER (*Aster eatonii*) Plants tall, to 48 inches. Leaves linear, very narrow, entire, and smooth. Heads pink or white, numerous, and arranged in racemes. East. and West. Wash.; moist habitats, such as along streams, in lowlands and foothills. Mid summer to early fall.

LEAFY ASTER (*Aster foliaceus*) Plants low to medium, 8-24 inches. Stems leafy with large basal leaves which are mostly entire or weakly toothed, smooth, and lanceolate. Flower heads purple, blue, or violet and several at tip of stem. East. and West. Wash.; moist, wooded habitats in the mountains. Mid summer to early autumn.

JESSICA'S ASTER (*Aster jessicae*) Foliage soft-hairy. Leaves very hairy and oval; mostly entire. Flowers pale violet. East. Wash.; open habitats, as well as streamsides, in the Palouse region; not common. Mid summer to early autumn.

WESTERN ASTER (*Aster occidentalis*) Plants low to medium (8-20 inches). Leaves entire and mostly smooth; lower leaves oblanceolate, or linear. Heads few and blue, violet, or purple. East. and West. Wash.; meadows and other open places in the lowlands, foothills, and mountains. Mid summer to early autumn.

THOROUGHWORTS (*Brickellia*) (Color Plate 62)

Perennial herbs (ours) with alternate or opposite, resinous leaves and small, white, yellow, or pink heads of disk flowers in cymes or panicles (rarely solitary). Involucral bracts numerous and conspicuously veined.

1. Leaves more or less oval-shaped and not toothed; petioles absent.
                         NARROW-LEAVED THOROUGHWORT
1. Leaves not oval-shaped (but broader) and strongly or weakly toothed; petioles present 2
2. Leaves triangular in shape and strongly toothed.
                         LARGE-FLOWERED THOROUGHWORT
2. Leaves not triangular in shape and weakly toothed.
                         SMALL-LEAVED THOROUGHWORT

*   *   *

NARROW-LEAVED THOROUGHWORT (*Brickellia oblongifolia*) Bracts striped green and white. East. Wash.; dry, rocky habitats in lowlands and foothills. Summer.

LARGE-FLOWERED THOROUGHWORT (*Brickellia grandiflora*) Flowers greenish to yellowish white. East. Wash.; rocky habitats in lowlands and foothills. Mid to late summer.

SMALL-FLOWERED THOROUGHWORT (*Brickellia microphylla*) Flowers whitish or purplish. East. Wash.; dry, rocky habitats in foothills and lowland canyons. Late summer and fall.

LUINAS (*Luina*) (Color Plate 62)

1. Leaves palmately lobed........................CUT-LEAVED LUINA
1. Leaves not palmately lobed......................................2
2. Leaves oval-shaped ....SILVER-BARK
2. Leaves not oval-shaped....................TONGUE-LEAVED LUINA

*   *   *

CUT-LEAVED LUINA (*Luina nardosmia*) Plants to 3 feet. Flowers yellow. Leaves large, alternate. Eastern slope of Cascades and East. Wash.; meadows and open woods. Late spring to mid summer.

SILVER-BARK (*Luina hypoleuca*) Plants 1-1½ feet tall. Flower yellowish. West. Wash.; rocky habitats, such as slides, outcroppings, and cliffs. Summer.

TONGUE-LEAVED LUINA (*Luina stricta*) Stems erect. Flowers pale yellow. Cascades; moist, subalpine meadows. Mid and late summer.

CUDWEEDS (*Gnaphalium*) (Color Plate 62)

1. Bristles of pappus joined at base and shed as a ring...PURPLE CUDWEED
1. Bristles of pappus not joined at base and not shed as a ring, but falling individually...2
2. Flowering heads large; involucre more than 3/16 inch high; plants un-branched or with only a few branches...........................3
2. Flowering heads small; involucre usually less than 3/16 inch high; plants usually with a number of branches................LOWLAND CUDWEED
3. Leaves with glandular hairs and sticky.............VISCOUS CUDWEED
3. Leaves without glandular hairs and not sticky.......................4
4. Plants annual or biennial, with weak taproots; leaf bases partly surrounding the stem ....CHILEAN CUDWEED
4. Plants perennial, with strong taproots; leaf bases not partly surrounding the stem ....SMALL-HEADED CUDWEED

*   *   *

PURPLE CUDWEED (*Gnaphalium purpureum*) Stems silvery. Leaves linear. Heads greenish purple and tightly clustered in short spike at tip of stem. West. Wash.; open places in lowlands. Late spring to fall.

VISCOUS CUDWEED (*Gnaphalium viscosum*) Stems and leaves white-woolly. Flowers yellowish. East. and West. Wash.; open woods, such as yellow pine forests. Mid summer to early autumn.

CHILEAN CUDWEED (*Gnaphalium chilense*) Plants to 24 inches with erect to prostrate stems which are gray-woolly and fragrant. Leaves broadly lanceolate and clasping. Heads yellowish and in roundish clusters near stem tips. East. and West. Wash.; moist, open places, particularly in lowlands; often prefers alkali flats. Summer and fall.

SMALL-HEADED CUDWEED (*Gnaphalium microcephalum*) Plants white-woolly, to 40 inches; odorless. Flowering heads whitish to pale yellow and clustered at ends of branches. East. Wash.; arid, open habitats, rocky places, and in forest burns. Mid summer to early autumn.

LOWLAND CUDWEED (*Gnaphalium palustre*) Plants low, to 12 inches. Flower heads whitish, in small clusters in axils of leaves and at tips of branches. East. and West. Wash.; wet, open habitats, such as alkali flats or dried beds of vernal sloughs. Late spring to fall.

PUSSY-TOES (*Antennaria*) (Color Plate 63)

Low, woolly perennial plants with alternate leaves and small, discoid heads that are solitary or in cymes. Pistillate and staminate heads on different plants. Involucral bracts papery. Plants tufted.

1. Heads 1 to a stem and terminal; plants usually less than 4 inches tall....2
1. Heads more than 1 to a stem; plants usually more than 4 inches tall.....3

2. Plants with long, threadlike stolons..........FLAGELLATE PUSSY-TOES
2. Plants without long, threadlike stolons..............LOW PUSSY-TOES

3. Plants forming dense mats; with many leafy stolons..................4
3. Plants not forming dense mats; without leafy stolons.................7

4. Tips of involucral bracts brownish or greenish......................5
4. Tips of involucral bracts whitish or pinkish........................6

5. Plants occurring in subalpine or alpine areas; tips of bracts sharp-pointed.
ALPINE PUSSY-TOES
5. Plants not occurring in subalpine or alpine areas; tips of bracts blunt.
BROWN PUSSY-TOES

6. Flowering heads in loose raceme or panicle....SLENDER EVERLASTING
6. Flowering heads in compact cyme................ROSY PUSSY-TOES

7. Bracts membranous and almost totally smooth.....................8
7. Bracts not membranous, but very hairy...........................9

8. Bracts whitish......................SILVERY-BROWN PUSSY-TOES
8. Bracts dark brown..................NARROW-LEAVED PUSSY-TOES

9. Leaves less than 1⅛ inches long..........PINEWOODS PUSSY-TOES
9. Leaves more than 1⅛ inches long.............................10

10. Plants small, less than 8 inches tall.............WOOLLY PUSSY-TOES
10. Plants larger, more than 8 inches tall...............TALL PUSSY-TOES

*　　*　　*

FLAGELLATE PUSSY-TOES (*Antennaria flagellaris*) Plants white-silky, to 2 inches high; in dense clusters. Leaves linear to linear-spatulate. Heads reddish, solitary. Cascades and East. Wash.; dry, open habitats in foothills and mountains. Mid spring to mid summer.

LOW PUSSY-TOES (*Antennaria dimorpha*) Plants low (to 1½ inches) in dense clusters. Leaves white-woolly, oblanceolate to linear-spatulate. Flower heads brownish or whitish. East. Wash.; arid, open habitats in lowlands and foothills. Spring.

ALPINE PUSSY-TOES (*Antennaria alpina*) Plants in leafy mats, to 4 inches high. Plants whitish-woolly. Leaves narrow and few. Heads yellowish. East. and West. Wash.; subalpine and alpine areas. Summer and early autumn.

BROWN PUSSY-TOES (*Antennaria umbrinella*) Plants low, to 7 inches. Leaves pointed and tipped with spines. Flower heads pale yellow and on stalks projecting well above matted leaves. East. and West. Wash.; subalpine and alpine areas. Summer.

SLENDER EVERLASTING (*Antennaria racemosa*) Plants low to medium (to 24 inches). Stems short with few leaves. Leaves oval to oblanceolate, smooth above and densely white-woolly below. Heads (bracts) greenish, brownish, or pinkish and borne in open racemes or panicles. Cascades and East. Wash.; open yellow pine woods in foothills and lower mountains. Late spring and summer.

ROSY PUSSY-TOES (*Antennaria microphylla*) Stems to 18 inches from leafy, prostrate mats. Foliage white-woolly. Leaves oblanceolate. Flower heads rosy orange. East. and West. Wash.; open, arid habitats in mountains; also open woods. Late spring and summer.

SILVERY-BROWN PUSSY-TOES (*Antennaria luzuloides*) Stems to 32 inches. Foliage silvery-woolly. Heads silvery-brown, in loose inflorescences. East. Wash.; open, rocky, and semi-wooded habitats in foothills and low to intermediate elevations in the mountains. Late spring to mid summer.

NARROW-LEAVED PUSSY-TOES (*Antennaria stenophylla*) Plants white-woolly and clustered. Leaves narrowly linear. Heads brownish, in small, dense clusters. East. Wash.; grasslands and open, yellow pine woods in lowlands and foothills. Late spring and early summer.

PINEWOODS PUSSY-TOES (*Antennaria geyeri*) Stems to 8 inches from woolly, leafy mats. Leaves oblanceolate. Flower heads pinkish or whitish and scattered. East. Wash.; open yellow pine woods. Mid to late summer.

WOOLLY PUSSY-TOES (*Antennaria lanata*) Plants tufted (to 6 inches). Foliage densely woolly. Lower leaves oblanceolate. Flower heads whitish. East. and West. Wash.; open, often rocky, places in the subalpine and alpine areas of the higher mountains. Mid to late summer.

TALL PUSSY-TOES (*Antennaria anaphaloides*) Flowering stems to 20 inches. Foliage white-woolly. Basal leaves narrowly lanceolate. Heads white to pinkish. East. Wash.; open slopes and woods in lowlands, foothills, and lower parts of mountains. Late spring and summer.

RAGWEEDS (*Ambrosia*)

1. Plants with succulent herbage occurring along saltwater beaches.
SILVER RAGWEED
1. Plants without succulent herbage and not occurring along saltwater beaches, but more inland................SPRING-FRUITED RAGWEED

*   *   *

SILVER RAGWEED (*Ambrosia chamissonis*) West. Wash.; sandy dunes and beaches along salt water. Summer and early autumn.

SPRING-FRUITED RAGWEED (*Ambrosia acanthicarpa*) East. Wash.; sandy banks along rivers. Mid spring to fall.

WOOLLY-HEADS (*Psilocarphus*)

Low-growing, white-woolly, annual plants with opposite, entire leaves, and heads solitary in leaf axils or at forks or tips of branches. Disk flowers only. Heads roundish and surrounded by leaves at base of head.

1. Mature plants with erect, upright branches and not entirely with matted growth form ....TALL WOOLLY-HEADS
1. Mature plants with prostrate, matted growth form......................2

2. Leaves thickly woolly; branches relatively stout. OREGON WOOLLY-HEADS
2. Leaves thinly woolly; branches threadlike . . . . . SLENDER WOOLLY-HEADS

* * *

TALL WOOLLY-HEADS (*Psilocarphus elatior*) Flowers purplish. East. and West. Wash.; moist swales and muddy beds of spring ponds. Late spring and summer.

OREGON WOOLLY-HEADS (*Psilocarphus oregonus*) Flowers purple. East. Wash.; dry beds of spring ponds and pools. Mid spring to mid summer.

SLENDER WOOLLY-HEADS (*Psilocarphus tenellus*) East. and West. Wash.; dry beds of spring ponds and wet swales. Flowers grayish. Mid spring to early summer.

POVERTY-WEEDS (*Iva*) (Color Plate 63)

1. Leaves triangular, petioled, and sharply toothed. BURWEED MARSH ELDER
1. Leaves oblong or long ovate, more or less sessile (without petioles) and not toothed . . . . POVERTY-WEED

* * *

BURWEED MARSH ELDER (*Iva xanthifolia*) Flowers greenish white. East. Wash.; moist, waste places in lowlands. Late summer and fall.

POVERTY-WEED (*Iva axillaris*) Flowers greenish white. East. Wash.; alkali flats and waste land in lowlands and foothills. Late spring to early fall.

WORMWOODS (*Artemisia*) (Color Plate 63; Fig. 72)

Strong-smelling, herbaceous plants (as included here) with alternate leaves, and numerous, small, rayless heads in panicled spikes or racemes. Flowers yellow, greenish, or brownish. Leaves often grayish or whitish hairy and deeply lobed.

Note: Only the herbaceous, non-shrubby species of this genus are included here.

1. Disk flowers fertile, with reproductive organs fully developed 2
1. Disk flowers sterile, with reproductive organs partly, or not, developed . . . 9
2. Plants biennial, arising from a slender taproot; leaves smooth.
                                      BIENNIAL WORMWOOD
2. Plants perennial, arising from a rhizome, rootstock, or stout taproot 3
3. Basal leaves well developed; stem leaves reduced in size 4
3. Basal leaves not well developed, or else absent; stem leaves well developed 5
4. Leaflets regularly 3-lobed . . . . THREE-FORKED WORMWOOD
4. Leaflets not regularly 3-lobed . . . . MOUNTAIN WORMWOOD
5. Leaves finely divided and very small . . . . MICHAUX'S WORMWOOD
5. Leaves coarsely divided and larger 6
6. Involucre noticeably broader than tall . . . . ALEUTIAN WORMWOOD
6. Involucre taller than wide, or as broad as tall 7
7. Leaves narrow, usually less than 1/2 inch wide . . . WESTERN WORMWOOD
7. Leaves broad, usually more than 1/2 inch wide 8

Figure 72.
Wormwood, *Artemisia.* Note the typical lobed leaves of the genus. Photographed by Yaich at "Hap's Hill" forest service campground which was named after Harold (Hap) Annen, pioneer in recreational development of the South Fork Stillaguamish-Mount Pilchuck region.

8. Disk flowers 2-8 in number.................SUKSDORF'S WORMWOOD
8. Disk flowers 10-25 in number................DOUGLAS'S WORMWOOD

9. Most leaves entire, not lobed...................DRAGON WORMWOOD
9. Most leaves lobed or cleft.................SILKY FIELD WORMWOOD

*　　*　　*

BIENNIAL WORMWOOD (*Artemisia biennis*) Foliage smooth; lower leaves twice pinnately divided. Heads arranged in crowded, leafy spikes, as well as in clusters in leaf axils. East. and West. Wash.; streamsides and rocky places in lowlands. Late summer and fall.

THREE-FORKED WORMWOOD (*Artemisia trifurcata*) Plants low and tufted. Leaves pinnately divided with each lobe further parted into (usually) 3 narrow lobes. Heads in spike or raceme on stalk projecting well above basal leaf cluster. Cascades and Olympics; sandy habitats in subalpine and alpine areas of mountains. Mid summer to early fall.

MOUNTAIN WORMWOOD (*Artemisia norvegica*) Leaves long petioled and pinnately divided. Heads yellowish and arranged in spikes projecting well above basal leaf clusters. East. and West. Wash.; subalpine woods and exposed, rocky places in the high mountains. Mid summer and early autumn.

MICHAUX'S WORMWOOD (*Artemisia michauxiana*) Leaves small and finely divided into toothed segments. Upper surface of leaves smooth; lower surface white-hairy. Heads pale yellowish, in long spikes. East. and West. Wash.; rocky habitats in subalpine and alpine areas of mountains. Late spring and summer.

ALEUTIAN WORMWOOD (*Artemisia tilesii*) Leaves entire, or with long, narrow, forward-pointing teeth or lobes. Plants low, usually less than 24 inches. Leaves smooth above, white-hairy below. Heads in loose panicle. East. and West. Wash.; rocky places in subalpine and alpine areas of the mountains. Mid summer to early autumn.

WESTERN WORMWOOD (*Artemisia ludoviciana*) Plants to 40 inches. Lower leaves oblanceolate and lobed or entire; upper leaves linear to oblanceolate, grayish or greenish above, white-hairy below, and entire or toothed. Heads in loose, branching clusters. East. Wash.; open, arid places, mostly in the mountains. Summer and early fall.

SUKSDORF'S WORMWOOD (*Artemisia suksdorfii*) Plants medium to tall (to 48 inches). Leaves lanceolate and entire (rarely toothed or lobed). Heads brownish, in dense branching clusters. West. Wash.; beaches and bluffs, either sandy or rocky, near salt water. Summer.

DOUGLAS'S WORMWOOD (*Artemisia douglasiana*) Plants medium to tall (to 60 inches). Leaves variable, entire or toothed or lobed; greenish above, white-hairy below. Heads borne in terminal panicles. East. Wash. and Columbia Gorge; near water in lowlands, particularly along streamsides. Summer.

DRAGON WORMWOOD (*Artemisia dracunculus*) Plants medium to tall (to 5 feet). Foliage smooth. Leaves linear to linear-lanceolate, entire (except for a few basal leaves which may be 3-cleft). Heads very small and scattered

329

along upper branches. East. Wash.; open, arid habitats in lowlands and foot-hills. Mid summer to early fall.

SILKY FIELD WORMWOOD (*Artemisia campestris*) Plants medium (to 20 inches). Leaves cleft into threadlike segments. Heads arranged in dense, leafy spikes. East. and West. Wash.; open, often rocky habitats in lowlands and foothills, but also occurring irregularly in high mountain areas. Mid summer to early autumn.

———————

Appendix

ENVIRONMENTAL DIVERSITY IN WASHINGTON STATE

Essays presented earlier in this book have indicated some physiographic reasons why the ecology of the state of Washington and adjacent regions is so varied. Perhaps a little more consideration of the matter may be of interest and value to the user of this guide, if only to emphasize the importance of some understanding of environmental complexity to whet the flower lover's interest in using the habitat for finding and studying wildflowers.

The accompanying map (Map I) indicates roughly the basic layout of the state, as separated into two unequal halves by the north-south trending Cascade Mountains. The western portion is cool and wet, while the eastern region possesses contrastive summer and winter climates and tends toward semi-aridity. Put in somewhat sharper focus, topographically, Western Washington contains the narrow Pacific coastal plain on its extreme western periphery; the Olympic Peninsula proper with its Douglas fir-hemlock forests, scattered gravelly prairies, sphagnum bogs, cedar-hemlock climax forests, spruce-cedar climax in the rainforests; and the sand dunes, high beach, salt marshes, and seashore meadows along the immediate ocean coast. The southwest coastal hills are largely unexplored biologically but are mostly heavily forested, being of relatively low summit elevation. The Puget Sound Basin has probably suffered more from the inroads of civilization than almost any other part of the state and much, if not most, of its original floras have been strongly altered or destroyed. The Cascade Mountains may be roughly divided into the humid west slope and the semi-arid east slope. Latitudinally, these mountains may also be classified into a northern group with the new North Cascades National Park complex as its heart, a slightly less towering middle portion (between Glacier Peak and Mount Rainier), and a slightly drier southern unit. East of the Cascades, the larger "half" of the state may be seen as comprised of the Okanogan Highlands to the north, bounded by the north-south Selkirk Ranges in the extreme northeast corner; the central Columbia Basin with the rolling Palouse hills near the Idaho border; the several ridges of the Yakima Folds to the west; the Blue Mountains in the extreme southeastern corner; and the Klickitat-Columbia Gorge region to the south.

Far from being an abstract discourse, this classification must have indicated to the observant flower student that challenges for studying varying environments, the discovery of rare endemics, and other floristic "goodies" abound in Washington. Proper planning of one's field explorations can yield rich harvests in ecologic experiences. Coupled with these botanical studies will be zoological ones as well, as the animals, many of them, depend strongly on vegetation for food, cover, and breeding sites. Variation in floras is usually mirrored in a parallel variation in faunas. Besides making possible a broader set of experiences with a wider diversity of kinds of plants and animals, such studies should indicate that a knowledge of plants, particularly their identification and ecology, is of considerable importance to zoologists, especially students of birds and mammals.

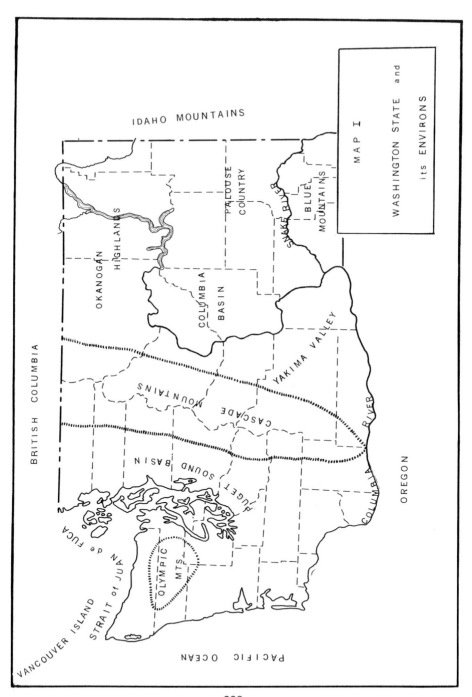

IDAHO MOUNTAINS

OKANOGAN HIGHLANDS

PALOUSE COUNTRY

COLUMBIA BASIN

SNAKE RIVER

BLUE MOUNTAINS

YAKIMA VALLEY

CASCADE MOUNTAINS

COLUMBIA RIVER

BRITISH COLUMBIA

PUGET SOUND BASIN

OREGON

STRAIT of JUAN de FUCA

VANCOUVER ISLAND

OLYMPIC MTS.

PACIFIC OCEAN

MAP I

WASHINGTON STATE and its ENVIRONS

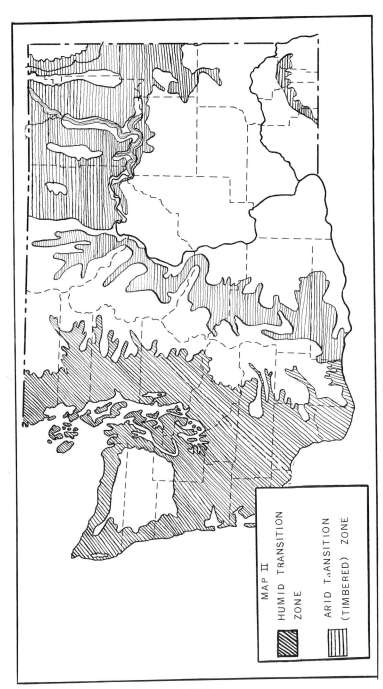

MAP II

HUMID TRANSITION
ZONE

ARID TRANSITION
(TIMBERED) ZONE

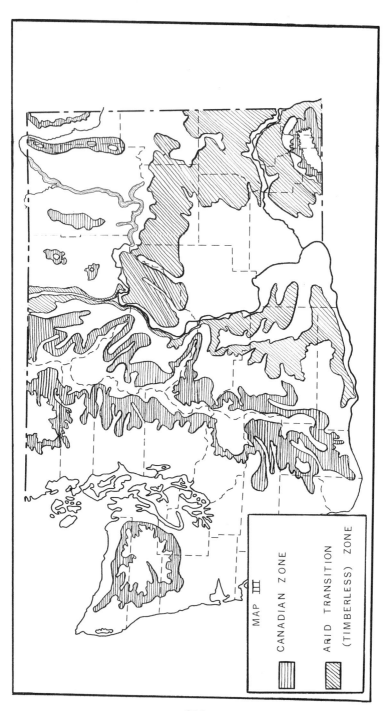

MAP III

CANADIAN ZONE

ARID TRANSITION
(TIMBERLESS) ZONE

334

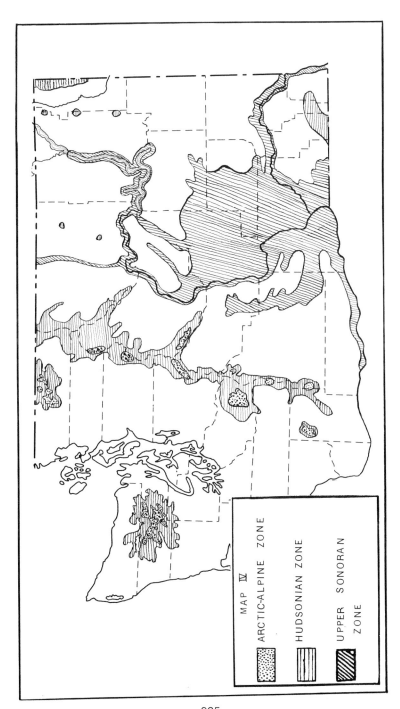

MAP IV

ARCTIC-ALPINE ZONE

HUDSONIAN ZONE

UPPER SONORAN ZONE

Patterns of Ecographic Description

A number of systems for describing and summarizing the variant ecology of Washington have been applied to the state. In the species accounts in this book, a very simple system has been employed for purposes of brevity. In such a system, references are made to such concepts as lowlands, uplands, montane and yellow pine forests, and subalpine and alpine areas. Brief consideration of some slightly more detailed patterns may be of interest.

According to the biotic province system of Lee R. Dice, as proposed in 1943, Washington may be assigned in its western part to the Oregonian Biotic Province and to the Palusian Biotic Province east of the Cascades. The senior author, in a series of papers in 1946 and 1947, assigned life belts to these biotic units. For example, that portion of the Oregonian Biotic Province in Western Washington would include the Puget Lowland Belt with its Littoral and Piedmont Sections, the Montane Forest Belt consisting of the hemlock-cedar forests of the mountain slopes, and the Alpine Belt with four subdivisions (brushy Sub-alpine Section; open, meadowy Intermediate-alpine Section; rocky, sparsely-vegetated Barren-alpine Section; and the icy, vegetation-devoid Arctic-alpine Section). In the eastern Palusian Province, one would encounter the Columbian Prairie Belt with its Sagebrush and Grassland Sections; the Montane Forest Belt with Yellow Pine and Pine-larch-fir Sections; and the Alpine Belt with the four sections mentioned earlier.

The Merriam life zone system as applied to Washington by C. V. Piper in the latter's 1906 monograph on the flora of the state was briefly outlined in an essay earlier in the guide. This system has been of immense value to a number of field students in classifying, on a broad scale, the environmental diversity of the state of Washington and the Pacific Northwest. Dr. Rex Daubenmire has prepared excellent, detailed classifications for the prairie and forested areas of Eastern Washington and Northern Idaho. The U.S. Forest Service is currently preparing a series of habitat classifications for various areas in the Northern Rockies for their land use evaluation work.

Several other systems of environmental classification have been published for our general region.

Adding to the aforementioned outline of the Merriam zones presented earlier in the book, Maps II, III, and IV indicate the general location of these zones in Washington. The accompanying album of photographs illustrate life zone characteristics, as given in the following list of figures:

Humid Transition Zone: Figs. 73, 74, 75
Canadian Zone: Figs. 76, 77, 78
Hudsonian Zone: Figs. 79, 80, 81
Arctic-alpine Zone: Figs. 82, 83, 84
Arid Transition (Timbered) Zone: Figs. 85, 86
Arid Transition (Timberless) Zone: Figs. 87, 88
Upper Sonoran Zone: Figs. 89, 90

Figure 73.
Humid Transition Zone: view of part of the Puget Sound Basin from
summit of Mount Issaquah. (Larrison)

Figure 74.
Humid Transition Zone: densely thicketed alder bottom. (Larrison)

337

Figure 75.
Humid Transition Zone: deciduous growth along river banks with distant
growth of conifers. (Larrison)

Figure 76.
Canadian Zone: montane forests of hemlock and cedar in canyon of the
South Fork of the Stillaguamish River. (Larrison)

Figure 77.
Canadian Zone: dense coniferous forest. (Larrison)

Figure 78
Canadian Zone: Larrison's camp midst cedars and hemlocks at Ohanepecosh
in Mount Rainier National Park. (Larrison)

Figure 79.
Hudsonian Zone: open forests and broken country in the Cascades. (Larrison)

Figure 80.
Hudsonian Zone: biologist's camp in mountain hemlock and yellow cedar of lower
part of zone at Pinnacle Lake on Mount Pilchuck. (Larrison)

340

Figure 81.
Hudsonian Zone: open meadows and scattered groves of subalpine fir at Sunrise in Mount Rainier National Park. (Larrison)

Figure 82.
Arctic-alpine Zone: snow fields and barren rock on south side of Mount Rainier. (Larrison)

341

Figure 83.
Arctic-alpine Zone: rocks and glaciers on northeast side of
Mount Rainier. (Larrison)

Figure 84.
Arctic-alpine Zone: rock field with scattered vegetation; Burroughs Mountain
in Mount Rainier National Park. (Larrison)

Figure 85.
Timbered Arid Transition Zone: open forested slopes. (Larrison)

Figure 86.
Timbered Arid Transition Zone: open yellow pine forest. (Larrison)

343

Figure 87.
Timberless Arid Transition Zone: open grass and forb covered slopes in
Palouse country near Idaho border. (Larrison)

Figure 88.
Timberless Arid Transition Zone: dense wildflower vegetation on moist
slope on Umptanum Ridge. (Larrison)

344

Figure 89.
Upper Sonoran Zone: densely-covered sagebrush flat. (Larrison)

Figure 90.
Upper Sonoran Zone: sagebrush and rocky cliffs in the Grand Coulee. (Larrison)

345

Habitat Diversity

A variety of habitats may occur within any life zone. These make up the lowest level of ecologic breakdown. Since many organisms, both plant and animal, show a strong preference for particular habitats, it follows that the field biologist must not only consider, in his search for plants and animals, the major environmental units, such as life zones, but the minor units, the habitats or associations. These latter, smaller-scale units are often controlled by soil or water pecularities of the exact sites in which they occur. The accompanying photographs (Figs. 91 through 102) give some examples of these ecologic controls.

Figure 91.
The open sea beach near the tide lines where environmental stresses prevent all but scattered vegetation. (Larrison)

Figure 92.
Scattered vegetation on dunes well above tide lines along sea beach (Larrison)

347

Figure 93.
Flowers and grasses on dunes on inner beaches on ocean coast. (Larrison)

348

Figure 94
Tiny, clustered flowers in seabeach sand where windblown stresses are great.
In this case, *Montia parvifolia*. (Larrison)

Figure 95.
Ideal wildflower habitat on open prairies: dense grasses
with scattered lupines. (Larrison)

Figure 96.
In open, arid areas, trees, shrubs, and flowers are crowded near
running water. (Larrison)

351

Figure 97.
Bed of wildflowers on moist slope where snowbanks linger into the spring. (Larrison)

Figure 98.
Low-lying flowers on the summit of a dry, wind-swept ridge. (Yaich)

353

Figure 99.
Scattered junipers, grasses, and wildflowers on a stabilized sand dune in the
Juniper Forest preserve northeast of Pasco. (Larrison)

354

Figure 100.
A well-drained, but moist, south-facing slope just east of Chinook Pass on the trail to Sheep Lake. An excellent place for a variety of wildflowers. (Yaich)

355

Figure 101.
Hot, dry, wind-driven sands in the dune area of the Juniper Forest preserve. A very poor place for all but a few highly adapted desert flowers. (Larrison)

Figure 102.
Oxyria plants growing in the gravel and shattered rocks of high alpine ridges: often among the highest occuring of wildflowers. (Thompson)

356

PHOTOGRAPHING FLOWERS

Photography is an excellent way of recording your flower "finds" and putting them on permanent file without collecting or unnecessarily injuring the plant. While, as in most hobbies, practice and experience are the best teachers, a few hints may be of value here.

First, as to camera. More and more professional flower photographers are using the larger cameras, such as the 2¼ x 2¼ or 4x5 inch models—for minimum enlargement for publication—but the amateurs and many "pros" still prefer the 35mm camera for its convenience. There are a number of excellent models of this latter type on the market, but the most useful ones combine a lens permitting close-up focusing (to at least 1½ feet), a fast lens speed (down to at least f/1.8), single lens focusing (for critical composition without parallax), and a through-the-lens light meter. Extension tubes or bellows and macro lenses permit extra close photographs.

Second, as to film. Most flower pictures are taken in color. A variety of film speeds and color balances are on the market, but we have noticed that most persons have definite ideas regarding the color emphasis the film they prefer provides. While it is often desirable to use a fast shutter speed to reduce blur from flower movement on breezy days, the fast films that make this possible have noticeably coarser emulsion grain and usually a "thinner" color density with less richness in colors. Certain films have less latitude for error than others. Jim Yaich prefers Agfachrome, particularly for its speed, but Larrison, after considerable experimentation, has returned to Kodachrome II for its deep colors and wider exposure latitude. The slower speed of the latter film may be compensated for by using a larger lens aperature, a time exposure, or electronic flash. It is often desirable to blur out the background by narrowing the depth of field through a wider lens aperature. By doing this, one can increase the shutter speed. Plenty of sunlight and calm days are still the flower photographer's best friends! Conversely, of course, a small lens opening deepens the field, if your background will not clutter up the picture. This brings up the most common error that the amateur flower photographer makes—taking a good picture of the flower but providing it with so complicated a background that it is hard to separate the flower from the branches, stems, leaves, or rocks against which it was photographed.

One should make a practice of photographing flowers against a distant background and using a larger lens opening to diffuse that background. While certain persons among the photographic camaraderie eschew the moving of plants, insisting on shooting them exactly where they grow, it may be necessary to remove a bloom or temporarily transplant a flower and prop it up or otherwise anchor it against the sky or at least a distant background. Accompanying this essay are several pictures of Yaich at work using this technique. Obviously, this should be done only when there are sufficient flowers present to allow the sacrificing of one. Colored cardboard backgrounds may also be used to good advantage.

Another common error made by beginners is the photographing of a white flower against a dark background and calculating the exposure on the basis of the background. Too much opening of the diaphragm or slowing the shutter will usually over-expose the flower and wash out all the detail of its petals, sepals, and flower parts. Unless you are good at re-calculating the exposure

Figure 103.
Close-up photography of a small plant which has been anchored in sand and placed in front of a cardboard to eliminate confusing background. (Larrison)

Figure 104.
Photographing a large flower on the side of a road against a distant background—the far side of the canyon. (Larrison)

358

Figure 105.
Photographing dutchman's breeches in the rainforest in cloudy weather with electronic flash. (Larrison)

Figure 106.
The delicate flowers of the yampah, *Perideridia,* shot against a purposely blurred background. (Paine)

359

Figure 107.
A bed of yellow avalanche lilies photographed to show habitat surroundings;
in this case, a snowbank flat in the mountains. (Larrison)

Figure 108.
A habitat study of yellow monkey flowers overhanging a mountain stream. (Larrison)

361

Figure 109.
Using a diffused, shadowy background for the delicate flowering spike
of the foamflower. (Yaich)

Figure 110.
Photographing small flowers against focused-out bare soil. (Yaich)

Figure 111.
Foxglove blossoms photographed against heavy shadow. (Patrick)

364

Figure 112.
Use of partially-diffused background to offset the delicate white flowers. (Larrison)

Figure 113.
Alternate use of light and shadow to provide proper background for this photograph of a small plant. (Yaich)

Figure 114.
Sand makes a good background for this example of the beach
silver-top, *Glehnia*. (Larrison)

by dead reckoning (it does no harm to under-expose the background), it may be well to bracket the originally computed shot with one exposure at a larger stop and one at a smaller. Generally, one of the pictures will have the proper exposure for giving the needed detail to the white flower.

Tripods are very handy and you should never be without one. For the 35mm cameras, a light, pack-sack tripod will be adequate.

A fourth common error of nature photographers is not getting the flower large enough on the film to enable it to be recognizable. One often has to decide whether he wishes to depict the whole plant with some of its habitat or to get an extremely close view, say of one or two blossoms. You must decide what you need or want. If you want a close-up of flower detail, get the camera as near as possible to the target. If, on the other hand, you wish the whole plant, move back a proper distance, but beware of recording a confusing background.

Rainforest photography is particularly difficult as most cameras' light meters do not accurately respond to the green light that filters down through the dense foliage, and thus pictures taken in such places are usually underexposed. Bracketing the exposure as given by the light meter will probably solve this problem.

Be sure that the details of the flower are sharp. The transparency is useless for projection or publication if the lines and colors are blurred. Give considerable thought to each photograph you make to insure its being the best you and your equipment can produce.

Analyze the flower photographs reproduced in other books. How were they taken? How was the composition arranged? How was the background handled? How would you have gone about taking the same picture if you had been the photographer? The photographs in Lewis J. Clark's recently published WILD FLOWERS OF BRITISH COLUMBIA should be carefully studied by any flower photographer. This book contains as fine a collection of color photos as any we have ever seen!

By all means get lots of practice. But practice is meaningless if you do not learn from your mistakes and experiments. The color plates in this book are the best we could take or borrow, but even some of them could well be improved upon. How would you have done it, should always be your thought on viewing a photographic reproduction.

Some directions on flower photography are included in photography manuals and a few flower guides. The black and white plates and their captions illustrating this essay will give you some further hints. Remember, study the picture in the viewfinder and be absolutely sure that it is the best you can make it!

INDEX

INDEX

INDEX

INDEX

INDEX

INDEX

374

INDEX

INDEX